Observatory Seismology

The National Academy of Sciences
of the
United States of America
offers Greetings upon the

CENTENNIAL ANNIVERSARY
of the

Regional Earthquake Observatories
at the University of California, Berkeley and Mt. Hamilton

By establishing the first permanent seismological stations in the Western Hemisphere, and initiating the network of stations that have yielded seismological information vital to the understanding of our dynamic earth, the University of California has been instrumental in laying the foundation of modern seismology.

Washington, D.C.
May 1987

Frank Press
President

Observatory Seismology

EDITED BY

J. J. Litehiser

An Anniversary Symposium
on the Occasion of the Centennial of the
University of California at Berkeley
Seismographic Stations

UNIVERSITY OF CALIFORNIA PRESS
Berkeley   Los Angeles   London

University of California Press
Berkeley and Los Angeles, California

University of California Press, Ltd.
London, England

Copyright © 1989 by The Regents of the University of California

Library of Congress Cataloging-in-Publication Data
Observatory seismology: an anniversary symposium on the occasion of the centennial of the
University of California at Berkeley seismographic stations/edited by J. J. Litehiser.
          p.   cm.
     "Held on the Berkeley campus the last week of May 1987"-Pref.
     Includes bibliographies and index.
     ISBN 0-520-06582-4 (alk. paper)
     1. Seismology—Congresses.   2. Seismometry—Congresses.
     3. University of California. Berkeley. Seismographic Stations—
     Congresses.   I. Litehiser, J. J. (Joe J.)
     QE531.027   1989
     551.2'2—dc19   89-30767
                                                                 CIP

Printed in the United States of America

1 2 3 4 5 6 7 8 9

Contents

Preface

In 1885 E. S. Holden, an astronomer and then President of the University of California, instigated the purchase of the best available instruments of the time "to keep a register of all earthquake shocks in order to be able to control the positions of astronomical instruments." These seismographs were installed two years later at Lick Observatory on Mt. Hamilton and on the Berkeley campus of the University. The stations have been upgraded over the years and joined by other seismographic stations administered at Berkeley, but their operation has never been seriously interrupted. Thus, 1987 marked one hundred years of continuous operation of the Seismographic Stations of the University of California at Berkeley—the oldest continuously operating stations in the Western Hemisphere.

The centennial of any institution is a time to reflect on its past accomplishments, to assess its present vitality, and to plan for its future contributions. In the case of the Seismographic Stations it was also recognized as an occasion for celebration by its fellows, staff, students, and friends. Therefore, a centennial anniversary symposium was planned and was held on the Berkeley campus the last week of May 1987. This volume, with a few revisions, additions, and losses, is a record of the technical papers presented as an important part of the anniversary symposium.

The original plan for the symposium's scientific program called for several addresses and twenty papers covering a wide range of topics of interest to observatory seismology, to be given in five sections of four papers each (see Appendix). Upon review of the papers submitted for this volume, however, it became clear that three overriding interests had emerged from different perspectives in papers of the various symposium sections: how best to record, archive, and share earthquake data; what the pattern of earthquake foci has to say about the tectonics of the crust; and how complex seismograms can be analyzed and interpreted to reveal the physical characteristics and processes of the Earth. In acknowledgement of this observation, the technical papers are reordered here under these three topics.

The stage for the twenty papers is set by two addresses. Dr. Robin Adams of the International Seismological Centre views Berkeley as a member of the world network of seismographic stations that produce the raw information on which studies of the distribution and mechanisms of earthquakes and the structure of the Earth are based. The effects of this information have often been of profound importance—in the delineation of the Earth's tectonically active zones, in the evaluation of earthquake hazard, and in the understanding of the earthquake source, to name a few instances.

In the second address, Dr. Bruce Bolt, Director of the Stations, lists some of the Berkeley network's specific contributions to seismology during its first hundred years of operation. Almost no aspect of observatory seismology is omitted from this list. Studies at the Seismographic Stations have led to important advances in understanding local seismicity, local and regional crustal structure and character, fault plane solutions, deep earth structure, seismometry, underground explosions, and earthquake prediction.

The papers of this volume, explicitly or implicitly, bear witness to the contributions of the Seismographic Stations of the University of California at Berkeley. They present a snapshot at the time of the anniversary symposium of the state of the art in observatory seismology and of speculation at the Stations' centennial about future advances. For those reading it in the several years following the symposium, it is hoped that this volume will serve as an historical document of the Stations' first one hundred years, as a compendium of current observatory practice, and as a glimpse into the future of seismology.

In the years to come, as the uncertain future of speculation becomes the present of fact and the present becomes the safe and serene past, it is hoped that readers will still be able to enjoy the thoughts and implied hopes of those gathered in Berkeley to indulge in the celebration of their science for a few days at the end of May 1987.

Joe J. Litehiser

PART ONE

Addresses

ONE

The Development of Global Earthquake Recording

R. D. Adams

THE PURPOSE OF SEISMOLOGICAL RECORDING

Seismological observatories and networks have to provide the raw information on which seismology is based. The obvious aim of seismological recording is the location of earthquakes, but there is a duality in observational seismology between the determinations of earthquake positions and of earth structure, for to find each, we need the other. Jeffreys and Bullen (1935) were faced with this problem in the determination of their travel-time tables and refined both tables and locations together, and this process of refinement continues.

Earthquake location in time and space is needed for a variety of reasons, for example, seismic hazard assessments for the engineering and insurance industries and to help local authorities in civil protection planning and preparedness endeavors. The position of earthquakes is also of scientific importance in delineating the Earth's tectonic activity, to show the broad pattern of its major zones and also to give details of occurrence in particular areas for scientific understanding of earthquake processes. An obvious example is the early mapping of the midoceanic ridges by earthquake locations before their bathymetric continuity was established.

Once the positions of earthquakes are known we can use the energy recorded from them to establish the properties of earth structure, including near-surface inhomogeneities and deeper structure and discontinuities, as in recent detailed studies of the core-mantle boundary (Morelli and Dziewonski, 1987). As well as velocity structure, we find the attenuative properties of the Earth from decay of body waves, surface waves, and free oscillations.

The final type of information available from seismograms helps reveal the mechanism of the earthquake source itself. This type of information has obvious scientific interest and often has a practical bearing on questions of

3

seismic hazard assessment. Source mechanism studies have developed from early work that depended only on the directions of the first motion of P-waves to a modeling of P-wave shape and to analysis of the entire waveform to give additional parameters such as the rupture-time history. It is satisfying that such determinations of source parameters are now closely linked, through techniques such as centroid-moment tensor solutions, with earthquake location, giving another example of a unified approach to seismological problems.

Our seismological observatories must provide the raw information necessary to solve these problems. Little, however, can be achieved by one station alone. Cooperation is the key to success, cooperation among countries, among agencies, and among individual stations to form networks on national, regional, and global scales.

HISTORICAL DEVELOPMENT OF EARTHQUAKE LOCATION

Pre-instrumental

In considering the development of earthquake location, we must not neglect the contributions made by noninstrumental seismology. The reporting of earthquake effects is still a major part of observational seismology and a useful adjunct to instrumental recording, but until a century ago it was the only method of studying earthquakes and their distribution. One of the earliest attempts at a global earthquake plot was a catalog produced by the Irish scientist Robert Mallet (1858). This was based entirely on felt reports, thus missing the details of major seismic features of the oceanic ridges, and showed a combination of population and earthquake distributions. Nevertheless, it was a creditable first approximation to a world seismicity map.

Among others prominent in early studies of global seismicity was the French observer Montessus de Ballore (1896), who published a paper with the impressive title "Seismic Phenomena in the British Empire" and realized the need to distinguish between places where earthquakes were reported felt and actual centers of vibration. He also produced early hazard maps, including one for the British Isles (fig. 1).

Good pre-instrumental information may still be subjected to analysis techniques developed later. An example is Eiby's (1980) analysis from the diaries of a clergyman in Wellington who meticulously noted the time and characteristics of aftershocks of the large 1848 earthquake in the north of the South Island of New Zealand. This provided good estimates of the relative numbers of large and small earthquakes (magnitude-frequency parameter b) and rate of decrease with time of the numbers of aftershocks (decay parameter p).

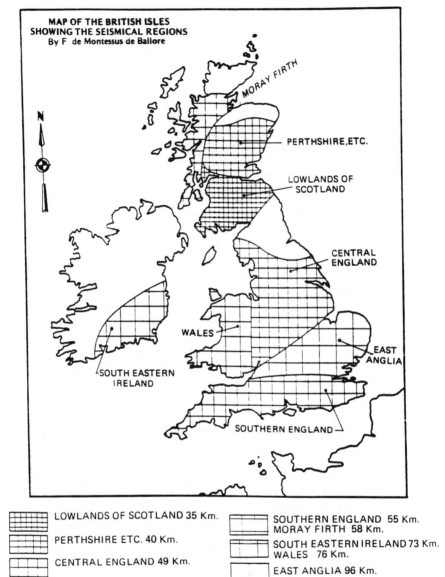

Figure 1. Hazard map of Britain (Montessus de Ballore, 1896). Distances given in kilometers are an arbitrary measure of seismicity inversely related to the number of earthquakes in a given region.

Early Instrumental Seismology on a Global Scale

World networks of seismographs, such as the Worldwide Standardized Seismographic Network (WWSSN), the Global Digital Seismographic Network (GDSN), and the Incorporated Research Institutions for Seismology (IRIS), are not new. Early outstations were set up by European countries, such as the German station at Apia in Samoa in 1902, but the first serious attempt at global coverage was the network of the British Association for the Advancement of Science (BAAS) established by Prof. John Milne on his return to Britain from Japan in the late 1890s. The Milne network at its peak had about ten stations in the British Isles and nearly thirty elsewhere throughout the world. The network comprised instruments of standard manufacture from which Milne collected readings at his home in the Isle of Wight in the first systematic analysis of global seismicity. From this enterprise, whose results were published as the *Shide Circulars* of the BAAS, there developed the International Seismological Summary (ISS) and, later, the International Seismological Centre (ISC). Under Milne, for the first time the true pattern of instrumentally determined global seismicity began to emerge, as shown in his earthquake map for 1899, which also shows the distribution of Milne seismographs (fig. 2; Milne, 1900).

We must remember that the knowledge of earth structure at that time was very elementary, and the instruments low in magnification (about 12), long in period (about 12 s natural period), and undamped, with surface waves as the main recordings. The general accuracy of location was surprisingly good, but naturally mistakes are apparent in the light of modern knowledge. One great strength of the network was its uniformity, which has helped in a recent reevaluation of Milne's locations of early events in West Africa (Ambraseys and Adams, 1986). Irrespective of details, it was often possible to establish by a similarity of reporting that certain stations were nearly equidistant from a given earthquake. We found that consistent locations could be found by using the reported time of the maximum oscillation, M, assuming it to be an Airey phase of velocity 2.8 to 3.0 km/s. In this way we could confirm the location of many early events, but some we found to be grossly misplaced. An example is the event of May 21, 1910, originally placed in Niger in Central Africa but found by us to be in Turkey, where there was confirmatory felt information (fig. 3).

Damped instruments of greater sensitivity were developed after about 1910, and fuller details of P and S phases were recorded but at the expense of uniformity of recording. By 1930 the number of recording stations had grown, and a map (fig. 4) compiled by Miss Bellamy (1936) of ISS shows well the main features of global seismicity, but with the details blurred by scatter. The stations at that time are shown in figure 5.

The number of stations grew steadily, and by 1951 about 600 were listed with their direction cosines in an ISS publication. The distribution of sta-

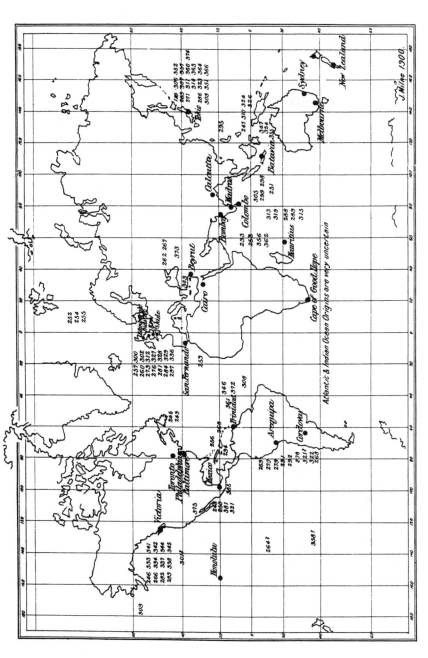

Figure 2. Global earthquakes and seismograph stations in 1899 (Milne, 1900). Epicenters are approximately indicated by numbers that refer to events in Milne's catalog.

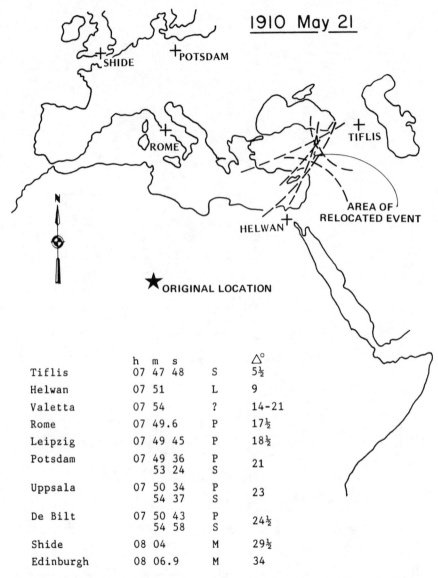

<table>
<tr><td></td><td>h m   s</td><td></td><td>△°</td></tr>
</table>

	h m s		△°
Tiflis	07 47 48	S	5½
Helwan	07 51	L	9
Valetta	07 54	?	14–21
Rome	07 49.6	P	17½
Leipzig	07 49 45	P	18½
Potsdam	07 49 36 53 24	P S	21
Uppsala	07 50 34 54 37	P S	23
De Bilt	07 50 43 54 58	P S	24½
Shide	08 04	M	29½
Edinburgh	08 06.9	M	34

Figure 3. Relocation to Turkey of an event originally placed in Niger (Ambraseys and Adams, 1986). Arrival times are given for stations with reinterpretation of phases and derived distances in degrees.

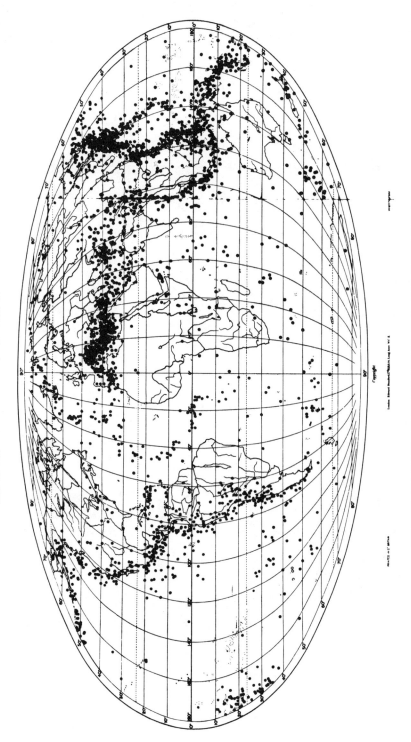

ORIGINS OF EARTHQUAKES FROM 1913—1930 INCLUSIVE.

Figure 4. Global earthquakes 1913–1930, showing scatter of features now better defined (Bellamy, 1936).

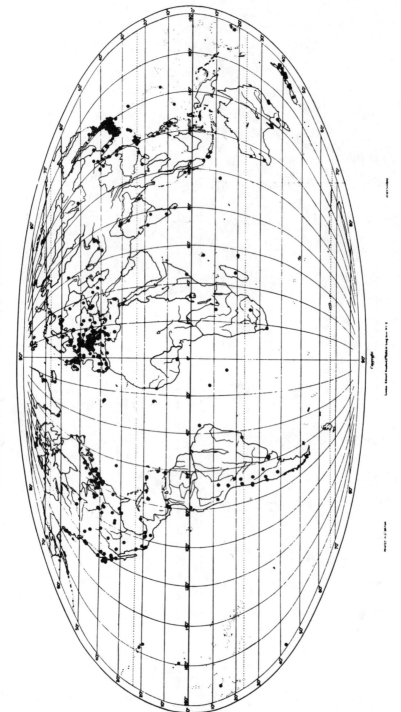

MAP OF THE WORLD ON AN EQUAL AREA PROJECTION.

SEISMOLOGICAL STATIONS.

Figure 5. Seismograph stations in 1936 (Bellamy, 1936).

tions, however, remained very uneven, with strong concentrations in North America and particularly in Europe. At the time the New Zealand station Roxburgh was installed in 1957, at latitude about 45°S, it was the most southerly regularly operated station in the world, still leaving the southernmost thirty percent of the world's surface with no station. The advent of the International Geophysical Year, and the installation of about 120 WWSSN stations in the late 1950s and early 1960s, changed the picture enormously; since then the coverage of recording stations has significantly improved.

Felt Reporting

The contribution to observatory seismology of felt information, even in present times, must not be underestimated. Properly documented felt reports can add valuable information, and in some parts of the world they still provide the most accurate locations. Felt reports of a small earthquake often give a more reliable location than can be determined from readings at a few stations, and a well-determined felt pattern for a large event will define the center of energy release, which may be closer to the centroid-moment tensor solution than to the less significant point of initation of rupture that is given by the instrumental hypocenter. Ambraseys and his co-workers (for example, Ambraseys and Adams, 1986) have developed formulae for estimating surface wave magnitude, M_s from isoseismal radii. These estimates have been shown to agree well with instrumentally determined values.

GLOBAL EARTHQUAKE LOCATION AT THE PRESENT TIME

The precision of earthquake location continues to improve. A recent example from the North Sea (Engell-Sørensen and Havskov, 1987) shows a much clearer pattern for 1985, when an improved station network was operating, compared with earlier years (fig. 6). On a global scale many small-scale tectonic features are now apparent in careful plotting of ISC data. Examples of these have recently been produced by Young et al. (1987) of the Ministry of Defence Seismological Unit in Britain (figs. 7, 8).

Despite these advances, some difficulties remain in global earthquake location, and some improvements could still be made.

In 1985, the period on which ISC is now working, about 1,400 stations reported each month, the largest events being reported by about 700 stations. For accurate location, however, it is the distribution of stations, rather than their number, that is important. More stations in seismically quiet, well-developed countries add little to location accuracy. It is true that a few strategically placed sensitive stations, particularly if they are arrays, can *detect* all major earthquakes, but give poor accuracy of location. Simple array locations of teleseisms are often many degrees in error and can have

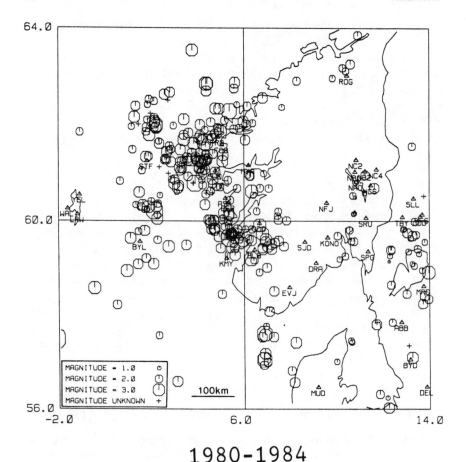

1980-1984

Figure 6*a*, *b*. Earthquakes in the North Sea, showing better-defined seismicity for the later period during which more stations operated (Engell-Sørensen and Havskov, 1987).

compensating errors of up to 6oo km in depth and one minute in origin time.

A few currently active stations in remote areas are still of immense value in effective global earthquake coverage. Examples are stations in the Antarctic and those like Raoul Island in the Kermadecs, which is still visited by ships only two or three times a year. Such stations are valuable even if local variations from a spherically symmetric velocity model are ignored.

Let me summarize the present-day status of global earthquake location as seen from ISC. Large major earthquakes are now well controlled in position, including depth, and mechanism. At the other end of the scale, in areas with

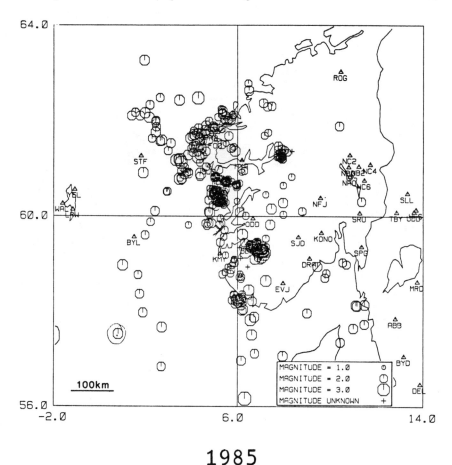

1985

close local networks such as California, Japan, and New Zealand, small local earthquakes can be detected and accurately located down to microearthquake levels. Many uncertainties remain, however, for small to moderate events in remote regions, including oceanic areas and sparsely inhabited continents.

The main difficulty in global earthquake location at the ISC is the "association" of individual readings into events. ISC locates about 25,000 events a year, or about one every twenty minutes. Therefore, it is not surprising that considerable ambiguity often arises as to which event a particular arrival belongs. This task is even more difficult at ISC because the analyst has to rely on reported times only, with no additional information on the character of the arrival to help discriminate between phases from teleseisms and local

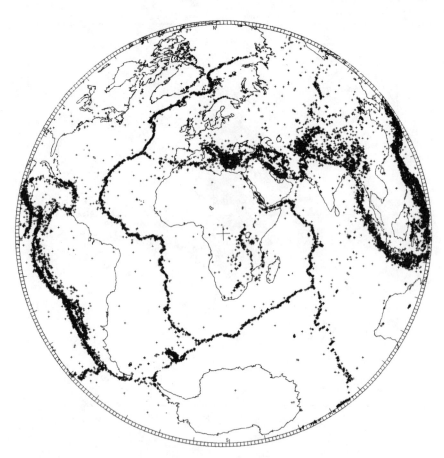

Figure 7. Detailed seismicity plot of ISC locations (Young et al., 1987).

events. Sometimes the inclusion or exclusion of a particular observation makes two solutions widely separated in position or depth equally plausible.

In addition to uncertainty of station association, detection is still poor in a surprisingly large area of the world. In 1983, for example, ISC found more than 2200 previously undetected new events (about 6 a day) of which 57 (about one a week) had a body-wave magnitudes, m_b, of 5.0 or greater. Most of the new events were found in remote areas around the Pacific, such as the Kermadec Islands, Sunda Arc, and New Guinea, but many also are found in highly active areas such as Turkey and South America, and a surprising number appear in well-developed countries where the national networks cannot locate events by themselves. An example of this is found in Europe, where new events tend to cluster near national boundaries where no one

country has enough information to locate an event, but the combined readings collected at ISC give a satisfactory solution (fig. 9; Adams, 1981).
Other new earthquakes have been found in areas previously thought to be
aseismic or of very low seismicity, such as Antarctica (Adams and Akoto,
1986).

Another emerging difficulty is analysis that is too automated. In particular, readings of distant events across small, dense networks can be interpreted as local events, either inside or very close to the network, if the records
are not carefully scanned for clues of character, for duration, and for later
phases. One example occurred on May 23, 1985, when the procedures used
at the U.S. National Earthquake Information Center (NEIC) found enough
readings from Fijian stations to produce a solution giving a shallow local
event, whereas incorporation of readings from more distant stations showed
that the earthquake was 500 km deep and nearly 1000 km away (fig. 10).
Perhaps the worst recent example is the misinterpretation at the Large Aper-
ature Seismic Array in Montana (LASA) of steeply arriving core phases as P
arrivals from the limit of P-wave distance. This results in a spurious "ring of
fire" at a distance of about 100° from LASA. In particular, such arrivals from
Pacific events form a fictitious zone of activity through Central Africa (fig.
11), which could easily be mistaken for a manifestation of the Cameroon
Volcanic Line (Ambraseys and Adams, 1986).

The other great uncertainty in earthquake location that persists is due to
the large-scale regional departures in velocity from the accepted models. In
particular, the main subduction zones have velocity anomalies of ten percent
or more that are ignored in standard processing. For large events located
with many teleseismic readings, the errors are minimal, but close stations
can exhibit very large residuals. At the other end of the scale, very small
events located only by very close stations cannot be greatly mislocated.
Intermediate-magnitude events located by a few regional stations can be
grossly mislocated, with small residuals arising not from accurate location
but from accommodation of inappropriate velocities by the least-squares
procedure. An example of this is a 1975 New Zealand earthquake, with a
solution from twenty local stations, which by a special study was shown
to be mislocated in both position and depth by about 50 km (fig. 12; Adams
and Ware, 1977).

Ideally, a complete three-dimensional velocity model of the Earth is
needed to ensure good earthquake location. Simple time corrections for stations and sources near areas of velocity anomalies are not enough without
considering azimuthal effects. For a first approximation, a "path correction"
for each source-receiver pair would give significant improvement.

The reliability of global earthquake location is steadily increasing, but
remaining uncertainties are not always appreciated by nonspecialists. Any
poorly recorded event in an unusual position should be carefully examined.

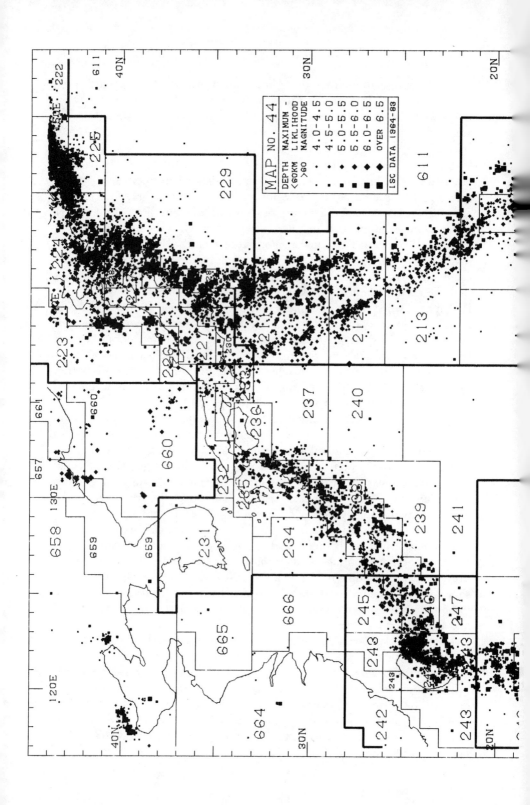

MAP NO. 44

DEPTH   MAXIMUM -   LIKLIHOOD   MAGNITUDE

	<60KM	>60
4.0-4.5	·	·
4.5-5.0	♦	■
5.0-5.5	♦	■
5.5-6.0	♦	■
6.0-6.5	♦	■
OVER 6.5	♦	■

ISC DATA 1964-83

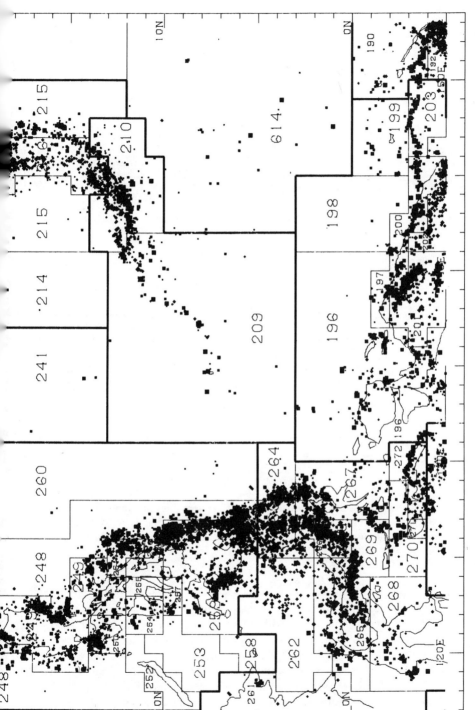

Figure 8. Detailed seismicity plot of ISC locations for the Philippine Sea area (Young et al., 1987).

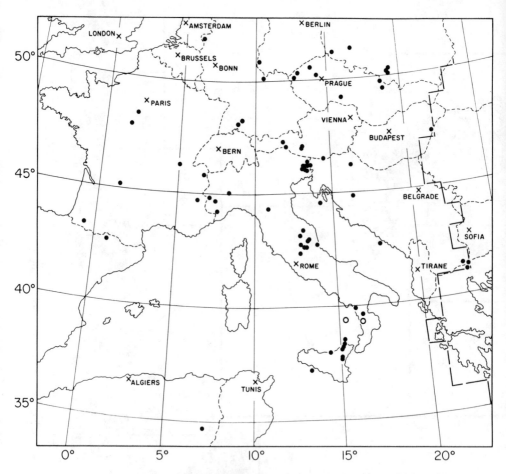

Figure 9. Previously undetected earthquakes in Western Europe found by the ISC "search" procedure. Note the clustering near international boundaries. Open symbols represent subcrustal earthquakes (Adams, 1981).

FUTURE DEVELOPMENTS

The world network can now adequately locate major earthquakes, and plans of organizations such as IRIS will ensure that detailed studies of their mechanisms can be carried out. It is the smaller events that need closer study, with better velocity models and readings from more and closer stations. The full global seismicity pattern can never be adequately monitored by one hundred or so well-placed sensitive stations. Whereas such a network might detect a large number of events, its accuracy of location would be poor. For example, the locations during a trial experiment in 1984 by stations con-

NEIC	May 23	18	24' 10.6	17.916 S	178.186 E	33km	NEIC	Less reliable solution
ISC *	May 23	18	22' 26.5	25.44 S	179.4 E	506km	1.47 3.8b	
29	obs		+0.55	+0.050	+0.11	+8.2	/20	/2
				171: South of Fiji				

Code	Station name	Delta deg	az. deg	ices npin	Op ID	ISC ID	hr	mn	sec	D	C resid	Op resid	ISC resid	wt.
S V A	Suva	7.33	353	E	EP	P	18	24	18.0	-			+0.7	:948
V U N	Vunikawai	7.41	353	I	IP	P	18	24	18.8	-			+0.8	.947
N D F	Nadi	7.85	346	I	P/PKP	P	18	24	24.5	+			+1.9	.907
S G E	South Ridge	7.92	350	I	IP	P	18	24	18.8	-			- 4.6	.262
Y S A	Yasawairara	8.85	349	I	IP	P	18	24	34.0	+			+0.9	.945
K R P	Karapiro	12.87	194	E	P/PKP	P	18	25	18				+3.0	.771
G N Z	Gisborne	13.22	185		P/PKP	P	18	25	19				+0.4	.951
	Gisborne			2	S/(SKS)		18	27	40		+2.8			
M N G	Mangahao	15.48	191	E	P/PKP	P	18	25	38				- 3.6	.633
	Mangahao			2	S/(SKS)		18	28	07		-12.3			
C D B	Cobb River	16.56	198		P/PKP	P	18	25	52				- 0.2	.952
W B 2	Warramunga Ar	41.74	268	E	EP	P	18	29	32.3				+0.1	.952
W R A	Warramunga Ar	41.75	268		P	P	18	29	32.3	+			0.0	.952
W R A	Warramunga Ar	vel=17	,az=103	,			18							
P L M	Palomar	84.22	49	E	EP	P	18	34	05				- 0.3	.952
S B B	Saddle Butte	84.35	47	E	EP	P	18	34	05.0				- 0.9	.945
I S A	Isabella	84.49	46	E	EP	P	18	34	07.0				+0.4	.951
J A S1	Jamestown	84.62	44	E	EP	P	18	34	08.0				+0.9	.945
C L C	China Lake	85.16	47	E	EP	P	18	34	09.0				- 0.8	.946
T P C	29 Palms	85.20	49	E	EP	P	18	34	10.0				- 0.1	.952
G S C	Goldstone	85.38	47	E	EP	P	18	34	11.0				+0.1	.952
G L A	Glamis	85.45	50	E	EP	P	18	34	12.0				+0.7	.947
B M N	Battle Mt	88.11	43	I	IP	P	18	34	24.0				+0.3	.951
S D D	Sodankyla	134.82	346	E	EPKP	PKP	18	40	33.0				- 13.6	.000
K J F	Kajaani	137.08	342	E	P/PKP	PKP	18	40	53				+2.2	.000
	Kajaani			2 E	ESKP	SKP2	18	43	37		-7.4		0.0	
S U F	Sumiainen	138.68	342	E	P/PKP	PKP	18	40	46				- 7.8	.000
	Sumiainen			2 I	ISKP	SKP2	18	43	41.2		-10.3		+1.4	
N U R	Nurmijarvi	140.87	340	E	P/PKP	PKP	18	40	59				+1.3	.000
U P P	Uppsala	143.33	345		P/PKP	PKP	18	41	00.0				- 1.9	.000
N B 2	NORSAR 2B	143.50	350		PKP	PKP	18	41	00.8				- 1.3	.000
H F S	Hagfors	143.93	348	E	PKP	PKP	18	41	01.4				- 1.5	.000
E K A	Eskdalemuir Ar	150.08	3		P	PKP	18	41	19.2	-			+6.0	.000
E K A	Eskdalemuir Ar	slo = 0	,											
C L L	Collmberg	152.14	342	I	P/PKP	PKP	18	41	25.1	-			+8.8	.000

Figure 10. The ISC computer solution for the earthquake of May 23, 1985. Note the false position found by the U.S. National Earthquake Information Center because its automatic location procedure misinterpreted readings at stations of a dense local network in Fiji.

tributing to the network sponsored by the Committee on Disarmament, Geneva, were significantly fewer and poorer than those found later by ISC for the same period. The greatest uncertainty in geometric location procedures is still in the determination of depth, and it is here that waveform modeling can make an important contribution.

What developments should be seen by the end of this century? Obviously, there will be an established global network of digital broadband stations, with a dynamic range high enough to record ground noise at the quietest sites but not subject to overload when recording strong motion from major earthquakes. We should also see more close networks in active areas and, in particular, many more stations in remote and oceanic regions, with a great

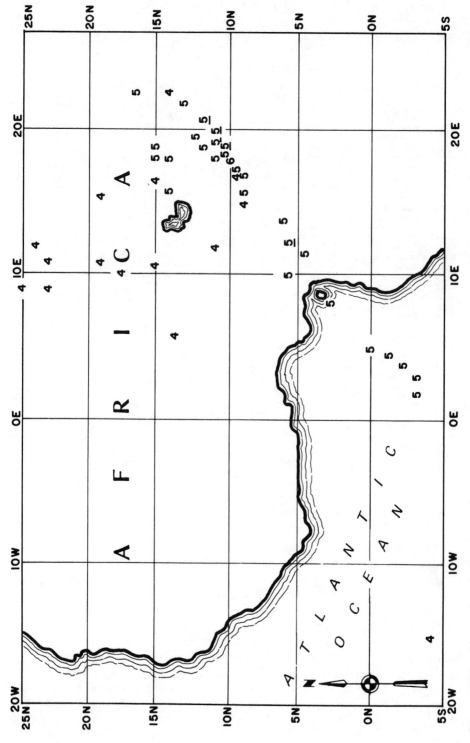

Figure 11. Spurious earthquake locations in Central Africa derived from misinterpretation of core phases on Pacific earthquakes recorded at the LASA array in Montana. Figures are assigned magnitudes, and underlining implies more than one event at the same location.

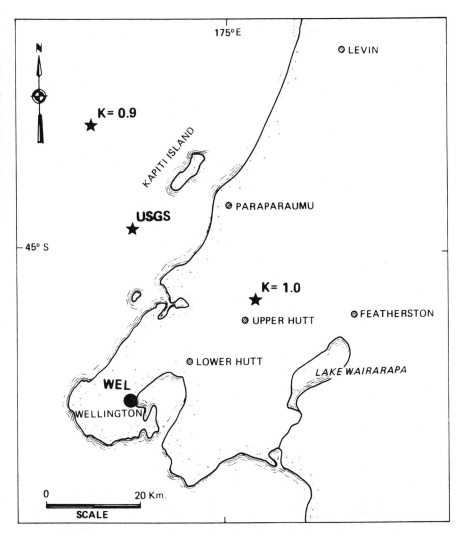

Figure 12. Mislocation of an intermediate-depth New Zealand earthquake. The position indicated by $k = 1.0$ is that found from the local network with a standard velocity model. The position marked "USGS" is that derived by the U.S. Geological Survey PDE service. That marked $k = 0.9$ is found by special study using a laterally changing velocity model, and is believed to be closer to the true position (Adams and Ware, 1977).

increase in the number of ocean-bottom seismographs. It has even been suggested that a succession of recording hydrophones be allowed to drift along the major ocean currents. Telemetry by land line, radio, or satellite will bring information for more rapid determination of earthquake parameters, but later, more refined processing will still be needed, as now, with careful monitoring by trained seismologists. The later analysis will include not only refinement of location, but modeling for depth and mechanism.

Observational seismology has come far in the last hundred years. There is every prospect that it will continue to develop and prosper.

ACKNOWLEDGMENTS

I thank Dr. P. W. Burton of the British Geological Survey for supplying early seismicity maps, and Mr. J. B. Young of the Ministry of Defence Seismological Unit, Blacknest, for permission to use previously unpublished plots of ISC earthquakes.

REFERENCES

Adams, R. D. (1981). ISC determinations of previously unreported earthquakes in Europe. In V. Schenk, ed. *Proceedings of the 2d International Symposium on the Analysis of Seismicity and on Seismic Hazard*, Czechoslovak Academy of Sciences, Prague, 132–139.

Adams, R. D., and A. M. Akoto (1986). Earthquakes in continental Antarctica. In G. L. Johnson and K. Kaminuma, eds., Polar Geophysics. *J. Geodynamics* 6: 263–270.

Adams, R. D. and D. E. Ware (1977). Sub-crustal earthquakes beneath New Zealand; locations determined with a laterally inhomogeneous velocity model. *N. Z. J. Geol. Geophys.*, 20: 59–83.

Ambraseys, N. N., and R. D. Adams (1986). Seismicity of West Africa. *Ann. Geophysicae*, 4B; 679–702.

Bellamy, E. F. (1936). *Index Catalogue of Epicentres for 1913–1930*. County Press, Newport, Isle of Wight. United Kingdom, 36 pp.

Eiby, G. A. (1980). The Marlborough earthquakes of 1848. *New Zealand DSIR Bulletin* 225, 82 pp.

Engell-Sørensen, L., and J. Havskov (1987). Recent North Sea seismicity studies. *Phys. Earth Planet. Inter.*, 45: 37–44.

International Seismological Summary (1951). The geocentric direction cosines of seismological observatories. County Press, Newport, Isle of Wight, United Kingdom, 18 pp.

Jeffreys, H., and K. E. Bullen (1935). Times of transmission of earthquake waves. Bureau Central Séismologique International, *Travaux Scientifiques*, Strasbourg, 11.

Mallet, R. (1858). Fourth report upon the facts and theory of earthquake phenomena. *Report of 28th meeting of British Association for the Advancement of Science*. John Murray, London, 1–136. (Plate XI).

Milne, J. (1900). *Fifth Report of the Committee on Seismological Investigations* Plate II,. British Association for the Advancement of Science, London.

Montessus de Ballore, F. de. (1896). Seismic phenomena in the British Empire. *Q. J. Geol. Soc. Lond.*, 52: 651–668.

Morelli A., and A. M. Dziewonski (1987). Topography of the core-mantle boundary and lateral homogeneity of the liquid core. *Nature*, 325: 678–683.

Young, J. R., R. C. Lilwall, and A. Douglas (1987). World seismicity maps suitable for the study of seismic and geographical regionalisation. *AWRE Report 07/87*. Her Majesty's Stationery Office, London.

TWO

One Hundred Years of Contributions of the University of California Seismographic Stations

Bruce A. Bolt

The first seismographs in the Western Hemisphere were installed at Lick Observatory and at the Berkeley campus of the University of California in 1887. Seismographs have recorded at these sites without serious interruption during the subsequent 100 years, making them the oldest continuously operating seismographic stations in the Western Hemisphere. This period coincided with vigorous growth in the physical knowledge of earthquakes and their sources and the application of seismic waves to geophysical problems. Earthquake recordings and associated analyses at Berkeley have made major contributions to these scientific advances.

Valuable measurements of many significant earthquakes in the United States and abroad have been made by the California stations, including seismograms from major regional earthquakes such as those in 1906 (San Francisco), 1927 (Lompoc), 1957 (San Francisco), 1966 (Parkfield), 1971 (San Fernando), and 1987 (Whittier Narrows). Crustal studies in Northern California were first carried out using recordings of local earthquakes. The Byerly fault-plane inverse method led to quantitative global analysis of earthquake mechanisms. Readings of arrival times and amplitudes of seismic phases, of great value for studies of deep Earth structure, were reported in Station *Bulletins*, U.S. Coast and Geodetic Survey (USCGS) and U.S. Geological Survey (USGS) catalogs, and the International Seismological Summary and International Seismological Centre lists. In particular, identification of exotic phases such as *PnKP*, *P'P'*, *PdP*, *SH diff*, and others have been of special inferential value. Developments in seismometry include the testing of the first regional network of stations (1960–61) in earthquake country using telephone telemetry; the introduction of broadband recording (1963 at Berkeley, followed by regional stations); the design (1980) of portable auto-

24

matic seismic wave processors; and the development (1985–87) of a regional digital seismographic system based on inexpensive PC microcomputers.

Recordings of both regional earthquakes and actual ground motions from nuclear tests in Nevada have played a significant role in discriminating between seismic wave patterns produced by underground nuclear explosions and natural earthquakes. The uninterrupted record of regional earthquakes (1910 to present) published in Station *Bulletins* permitted, for example, the detection of an approximately 22-year cycle in the occurrence of characteristic earthquakes near Parkfield along the San Andreas fault; currently this is the only official earthquake prediction (for 1988 ± 5 years) yet released in the United States. Finally, new ideas on the application of strong-motion seismology to engineering have emerged at the Seismographic Stations.

THE AGE OF ASTRONOMERS

In his thorough history of the Stations* operated out of the University of California at Berkeley, Louderback (1942) makes the point that the installation of seismographs at Lick Observatory (Mount Hamilton) and the Students' Observatory on the Berkeley campus were organized under the same plan, with fundamentally identical instrumentation (fig. 1). At the instigation of E. S. Holden, who was President of the University in 1885, the best instruments available at the time, designed by Prof. J. A. Ewing, arrived from England in 1887. The official inauguration of Lick Observatory was not until June 1888, a circumstance that sometimes causes confusion in relation to the date of start-up of the seismographs. In fact, Holden had the Ewing pendulums installed at Lick Observatory the previous year, and the first record reported was of a local earthquake on April 24, 1887. At Berkeley, the first indicated record (on the Ewing Duplex Pendulum) was of an explosion at a powder works in North Berkeley on August 11, 1887; the first earthquake to be recorded was on August 19, 1887, at 1:02 A.M.

The early seismological developments at Lick and Berkeley were due largely to the interest of astronomers. Holden became the Director of Lick Observatory after its completion in 1888. Initially, he was concerned primarily with astronomical aspects, stating that the seismographs were required "to keep a register of all earthquake shocks in order to be able to control the positions of astronomical instruments." Evidently, his interests broadened in that he published a catalog of Pacific Coast earthquakes (1897–

---

*In the following discussion, "Stations" will be used to refer to the Seismographic Stations of the University of California at Berkeley. Originally, the designation was simply University of California. Thus, the Stations are arguably the oldest organized research unit, both of the University of California and of the Berkeley campus.

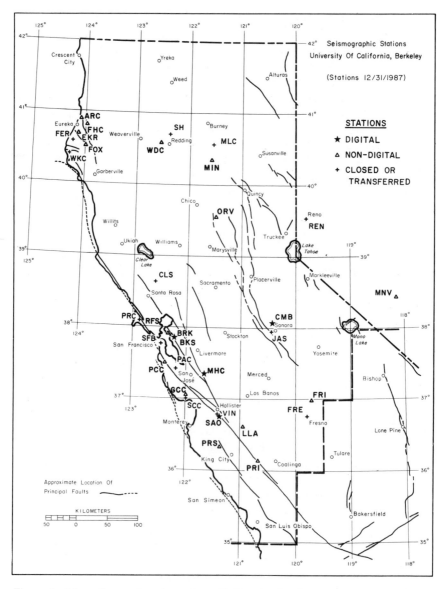

Figure 1. Map of central and northern California showing various seismographic stations of the University of California at Berkeley network that operated for a year or more since 1887 through 1987. The stations at Reno (REN) and Mina (MNV), Nevada were also part of the UCB network for a period.

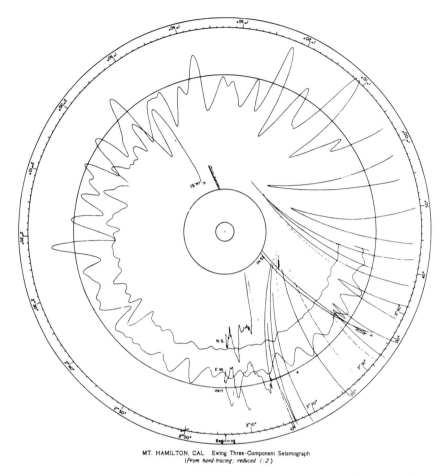

MT. HAMILTON, CAL. Ewing Three-Component Seismograph
(From hand-tracing; reduced 1:2)

Figure 2. Ground-motion recording of the 1906 San Francisco earthquake made at Lick Observatory, Mt. Hamilton, California, by the Ewing three-component seismograph.

1906), later incorporated into the famous Townley-Allen Earthquake Catalog (1939). Holden's catalog, although not the first in the world, was perhaps the first in the United States. By the turn of the century, a coordinated group of nine seismographic stations in Northern California and Nevada had been established at local astronomical observatories, such as that at Carson City, Nevada. These instruments, including the original Ewing seismographs, were therefore in place to record the great 1906 earthquake, but their ground-motion response was too limited to play an incisive role in the studies of the mechanism of that earthquake. The only seismogram (see fig. 2) that has had much scientific consequence was from the conical pendulum.

THE 1906 EARTHQUAKE

The occurrence of this destructive earthquake began a new era in seismology
in the United States and especially at the University of California at Berkeley. The Seismological Society of America was organized in San Francisco
in 1906 with George Davidson as President and Prof. G. D. Louderback of
Berkeley as the first Secretary. The period saw fresh impetus to observational
seismology, and new instruments were installed at the University's Seismographic Stations. For example, Prof. F. Omori of Tokyo University provided
in 1906 a two-component horizontal seismograph from Japan. Later, two
Bosch-Omori pendulum instruments were operated by the University of
California, one at Berkeley (1910 to 1961) and a less massive one with two
horizontal components at the subsidiary station at Ferndale (1933 to 1962).
The latter was transferred* from the Seismographic Stations on "permanent
loan" in 1963 to that city, where it is now on display in a special earthquake
museum (see fig. 1). By 1910, an 80-kg Wiechert vertical seismograph had
arrived at Berkeley from Germany, and the next year a 160-kg horizontal and
an 80-kg Weichert vertical component seismograph were installed at Lick
due to a generous gift from W. R. Hearst. Up until the 1950s, the station at
Mt. Hamilton continued to be operated by the astronomical staff, whereas
the Berkeley instruments were tended initially by the Engineering Department and from 1910 by members of the Department of Geological Sciences
(then called the Department of Geology and Mineralogy).

It is appropriate to stress here the importance of some of the figures
associated with the Seismographic Stations in the first two decades of the
century. H. O. Wood was on the academic staff at Berkeley and was associated with the earthquake recordings there until his departure for the Volcano Observatory in Hawaii in 1912. (It is unfortunate that Wood seems
to have taken with him to Hawaii, either then or later, a selection of seismograms of key earthquakes from the Berkeley collection. Despite my attempts
to find them, these seismograms have never been recovered.) Wood later
played an extremely important role in the development of the Southern California network beginning at the California Institute of Technology in
Pasadena in 1932. While at the University of California, Wood gave a course
in seismology (Geology 114) in 1911 and 1912, which may have been the first
in the subject in the United States. The course was continued from 1912 to
1921 by E. F. Davis, subsequently chief geologist and vice-president with
Shell Oil. J. P. Buwalda inherited it in 1922, after which he became chairman
of the Department of Geology at the California Institute of Technology. In
1923, J. B. Macelwane, who obtained a Ph.D. in physics at Berkeley, was
appointed Assistant Professor by Andrew C. Lawson. He was responsible for

*My action led to a Resolution by the California Assembly asking me not to close this earth-
quake station.

the seismographs and taught seismology, including a graduate course, until he went to St. Louis in 1925.

There is no evidence that Lawson either taught seismology or was directly associated with the seismographs. Nevertheless, the interest of such a figure, with powerful influence both in U.S. geological circles and in the University, ensured the continuous operation of the Seismographic Stations and the strengthening of seismology within the Department of Geological Sciences. Lawson's seminal contribution to the field was the *Report of the State Earthquake Investigation Commission* (1908), which he contributed to and edited. In this report, H. F. Reid proposed the elastic rebound theory of earthquake generation by sudden fault slip. This model was adopted as realistic by subsequent seismologists at Berkeley.

THE DIRECTORSHIP OF PERRY BYERLY, 1925–1962

The period during which direction came from Perry Byerly coincided with striking advances in the science of seismology, many of which depended on contributions from the Berkeley Stations. Their operation during these thirty-eight years provided the first reliable and homogeneous catalog of earthquakes in Northern California and surrounding areas. The *Bulletin of the Seismographic Stations* (of direct value to California citizens) began in 1910 and has continued until the present. It is the primary source of information on earthquakes and locations (and locally assessed magnitudes, after 1942) and is consulted often for both research and practical seismic hazard evaluation.

Some details of Byerly's incumbency up to 1942 are set out in Louderback's history (1942). For an assessment of his main contributions to seismology the reader is referred to Bolt (1979). During his tenure, Byerly worked as a professor in the Department of Geological Sciences, which became the Department of Geology and Geophysics in 1947. In the postwar period, the Stations were affected by the general reorganization of research groups at the University of California at Berkeley with the creation of a formal scheme of Organized Research Units (ORUs). These units were and are meant to act as interdepartmental research centers where graduate student training and faculty research can be concentrated on a broad subject in a profitable way.

After World War II, the staff remained small until the first significant increase in 1956, with the appointment of a professional research seismologist as assistant to Byerly, who was under unusual pressure in maintaining the work of the Stations along with a full teaching and research load. The first research seismologist to be appointed on the Station budget was Dr. D. Tocher (1956–1964). Tocher, a Ph.D. student of Byerly's, returned from Harvard to fill the position. Although the budget increased little in the 1950s, more modern instrumentation was introduced at Berkeley and Mount Hamilton. The number of stations, with a considerable variety of seismographs, increased to fifteen by 1960, including cooperating stations in Nevada (at Fallon, Reno, Ruth, and Yerington) and Oregon (at Corvallis). Of special research importance was the early operation of Wood-Anderson instruments. For a considerable time the Berkeley Station was also responsible for the Reno Station (1948–1963) and the Branner Station (1947–1968) at Stanford University. Byerly cleverly managed the expansion by using facilities generously offered by colleges like Fresno and Humboldt State College. A full listing of the growth of the Stations and their instrumentation is given in Bolt and Miller (1975). Special credit must be given during these years to the instrumental, organization, and diplomatic skills of W. C. Marion, chief technician at the Stations from 1953 to 1975.

Another major step forward was taken with the Observatory work in 1961. This growth was a direct result of the upgrading of seismology nationally as part of the scientific effort stimulated by negotiations for a test-ban treaty for underground nuclear explosions. It was quickly realized during early discussions with the Soviet Union and Great Britain (Byerly was a U.S. advisor at the test-ban treaty talks in Geneva in 1958) that observational seismology had not kept up with available technology. From the very beginning of surface and underground testing, the Berkeley Stations recorded ground motions from some of the largest explosions. For example, Prof. Edward Teller tells of confirming the detonation of the nuclear device "Mike" at Eniwetok atoll, Marshall Islands, by watching the galvanometer light spot of a seismograph move "wildly" in the seismological vault in Haviland Hall. Some details of these Berkeley contributions can be found in Bolt (1976).

Two important steps were taken at this time using research grants from Project VELA UNIFORM of the Advanced Research Project Agency of the Department of Defense. One was the tunnel driven into the Berkeley Hills above the campus to create a less noisy recording vault, subsequently called the Berkeley Byerly station (BKS). This vault became the site in 1959 of newly designed seismographs that were part of the Worldwide Standard Seismographic Network (WWSSN). The second step, largely under the supervision of D. Tocher, W. C. Marion and R. Sell, was installation in northern California of the first regional network of seismographic stations telemetered by commercial telephone lines (see "Seismicity" below).

THE DIRECTORSHIP OF BRUCE A. BOLT, 1963–1989

The author of this historical account was appointed Director to succeed Byerly in February 1963. His directorship continued until June 30, 1989.

Major changes in observational power and research breadth took place during this quarter century (see "Seismological Contributions" below). The network was consolidated to allow continuous operation, largely with state funds included in the University budget. These state research funds came under considerable pressure at various times during these twenty-five years, and battles had to be fought to maintain the budget at adequate levels. Some older stations, such as Fresno and San Francisco, had to be closed for reasons of economy. A major success was the special addition by the state of $80,000 per year to the operating budget after the 1971 San Fernando earthquake. The University subsequently incorporated these funds into the regular budget.

In 1964, the seismological strength of the Department of Geology and Geophysics was increased by the appointment of Dr. T. V. McEvilly from St. Louis University, where first Macelwane and later a distinguished alumnus from the Seismographic Stations, Prof. W. Stauder, had gone to teach. McEvilly was appointed Assistant Director of the Seismographic Stations in 1968. Also in 1968, L. R. Johnson came from the California Institute of Technology as a Professor in the Department of Geology and Geophysics and became an Associate at the Stations. Other Associates appointed have been D. Tocher, M. Niazi, D. R. Brillinger, J. Penzien, and E. Majer. The key position of Research Associate at the Stations changed occupants several times during the period: Dr. C. Lomnitz (1964–1968), Dr. M. Niazi (1968–69), Dr. U. Chandra (1969–1970), Dr. R. D. Adams (1970–1971), Mr. W. K. Cloud (1971–1976), and Dr. R. A. Uhrhammer (1976–present). Dr. Tocher left the staff in 1965 for earthquake research at the USCGS (later to become the National Oceanographic and Atmospheric Agency—NOAA). A second Research Seismologist, Dr. R. Clymer, was appointed in 1981, using federal research funds.

At the beginning of 1963, there were sixteen stations in the network (fig. 1): the central station on the Berkeley campus now had four vaults (in Haviland Hall, the Main Library, the Earth Sciences Building, and an adit in Strawberry Canyon). The stations at Ferndale, the University of San Francisco, and Fresno were closed and new stations opened at other more suitable sites. The important Wilip-Galitzin seismographs, which had operated at Berkeley from 1930, were also shut down in 1965 because of redundancy with the WWSSN recordings (details can be found in Bolt and Miller, 1975). The Bosch-Omori instruments at Berkeley were removed for public display at the J. D. Randall, Jr., Museum, San Francisco, and at the Lawrence Hall of Science, Berkeley.

A major new research direction instituted at the Stations during the early part of this period was marked by the construction of a specialized field observatory on the San Andreas fault near Hollister. This station, built on land deeded to the University by Mr. and Mrs. Howard Harris and called the San Andreas Geophysical Observatory (SAGO), was designed as a multipurpose geophysical observatory that would measure basic aspects of crustal strain fields and near-field shaking associated with local earthquakes. It was inaugurated in 1968 after construction by the staff and graduate students, funded largely by private donations. SAGO continues operation at the present time in a reduced mode. It was perhaps before its time. In retrospect, before the research grant support of the Federal Earthquake Hazard Reduction Programs of the 1970s, the Seismographic Stations had neither the resources nor manpower to maintain such an ambitious and novel field observatory at the necessary high scientific level. Even today, there are still few such monitoring installations in the world. (In the 1980s a broadly similar concentration of field sensors was installed in the Parkfield area in response to an earthquake prediction. See "Prediction" below).

Another priority at the Stations was development of seismographs recording both period and amplitude over broader dynamic ranges than the WWSSN system. The first very-long-period seismographs (systems whose pendulum and galvonometer free periods are $T_0 = 45$ s, $T_g = 300$ s) commenced operation at Berkeley in 1964, and continuous magnetic-tape analog recording also began in that year. This project culminated in 1987 with the development of a digital broadband system of stations including Berkeley, Mt. Hamilton, SAGO, Oroville, Whiskeytown, and a new permanent station (CMB) at Columbia College, Tuolumne County, in the Mother Lode country.

SEISMOLOGICAL CONTRIBUTIONS AT BERKELEY

The main contributions to knowledge of earthquakes by staff and students working at the Seismographic Stations may be grouped under five headings: continuous earthquake observations, teaching, research, public information, and consulting.

It it hard to overemphasize the value of maintaining continuity of earthquake recording. Many historically important seismological observatories around the world have, to the detriment of the science, succumbed to attack on the grounds of the slowness of short-term scientific return. In fact, it is not difficult to show that long-term observation of earthquakes is crucial for many key purposes. Earthquakes are not well-controlled experiments whose time, size, and place can be chosen. Mechanisms differ, wave trains through the complicated structure of the Earth's interior vary, and the vital statistical basis for seismological hazard assessment often accumulates slowly.

As mentioned earlier, this paper does not treat the gamut of seismological research work at the University of California at Berkeley but rather the much more limited aspects related to the existence of the Seismographic Stations. The former subject is much broader than the latter but, of course, the two overlap and interrelate. An early assessment is given by Byerly in a 1958 lecture in which he referred to "The cradle of seismology in the United States." Indeed, a great many seismologists have been trained and worked on earthquake problems at Berkeley in the last century. Most, but by no means all, were associated significantly with the Seismographic Stations. Others carried out their research almost entirely within the Department of Geology and Geophysics (under its various titles), the College of Engineering, the Department of Statistics, and elsewhere.

As part of the preparation for this paper, several seismological alumni who took part in graduate studies at the Seismographic Stations were asked to provide a list of the main scientific contributions of the Stations. All those canvassed emphasized the role of the Stations, its staff, and its students in teaching and public service. The facilities of the Stations have been long used for demonstrations of observatory practice and analysis to undergraduates in various geology and geophysics classes. Also, for many years, seismograms and other materials from the Stations have been incorporated in laboratory work for undergraduates and graduates studying earthquakes. Even when not using directly measurements made at the Stations, most students who have taken degrees in seismology at Berkeley have familiarized themselves with the earthquake observational program at the Stations and participated in the systematic and routine reading of seismograms, particularly from the WWSSN instruments at BKS. For this reason, Perry Byerly (1958) used the term "cradle of seismology" when referring to the Berkeley program. On the public service side, the Stations receive hundreds of visits from the public each year, particularly groups of schoolchildren. On request, staff at the Stations also frequently provide as a public service information on past records of earthquakes and current earthquake activity.

As part of its public involvement, the Stations' past two directors, assistant director, and senior staff have acted as consultants to a greater or lesser extent to many public and private projects involving earthquake hazard assessment. This consulting work has ranged from membership (Bolt) on the State Seismic Safety Commission, to advice to public utilities on seismic questions related to power-generating plants and dam safety, to overseas studies on ground-motion inputs for engineered design such as for the Jamuna Bridge project of the World Bank in Bangladesh and the High Aswan Dam in Egypt.

Seismicity

The distribution of past and present stations, operated as part of the University of California at Berkeley network for more than one year up to December, 1987, is shown in figure 1*. The network has evolved as oppor-

---

*A temporary near-field network of seismographs was operated in Bear Valley, along the San Andreas fault (see Section on "Strong Motion Seismology").

tunities and restraints changed over the years, but the original stations at Berkeley and Mount Hamilton have always been maintained. Based on the recordings at the Stations, the *Bulletin of the Seismographic Stations* has been produced each year since 1912 (for example, Uhrhammer et al., 1985) to tabulate recorded local earthquakes (above a magnitude threshold of about 2.5). It is an uninterrupted record of seismicity containing over 150,000 earthquakes and is the primary source for earthquake epicenter maps for northern California. It is used for earthquake risk assessments and statistical predictions of future earthquakes. For example, the *Bulletins* permit the calculation that the odds of an earthquake of magnitude 6 or greater in the central and northern part of the state are, on average, 1 in 5 per year. A map of epicenters from 1985 to 1986 above Richter magnitude 4 is shown in figure 3.

Measurements of the main seismic phases of all significant local, regional, and teleseismic earthquakes are distributed to appropriate scientific centers throughout the world. Each week, measured arrival times and amplitudes are sent to the National Earthquake Information Center (USGS) in Boulder, Colorado, and each month, a listing of the main phases from major earthquakes is published. Each six months, magnetic tapes are sent to the international center (the ISS up to 1960 and subsequently the ISC in Newbury, England). There are on file at the Stations over 300,000 paper seismograms and over 500 magnetic tapes containing earthquake recordings. The guiding philosophy has been to record continuously rather than only during intervals triggered by seismic events so that research workers can have access to complete ground motions. Nevertheless, with the shift to tape recordings, more and more continuous records have eventually been "dubbed," with significant events saved on library tapes (now compact disks).

Research at the Stations has concentrated on special studies of local earthquakes. This policy is based on an early recommendation of H. O. Wood that California seismographic networks should be used to study local earthquakes in detail. The great Report of the 1906 San Francisco earthquake by the State Earthquake Investigation Commission (Lawson, 1908) reproduces seismograms from stations of the local network, including records from Lick Observatory and Berkeley (fig. 2).

Many analyses of aftershock sequences within the northern California area have been made over the years. Perhaps the first detailed study in the United States was that of the Nevada sequence of 1932 by the late Prof. James T. Wilson, then a Ph.D. student of Perry Byerly's and that of Parkfield in 1934. The analysis of sequences was later extended by Prof. A. Udias and others working at the Stations.

Observatory requirements have led to an emphasis on improved ways to estimate the parameters of earthquakes. In 1963, one of the first computer-based programs to calculate local earthquake hypocenters by least-squares

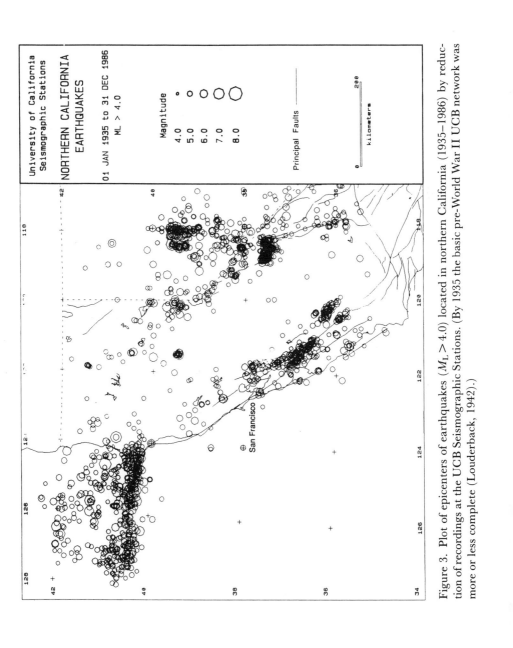

Figure 3. Plot of epicenters of earthquakes ($M_L > 4.0$) located in northern California (1935–1986) by reduction of recordings at the UCB Seismographic Stations. (By 1935 the basic pre-World War II UCB network was more or less complete (Louderback, 1942).)

adjustments was placed into routine use at Berkeley. The program, called LOCAL, became a basis for computer codes using more detailed procedures developed at the USGS and elsewhere. Similarly, the group-location method for joint location of earthquakes was developed at the Stations by Dr. J. Dewey for teleseisms and by staff for local earthquakes. In 1980, the Berkeley network became the first in the United States to publish routinely seismic moments (M_0) of earthquakes estimated directly from measurements of Wood-Anderson seismograms.

As mentioned before, the first telemetry network of regional extent in the world began operating at Berkeley in 1961. At its maximum density, the network in the Coast Ranges consisted of nine stations with short-period Benioff seismographs all telemetered by commercial telephone lines to the central campus station. Recordings on 16-mm continuously processed film ("develocorders") and paper helical strips ("helicorders") of sixteen telemetry stations continue in 1989 to be read daily. The uniform recording and precise timing of this network soon demonstrated an order of magnitude increase in the precision of local hypocenter estimation. It was established that the depth of earthquakes in central California was shallower than had been thought—ranging mainly between 5 and 10 km, with the base of the seismogenic zone at about 15 km. This result corrected an assumption, based on an earlier inference from experience in Europe, that *most* earthquake foci occur at depths of about 15 km (near the "Conrad discontinuity"). In addition, the severe location bias from lateral crustal heterogeneity (up to 5–10 km) was demonstrated. Nevertheless, with appropriate adjustments it was shown that the hypocenters of earthquakes in the California Coast Ranges concentrated along main active faults such as the San Andreas, Hayward, and Calaveras. These results led to great improvements in the technique of mapping active faults, including submarine transform faults, using epicenter locations. (The association between surface faults and foci in southern California proved later to be somewhat less definite.)

Crustal Studies

Early work by Byerly and his students, using both local earthquakes and gratuitous explosions in the area, defined in a general way the structure of the central California crust. By 1963, the depth of the Mohorovičić discontinuity under the Central Coast Ranges was determined to be about 22 km, a figure not much revised since. Later work concentrated on structural variations across the San Andreas fault (see McEvilly and Feng, 1983).

A major step in crustal tectonics was the discovery of seismological evidence for a root under the Sierra Nevada. A. C. Lawson, had predicted such a root on the basis of isostasy, and in 1938 Byerly reacted by comparing the arrival time of P waves at the Fresno station on the west side of the Sierra with the arrival time at the Tinemaha station (run by the California Institute of Technology) on the east side of the Sierra Nevada. Byerly found a delay of several seconds at Tinemaha from earthquake sources in the northeast Pacific, thus indicating lower than normal seismic velocities under the range. Research on this subject has continued, using special field profiling and ray tracing.

Work has also used surface-wave observations. A major concept was introduced into seismology in 1953 by J. F. Evernden, who used Wood-Anderson instruments around the Bay area as an early seismic array. Cross-correlation enabled direct measurement of phase velocities of Rayleigh waves and hence the inference of crustal structure. Previously, single-station methods had been limited to comparisons of group velocity. Later work by Dr. T. Mikumo with surface waves involved the structure of the Sierra Nevada.

In the last decade, field investigations from the Seismographic Stations have used artificial sources. In 1974 a Vibroseis reflection survey was used for the first time, to study the structure of the San Andreas fault zone; measurements yielded very precise differences in travel times useful in calculating strain in the crust. These studies were aimed at detecting precursors to large earthquakes (McEvilly and Clymer, 1981).

Earthquake Mechanisms

The first inversion of first motions using teleseisms was carried out by Byerly in the period 1928–1938, based on ideas developed in Japan by H. Nakano for local earthquakes. The scheme involved the use of polarities of P-waves to define patterns of compressions and dilations arising from fault geometries of various kinds. After some resistance from other seismologists (such methods were not used, for example, at the Seismological Laboratory at the California Institute of Technology until 1952) they have become an essential part of the seismologist's tool kit.

By 1958 Byerly's P-wave methods had been extended by W. Stauder and others to S-wave polarizations. Use and extension of this inversion algorithm has continued at the Stations (see, for example, Dehlinger and Bolt, 1987). The other two tools of most importance to observational seismology are epicenter-location methods and magnitude estimation. The former was discussed in the previous section. The latter, developed largely at the California Institute of Technology by C. F. Richter, B. Gutenberg, H. Kanamori, and others, has not been the subject of much work at Berkeley, but the continuous estimation of magnitudes at the Stations using the network Wood-Anderson seismographs has been important in establishing a calibrated estimation basis.

With the introduction of three-component sets of long-period instruments at Berkeley in 1964, many records of waveforms of earthquakes and underground nuclear explosions accumulated. Various papers were published based on fits of theoretical seismic motions to these forms and on comparisons between the characteristics of earthquake and explosion sources

(McEvilly and Peppin, 1972). More recently, the application of pattern recognition theory is being tried, exploiting digital three-component recordings over a wide frequency band and interactive computer graphics displays.

After the 1966 Parkfield earthquake, the U.S. Geological Survey began to build up an experimental telemetry network of short-period vertical-component stations in California along the San Andreas fault system between Parkfield and Santa Rosa. Partly in response to the destructive 1971 San Fernando earthquake, this network was rapidly expanded to over 300 stations in northern California; extensive data on microearthquakes down to unit magnitude have now accumulated. This detailed information complements the monitoring of the larger earthquakes ($M_L > 3.0$) by the Berkeley network. The multitude of such stations has also permitted more extensive use of fault-plane solutions of small local earthquakes to study the tectonics of California. Indeed, the first check of the plate tectonics paradigm in California was the validation of the San Andreas system as a transform fault using recordings from the Berkeley telemetry network (Bolt et al., 1968).

One of the unique contributions of the Seismographic Stations has been the study of fault creep (Tocher, 1960). Not only were quantitative slip measurements made over many years at the Cienega Winery near Hollister (fig. 4) but a long time series of displacements on the Hayward fault has been recorded with a differential slip meter installed in a water diversion tunnel under Memorial Stadium on the Berkeley campus. The latter consistently show a right-lateral slip rate of approximately 2 mm per year.

The introduction of broadband recording has also led to seminal publications on earthquake generation mechanisms. For example, one of the earliest studies of directivity due to the rupture of a fault was carried out on the 1966 Parkfield earthquake (Filson and McEvilly, 1967) using Love waves recorded at Berkeley by long-period seismographs.

Deeper Structure

From the beginning, data from the Stations have been used for the study of the structure of the deep Earth. Investigators have used Berkeley network seismograms directly or readings reported in the *Bulletin of the Stations* and the International Seismological Summary (ISS) and its successor, the International Seismological Centre (ISC) catalog.

One of the first major contributions was isolation of the "20° discontinuity" in P travel times, interpreted as a first-order discontinuity in the Earth at a depth of about 400 km. This result arose from Byerly's analysis of travel times from the large Montana earthquake in 1925. The 1960s saw a flourishing of work on the fine structure of the Earth's interior. Mention can be made of the location and definition of such phases as *PdP* (*P*-waves reflected from the top of structure in the upper mantle); *P diff* (long-period P-waves diffracted along the boundary of the Earth's core); *SH diff*; *PnKP*

Figure 4. Photograph of D. Tocher at the offset culvert at the Cienega Winery (about 1970) near Hollister, where it is intersected by the San Andreas fault. The first systematic measurements of fault creep were set up here by Tocher while at the Seismographic Stations.

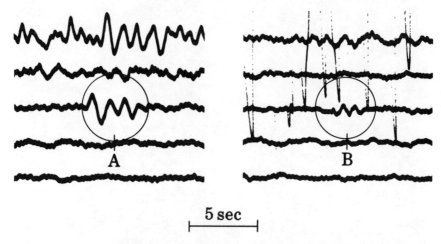

Figure 5. Portions of seismograms recorded by the short-period vertical-component seismograph at the Jamestown station of the UCB network (see fig. 1). The wave packet A is the core phase *P4KP*, and B is *P7KP*.

(multiple reflections within the liquid core of the Earth); *P'P'* and *P'dP'* (core waves reflected near the antipodes); and *PKiKP*. Inferences and theoretical work have been stimulated substantially by exotic observations of such types, many of which have now been reproduced in textbooks (see Bolt, 1982).

Consider one illustration of the care and completeness with which phases on seismograms have been read and cataloged over the years by staff and students. The phase P7KP, which is reflected seven times within the core at the mantle boundary, was identified (fig. 5) on seismograms from the Jamestown station in 1970. Two years later Dr. G. Buchbinder in Canada independently found that the even rarer phase P13KP had been listed among the unrelated phases in the *Bulletin of the Berkeley Stations*.

Other pioneer work on Earth structure involved use of the Berkeley telemetry regional network in the California Coast Ranges in the 1960s. Azimuthal anomalies in travel times were associated (Nuttli and Bolt, 1966) with undulations of the low-velocity zone in the lithosphere. It later became standard practice to incorporate such anomalies in all constructions of global seismic travel times.

The work at the Stations has been influential in other ways in the development of global and regional travel-time tables. For example, the 1968-PKP times of Bolt are still used as a standard by the USGS (NEIC) for the preliminary determination of epicenters, and the statistical work of H. Freedman helped lay a probability basis for the development of the 1968 P travel times.

A major effort has also been carried out on measurement and interpretation of free oscillations of the Earth (Bolt and Brillinger, 1979). Work began with measurements by Dr. A. Nowroozi of ground amplitudes and frequency spectra of spheroidal and torsional modes after the 1964 Alaskan earthquake using long-period pendulums of the Berkeley station. This was followed up by theoretical studies using finite-element models and complex demodulation methods. The growth of the regional broadband system provided comparisons of spectral estimates from stations a few hundred kilometers apart (Hansen, 1982). The Hansen study yielded some of the best-resolved estimates of the Q attenuation factor in the Earth.

Seismometry

As mentioned above, the early history of the Stations saw the development of the first cooperating seismographic network in the United States (Louderback, 1942). In later years, new cooperative arrangements were established with many centers and organizations. The California Department of Water Resources, motivated by a need to monitor the seismic safety of dams and aqueducts, assisted with the stations JAS, ORV, and now with CMB, at Columbia Community College (see fig. 1). The National Park Service assisted within Lassen National Park with MIN and MLC and at Whiskeytown (WDC). The Bureau of Reclamation had established the Shasta Dam (SH) station in 1942 with reservoir-induced seismicity in mind; its operation was transferred to Berkeley in 1952. The most sustained federal support has been first from the USCGS and since 1975 from the USGS (especially with the WWSSN station at BKS and the DWWSSN station at JAS and CMB).

The theory of the seismograph has also been developed over the years at the Stations by Byerly, J. Eaton, P. Rodgers, and others. An often-referenced paper on the history of seismometry to 1900 was published by Dewey and Byerly (1969).

At the San Andreas Geophysical Observatory (SAGO), described in a previous section, many new types of sensors were designed and deployed. In addition to seismographs and accelerometers, equipment included telluric current meters, strain meters, and microbarographs. The first special microbarograph had been designed by the engineering staff and installed at BKS in 1963. Its successes include recordings of atmospheric oscillations from the 1964 Great Alaskan earthquake and the 1980 eruption of Mount St. Helens.

A major design effort (McEvilly and Majer, 1982) at the Stations was an automated seismic processor (ASP) for microearthquakes, based on microchip technology. The prototype portable instrument was a sixteen-channel system. This development, later the basis for larger commercial instruments, won an award as one of the top technological innovations of 1984.

A major development in the last several years had been the design of a

87 225 14h01m00.00s   14h06m00.00s

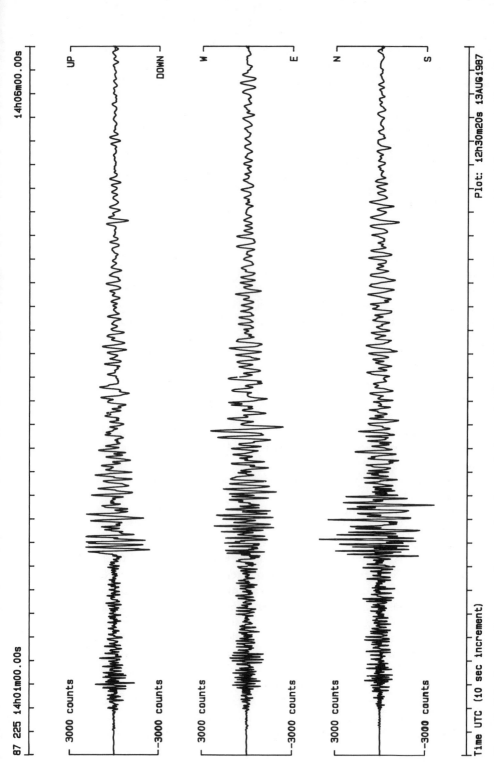

UP

DOWN

3000 counts

-3000 counts

W

E

3000 counts

-3000 counts

N

S

3000 counts

-3000 counts

Time UTC (10 sec increment)   Plot: 12h30m20s 13AUG1987

Figure 6. Seismic waves from an underground nuclear explosion at the Nevada Test Site recorded by the broadband digital seismographs at Mt. Hamilton on August 13, 1987.

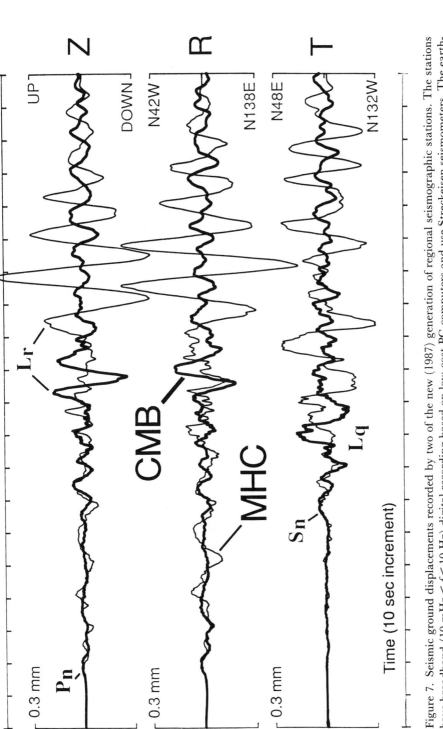

Figure 7. Seismic ground displacements recorded by two of the new (1987) generation of regional seismographic stations. The stations have broadband (10 mHz < f < 10 Hz) digital recording based on low-cost PC computers and use Streckeisen seismometers. The earthquake was centered at Whittier Narrows, Southern California, on October 1, 1987, with M = 6.0 (BKS), M = 1.3 × 10^{25} dyne-cm (BKS).

Underground Explosion Discrimination

A number of graduate students who studied at the Seismographic Stations have become leading figures in research on discrimination between natural earthquakes and underground nuclear explosions. Specially sustained work on this subject (carried out away from the Stations) is due to C. Romney and J. F. Evernden. One of the major contributions of the Stations has been the continued seismographic recording of underground nuclear explosions fired at the Nevada Test Site and elsewhere. Analog tape recordings of these events began at Berkeley in 1964 and have continued in analog and digital form to the present time. This library is one of the most extensive sets of intermediate- and broadband recordings of such explosions in the world (see fig. 6).

From early in the VELA UNIFORM program (see Bolt, 1976), a series of investigations on related problems has been carried out at the Stations. The program was begun by Tocher and Byerly (1960–1963), continued by Bolt (1963–1965), and subsequently pursued as a major research enterprise by McEvilly and Johnson. Many publications have resulted from the work; a recent account of some of the main results associated with the latter two seismologists and research assistants is given in Johnson and McEvilly (1985).

In summary, these results include the validation of short period P_g discriminants, using recordings at the Jamestown station, and tests of the effectiveness of M_s/m_b discriminants for $M_L < 4.0$, made possible through recordings of local earthquakes by the broadband Berkeley system. The same data base has allowed various types of modeling of small earthquakes. An extensive set of observations in the near field of small to moderate earthquakes was made in the 1970s at Stone Canyon and Bear Valley, south of SAGO, and later by operating portable seismographs near the Nevada Test Site (see also "Strong Motion Seismology" below).

PREDICTION

Earthquake prediction in time and place has been approached with caution at the Seismographic Stations. It was felt that early claims of imminent and almost universal success were extravagant, given the great geological complexities involved.* Because, however, prediction in a testable form is the mark of a quantitative science, the subject has by no means been neglected.

Two aspects have been stressed: the uncertainties in tempo-spatial forecasts, and the estimation of seismic hazard. The standardized operation of

---

*See, for example, testimony of T. V. McEvilly at Field Hearings on S.B. 1473 and S.B. 1474, 27 April 1973, Senate Commerce Committee, Subcommittee on Oceans and Atmosphere, San Francisco, California.

both the Berkeley telemetry short-period network and the broadband systems was recognized as allowing the estimation of practical sensitivity levels. Such threshold levels are essential if certain hypothesized earthquake precursors are to be credible. One of the first results was deflation of the claims of precursory travel-time anomalies. Studies using quarry blasts and Nevada Test Site explosions as known sources of seismic waves showed that any variations are well within the scatter of the measurement errors common at the time. No systematic effect could be detected with confidence by routine methods.

One prediction that has gained recent notoriety is based on a demonstration of past periodicity of moderate characteristic earthquakes near the town of Parkfield (Bakun and McEvilly, 1984) in earthquake recordings by the Berkeley network over its hundred-year history. Parkfield lies near the San Andreas fault in a rural region remote from populated centers. The San Andreas fault trace is clearly visible in bedrock just north of Parkfield. The seismographic record established that moderate-sized earthquakes (M_L 5.5 to 6.0) occurred near Parkfield in 1901, 1922, 1934, and 1966. (See the 1922 Parkfield seismogram written at Berkeley in fig. 8.) There was also evidence from felt reports of similar earthquakes in 1857 and 1881. In addition, available seismograms permitted quantitative estimates of size and location for the earthquakes of March 10, 1922, June 8, 1934, and June 28, 1966. These dates predict an almost constant recurrence time of about twenty-two years (with the exception of the 1934 fault slip). Repetition of this cyclic pattern makes the next Parkfield earthquakes expected about 1988, with appropriate allowance for statistical variation. Work on characteristic earthquakes, postulated to be typical of various parts of active faults, can be done only in regions where calibrated seismograms over long periods are available.

On a different aspect of earthquake prediction, estimations of hazard recurrence statistics in northern California have been developed at the Stations over the years by researchers C. Lomnitz, R. A. Uhrhammer, L. Knopoff, and many others, using the basic seismicity information published in Station *Bulletins*.

Strong Motion Seismology

Finally, it should be mentioned that earthquake prediction relates not only to time, size, and place, but also to the forecasting of the strong ground motions that constitute an earthquake. Considerable work has been done by W. D. Smith, L. Drake, and others on the development of finite-element programs and algorithms for seismic wave propagation in realistic geologic structures such as continental boundaries, mountain roots, and alluvial valleys.

The testing of such numerical predictions of seismic shaking at the surface of complex structures depends on appropriate recordings of strong ground

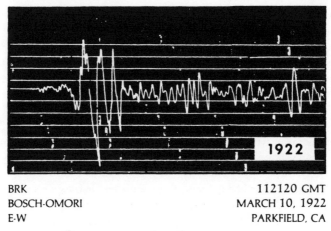

BRK   112120 GMT
BOSCH-OMORI   MARCH 10, 1922
E-W   PARKFIELD, CA

Centennial Anniversary
U.C. BERKELEY SEISMOGRAPHIC STATIONS
1887-1987

1986
CHARDONNAY
ALEXANDER VALLEY

PRODUCED AND BOTTLED BY WILSON-COLE CELLARS
HEALDSBURG, CA. ALC. 13 % BY VOL. CONTAINS SULFITES

Figure 8. The east-west component of ground motion at the Berkeley station recorded by the Bosch-Omori seismograph on March 10, 1922, from an earthquake source near Parkfield, California. The recording is part of the basis of the "Parkfield Prediction Experiment" (1988 ± 5 years). Reproduced on a wine label printed for the Centennial Symposium, May 28–30, 1987.

relatively inexpensive digital broadband network (BDBN) for the UCB network. The design philosophy was to use off-the-shelf items and PC computers of the XT/AT type. The operation at the Mt. Hamilton station (MHC) commenced in May 1987 and at Berkeley in June 1987. Records from this new system (ultimately to consist of ten digitally recording stations in central California) are shown in figures 6 and 7.

A recent innovation in microearthquake monitoring, achieved jointly with the Earth Sciences Division, Lawrence Berkeley Laboratory, has been the installation and operation of an array at Parkfield with digital telemetry recording 500 samples per second for each component. The ten stations, each with three components, are capable of being triggered by earthquakes as well as recording waves from controlled artificial sources.

motions. To this end, a program of instrumentation with strong motion accelerographs was commenced in 1967 and later strengthened with the appointment of W. K. Cloud, formerly head of the USCGS Field Investigation Office, as Research Seismologist at the Stations. In 1968, a cased borehole 500 feet deep was drilled in the gouge zone of the Hayward fault on the Berkeley campus for various instrumention. In 1976, downhole strong-motion accelerometers were installed in a hole bored in bay mud at the University's Richmond Field Station. This facility has yielded important new information on the depth variation of seismic ground motion (Johnson and Silva, 1981).

Background moderate seismicity along the Bear Valley segment of the San Andreas fault provided valuable measurements of near-field ground motions in an intensive study using a special network of strong-motion seismographs. In this "Near Field Project," funded under VELA UNIFORM, nine three-component broadband seismographs were operational from 1973 to early 1977 and resulted in improved methods for resolving hypocenters and fault mechanisms (see Johnson and McEvilly, 1985).

In 1979 a digital accelerometer system for a dense strong-motion array was designed and tested by the staff at the Seismographic Stations. The array, called the Strong Motion Array Taiwan-One (SMART 1), was installed in northeast Taiwan, which is currently much more seismically active than California. The project has been carried out in close cooperation with scientists at the Institute of Earth Sciences of the National Research Council in Taiwan. The results have been gratifying, with a substantial number (over fifty) of earthquakes triggering the array of thirty-seven digital instruments in seven years. Numerous research papers of both seismological interest and engineering applicability have been published to date (see Loh et al., 1982), and work on this important array is continuing.

Strong-motion field seismographs have also been used in the context of seismic source discrimination in an extended experimental program of near-source recordings at the Nevada Test Site, begun in 1969. Concomitant wave-propagation and moment-tensor modeling have resulted, and the work continues (Stump and Johnson, 1984).

CONCLUSIONS

This history of the development of the first seismographic observatories in the United States commenced by discussing "the Age of Astronomers." By 1970, seismological observational work had greatly expanded and become more diversified. "The Age of Prediction" began in response to major programs of research on earthquake forecasting in the United States and many other earthquake-prone countries, notably Japan, China, and the Soviet Union. This new research focus, as well as growing public concern about seismic hazards, led to increased federal and state research funds and the establishment of many complementary networks of seismographs in North America. In California, as described earlier, the most notable network, consisting of telemetered short-period instruments to record microearthquakes, was developed and operated by the USGS. Other special seismographic networks in the region were operated by the Department of Water Resources near large water-storage facilities, by the Lawrence Livermore National Laboratory in the vicinity of Livermore Valley, and by the Pacific Gas and Electric Company, in both the northern part of the state around Humboldt Bay and, since 1986, the vicinity of the Diablo Canyon nuclear electric generating plant.

The addition of other modern special-purpose seismographic networks in central and northern California requires reevaluation of the earlier justifications for the continuation of the Berkeley network. My own view is that the University of California should not engage in merely routine recording; justification must depend on nonredundant observations (fig. 7), related fundamental research, support for teaching of undergraduates and graduates, and essential public education and information.

Future observational developments at the Stations are likely to be influenced by newly announced plans for a national network of broadband seismographic observatories under the auspices of the USGS. The scheme includes real-time transmission of digital data from each network station by satellite links to the regional central Stations (for example, Berkeley) and a National Earthquake Center. The provision at permanent observatories for continuity of earthquake surveillance, comprehensive seismic-wave recording, and cataloging of both small and great earthquakes at all distances remains a very worthwhile scientific enterprise. It is fundamental both to seismic-hazard evaluation and to a deeper understanding of geophysical processes and Earth properties.

The final question is: What have been the major scientific contributions of the Berkeley Stations? The answer must start with the continuous uniform recording of earthquakes from their beginning, with measurements of local, regional, and distant earthquakes. Such integration is still rare at other earthquake observatories around the world. The resulting precise measurements of earthquakes have been incorporated into innumerable studies of seismicity and Earth structure. The early goal of advancing seismology through an observational program has been achieved. The Stations have been consistently supported by the University of California from state funds over the years, although the level of fiscal support has fluctuated, particularly when state budgetary restrictions have affected all Organized Research Units. The Stations have provided key information in the international quest for adequate means to verify a nuclear weapons test-ban treaty. Many productive U.S. and foreign seismologists have received their observational training and insights as participants in research programs at the Stations.

Overall, both the seismological profession and the general community can be grateful to the University of California for a century of continuous commitment to earthquake studies.

ACKNOWLEDGMENTS

I am most grateful to numerous colleagues and seismological alumni of the Seismographic Stations for comments and insights on the historical record. Especially, I benefited from many hours of conversation and philosophizing on earthquake studies with the late Perry Byerly, who became not only a mentor but a close friend. A draft of this paper was much improved by the generous scrutiny of W. Bakun, J. Eaton, J. Filson, T. V. McEvilly, W. C. Marion, M. Niazi, G. Oakeshott, W. Stauder, and R. A. Uhrhammer, although my emphases and judgments do not always coincide with their views.

It should be made clear that cases quoted in the text represent only a small sample of the published research performed at the Seismographic Stations by associated faculty, visiting scholars, and graduate students over the last 100 years. The history is given, of course, from my own perspective and emphasizes observatory-related work. Details on publications can be found in the *Annual Reports* of the Organized Research Unit, on file at the Stations. More technical material is contained in the introductory section of the *Bulletins of the Seismographic Stations* (1910–1987). Not all studies mentioned in the text are specifically referred to in the list of references. Many supporting publications can be found under the mentioned author's name in the *Bulletin of the Seismological Society of America*.

REFERENCES

Bakun, W. H., and T. V. McEvilly (1984). Recurrence models and Parkfield, California, earthquakes. *J. Geophys. Res.*, 89: 3051–3058.

Bolt, B. A. (1976). *Nuclear Explosions and Earthquakes*. W. H. Freeman, New York.

———. (1979). Perry Byerly—A memorial. *Bull. Seism. Soc. Am.* 69: 928–945.

———. (1982). *Inside the Earth*. W. H. Freeman, New York.

———. (1985). The development of earthquake seismology in the western United States. In *Centennial Special Volume 1, Geol. Soc. Am.*, 471–480.

Bolt, B. A., and D. R. Brillinger (1979). Estimation of uncertainties in eigenspectral estimates from decaying geophysical time series. *Geophys. J. R. Astr. Soc.*, 59: 593–603.

Bolt, B. A., T. V. McEvilly, and C. Lomnitz (1968). Seismological evidence on the tectonics of central and northern California and the Mendocino escarpment. *Bull. Seism. Soc. Am.*, 58: 1725–1767.

Bolt, B. A., and Roy D. Miller (1975). *Catalog of Earthquakes in Northern California and Adjoining Areas: 1 January 1910–31 December 1972*. Seismographic Stations, University of California, Berkeley, 1–567.

Bolt, B. A., R. A. Uhrhammer, and J. E. Friday (1988). A PC-based broadband digital seismograph network. *Geophys. J. R. Astr. Soc.*, 93: 565–573.

Bullen, K. E., and B. A. Bolt (1985). *Introduction to the Theory of Seismology.* Cambridge University Press, New York.

Byerly, P. (1958). The beginnings of seismology in America. *Symposium on Physical and Earth Sciences.* University of California, Berkeley.

Dehlinger, P., and B. A. Bolt (1987). Earthquakes and associated tectonics in a part of coastal central California. *Bull. Seism. Soc. Am.*, 77: 2056–2073.

Dewey, J. W., and P. Byerly (1969). The early history of seismometry (to 1900). *Bull. Seism. Soc. Am.* 59: 183–227.

Filson, J., and T. V. McEvilly (1967). Love wave spectra and the mechanism of the 1966 Parkfield sequence. *Bull. Seism. Soc. Am.*, 57: 1245–1259.

Hansen, R. A. (1982). Simultaneous estimation of terrestrial eigenvibrations. *Geophys. J. R. Astr. Soc.*, 70: 155–172.

Johnson, L. R., and T. V. McEvilly (1985). Regional studies with broadband data. In *The VELA Program, a Twenty-five Year Review of Basic Research.* Defense Advanced Research Projects Agency, Rosslyn, Virginia, 146–182.

Johnson, L. R., and W. Silva (1981). The effects of unconsolidated sediments upon the ground motion during local earthquakes. *Bull. Seism. Soc. Am.*, 71: 127–142.

Lawson, A. C. (1908). *The California Earthquake of April 18, 1906:* Report of the State Earthquake Investigation Commission. Carnegie Institution, Washington, D.C.

Loh, C. H., J. Penzien, and Y. B. Tsai (1982). Engineering analysis of SMART 1 array accelerograms. *EESD*, 10: 575–591.

Louderback, G. D. (1942). History of the University of California Seismographic Stations and related activities. *Bull. Seism. Soc. Am.*, 32: 205–229.

McEvilly, T. V. (1980). Memorial to Don Tocher. *Bull. Seism. Soc. Am.*, 70: 400–402.

McEvilly, T. V., and R. Clymer (1981). Travel-time monitoring with Vibroseis. *Bull. Seism. Soc. Am.*, 71: 1903–1927.

McEvilly, T. V., and R. Feng (1983). Interpretation of seismic reflection profiling data for the structure of the San Andreas fault zone. *Bull. Seism. Soc. Am.*, 73: 1701–1720.

McEvilly, T. V., and E. L. Majer (1982). ASP: An automated seismic processor for microearthquake networks. *Bull. Seism. Soc. Am.*, 72: 303–325.

McEvilly, T. V., and W. Peppin (1972). Source characteristics of earthquakes, explosions, and afterevents. *Geophys. J. R. Astr. Soc.*, 31: 67–82.

Nuttli, O., and B. A. Bolt (1966). P wave residuals as a function of azimuth. *J. Geophys. Res.*, 71: 5977–5985.

Rodgers, P. (1968). The response of the horizontal pendulum seismometer to Rayleigh and Love waves, tilt, and the free oscillation of the Earth. *Bull. Seism. Soc. Am.*, 58: 1384–1406.

Stump, B. W., and L. R. Johnson (1984). Near-field source characterization of contained nuclear explosions in tuff. *Bull. Seism. Soc. Am.*, 74: 1–26.

Tanimoto, T., and B. A. Bolt (1983). Coupling of torsional modes in the Earth. *Geophys. J. R. Astr. Soc.*, 74: 83–95.

Tocher, D. (1960). Creep on the San Andreas fault. *Bull. Seism. Soc. Am.*, 50: 396–403.

Uhrhammer, R. A., A. J. Lomax, and R. McKenzie (1985). *Bulletin of the Seismographic Stations*, University of California, Berkeley, 54: 1–88.

PART TWO

Past and Future Development of the Seismological Observatory

THREE

International Seismology in the Digital Era

Michael J. Berry

INTRODUCTION

The Centennial Celebration of the opening of the first seismographic stations in North America at Mount Hamilton and Berkeley in 1887 is a fitting time for the seismological community to take stock of its affairs. Instrumental seismology's first century can be characterized by the very significant progress achieved in understanding the internal structure and dynamic properties of the Earth through the analysis of data from photographic recording seismographic networks and the development of efficient international mechanisms for archiving and distributing network data. As the older analog networks are replaced by more powerful digital types, the challenge for the international seismological community will be to ensure that the efficient mechanisms developed in the analog era are modified or replaced by similarly efficient mechanisms for archiving and distributing digital data. It is the purpose of this discussion to identify where changes will be required and to suggest the nature of some of these.

THE INTERNATIONAL SEISMOLOGICAL CENTRE (ISC)

In the early 1960s it was generally recognized that a new organization was needed to bring together all available seismic phase data in order to produce a definitive catalog of global seismicity. After numerous meetings and consultative committees, the International Seismological Centre (ISC) was formed as a direct descendant of the older International Seismological Summary (ISS) based in the United Kingdom and of the Bureau Central International de Seismologique (BCIS) based in France. The Centre's mission was similar to those of the earlier organizations, but the Centre differed importantly in being more adequately funded by supporting members, initially from several countries. Although the original membership was not great, it has grown steadily to include some forty organizations from nearly as many countries.

The objectives of the ISC as set out in its Working Statutes are the collection and analysis of terrestrial seismic events for the advancement of scientific knowledge of earthquakes, their prediction, and their modification. The principal tasks of the Centre are:

1. To collect seismogram readings from station networks throughout the world in cooperation with other seismological data centers and organizations.
2. To edit and preserve the readings for analysis in computer-readable form.
3. To compute focal coordinates and magnitudes for each event for which adequate data are available and to publish monthly a bulletin containing the fullest possible listing of original data and the parameters derived therefrom.
4. To prepare and publish a regional catalog of earthquakes.
5. To undertake such research and development efforts as may be relevant to improving the execution of the abovementioned tasks, and which are within the terms of these statutes.
6. To provide such other services to institutions or individual scientists and engineers throughout the world as are compatible with the execution of the abovementioned tasks, and with the data and facilities available within the Centre.
7. To undertake such other relevant activities as may be approved by the Governing Council on its own motion or on the recommendation of the Executive Committee.

At the beginning it was planned that the ISC would also establish a microfilm bank, and in fact the United States Coast and Geodetic Survey (USCGS) sent the Centre the 1964 output from the Worldwide Standardized Seismographic Network (WWSSN), which included microfilm from the Canadian network, and negotiations were well advanced with the Academy of Sciences of the USSR for copies of Soviet seismograms (J. H. Hodgson, personal communication). However, this activity has not continued owing to lack of funds.

Today the ISC is a lean, well-run organization, collecting some 1,200,000 seismic phase data from over 1,500 seismographic stations distributed around the globe to locate more than 25,000 earthquakes each year. The Centre also reports the earthquake locations estimated by other organizations which individually have access to fewer data as preliminary input, and uses "free search" computer routines to find events that have not been reported. The Centre has neither the staff nor the facilities to study waveform data.

The strength of the ISC catalog of earthquakes and the associated phase arrival data base lies in its completeness and comprehensive global coverage and in the uniformity of its techniques over the years. It cannot, of course, improve on the locations of events that have occurred within dense local or regional networks, but for those parts of the globe without such coverage it provides the definitive focal parameters.

The parameters of large events are now being calculated by seismologists at Harvard and the United States Geological Survey by the analysis of digital waveforms from the available broadband stations. These solutions are routinely published by the USGS in the National Earthquake Information Service (NEIS) monthly summaries. As the global digital networks develop, other organizations also are likely to make estimates of these parameters. The ISC, for its part, will provide the definitive information for intermediate magnitude events (less that magnitude 6.5), particularly in regions poorly monitored by local seismographic stations. The Centre will also, surely, continue to collate, archive, and distribute the definitive cumulative files of phase data and earthquake epicenters. The value of these files grows with time, and studies by Morelli and Dziewonski (1987) and others demonstrate the wealth of information the files contain on the heterogeneous nature of the Earth's interior. The earthquake catalogs themselves also are proving to be increasingly valuable as fundamental input to assessments of earthquake hazard. The importance of the catalogs will, of course, also continue to develop as they span longer periods of time.

In the future, as data from global networks become readily available, it will be natural for the ISC to wish to use such data to refine its estimates of earthquake focal parameters. Such a change from current practice is likely to receive support from the ISC's Governing Council, but the change will not be possible without extra resources, always difficult to acquire.

As the global digital networks develop, an international data center will be needed to collate, archive, and distribute the digital waveforms to the international seismological community. Such a role for the ISC would be fully compatible with its mandate, but again would require additional financial support.

THE IASPEI COMMISSION ON PRACTICE

In his "Notes on International Seismology for the History of the Dominion Observatory," J. H. Hodgson (personal communication) traces the development of the ISC from the earlier ISS and BCIS. Numerous committees were formed during that period under the auspices of UNESCO and the International Association of Seismology and Physics of the Earth's Interior

(IASPEI). Some had ambitious mandates and produced appropriately ambitious "wish lists"; others were more focused. One result, as explained above, was the founding of the ISC as a nongovernmental body, supported by member institutions, with generally one member from each supporting country. While the ISC is independent of other organizations, it ensures close ties with IASPEI by having one IASPEI appointee on its executive committee. It has become traditional for IASPEI to appoint the chairman (or one of the co-chairmen) of its Commission on Practice to this position.

IASPEI conducts its affairs through Commissions, loosely coordinated by a Bureau made up of the Executive Committee. Naturally the number and mandate of Commissions has evolved with time in response to the demands of science and the interests and ambitions of the scientists involved. There are, therefore, no formal mandates established for the Commissions, but their names clearly indicate the focus of their interests.

The Commission on Practice had become particularly active in recent years, and the scope of its current activities can be seen in its committee structure. It has four Subcommissions, each with Working Groups:

1. Subcommission on Quantification with Working Groups on Pre-instrumental Observations, Analog Recordings, and Digital Recordings.
2. Subcommission on Data Exchange with Working Groups on Telegraphic Formats, Historical Seismograms and Earthquakes, Guide to International Data Exchange, Seismic and Geographic Regionalization, and Digital Data Exchange.
3. Subcommission on Digital Seismology with Working Groups on Digital Seismometry, Unification of International Networks, Space-oriented Seismology, Digital Seismogram Interpretation, and Digital Data Exchange.
4. Subcommission on Algorithms (jointly with the Commission on Seismological Theory) with a Working Group on Interdependence of Earthquake Parameters and Earth Structures.

Many of the subjects covered by the Commission are clearly of direct relevance to the work of the ISC. The linkage is important and functioning. On important matters, the IASPEI representative brings formal resolutions of the Commission to the ISC Executive, where they can be fully considered; on a less formal basis, the IASPEI representative provides a source of advice and an insight into the concerns of the Commission.

Digital seismometry and practice has been a subject for IASPEI consideration for at least a decade. However, recent developments have made this subject of central importance to the future of seismology, and it is now being discussed in a number of other forums.

FEDERATION OF DIGITAL BROADBAND SEISMOGRAPHIC NETWORKS

At a meeting convened, in 1986, during joint meetings of the German Geophysical Society and the International Lithosphere Program in Karlsruhe, Federal Republic of Germany, twenty-four seismologists from some twenty institutions agreed upon the need for a new organization to facilitate coordination among the various groups now actively planning the deployment of large regional or global digital seismographic networks. The following text was adopted unanimously at the meeting and provides a succinct statement of the mission of the organization.

> The international seismological community recognizes new opportunities within its field for improved understanding of the internal structure and dynamical properties of the Earth provided by recent developments in seismograph network technology.
>
> It also recognizes that rapid access to seismic data from arrays of modern broadband digital instruments wherever they might be is now possible.
>
> The developments include greatly improved broadband seismographic systems that capture the entire seismic wave field with high fidelity, efficient and economical data communications and storage, and widely available, powerful computing facilities.
>
> In view of the above, and to take advantage of existing developing global and regional networks, it is considered that the federation be formed to provide a forum for:
>
> —developing common minimum standards in seismographs (e.g., bandwidth) and recording characteristics (e.g., resolution and dynamic range);
>
> —developing standards for quality control and procedures for archiving and exchange of data among component networks; and
>
> —coordinating the siting of additional stations in locations that will provide optimum global coverage.
>
> The federation welcomes the participation of all institutions committed to the deployment of broadband seismographs and willing to contribute to the establishment of an optimum global system with timely data exchange (Romanowicz and Dziewonski, 1986).

The founding meeting of the Federation was held in Kiel in August 1986 when four working groups were established. These are:
   I. Siting Plans
   II. Digital Broadband Seismograph Specifications
   III. Data Collection and Exchange Formats
   IV. Data Centres

Strictly, the activities of the new Federation do not duplicate those of the IASPEI Commission on Practice, since membership in the Federation is limited to interested institutions operating broadband networks, while the

Commission is open to all practicing seismologists. In practice, of course, the activities overlap considerably, many of the same topics being considered by potentially many of the same seismologists. The relationship between the Commission on Practice and the ISC may provide a useful model to resolve the overlap. Some of the more purely technological aspects of the Commission program could be transferred to the Federation for its consideration, and appropriate liaison could be ensured by having the Chairman of the Commission an ex-officio member of the Federation's Executive Committee.

THE GENEVA NETWORK

While the seismological community in general is actively developing a global digital seismographic network to study the heterogeneous nature of the Earth's interior and to improve understanding of the distribution and nature of earthquakes, a smaller group of seismologists is actively planning a network for a more narrowly focused objective. It has long been recognized that seismological techniques can provide one of the principal means of monitoring compliance with the provisions of a Comprehensive Test-Ban Treaty when such a treaty is successfully negotiated among nations. To this end the Conference on Disarmament, meeting in Geneva, has formed a Group of Scientific Experts (GSE) to develop specifications for a global network whose mission it would be to provide the necessary seismological data to national states to enable them to make judgments about possible treaty violations. The motivation, therefore, for this "Geneva Network" is political, rather than scientific, and its creation will be determined by considerations other than those that motivate the member networks of the Federation. Nevertheless, the considerations of the Geneva Group are relevant to all organizations concerned with global seismology. First, for many countries the seismographic stations that will form components of the Federation's global network will be the same stations identified for the Geneva Network. Second, the mechanisms being proposed for the rapid exchange of phase and digital waveform data, which will be the essence of the Geneva Network operation, may be useful models for consideration by the Federation, although without the absolute requirement of extremely fast data exchange.

The essence of the data-exchange model being developed by the GSE is the concept of a number of International Data Centres (IDC) supplied with phase, waveform, and earthquake parameters by National Data Centres (NDC) which, in turn, collect their data from the identified stations of their own networks. Figure 1 illustrates the model as developed in the spring of 1987. Clearly, the imperatives of the Geneva Network are such that redundancy of operation is necessary, and this will come at a high cost. Although the international seismic data exchange system depicted in figure 1 is a pre-

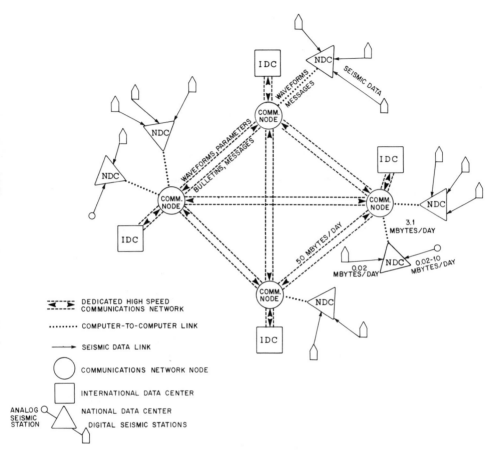

Figure 1: Global communications concepts for international seismic data exchange currently envisaged by the Conference on Disarmament Scientific Expert Group. Adapted from figure 10 of USA Working Paper GSE/US/44, "Technical Concepts for a Global System for Seismic Data Exchange," March 1987.

liminary conceptual design, if superpower and other international discussions of a test-ban treaty lead to implementation in the near future, it will have profound implications for global seismology. It is intended with this system that measured parameters (arrival times, amplitudes, etc.) and digital waveforms for all detected seismic events be transmitted to the IDCs within twenty-four hours. More than one IDC will be analyzing these data; the IDCs will reconcile differing hypocenter and magnitude parameters among themselves; and seismic event bulletins will be transmitted to participating countries within six days. A new feature of this system will be the use of waveform data to improve on event bulletins produced currently (for example, ISC, NEIS) by automatic association of parameter data. Since the emphasis of the Geneva system will be on the best possible event bulletins for small seismic events, it will not be likely to duplicate current attempts at waveform analysis of larger global earthquakes using Global Digital Seismographic Network (GDSN) and other digital data.

WORLD DATA CENTRES

The World Data Centres (WDC) were set up by the International Council of Scientific Unions (ICSU) during the International Geophysical Year of 1957 to facilitate the ready exchange of geophysical data throughout the international scientific community. The primary WDC for seismology, WDC-A, is operated by the United States from the offices of the National Oceanic and Atmospheric Administration (NOAA) and the USGS near Denver, Colorado. For more than twenty years WDC-A has provided an invaluable service to the seismological community by providing microfilm, at moderate cost, of all the seismograms written by the Worldwide Standardized Seismographic Network (WWSSN) and the Canadian Standard Network (CSN). There is no doubt that many of the major advances in our knowledge of the internal structure and dynamics of the Earth during this period have come from the widespread analysis of data distributed by the WDC-A from these networks.

As limited digital networks have been developed in the last decade, seismologists have come to recognize the convenience and power of the higher dynamic range data. The result has been a steady decline in the demand for microfilm of analog seismograms.

Recognizing the need for more orderly and convenient access to the digital data from several digital networks (RSTN, SRO, ASRO, IDA, DWWSSN), the USGS has started distributing event data on compact discs (CD-ROMs). These are inexpensive to reproduce once the initial master has been created. This innovative approach offers the promise that the seismological community will have access to data from the digital networks in the same (or better) fashion as from older analog networks.

DATA VOLUMES

The volume of data produced by a fully developed global digital network is large. It is, therefore, essential that its dimensions be fully recognized when considering how this digital output can be made conveniently available to the user community.

In its proposal for a New Global Seismographic Network, the Incorporated Research Institutions for Seismology (IRIS, 1984) notes:

It should be pointed out that even with 100 operational stations, the aggregate data rate of 25 Kbyte/sec is not high for either modern telecommunications networks or small computers, . . . the big jobs—big in the sense of computational effort and equipment needed—are the organization, archival and dissemination of the data.

Data volumes are easy to calculate. A broadband station will probably sample each of its three orthogonal components twenty times/per second, with perhaps three additional channels sampled once per second. If we assume 4 bytes of 8 bits/byte (32 bits/sample), one station will produce 252 bytes/s. A 100-station network would then produce about 800 gigabytes (Gb) per year.

These are large volumes, but if only triggered data are kept, the data can be reduced by a factor of eight (equivalent to saving twenty minutes of data for all events greater than magnitude 5 from all network stations). If the data are also compressed before recording, a further reduction by a factor of four (to approximately one byte per sample) should be possible (IRIS, 1984).

Recording media vary greatly in their capacity to hold data. The community is thoroughly familiar with digital tapes, and although the USGS is now distributing CD-ROMs, optical discs are not yet in common use. The following table sets out the numbers:

Medium	Capacity	Volumes/year		
	(Gb)	Compressed	Triggered	Both
6,250-bpi tape	0.12	1,656	828	207
CD-ROM	0.60	331	166	41
Optical disc	3*	66	33	8

* or greater

Thus, a global digital network of the sort planned by IRIS (100 stations) will produce data volumes requiring the capabilities of the latest technology.

FEDERATION DATA CENTRES

The new Federation of Digital Broadband Seismographic Networks seeks to develop a global network with optimum station distribution. The number to be drawn from networks of the Federation members will depend upon two separate factors: the availability of stations meeting Federation specifications and the ability of the Federation to archive and distribute the network data.

It now seems likely that a significant number of broadband digital stations meeting at least minimum Federation specifications will be deployed around the world. The USGS, IRIS, GEOSCOPE project (Romanowicz et al., 1984), and ORFEUS (Nolet et al., 1986) together will provide over 150 stations within five years. Several other national networks are also under development, promising to raise the number of stations available to the Federation to approximately 200.

To fulfill its mandate, the Federation must develop procedures for the archiving and exchange of data among component networks. The Federation, as an unfunded organization, cannot, of course, operate a data center itself; however, it is clear that each component network, global (GDSN, IRIS, or GEOSCOPE), regional (ORFEUS), or national (for example, the Canadian Network of Digital Seismometers, or CANDIS) will develop its own data center to meet its own needs.

In a report to the Federation on data center cooperation, Husebye et al. (1986) propose the following objectives for a Federation Data Centre (FDC):

1. Free access to any network data for any researcher associated with one of the member networks.
2. Pooling of network data in such a way that any center possesses a complete copy of all data available at least at 1-Hz sampling. However, for intermediate-period body-wave analysis, 4- to 10-Hz sampling would be more useful.
3. Easy retrieval of pooled network data for any qualified user at the user's expense.

These authors note that, despite considerable progress in mass storage technology, it is not considered realistic that all broadband data, using the original sampling of 20 Hz (or higher), can be available at all centers, at least for the time being.

Husebye et al. (1986) propose a hierarchy of data centers to progressively accumulate the data. At the first level, National Data Centres would collect the data from their own stations, apply essential quality control, archive the complete data set, and forward an edited set of data (to agreed criteria) to a Regional Data Centre (RDC), for example, the ORFEUS Data Centre. The RDC would make data available to all local participants, especially for regional studies of smaller magnitude events when data from distant global stations would be of little or no value. After archiving and possible further editing (again to agreed specifications), the RDCs would forward their data to the international center that acts as the Federation Data Centre.

Operating in parallel with national networks and regional consortiums will be independent networks of global extent. These networks will also operate data centers (Global Data Centres, or GDCs). It is the suggestion of Husebye et al. that one of the GDCs accept the responsibility for operating the Federation Data Centre. This is a realistic proposal, but a major responsibility for the center that accepts the role. Following the successful example of the analog era, it would be ideal if the GDC accepting the role of Federation Data Centre were to be under the ICSU World Data Centre umbrella.

The model proposed by Husebye et al., similar in concept to that developed for the international data centers of the Geneva Network, takes maximum advantage of the data centers already operating or planned. The Federation must now define the criteria for editing data at each level of data center and, of course, identify the Federation Data Centre itself.

SUMMARY

The first century of instrumental seismology has seen remarkable progress in determining the internal structure and dynamic properties of the Earth. In large measure this progress has been achieved by the operation of well-calibrated seismographic networks writing photographic records and the efficient and wide distribution of the data and seismogram copies from the networks to the seismological community.

The challenge in the rapidly developing digital era will be to ensure that the superior data from the new networks are also made available widely, efficiently, and in an easily used format. This will require careful consultation throughout the community and some adjustment in the roles and responsibilities of several of the international organizations for seismology, both to reduce unproductive overlapping activities and to address new problems and opportunities in a constructive fashion.

ACKNOWLEDGMENTS

I would like to thank P. W. Basham, R. G. North, R. D. Adams, J. H. Hodgson, and E. R. Engdahl for their helpful comments on the first draft of this manuscript.

REFERENCES

Husebye, E. S., R. P. Massé, and S. S. Alexander (1986). *Network Federation—Data Center Cooperation.* A working group report to the Federation of Digital Broadband Seismograph Networks, San Francisco, December 1986, 10 pp.

Incorporated Research Institutions for Seismology (1984). *Science Plan for a Global Seismographic Network*, Washington, D.C.

Morelli, A., and A. M. Dziewonski (1987). Topography of the core-mantle boundary and lateral homogeneity of the liquid core. *Nature* 325: 678–683.

Nolet, G., B. A. Romanowicz, R. Kind, and E. Wielandt (1986). *ORFEUS, Science Plan, Observatories and Research Facilities for European Seismology*, Utrecht, the Netherlands.

Romanowicz, B. A., M. Cara, J. F. Fels, and D. Rovland (1984). GEOSCOPE: A French initiative in long-period three-component global seismic networks, *EoS, Trans. Am. Geophys. Un.*, 65: 753–754.

Romanowicz, B. A., and A. M. Dziewonski (1986). Toward a federation of broadband seismic networks. *Trans. Am. Geophys. Un.*, 67: 541–542.

FOUR

The Global Seismographic Network: Progress and Promise

Adam M. Dziewonski

INTRODUCTION

The opening of the Berkeley stations preceded by two years the first documented teleseismic observation. According to Bolt (1982), E. von Rebeur Pashwitz interpreted the disturbances recorded by horizontal pendulums at Potsdam and Wilhelmshaven as caused by the earthquake in Tokyo of April 18, 1889. After that, progress in global seismology was rapid. The first global networks were established at the turn of the century. This coincided with the beginning of international cooperation in seismology; the systematic determination of epicenters of the world's large earthquakes reaches as far back as 1899.

The rewards were not long in coming. In 1906 Oldham discovered the liquid core, and in 1909 Mohorovičić reported the discontinuity between the crust and the mantle. By the end of the 1930s the conceptual image of the spherically symmetric model of the elastic properties of the Earth's interior was essentially complete. It was also rather accurate. Travel-time tables of Jeffreys and Bullen, first published in 1939, are still used to locate earthquakes by the National Earthquake Information Centre (NEIC) of the U.S. Geological Survey (USGS) and by the International Seismological Centre (ISC). Important progress was made in the 1960s in the recovery of the fine structure of the upper mantle and in observations of free oscillations of the earth. It is significant, however, that this progress depended on the availability of waveform data to the researchers' data.

Studies using waveform data from a widely distributed network of stations were difficult until copies of the centralized information were made available. This, in addition to the uniformity of the instrumental responses, was the principal advantage of the Worldwide Standardized Seismographic Network (WWSSN) established twenty-five year ago. The majority of the stations of this analog network, which once had 125 installations, are still operational.

The first two global networks with digital recording became operational in the mid-1970s. These were the International Deployment of Accelerometers (IDA; Agnew et al., 1976) and the Global Digital Seismographic Network (GDSN; Peterson et al., 1976) operated by the USGS. They were complementary in their response: IDA was designed to record ultralong-period waves, while GDSN has the highest sensitivity in the passband important for discriminating between nuclear explosions and earthquakes. Both suffered, however, from a rather limited dynamic range. The digital array installed in Gräfenberg, West Germany, in 1976 did much to convince the seismological community of the advantages of broadband recording (Harjes and Seidl, 1980).

Data from the early digital networks made a very significant contribution to seismology; some say that seismic tomography (Anderson and Dziewonski, 1984) will cause a new revolution in earth sciences. There has been progress in the routine quantification of earthquakes. The two figures shown here are meant to convey what is being done.

Figure 1 is a view of the Earth from a point 35,000 km from its center. The surface has been cut with a spherical triangle, each of its sides 10,000 km long. Velocity anomalies are mapped with a variable density of shading: the slowest velocities are the lightest. This is a composite picture, showing shear-velocity anomalies in the upper mantle, retrieved from mantle-wave analysis by Woodhouse and Dziewonski (1984), compressional velocity anomalies in the lower mantle, obtained from travel-time residuals by Dziewonski (1984), and compressional velocity anomalies obtained from observations of splitting of normal modes by Giardini et al. (1987). While progress continues—there are now shear-velocity models of the lower mantle from waveform inversion, and it had been proposed that the inner core is anisotropic—the important fact to notice is that images of the Earth's interior are being built from various types of data from very different frequency ranges.

Figure 2 shows eighty-eight centroid-moment tensor (CMT) solutions obtained from the analysis of GDSN data for a single month, March 1987 (Dziewonski et al., 1987). The CMT method was developed by Dziewonski et al. (1981) and later generalized by Dziewonski and Woodhouse (1983) to incorporate mantle waves. Woodhouse and Dziewonski (1984) developed algorithms for the direct and inverse problems for lateral heterogeneity; since 1984 the CMT solutions have been derived using synthetic seismograms and differential kernels corrected for aspherical structure. With the analysis extended back in time to 1977, the total number of CMT solutions for the last

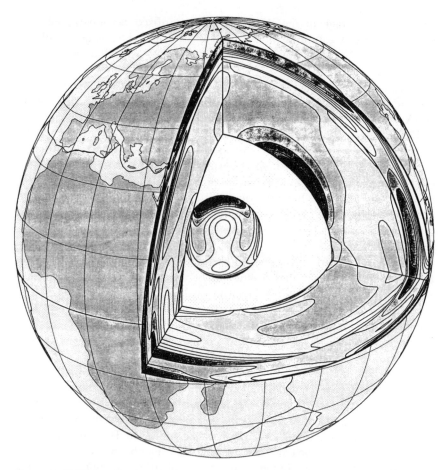

Figure 1. "Window into the Earth." A perspective view from a distance of 35,000 km to the Earth's center, showing regions of fast (dark) and slow (light) seismic velocities in the mantle and in the inner core. Upper mantle model is determined from inversion of long-period waveforms, lower mantle from travel times of body waves, and inner core from splitting of free oscillation spectral peaks. Computer graphics by John Woodhouse, Harvard University.

Figure 2. Centroid-moment tensor solutions for eighty-eight earthquakes occurring during March 1987 (Dziewonski et al., 1987). Although difficult to distinguish in this figure, both moment-tensor (shading) and best-double-couple solutions (solid lines) are shown. Beachball diameter is a linear function of magnitude; the smallest M_0 shown is 5×10^{23} dyne-cm, the largest (off the coast of Chile), 5×10^{27} dyne-cm.

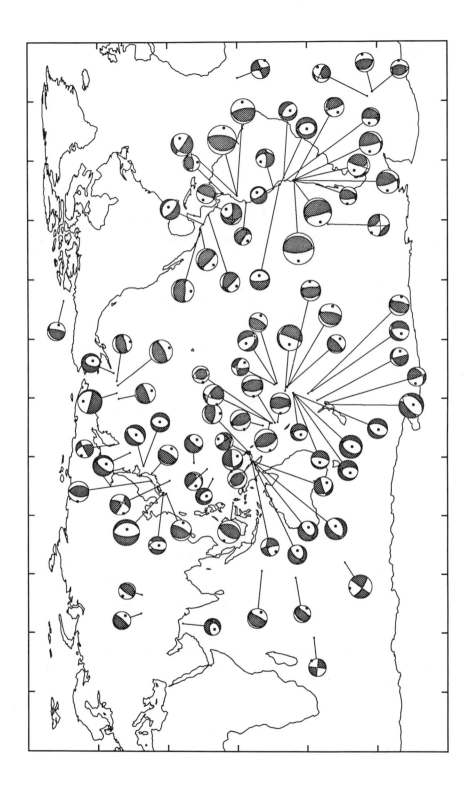

eleven years stands at about 6,500. This data set allows us to investigate in detail spatiotemporal variations in regional stress release.

The figures were selected arbitrarily only as illustrations. When the "Science Plan for a New Global Seismographic Network" was prepared by the Incorporated Research Institutions for Seismology (1984), as many as thirty-four scientists from sixteen institutions contributed to it. Science plans were also prepared for GEOSCOPE, a global network operated by French universities (Romanowicz et al., 1984), and ORFEUS (Observatories and Research Facilities for European Seismology), an association of fifteen western European countries. Chapter 3 in this volume, by M. J. Berry, describes the formation and objectives of the Federation of Digital Broadband Seismographic Networks in the context of the international exchange of seismic data. The Federation will adopt minimum common standards for the response and dynamic range of the stations of member networks. The Federation may also adopt optimum standards. These, as preliminary discussions indicate, could be very close to those chosen by IRIS when it formulated the design goals for its Global Seismographic Network (GSN) stations. The description of a GSN station and progress toward its implementation are the subject of this chapter.

THE VERY BROAD BAND SEISMOGRAPH

A meeting of the Ad Hoc Group on Global Seismographic Network was held in July 1983. Its report was an essential step toward the establishment of the GSN project. At the same time, less than thirty miles away, the final touches were being put on the first operational Very Broadband (VBB) Seismograph System with digital recording (Wielandt and Steim, 1986).

The idea of a VBB system is often credited to Plesinger (Plesinger and Horalek, 1976) who, in 1972, installed a system with a response flat to ground velocity from 0.3 to 300 seconds at Kasperske Hory, Czechoslovakia. The signals were recorded on magnetic tape using FM modulation. With the response falling off as ω^2 at long periods there was enough sensitivity to record not only the gravest modes of free oscillations of the Earth, but also the tides. At short periods, frequencies up to 5 Hz could be easily captured, and thus the entire band needed to record teleseismic signals could be accommodated.

Wielandt and Steim (1986) put it this way: "The most obvious argument in favour of such a VBB system is that is does not *a priori* determine the seismological research. Every user would simply extract that band of frequencies in which he is interested, unrestricted by any artificial subdivision of the spectrum."

The GSN "Design Goals" document (IRIS, 1985) states several basic requirements:

1. The sensitivity must be sufficient to resolve seismic signals at the level of the lowest ambient noise within the band from 0.3 mHz to 5 or 10 Hz.
2. The system should record on scale the largest teleseismic signals—say, an earthquake with $M\omega = 9$ at $30°$.
3. The linearity of the system should be such that signals near the ground noise minimum can be resolved in the presence of the maximum ground noise at other frequencies (microseismic storms).

Wielandt and Steim argue that it is possible to meet these requirements with a single data stream generated by a feedback system with a response flat to velocity between a frequency of 5 Hz and a period of 360 s. A much larger body of evidence related to this point can be found in Steim (1986).

The wide band of frequencies, with a significant variation in the spectral power within this band imposes important requirements on the other elements of the system, namely the analog-to-digital (A/D) converters. The need for a 140-db operating range could be met with a gain-ranging system; it could also be met with an A/D converter having a 24-bit resolution, undoubtedly more expensive and initially subject to serious doubts as to whether it could be realized.

Figure 3a, from Steim (1986), demonstrates the results of a test carried out in parallel on two high-resolution digitizers of different design. Two tones were used, one signal of 0.03 Hz with an amplitude of $\pm$ 5,000,000 counts and the other of 1 Hz with an amplitude of $\pm$ 5 counts, a million times smaller. The top two boxes show the unfiltered outputs from both digitizers, while the bottom two show the results after processing by a high-pass digital filter. A signal of 1 Hz is clearly present in both outputs, and it appears that distortion might have been introduced in part by the analog input, since the noise components in the two time series are somewhat similar. Figure 3b is a frequency-domain representation of the same test. The peak at 1 Hz with an amplitude of $- 120$ db is about 30 db above the noise level. It has been demonstrated, therefore, that high-resolution A/D converters work. But are they worth the additional cost?

The following two examples also come from the work of Steim (1986). One of the experimental versions of the system developed at Harvard used a gain-ranged A/D converter with a 15-bit mantissa. With the sensitivity set at a reasonable level, it is only for earthquakes with magnitudes above 7.5, at teleseismic distances, that the need for gain ranging arises. Therefore, not until the Michoacan earthquake of September 19, 1985, was an offset of four counts between the zeros of the high-gain and low-gain channels discovered.

In the middle of figure 4 is a plot of the original VBB trace of the vertical component of the large September 21 Michoacan aftershock. No evidence of distortion can be seen. At the top are two traces obtained by filtering the

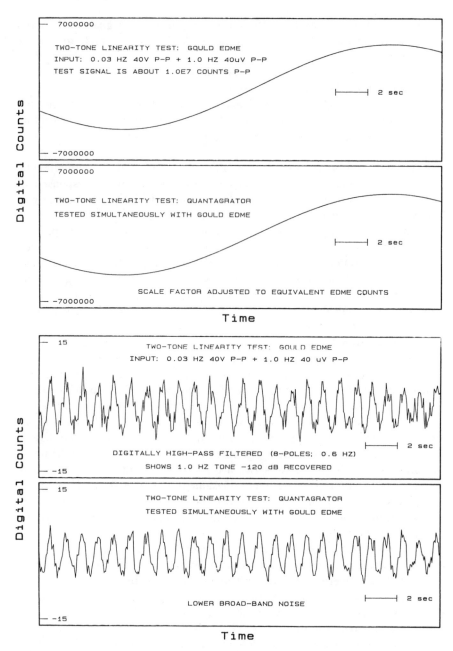

Figure 3a. A two-tone test of two 24-bit A/D converters of different design and manufacure. A 0.03-Hz tone and a 1-Hz tone, one million times smaller, are applied simultaneously to the two encoders. The 1-Hz tone (lower two panels) is visible after high-pass filtration. From Steim (1986).

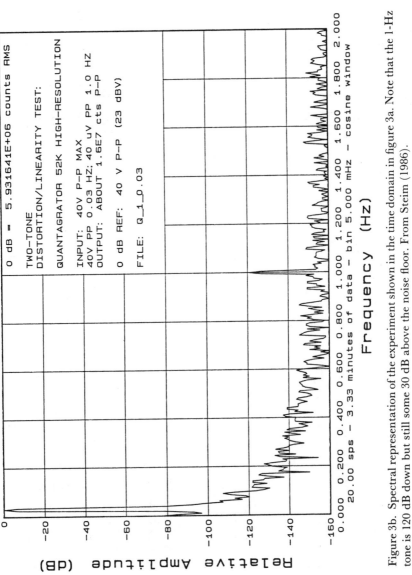

Figure 3b. Spectral representation of the experiment shown in the time domain in figure 3a. Note that the 1-Hz tone is 120 dB down but still some 30 dB above the noise floor. From Steim (1986).

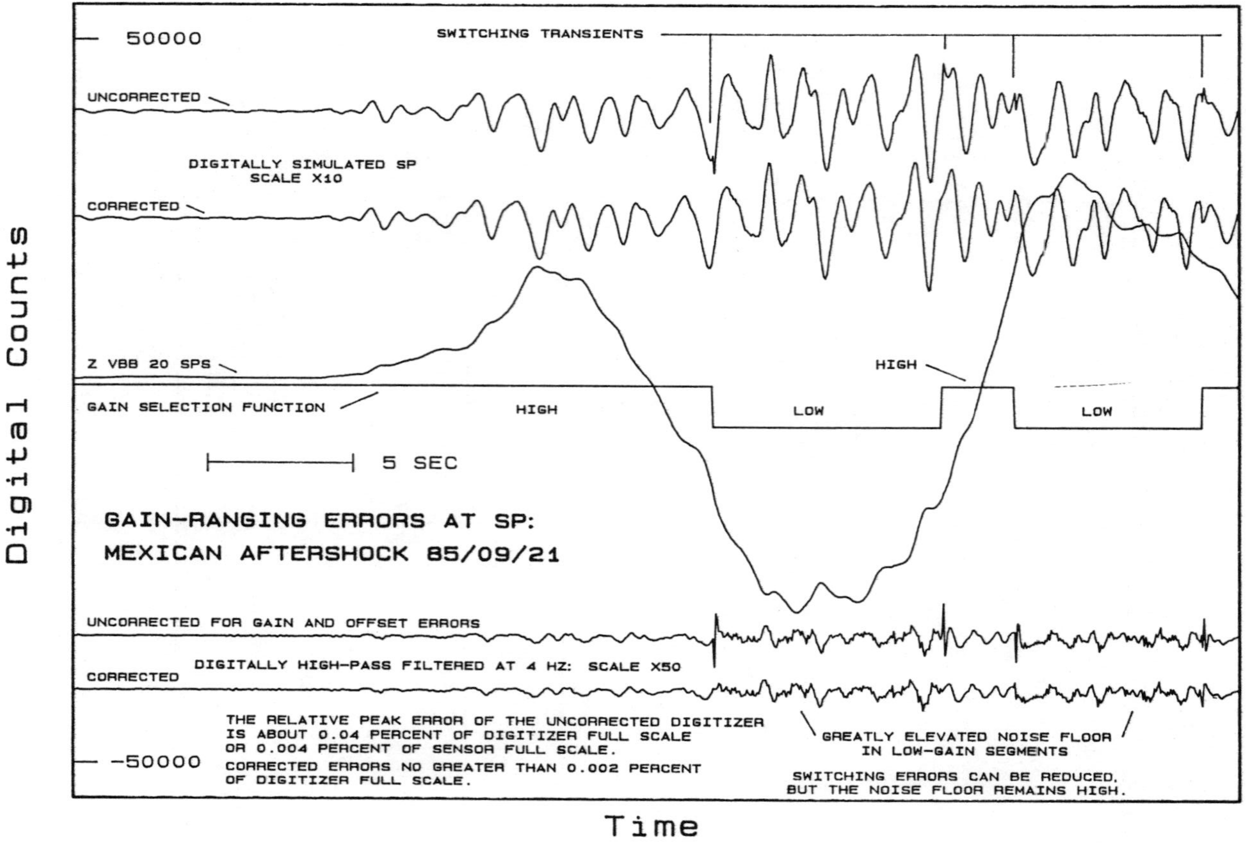

Figure 4. Quantization and offset errors at frequencies above 1 Hz, shown for the gain-ranged digitizer recording of the Michoacan aftershock of September 21, 1985. See text for discussion; from Steim (1986).

VBB record with a short-period WWSSN response. The top trace shows distinct glitches at the times of gain switching. The errors appear to be largely removed when correction for the zero offset is applied. The bottom pair show the same VBB record processed by a 4-Hz high-pass filter. The spikes due to gain switching are now the most prominent feature, and even correction for zero offset does not remove them completely. What cannot be corrected at all is the high noise floor, which is particularly noticeable at high frequencies of the low-gain channel.

Gain-switching errors can also be important at very long periods. Figure 5 (top) shows the very-long-period recording of both the main shock and the largest aftershock of the Michoacan earthquake. In both cases significant distortions are visible immediately after the R_1 arrivals. This is because the zero offset causes an overall bias when the gains are switching. In this case, correction for the offset seems to remove the distortion to a large extent.

It is next to impossible to assure perfect accuracy of the gain steps and matching of the zero levels. This is particularly true with regard to field-deployed instruments. Electronic parts can age differently, and the perfor-mance of instruments may change with time. In addition to the above argu-ment against gain switching, there are other reasons to use 24-bit digitizers in the VBB system. Winterly marine microseisms can be 4,000 time larger in ground velocity that the ground noise in the free oscillation band. This factor could be 200,000 for a response flat to acceleration.

In 1987, as an interim step toward improving the quality of digital data, IRIS, in cooperation with the USGS, installed VBB sensors at five stations already equipped with digital data loggers: College, Alaska; Afiamalu, Samoa; Kevo, Finland; Charters Towers, Australia; and Toledo, Spain. A preliminary version of the GSN station (to be described below), which in-cludes 24-bit digitizers, will soon be deployed at several U.S. sites: College, Alaska; Kipapa, Hawaii (in cooperation with GEOSCOPE); Cathedral Caves, Missouri; Pasadena, California; and Harvard, Massachusetts. These stations will be equipped with a dial-up system, and it will be possible for individual seismologists to retrieve data from them in quasi-real time.

IRIS also cooperates with the IDA project. New VBB stations have been deployed at Piñon Flats, California, and on Easter Island. Early upgrades are scheduled for Eskdalemuir, Scotland, and Sutherland, South Africa.

A state-of-the-art Data Collection Center is being developed jointly by IRIS and the USGS at the Albuquerque Seismological Laboratory. It is planned that the vastly increased data volume (GSN stations will be record-ing all three components of VBB data continously at twenty samples per second) will be handled using new optical mass-storage media.

Other member networks of the Federation are also accepting the VBB response. The very first network station using this response is a GEOSCOPE

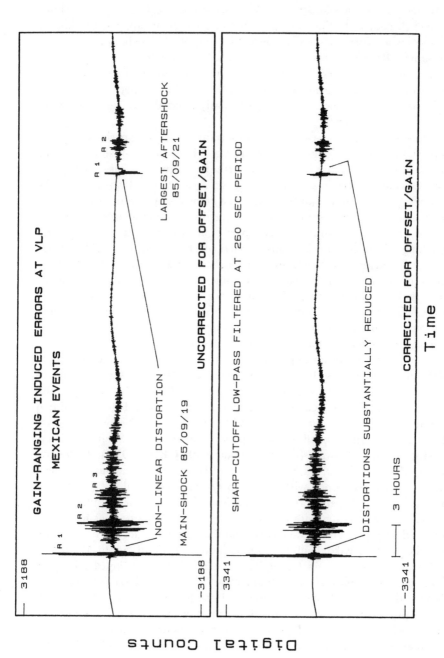

Figure 5. Very-long-period recordings of the Michoacan earthquakes of September 19 and 21, 1985, before (top) and after (bottom) correction of gain-ranged digitizer for offset and gain errors. From Steim (1986).

installation in Japan. Canada, Italy, Germany, and others are also installing VBB stations.

DESCRIPTION OF A GSN STATION

The Science Plan for New Global Seismographic Network (IRIS, 1984) documented the need for a broadband station with certain characteristics. This issue was followed up in greater detail in the Design Goals for GSN (IRIS, 1985). Both documents had a distribution of about 500 copies, roughly half sent to scientists outside the United States. In the spring of 1986 these documents were translated into design specifications and submitted to IRIS's administration.

In April 1987, following appropriate procurement procedures, IRIS entered into a contractural agreement with Gould, Inc., for construction of a prototype station processor. The choice of the architecture of the system was guided by several considerations:

1. Meeting of the scientific objectives
2. Reliability and ease of maintenance
3. Modularity and minimal dependence on unique products
4. Feasibility of future upgrades and modifications of the chosen elements of the system
5. Scientific and operational benefits for the host organization

Figure 6 is a block diagram of the system. The two principal components are the data-acquisition unit (DA) and the data-processing unit (DP). They are connected by a serial link or any form of telemetry, from telephone lines to satellites. The following is a brief description of the major features of a GSN station.

Data-Acquisition (DA) Module

The DA is the heart of the system. With only minor software modifications, relative to the agreed-upon specifications, and the addition of a tape recorded, this unit would be, in principle, capable of fulfilling the principal objective of the entire system, namely, the acquisition and recording of data.

The major components of the DA system are:

1. A very broadband seismic sensor system. The STS-1V(H)/VBB, built by Streckeisen & Co., is a set of sensors that satisfy the IRIS design goals for installation in a vault.
2. A high-resolution digitizer/calibrator unit (HRDCU). This is a three-channel 24-bit formatted digitizer/calibrator for use with the VBB sensors. Its data rate is twenty samples per second (sps) per channel.

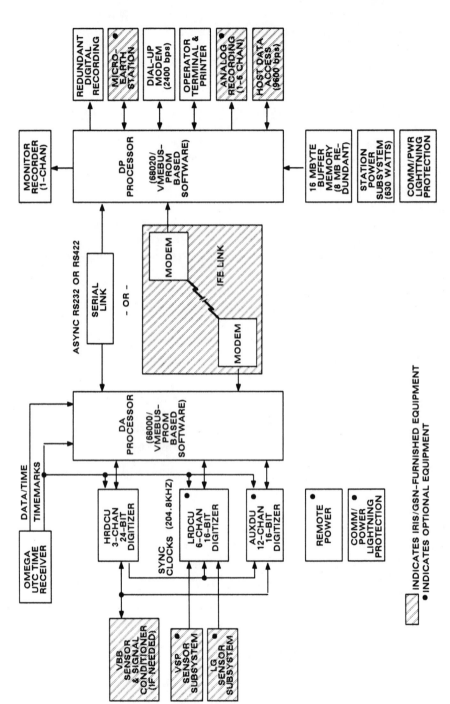

Figure 6. Block diagram of the prototype GSN station. From report U87-260 by Gould Inc.

3. Kinemetrics OMEGA UTC time receiver.
4. Auxiliary digitizer unit (AUXDU). This is for monitoring various state-of-health parameters of the VBB system and, optionally, other parameters such as atmospheric pressure or geomagnetic field. Data rates are programmable.
5. Optional low-resolution digitizer-calibrator unit (LRDCU). This is for digitizing the output of additional sensors.
6. Optional very-short-period (VSP) sensor system. "Design Goals" suggested a sampling rate of 100 sps. Consideration is being given to increasing it up to 200 sps.
7. Low-gain (LG) sensor subsystem. This was originally thought of as a means to extend the dynamic range of the VBB system and could serve as a strong-motion monitor. Its sampling rate is the same as that of the VSP system. There could be a limitation on the aggregate data rate of the VSP and LG channels (about 600 sps total—all sensors and all components).
8. Data-acquisition unit (DA). This is based on a 68000 or 68020 CPU with a VME bus, operating under an OS-9 operating system and special application software. The DA processor interfaces with the three GSN digitizers (HRDCU, LRDCU, and AUXDU) and with the data-processor unit (DP). All interfaces are bi-directional. The major data-manipulation functions of the DA processor are to collect data from the three digitizers, time tag data blocks, compress VBB data, perform VSP and LG event detection, and transmit data to the DP.

Data-Processor (DP) Module

The DP module provides the means for on-site and remote monitoring of system performance, communications with remote users, digital and analog recording of data, maintenance of data buffers, display of data for a selected time window on a graphic terminal, and many other functions. Its principal role is the enhancement of the functions of the DA unit, on-site quality control, and providing station personnel and remote users with information on seismic events.

The station DP consists of commercially available hardware modules and is based on a standard VME bus. Figure 7 gives some details of the DP configuration. The computing power of the 68020 chip is such that only a small fraction of its capacity will be used for the planned tasks, which leaves much room for expansion. Even now it is a fairly complex, sophisticated system.

Figure 8 is a block diagram of the DP unit's data-manipulation functions. The VBB data are decompressed so that they can be processed through a series of digital filters that produce short-period (SP), long-period (LP; 1 sps), and very-long-period (VLP; 0.1 sps) data. The LP and VLP data

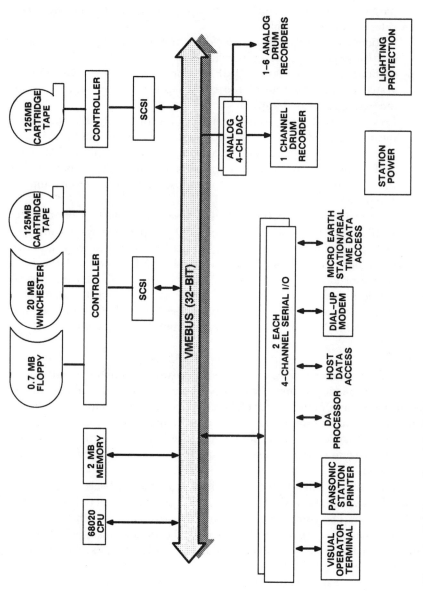

Figure 7. Configuration of the GSN station data processor (DP). From report U87-260 by Gould Inc.

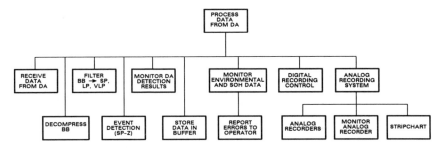

Figure 8. Data processing functions carried out by the DP unit. U87-260 by Gould Inc.

streams are obtained using finite-impulse-response (FIR) filters with a very sharp corner near the edge of the passband. This assures retention of the maximum information in the passband and may modify the way in which seismologists evaluate the usefulness of various data streams.

Figure 9 is taken from Steim (1986). It shows the original VBB channel and five channels derived from it. There is a twenty-second delay caused by a FIR filter. The trace labeled LP is obtained from the VBB stream using a 201–points FIR filter. It is clear that is contains most of the information present in the VBB stream, but with twenty times fewer samples. It very well may be that this will be the most frequently used data stream, particularly because of its relatively light archival burden. The other data streams shown contain less high-frequency energy, with the simulated SRO-LP channel representing an extreme. The VBB response is particularly convenient for a stable recovery of the ground displacement function (bottom trace).

The command, control, and algorithmic functions executed by DP are shown in figure 10. Rather than discuss them in detail, let us list functions that the operator can execute from the system console without interrupting acquisition of data:

1. Adjust the scale and select active analog monitor channels, including the selection of simulated WWSSN and Seismic Research Observatory (SRO) response functions.
2. View a continuously updated full-screen status display that shows a snapshot of all data channels, the internal and received UTC time, and several other system parameters.
3. View the system event log.
4. Change the tape cartridge without loss of data.
5. Examine the status of active processes.
6. View selected data waveforms from buffers or in real time.
7. Set, change, or display event-detection parameters.
8. Exchange message text over the real-time and dial-up ports.

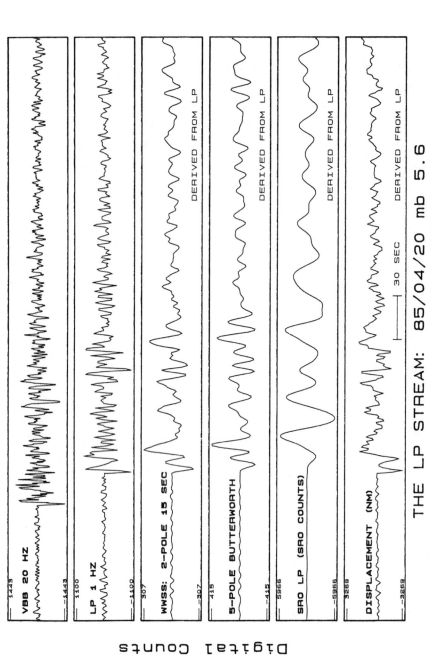

THE LP STREAM: 85/04/20 mb 5.6

Figure 9. The information content of the "broadband" 1-Hz LP data stream, obtained by processing VBB data with a FIR filter with a very sharp roll-off near the edge of the passband. The four lower traces, showing alternative responses, are derived from the LP data stream. The 20-s delay is due to the finite length of the FIR filter. From Steim (1986).

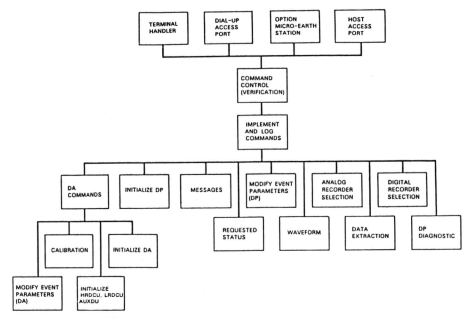

Figure 10. Command, control, and diagnostic function structure within the data-processor (DP) unit. From Gould Inc. report U87-260.

9. Control and set up a calibration cycle or program the onset time of a calibration sequence to be recorded with the station data.
10. Run a calibration analysis as a low-priority background job.
11. Log messages and the results of calibration to the system's mass-storage device.

Many of the functions described above can be performed through a dial-up port, which allows for frequent checks of station performance from the network maintenance center.

It is expected that a prototype of the GSN system will be delivered in the fall of 1988 and, following tests, production units will be ordered. The first ten, budget permitting, will be deployed in 1989.

A TRULY GLOBAL NETWORK

The report of the Ad Hoc Group on Global Seismographic Network, prepared in July 1983, reads:

> We envisage a network consisting of 100 [digital seismographic] stations of wide dynamic range covering frequencies from a fraction of a milliHertz to several Hertz or higher.

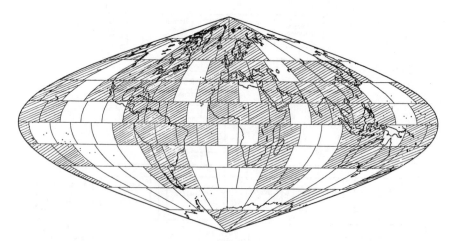

Figure 11. Inadequacy of future global coverage by land-based stations. Shaded areas show blocks that will contain, by 1992, at least one station satisfying the Federation standards.

   The Network would be a major research facility for earth scientists studying the structure and dynamics of our planet. The concept of an integrated set of instruments operating in unison, with widespread and convenient access to global data by a large number of users is a natural step in the evolution of seismology.

What is not clear from this quotation is that all these instruments would be land-based. Even though deployment on oceanic islands would help to alleviate some of the imbalance in distribution, islands are anomalous features in the ocean floor and are characterized by a high level of seismic noise. It is clear that without a complement of permanent ocean-bottom or sub-bottom observatories it will not be possible to examine with uniform resolution either the stress release in the Earth or its internal laterally varying structure.

While important progress is being made in the deployment of land-based stations through efforts such as that of the IRIS initiative in the United States, the GEOSCOPE Project in France, and the activities of other members of the Federation, nonetheless, as figure 11 shows, there are clear limits to the quality of global coverage obtainable in this way. The surface of the Earth has been divided into 128 regions of roughly equal area. Regions in which there will be a Federation station with "global" characteristics by 1992 are marked by hatching. Most of the large "white" areas, except for the Soviet Union, are in the major ocean basins.

The proposal of permanent geophysical observatories on the ocean bottom received strong support during the COSOD II (Conference on Scientific

Ocean Drilling) meeting held in Strasbourg, France, in July 1987. While the official report of the COSOD II proceedings is yet to be published, the text below appears to represent the consensus of the participants directly involved in this issue.

The desirability of establishing ocean bottom and sub-bottom geophysical observatories in conjunction with drill holes has been obvious from the start of the deep sea drilling program. But no such observatories have been established for two principal reasons. First, that rocks cored from the drill holes have, by far, been the most important reason for drilling the cores. Second, it has not been clear that the requisite technology has been available for the various aspects of such observatories: development of the bottom and sub-bottom instruments, their emplacement, their maintenance and data retrieval. The reason for tying the ocean bottom/sub-bottom observatories to the drilling program is three-fold. First, that it is very important to have information about the subsurface at the site of the observatories. Second, that emplacing instruments in the borehole reduces noise levels significantly for some instruments (Shearer and Orcutt, 1987). Third, that some experiments specifically require the emplacement of instrument at different levels in the boreholes.

It is critical for ocean bottom seismic observatories to supplement the land-based coverage and to become an essential part of the global observing system during the next decade. Both short period and long period seismic observations are extremely important. Deployment on the ocean floor of a very broad band seismograph system . . . would be ideal. The primary purpose of this type of an observatory would be to monitor seismic activity on the ocean floor, and to record information needed in studies of earth structure and earthquake source mechanism.

Important technological problems remain to be solved. Partly as a result of the COSOD II discussions, new initiatives are developing that involve both the oceanographic and the seismological communities. The first step will be to evaluate the pilot projects that should be undertaken as soon as possible.

There is an unusual opportunity that will develop during the next few years, which should accelerate the process. The telephone companies are now changing to transoceanic cables using fiber-optic technology. This means that old, still functional cables will be abandoned. These cables could well be used to power and transmit in real time data from ocean bottom stations. Indeed, POSEIDON, a very imaginative project proposed by Japanese seismologists, assumes a major deployment of permanent ocean bottom stations in the western Pacific, using the underwater communication cables.

There is a chance, perhaps the greatest during the entire first century of global seismology, of covering the world with instruments of high quality and performance that few of us dared to dream of only a few years ago. An important vehicle for this development will be the largest ever Earth-oriented international scientific program: The Global Change. It is, to a large degree, up to us to convince the rest of the geoscience community that seismology and seismographic stations are indispensable tools for a comprehensive study of our changing environment.

REFERENCES

Agnew, D., J. Berger, R. Buland, W. Farell, and F. Gilbert (1976). International Deployment of Accelerometers: A network for very long period seismology. *EOS, Trans. Am. Geophys. Un.*, 57: 180–188.

Anderson, D. L., and A. M. Dziewonski (1984). Seismic tomography. *Scientific American*, 251: 60–68.

Bolt, B. A. (1982). *Inside the Earth: Evidence from Earthquakes*. W. H. Freeman, San Francisco, 191 pp.

Dziewonski, A. M. (1984). Mapping the lower mantle: Determination of lateral heterogeneity in P-velocity up to degree and order 6. *J. Geophys. Res.*, 89: 5929–5952.

Dziewonski, A. M., T. A. Chou, and J. H. Woodhouse (1981). Determination of earthquake source parameters from waveform data for studies of global and regional seismicity. *J. Geophys. Res.*, 86: 2825–2852.

Dziewonski, A. M., G. Ekström, J. H. Woodhouse, and G. Zwart (1988). Centroid-moment tensor solutions for January–March, 1987. *Phys. Earth Planet. Inter.*, 50: 116–126.

Dziewonski, A. M., and J. H. Woodhouse (1983). An experiment in the systematic study of global seismicity: Centroid-moment tensor solutions for 201 moderate and large earthquakes of 1981. *J. Geophys. Res.*, 88: 3247–3271.

Giardini, D., X. D. Li, and J. H. Woodhouse (1987). Three-dimensional structure of the Earth from splitting in free oscillation spectra. *Nature*, 325: 405–411.

Harjes, H. P., and D. Seidl (1980). Digital recording and analysis of broad-band seismic data at the Gräfenberg (GRF) array. *J. Geophys.*, 44: 511–523.

Incorporated Research Institutions for Seismology (1984). *Science Plan for New Global Seismographic Network*. IRIS, Washington, D.C., 130 pp.

——— 1985. *Design Goals for New Global Seismographic Network*. IRIS, Washington, D.C., 31 pp.

Peterson, J., H. M. Butler, L. G. Holcomb, and C. R. Hutt (1976). The seismic research observatory. *Bull. Seism. Soc. Am.*, 66: 2049–2068.

Plesinger, A., and J. Horalek (1976). The seismic broadband recording and data processing system FBV/DPS and its seismological applications. *J. Geophys.*, 42: 201–217.

Romanowicz, B., M. Cara, J. F. Fels, and D. Rouland (1984). GEOSCOPE—A French initiative in long-period three-component global seismic networks. *EOS, Trans. Am. Geophys. Un.*, 65: 753–754.

Shearer, P. M. and J. A. Orcutt (1987). Surface and near-surface effects on seismic waves—theory and borehole seismometer results, *Bull. Seism. Soc. Am.*, 77, 1168–1196.

Smith, S. W. (1987). IRIS-A university consortium for seismology, *Rev. Geophys, Space Phys.*, 25, 1203–1207.

Steim, J. M. (1986). *The Very-Broad-Band Seismograph System*. PH.D. Diss., Harvard University, Cambridge, 183 pp.

Wielandt, E., and J. M. Steim (1986). A digital very-broad-band seismograph. *Annales Geophysicae*. Series B, Terrestrial and Planetary Physics, 4: 227–232.

Woodhouse, J. H., and A. M. Dziewonski (1984). Mapping the upper mantle: Three dimensional modeling of earth structure by inversion of seismic waveform. *J. Geophys. Res.*, 89: 5953–5986.

FIVE

Large-Scale Processing and Analysis of Digital Waveform Data from the USGS Central California Microearthquake Network

W. H. K. Lee and S. W. Stewart

In 1966 the U.S. Geological Survey (USGS) began to install a microearthquake network along the San Andreas fault system in central California. Its main objective was to develop techniques for mapping microearthquakes in order to study the mechanics of earthquake generation (Eaton, Lee, and Pakiser, 1970). The network was designed to telemeter seismic signals from field stations to a recording and processing center in Menlo Park, California. Its instrumentation has been described by Lee and Stewart (1981).

By 1987, this network had grown to over 350 stations in northern California (fig. 1) and is believed to be the largest local earthquake network in the world. At present, about 500 channels of seismic signals are being monitored in real time as some stations send in one high-gain vertical-component signal and three low-gain three-component signals. We also receive seismic signals from some stations operated by the USGS, Pasadena; University of Nevada (UNV), Reno; Lawrence Livermore Laboratory (LLL); California Division of Mines and Geology (CDMG); California Division of Water Resources (CDWR); and University of California (UC), Berkeley.

The purpose of this paper is to describe briefly the present data acquisition and processing system, and to summarize our current effort in processing and analyzing waveform data. The volume of data we handle is huge and required special attention.

CUSP DATA ACQUISITION AND ROUTINE PROCESSING

The CUSP (Caltech-USGS Seismic Processing) system consists of on-line real-time earthquake waveform data acquisition routines, coupled with an off-line set of data reduction, timing, and archiving processes. It is a complete system for processing local earthquake data in that all processing steps fol-

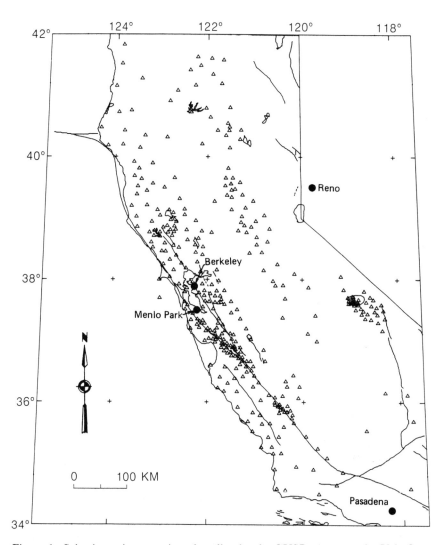

Figure 1. Seismic stations monitored on-line by the CUSP system at the U.S. Geological Survey, Menlo Park. Some selected stations operated by the California Department of Water Resources, California Division of Mines and Geology, California Institute of Technology, Lawrence Livermore National Laboratory, University of California (Berkeley), and University of Nevada (Reno) are also included.

lowing detection of the seismic event, to final cataloging, archiving, and retrieval of data, are scheduled and verified by the CUSP system.

CUSP is an evolutionary outgrowth of previous systems designed and developed by Carl Johnson while at Caltech and then with the USGS in Pasadena, California (Johnson, 1979 and 1983). Various implementations of CUSP are now operating in southern California (Caltech-USGS, Pasadena), central California (USGS, Menlo Park), and Hawaii (Hawaiian Volcano Observatory). The version running in Menlo Park was modified considerably by Peter Johnson, Sam Stewart, Bob Dollar, and Al Lindh to meet the specific needs of our network. Hardware includes two PDP 11/44 computers made by Digital Equipment Corp. (DEC), two 512-channel analog-to-digital converters, four dual-ported magnetic disk drives, two 6250 BPI magnetic tape drives, a VERSATEC plotter, a line printer, real-time clocks, and several display terminals.

The CUSP system as implemented for the Central California Microearthquake Network was the first of its two DEC PDP 11/44 computers (referred to as 11/44A) for real-time, on-line earthquake detection and data acquisition (fig. 2). The 11/44A monitors up to 512 signals in real time and writes out digitized waveform data to magnetic disk storage for events it interprets to be seismic. Currently, 500 signals are digitized at 100 samples per second. About two or three times a day, the digitized waveform data of detected events are automatically transferred to the second DEC PDP 11/44 (referred to as 11/44B), where initial CUSP processing takes place. Such transfer is made possible by the use of dual-ported magnetic disk drives. While the waveform data are still on disk, earthquake events are timed by means of a CUSP-controlled interactive graphics timing system, and archiving and other functions are performed. The event waveform data are archived on high-density 6250 BPI magnetic tapes, and all data except the digitized waveform data are then transferred to a DEC VAX/750 computer for final data reduction. Thereafter, the complete data sets are available for general use on the DEC VAX/750 computer.

A primary design feature of CUSP is that "all" information known to CUSP about an earthquake is contained in one file, and the digitized traces associated with that earthquake are contained in a separate file. These are known as "MEM" files and "GRM" files, respectively (fig. 2). For reasons of rapid data-base manipulation, MEM files are written in a compact, database-specific format. For compact storage, GRM files are written in DEC integer binary format. MEM files are collected each day on a "Daily Freeze" tape, and GRM files are archived on "Arkive" tape(s). Each local earthquake timed and located on the DEC PDP 11/44B computer has a "TROUT" plot produced on a VERSATEC plotter. These plots are a summary of the hypocenter information along with a plot of the seismic traces that entered into the earthquake location solution. Daily Freeze tapes are

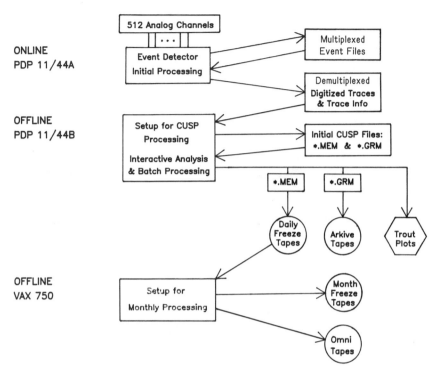

Figure 2. Schematic diagram showing the CUSP system processing steps and products.

combined each month into a "Monthly Freeze" tape. Also for each month, the hypocenter summary and phase data files in HYPO71 format (Lee and Lahr, 1975) and the station coordinate file are written on an "Omni" tape in DEC ASCII format for general use, especially on other computers.

The volume of data processed by the CUSP system is huge. Each year, about 15,000 earthquakes are routinely analyzed, and about 50 gigabytes of digital waveform data are archived. The system is remarkably robust. The off-line 11/44B computer is used as backup for the on-line 11/44A computer in case of emergency or routine hardware maintenance. Data loss occurs rarely and is usually due to electric power fluctuation or failure. System up-time is better than 99.7 percent. Because the station coverage is sparse in places, event coverage is not uniform throughout the network area, especially near the edges. Nevertheless, statistical analysis indicates that records of seismic events occurring within the network are complete for magnitude 1.5 and greater. Figure 3 shows the earthquake epicenters as determined by the CUSP system for 1984–1986. Most earthquake activity is along the San Andreas fault system and in the Coalinga and Long Valley area (due to after-

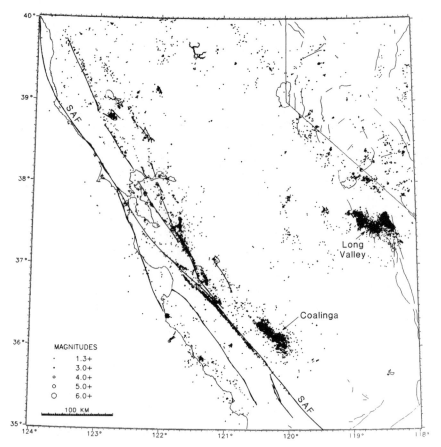

Figure 3. Map showing the earthquake epicenters as determined by the CUSP system for the period 1984–1986. SAF denotes the San Andreas fault.

shocks of the 1983 Coalinga earthquake and the 1984 Round Valley earthquake). Epicenters are systematically displaced to the west from the San Andreas fault trace because of the simplified crustal model used in the routine location of earthquakes. Systematic bias also may be seen on other faults (not named in fig. 3).

SETTING UP CUSP DATA FOR EXTERNAL PROCESSING

The CUSP system was designed and is used for the systematic detection, processing, and cataloging of data from earthquakes that occur within a seismic telemetry network. Its configuration is optimized for rapid processing of many local events. In its present form, the CUSP system is not intended for

1. Processing Small Data Sets

2. Processing Large Data Sets

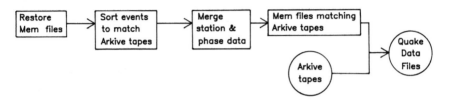

Figure 4. Two schemes for setting up CUSP data for processing outside the CUSP computing environment.

use as a research tool. Furthermore, CUSP data are optimized for use in the CUSP environment on DEC computers. Because of the limited computer facilities at the USGS, advanced processing and analysis of moderate to large quantities of seismic waveform data usually have to be carried out on more powerful general computers outside the CUSP computing environment. For this reason, we have implemented two schemes for setting up CUSP data for external processing.

Figure 4 illustrates the two schemes, one for processing "small" data sets and the other for processing "large" data sets outside the CUSP environment. "Small" means a few hundred earthquakes requiring about ten high-density 6250 BPI magnetic tapes to store their waveform data. "Large" means several tens of thousands of earthquakes requiring about 1,000 high-density tapes. The goal of both schemes is to produce an earthquake data file that has all the data for a given earthquake in a form that can be read by any computer. A typical earthquake data file contains about five megabytes. The earthquake data file is organized in a manner described by Lee, Scharre, and Crane (1983). It is designed to be complete, that is, containing index information, a description of the data, specifications of all data formats, recording stations, and earthquake summary, phases, and waveform data. In other words, all the necessary data for studying a particular earthquake are contained in its earthquake data file.

Traditionally, earthquake data are organized in a manner suggested by the nature of the data. For example, instrumentaion and operational information is contained in the station files, arrival times and amplitudes in the phase files, and digital waveform data in the trace files. Description and format for these files are usually written on paper and sometimes included in publications. However, there is a tendancy to update station files and phase files, introduce new formats, move data files onto different computers, and lose paper notes. Before long, it is almost hopeless to reconstruct a complete data set for a group of earthquakes. In view of this difficulty, when working outside the CUSP environment, we have chosen to put all the necessary information for an earthquake into one independent data file.

CODA PROCESSING AND ANALYSIS

In the past several years, there has been considerable interest in studying coda waves from local earthquakes and, in particular, estimating the quality factor Q using coda waves (Herrmann, 1980; Singh and Herrmann, 1983; Biswas and Aki, 1984; Jin, Cao, and Aki, 1985; Novelo-Casanova et al., 1985; Scherbaum and Kisslinger, 1985; Jin and Aki, 1986; Lee et al., 1986; Novelo-Casanova and Butler, 1986; Sato, 1986; Rogers et al., 1987; and Peng et al., 1987). Laboratory experiments indicate that microfracturing should occur prior to earthquakes. Because fractures greatly attenuate seismic waves, temporal variation of coda Q may be a useful precursor for earthquake prediction.

According to Aki and Chouet (1975), the coda amplitude $A(\omega \mid t)$ at angular frequency ω and lapse time t (measured from the origin time) is given by

$$A(\omega \mid t) = c(\omega)t^{-\alpha}e^{-\omega t/2Q} \qquad (1)$$

where $c(\omega)$ represents the coda source factor, α is a constant that depends on geometrical spreading, and Q is the quality factor. By performing linear regression of $\ln(At^{\alpha})$ versus t, we may obtain Q^{-1} from the slope of fit, b, by

$$Q^{-1}(\omega) = 2b/\omega = b/(\pi f) \qquad (2)$$

where f is the frequency in cycles/second.

Lee et al. (1986) began a systematic study of coda Q using the CUSP data from the Central California Microearthquake Network (fig. 5A). For this type of study, the digitized seismic waveform data (100 samples/second), together with auxiliary data such as origin time, hypocenter location, and magnitude, are first organized as earthquake data files in the manner described by Lee, Scharre, and Crane (1983). Using this scheme, we can select any station record from any earthquake with ease because the computerized system keeps track of the data records. For a selected earthquake, a record section is generated with the seismic traces arranged by increasing epicentral distance. From this record section, a data analyst decides whether or not this earthquake has a sufficient number of "good" stations (usually twenty or

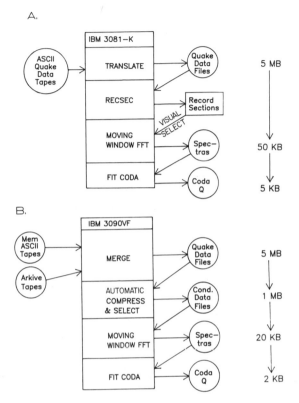

Figure 5. (A) Coda-processing scheme at the SLAC Center (top); (B) coda-processing scheme at the IBM Center (bottom).

more) and decides which station records have high enough signal quality to be processed.

Judgment of signal quality is rather subjective: for our study, "good" station records were those with coda amplitudes several times larger than the noise amplitudes preceding the earthquake, and station signals with spikes were rejected. For each selected station, a fast Fourier transform was performed on the data in overlapping moving windows for the entire station record. The resulting power spectra were then corrected for instrument response, and spectral averages over five consecutive octave frequency bands (centered at 1.5, 3, 6, 12, and 24 Hz) were obtained for each window. Typically, we used a window size of 512 data samples (corresponding to 5.12 s) and advanced the window by 2.56 s.

To avoid contamination by body and surface waves, only coda data collected at lapse times greater than twice the S travel time were included in the analysis, following the criterion for a common decay curve given by Rautian and Khalturin (1978). We then corrected the coda amplitude for geometrical spreading using Sato's (1977) formula, which is appropriate for coda waves in the near field. The logarithm of the corrected spectral amplitude was linearly related to the lapse time according to the single back-scattering theory of coda waves, that is, equation (1), and Q^{-1} was then calculated from equation (2). We commonly performed linear regressions in four coda time windows (10 to 25 s, 20 to 45 s, 30 to 60 s, and 50 to 100 s) to estimate Q^{-1}.

The procedure described above was performed using an IBM 3081 mainframe computer at the Stanford Linear Accelerator Center (SLAC) as shown in figure 5a. This computer is powerful enough to allow all the analysis in the interactive mode, that is, the computer keeps up with the actions taken by the analyst. Typically, five megabytes of input data for an earthquake are reduced to two kilobytes of results.

The SLAC procedure was designed to process "small" data sets of a few hundred earthquakes and to allow the analyst to quickly modify the program for particular research needs. However, it is not efficient for processing "large" data sets of tens of thousands of earthquakes. For "large" data sets, we are implementing a scheme using an IBM 3090 model 200/VF supercomputer at the IBM Palo Alto Scientific Center, as shown in figure 5b. First, MEM files are restored back to the CUSP data base on our VAX 750 computer, and events are sorted to match the order of the event on a given Arkive tape. Station and phase data are extracted from the CUSP data base and then written on an ASCII formatted tape. This MEM ASCII tape and the corresponding Arkive tape are taken to the IBM Center and put onto an on-line disk storage device. Data from these two tapes are merged into earthquake data files.

Each earthquake data file contains the relevant information about the particular earthquake (hypocentral location, magnitude, etc.) and a large number of digitized seismograms from the recording stations. The automatic selection of stations is based on their location with respect to the epicenter and the quality of their signals. For stations within an appropriate epicentral distance for the event magnitude, we compare the background noise level with the amplitude level for the P and S waves and also with a portion of the coda. If the signal-to-noise ratio is not greater than 4 for the P and S waves and 2.5 for the coda, the seismogram is rejected. The length of the seismogram is also trimmed to twice the length of the coda expected theoretically for the event magnitude.

Because the CUSP system is extremely conservative in saving digital waveform data and generates more data than necessary for waveform analysis, it is possible to greatly reduce the amount of data by the above procedure. This is demonstrated in figure 6. Here, several traces with low seismic energy or with high noise are eliminated, and the excess pre-event and postevent

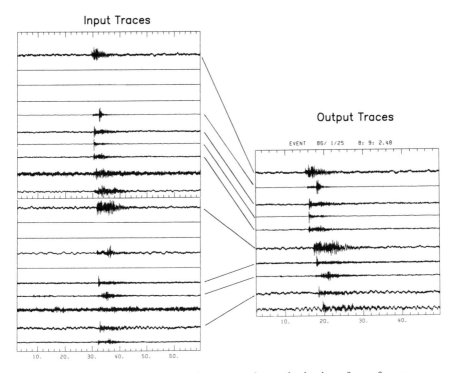

Figure 6. An illustration of automatic compression and selection of waveform traces.

data from "good" traces are trimmed. Actually, figure 6 shows seismic traces arranged according to increasing epicentral distance and illustrates data from only the first twenty stations. Because seismic energy usually decreases with increasing epicentral distance, the number of "good" traces also decreases rapidly. In general, 80 percent of the raw data is eliminated through such automatic selection and compression.

SOME SELECTED RESULTS ON CODA ATTENUATION

Table 1 summarizes the processed data sets. Results from the Long Valley data sets are described in Lee et al. (1986) and Peng et al. (1987). Results from the Big Bend area of California will be described in Peng's Ph.D. thesis. We have completed an analysis of a three-month period (April to June 1984) for all "good" earthquakes in central California. By "good" we mean an earthquake with "good" signals from at least twenty stations, or typically an earthquake with magnitude between 2 and 3, depending on the source location with respect to our network. We have also studied selected quarry blasts and nearby earthquakes for entirely different purposes. Because the coda-

TABLE 1.   Summary of Coda Q Studies

Region	Period	No. Quakes	No. Traces	Total Bytes
Processed at SLAC				
Long Valley	4/84–1/85	150	15,000	1×10^9
Big Bend	4/84–9/85	300	15,000	1×10^9
Central California	4/84–6/84	300	30,000	2×10^9
Selected quarries	4/84–10/85	400	20,000	1×10^9
Being Processed at IBM				
Central California	4/84–6/87	50,000	2,500,000	1.5×10^{11}

processing scheme at SLAC can be quickly modified for other research purposes, we have used it to study spectral differences between quarry blasts and nearby shallow earthquakes. We are just beginning a systematic processing of all CUSP digital waveform data since April 1984 at the IBM Center. Our aim is to determine the temporal and spatial variations of coda Q in central California. In addition, this processing will condense the CUSP archived data to a more manageable volume and also convert the data to a form that can be used more easily on other computers not running the CUSP system.

DISCUSSION

The history of earthquake seismology suggests that major advances have been made shortly after an accumulation of sufficient amounts of seismic data of a quality that surpasses that of earlier data. For example, shortly after a few hundred seismographs were established around the world in the early 1900s, the gross structure of the earth's interior was quickly established. By the 1930s, determinations of seismic velocities, density, and other physical parameters for a spherical earth model were completed by Keith Bullen, Harold Jeffreys, and Beno Gutenberg. The establishment of the Worldwide Standardized Seismograph Network in the early 1960s (with seismograms readily available) enabled the study of global seismicity and focal mechanisms on a scale that was not previously possible. As a result, earthquake seismology made significant contributions to the theory of plate tectonics in the late 1960s.

Microearthquake networks became popular in the 1960s, and by now there are about 100 local earthquake networks worldwide. Because of the voluminous amount of data they generate, it is very difficult for network operators to keep up with the data. Early effort was concentrated in processing phase data and the precise location of earthquakes. The amount of phase data for the Central California Microearthquake Network, for example, is about twenty-five megabytes per year. A few years ago, various local networks began to acquire digital waveform data. The amount of digital data suddenly increased 2,000-fold to about fifty gigabytes per year for the Central California Microearthquake Network. We are just learning how to cope with this vast amount of data, which requires special attention to data organization and the setting up of efficient data processing and analyses schemes. We hope that this present effort in large-scale processing and analysis will provide a foundation for the study of local earthquakes and earth structure in greater detail and for testings various hypotheses about earthquake generation.

ACKNOWLEDGMENTS

The work described here was made possible by Carl Johnson's development of the CUSP system and the dedicated efforts of many of our colleagues at the USGS. In particular, we are indebted to Kathy Aviles, Bob Dollar, Peter Johnson, Shirley Marks, Gail Nishioka, Dean Tottingham, and Carlos Valdes. We thank the International Business Machines Corporation for generously providing the necessary computer facilities for our large-scale data processing and analysis under their Academic Research Support Program. We also thank Kei Aki and his students for collaboration, and Bruce Bolt for inviting us to present this paper at the Centennial Symposium of the UC Seismographic Stations.

REFERENCES

Aki, K., and B. Chouet (1975). Origin of coda waves: Source, attenuation and scattering effects. *J. Geophys. Res.*, 80: 3322–3342.

Biswas, N. N., and K. Aki (1984). Characteristics of coda waves: Central and south-central Alaska. *Bull. Seism. Soc. Am.*, 74: 493–507.

Eaton, J. P., W. H. K. Lee, and L. C. Pakiser (1970). Use of microearthquakes in the study of the mechanics of earthquake generation along the San Andreas fault in central California. *Tectonophys.*, 9: 259–282.

Herrmann, R. B. (1980). Q estimates using the coda of local earthquakes. *Bull. Seism. Soc. Am.*, 70: 447–468.

Jin, A., and K. Aki (1986). Temporal change in coda Q before the Tangshan earthquake of 1976 and the Haicheng earthquake of 1975. *J. Geophys. Res.*, 91: 665–673.

Jin, A., T. Cao, and K. Aki (1985). Regional change of coda Q in the oceanic lithosphere. *J. Geophys. Res.*, 90: 8651–8659.

Johnson, C. E. (1979). Cedar—An approach to the computer automation of short-period local seismic networds. Ph.D. diss., California Institute of Technology, 332 pp.

———(1983). CUSP—Automated processing and management for large, regional seismic networks (abstract). *Earthquake Notes*, 54: 13.

Lee, W. H. K., K. Aki, B. Chouet, P. Johnson, S. Marks, J. T. Newberry, A. S. Ryall,

S. W. Stewart, and D. M. Tottingham (1986). A preliminary study of coda Q in California and Nevada. *Bull. Seism. Soc. Am.*, 76: 1143–1150.

Lee, W. H. K., and J. C. Lahr (1975). HYPO71 (revised): A computer program for determining hypocenter, magnitude, and first motion pattern of local earthquakes, *U.S. Geol. Surv. Open-file Rept. 75–311*, 116 pp.

Lee, W. H. K., D. L. Scharre, and G. R. Crane (1983). A computer-based system for organizing earthquake related data. *U.S. Geol. Surv. Open-file Rept. 83–518*, 28 pp.

Lee, W. H. K., and S. W. Stewart (1981). *Principles and Applications of Microearthquake Networks*. Academic Press, New York, 293 pp.

Novelo-Casanova, D. A., E. Berg, V. Hsu, and C. E. Helsley (1985). Time-space variation, seismic S-wave coda attenuation (Q^{-1}) and magnitude distribution for the Pelatan earthquake. *Geophys. Res. Lett.*, 12: 789–792.

Novelo-Casanova, D. A., and R. Butler (1986). High-frequency seismic coda and scattering in the northwest Pacific. *Bull. Seism. Soc. Am.*, 76: 617–626.

Peng, J. Y., K. Aki, B. Chouet, P. Johnson, W. H. K. Lee, S. Marks, J. T. Newberry, A. S. Ryall, S. W. Stewart, and D. M. Tottingham (1987). Temporal change in coda Q associated with the Round Valley, California, earthquake of November 23, 1984. *J. Geophys. Res.*, 92: 3507–3526.

Rautian, T. G., and V. I. Khalturin (1978). The use of the coda for determination of the earthquake source spectrum. *Bull. Seism. Soc. Am.*, 68: 923–948.

Rogers, A. M., S. C. Harmsen, R. B. Herrmann, and M. E. Meremonte (1987). A study of ground motion attenuation in the southern Great Basin, Nevada-California, using several techniques for estimates of Q_s, log A_o, and coda Q. *J. Geophys. Res.*, 92: 3527–3540.

Sato, H. (1977). Energy propagation including scattering effects, single isotropic approximation. *J. Phys. Earth*, 25: 27–41.

———. (1986). Temporal change in attenuation intensity before and after the eastern Yamanashi earthquake of 1983 in central Japan. *J. Geophys. Res.*, 91: 2049–2061.

Scherbaum, F., and C. Kisslinger (1985). Coda Q in the Adak seismic zone. *Bull. Seism. Soc. Am.*, 75: 615–620.

Singh, S., and R. B. Herrmann (1983). Regionalization of crustal Q in the continental United States. *J. Geophys. Res.*, 88: 527–538.

SIX

Distributed Intelligence in Regional Networks

D. W. Simpson and D. H. Johnson

INTRODUCTION

In their basic principle of operation, networks of seismograph stations have changed little since the time of Milne or the original Berkeley network in the early part of this century (see chaps. 1 and 2 of this volume); their purpose has been to provide the seismologist with a continuous record of ground motion as a function of time. Sensors, timing, and recording systems have improved, and communication between stations and the seismologist has speeded up—from mail, to telex, to radio and satellite telemetry—but the basic concept of individual stations reporting information on arrival times of different seismic phases is still the most common form of network operation.

Networks can be viewed as operating in a fundamentally different mode if the network as a whole (rather than individual stations) is considered the basic sensing unit, using the distributed nature of the network to derive spatially dependent parameters. It is in this mode that arrays such as LASA and NORSAR are used to determine apparent velocity and azimuth of approach of wavefronts crossing the array or to improve the signal-to-noise ratio through phased summation. Earthquake monitoring networks such as CAL-NET can use the simultaneous collection of data from distributed stations for real-time location of earthquake hypocenters (Stewart, 1977). Networks also take on a different mode of operation when sufficient computational power (intelligence) is placed at the sensor to allow decisions to be made on the nature of the signals being received. Event detection (comparing short-term and long-term averages of the received time series) in common use in portable digital recorders is a simple example of this decision-making capability (Ambuter and Solomon, 1974). At a much higher level is the Automated

99

Seismic Processor (ASP; McEvilly and Majer, 1982), an example of the use of "distributed intelligence," in the sense of the title of this paper, combining both sensor intelligence and distributed network processing to derive parameter data and earthquake locations in a local network application.

Among the most active areas of current development in computer technology are networking (both local and wide-area) and distributed processing. In concept, these developments have direct relevance to regional seismograph networks, and, in practice, many of the specific hardware developments and protocols for data communication now emerging from the computer industry can be directly incorporated into seismograph network design.

REGIONAL NETWORKS

Since the mid-1960s, the use of networks telemetering relatively low-dynamic-range narrow-bandwidth data to a central recording station (Lee and Stewart, 1981) has served well the purpose of studying the spatial and temporal distribution of regional earthquakes. The low cost per station has allowed a relatively large number of sites. The high magnification at high frequencies, and recording at a central station with a common time base, have allowed the accurate timing of the arrival of body waves from regional earthquakes. Both of these factors—a dense network and common timing—are necessary to provide accurate locations and a sensitive detection threshold in seismicity studies. There have been trade-offs, however. Inherent in the low cost of analog telemetry are severe restrictions on dynamic range (typically less than 50 dB) and bandwidth (1–20 Hz). The major factor limiting the quality of recorded data is analog telemetry over audio-grade lines—usually by telephone. With rising telephone costs, maintenance of this weakest link in the system has also become one of the major costs in operating the networks. Actual operating costs have been lowered in some networks through the use of radio telemetry and excess capacity on existing microwave links, but the real costs of land-line telemetry remain high.

The proliferation of dense telemetered networks has provided an increasingly clear picture of the spatial distribution of major seismic source zones. While it is necessary to maintain our ability to define the spatial and temporal distribution of earthquakes, it is also important that we learn more about the sources themselves—their spectral content and dynamic characteristics—and about the attenuating properties of the crust. Such information is essential in any assessment of the shaking to be expected from moderate to large earthquakes. To carry out these studies requires data of significantly higher quality—in both bandwidth and dynamic range—than that attainable with analog telemetry.

With currently available digital technology, there are few, if any, technical limitations to producing data of the required quality. Constraints are imposed by cost, due not so much to the price of individual components but to the impact of increased data density on telemetry and data storage. Improved data quality usually implies increased data quantity (greater bandwidth) for the same total signal duration. The main operational costs in land-line telemetry are related to the amount of data transmitted and collected and the distance over which they are telemetered. Bandwidth limitations and economic considerations limit the transmission of continuous high-quality digital data by telephone. One voice-grade telephone line can carry up to eight continuous seismic channels in analog form, but the quality of most long-distance telephone lines is often not even sufficient to carry three channels of limited-bandwidth (16 bit, 20 Hz) digital data.

With new seismometer designs and modern digital technology, it is now possible to record ground motions over the entire frequency band and amplitude range necessary to provide on-scale recording of ground motions, from background noise to the expected shaking from nearby large earthquakes (fig. 1). Portable digital recorders, broadband global stations, experiments in digital and satellite telemetry, and "smart" station modules have shown that there are no fundamental problems in developing the component parts of the complete seismological network. The challenge now lies in how to put the pieces together in a coherent network at a reasonable cost. By careful consideration of the telemetry and recording philosophy used, it should still be possible to vastly improve the quality of data and retain the same monitoring capability, while at the same time significantly reducing the operating cost for the network.

A DISTRIBUTED NETWORK

Figure 2 shows the main components of a generic regional seismic network and its communication links and summarizes the way these components are connected. This organization stresses the complementary nature of the two primary purposes of regional earthquake recording: kinematics and dynamics.

Kinematics is the study of the spatial and temporal distribution of earthquakes. It involves continuous monitoring and the production of earthquake catalogs, and requires accurate location and size estimation, implying precise timing and a high density of stations. Technical emphasis is on many, low-cost, high-sensitivity stations and near real-time access to data.

Dynamics is the study of ground motions and waveforms in terms of the earthquake source and propagation effects. This requires high-fidelity recording of ground motion. The technical emphasis is on broadband, high-dynamic-range digital instrumentation at a few high-quality stations. Real-time access to data is not as critical as for the kinematic role.

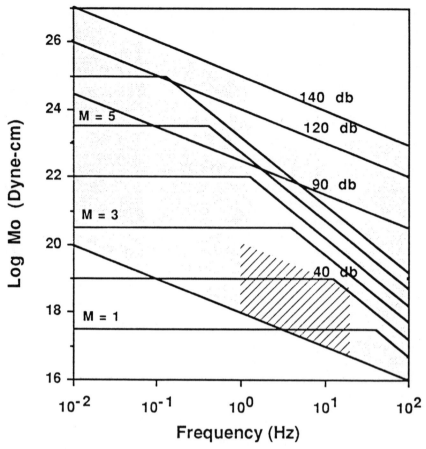

Figure 1. Displacement spectra for earthquakes of magnitude 1 to 6 (after Lee and Stewart, 1981) and schematic response of the instrument systems. The cross-hatched region is an approximation to a band-limited (1–20 Hz), 40-dB-dynamic-range system with a velocity-sensitive seismometer typical of many analog telemetered systems. The shaded area represents a "broadband" (100 s–100 Hz) system with 140 dB dynamic range. Digital recording and telemetry systems with these characteristics are now in use (Berger et al. 1984; Borcherdt et al., 1985), and single sensors covering almost the entire bandwidth and dynamic range are available (Wielandt and Streck-eisen, 1982).

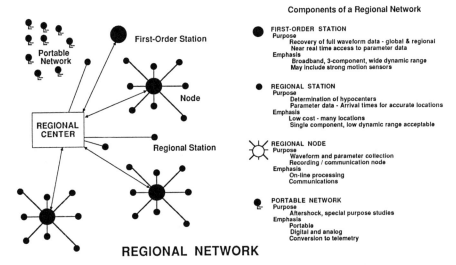

Figure 2. Components of a regional network. In this example, all regional nodes are also first order stations.

Levels of Field Instrumentation

Three levels of field instrumentation are shown in figure 2, regional, first-order, and portable stations, each designed to address a different monitoring requirement. In practice these network components may considerably overlap.

Regional stations Regional stations are numerous, have high sensitivity (single component, narrow band acceptable), and are aimed primarily at satisfying the kinematic role of the regional network. That is, this type of station satisfies the basic goal of providing high-resolution mapping of the maximum number of earthquakes. In a distributed network, these stations can still provide continuous data to a regional node, but future developments may permit some or all such stations to transmit, on demand, only derived parameter data (arrival times, amplitudes, duration, etc.).

First-order stations First-order stations are fewer in number but much higher in quality, and are aimed at satisfying the dynamic role of regional networks. That is, their purpose is to provide broadband (10s of seconds to 10s of Hz) on-scale, digital recording of larger events for studies of the source and propagation path of regional and local earthquakes. At some locations, stations of even broader bandwidth (to 1000s of seconds), intended for global or national studies, can serve the regional purpose as well.

Portable stations A "rapid deployment force" of portable instruments is necessary to allow dense coverage during an aftershock sequence for high-resolution mapping of the spatial and temporal variation of activity in the focal zone. In addition, these instruments may be used for special studies, usually with specific objectives and of limited duration. These studies may involve a small portable telemetered network in addition to the usual self-contained portable instruments.

Network Interconnections

The way a network functions is determined by its communication links and nodes. The schematic diagram in figure 2 could represent the current type of telemetered network if most of the stations were of the same type (single-component vertical), communication links were all continuous analog telemetry, nodes had no intelligence but were only mixing points for multiplexed telemetry signals, and all recording and signal processing took place at the regional center. This would then represent a low-order subset of the fully distributed network.

In analogy with the concepts of local-area networks (LANs) and distributed processing that are rapidly gaining ground in the computer industry, the network configuration in figure 2 begins to take on the appearance of a modern distributed network, as more of the processing takes place at the remote field sites and nodes. Such a distributed network relies on placing as much computing power as possible at the originator (field station) and developing a sophisticated communication network to distribute the data.

Nodes Two obvious ways to decrease telemetry costs are to transmit shorter segments of data and to telemeter them over shorter distances. The purpose of the regional node within a distributed seismic network is to concentrate data collection by providing the functions of local recording, data storage, communication control, and on-line processing of incoming data. Only data of interest need be transmitted from the node to the regional center. The most condensed type of data is parameter information, such as determinations of arrival times or amplitudes from individual stations, or computed locations of events based on data from multiple stations. Even if high-quality parameter data are available, original waveform data will still be needed for research purposes or confirmation of automatic analysis, but the need for full waveform data in real time is not usually as important as for parameter data. Nodes can serve to collect waveform data as well, either providing local recording or storing and transmitting data (not necessary in real time) to a regional center.

Communication links In an analog telemetry network, communication links are simplex (one-way) and continuous. They serve only to transmit data from a field site to a central facility where all processing and recording take place. As more decision-making capability is provided at remote sites, allowing the identification of data segments of interest, continuous telemetry becomes unnecessary. In some cases, the communication of waveform data to the regional center in an "event detected" system could be as simple as mailing weekly tapes. The system begins to take more complete advantage of the distributed processing capability when duplex (two-way) or multiple (dial-in) access is available, providing full communication and allowing interrogation and control of the remote station from the regional center, in addition to data retrieval. A more advanced form of communication in such a system is realized when each node (or station) can connect directly to the others, duplicating many of the advantages of continuous telemetry to a central station, but reducing costs by using the communication links ony when necessary. A communication link itself can take many forms—dial-up telephone, radio, satellite, fiber-optic cable—and may well change with time as new technologies become available. Data transmission formats (protocols) for computer communication are relatively insensitive to the mode used for the communication link except in limiting data rates.

The above scenario describes only one conceptual distributed network. As with distributed processing in computing, two of the major advantages of such a network are its flexibility and the ease with which new technologies can be incorporated. The routing of communications and the type of equipment at field stations or nodes can respond to local requirements and evolve with time without major impact on the operation of the entire network. For some network functions, the stations can be "dumb," simply providing continuous data to a node where processing takes place (as in most current telemetered networks). In other applications, cost or logistic constraints may make it advantageous to place more intelligence at the remote field site. If the hardware configuration of the network is sufficiently flexible, data from remote stations with different capabilities can be mixed, and changes in network configuration can be controlled by software.

L-DGO REGIONAL RECORDING SYSTEM

As part of field programs for the study of seismicity and seismotectonics in the Caribbean, Alaska, and Central Asia, the Lamont-Doherty Geological Observatory (L-DGO) began the development in 1978 of a data acquisition system for telemetered seismic networks specifically designed for operation in remote environments with limited maintenance requirements. As such, the data acquisition system operated as a low-level regional center (figure 2), collecting data continuously from field stations and providing event detection and recording capability. With additional processing capabilities, initially developed for use in the L-DGO network in the Shumigan Islands, Alaska, the system now includes both data acquisition and an on-line processor. In

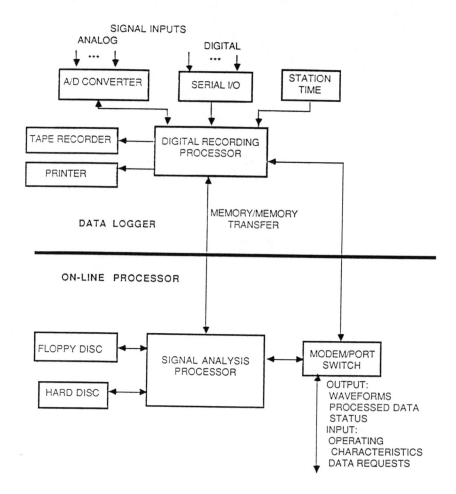

LDGO Regional Station Recording System

Figure. 3. An example of a regional network recording system. The data logging, on-line processing, and communication capabilities serve many of the functional needs of the regional centers in figure 2.

this configuration (figure 3) it will act as the regional node in a current upgrading of L-DGO's regional network for monitoring seismicity in New York State and surrounding areas.

The system consists of two functionally related but independent parts: a data acquisition system and an on-line processor.

Data Acquisition System

A stand-alone digital recording system is capable of accepting analog data from up to thirty-two remote stations (via telephone, radio, or direct connection) plus four channels of digital data. Both continuous and triggered data can be recorded. Time is locked to UTC via a satellite time-code receiver. Event detection is performed within the acquisition system (independently of the on-line processor). Recording is on cartridge tape. Local recording on helicorders can be used to provide continuous monitoring. Remote access via modem allows checking system status and modification of recording parameters.

On-line processor

"Loosely coupled" to the data acquisition system is an on-line processor, which acts as the primary data analysis and communication controller for the node. Data are transferred from the acquisition system to the on-line processor but, to insure continued data acquisition independently of the on-line processor, the processor provides no control to the data acquisition system. In the current stages of the development of the distributed network concept, it is intended that the on-line processor be as flexible as possible to allow experimentation with analysis and communication techniques. Current analytical capabilities include picking of P- and S-wave arrival times, calculating duration magnitude, and event location. The operating system for the on-line processor is a commercial version of UNIX (XENIX), to encourage program development of larger computers while providing relatively easy program transfer, and to allow use of the extensive communication protocols available as part of UNIX. Programs and data, both parameter and limited amounts of waveform data, can be easily transferred to and from the system via dial-up modem. Until broader-band communication links are available (for example, national or regional computer networks), the primary mode of retrieval of larger quantities of waveform data will be weekly mailings of cartridge tape.

CONCLUSION

The use of digital technology in seismograph instrumentation has already greatly improved the quality of data available for studying earthquake sources, especially in broadband teleseismic recording with global networks and the near-field recording of local earthquakes on portable instruments. Developments in computer networking and distributed processing present the possibility of additional improvements in the quality of waveform data gathered from regional networks, and major advances in data analysis and communication. With sufficiently powerful field hardware at remote sites and an effective and reliable communication system, a distributed network has enough intrinsic flexibility to allow its reconfiguration under software control. This holds potential for growth and provides an efficient means of optimizing data retrieval and analysis for particular scientific and monitoring goals.

ACKNOWLEDGMENTS

The manuscript was reviewed by Art Lerner-Lam and John Taber. The work was partially supported by the U.S. Geological Survey Cooperative Agreement, number 14-08-0001-A0261, and the U.S. Nuclear Regulatory Commission, contract number 04-85-113-02. Lamont-Doherty Geological Contribution, number 4182.

REFERENCES

Ambuter, B. P., and S. C. Solomon (1974). An event-recording system for monitoring small earthquakes. *Bull. Seism. Soc. Am.*, 64: 1181–1188.

Berger, J., L. M. Baker, J. N. Brune, J. B. Fletcher, T. C. Hanks, and F. L. Vernon (1984). The Anza array: A high-dynamic range, broadband, digitally radiotelemetered seismic array. *Bull. Seism. Soc. Am.*, 74: 1469–1481.

Borcherdt, R. D., J. B. Fletcher, E. G. Jensen, G. L. Maxwell, J. R. Van Schaak, R. E. Warrick, E. Cranswick, M. J. S. Johnston, and R. McClearn (1985). A general earthquake observation system (GEOS). *Bull. Seism. Soc Am.*, 75: 1783–1825.

Lee, W. H. K., and S. W. Stewart (1981). *Principles and Applications of Microearthquake Networks*. Academic Press, New York, 293 pp.

McEvilly, T. V., and E. L. Majer (1982). ASP: An automated seismic processor for microearthquake networks. *Bull. Seism. Soc. Am.*, 72: 303–325.

Stewart, S. W. (1977). Real-time detection and location of local seismic events in central California. *Bull. Seism. Soc. Am.*, 67: 433–453.

Wielandt, E., and G. Streckeisen (1982). The leaf-spring seismometer: Design and performance. *Bull. Seism. Soc. Am.*, 72: 2349–2367.

SEVEN

Seismographic Recording at Berkeley (1887–1987)

Robert A. Uhrhammer

INTRODUCTION

The University of California has operated a seismographic station network since 1887. During the past century the equipment at the stations has evolved from low-magnification mechanically recording instruments to the latest generation of broadband instrumentation utilizing digital telemetry and recording. Currently, the Seismographic Stations house a wide range of instrumentation designed to record various aspects of ground motion from local, regional, and distant events. This is necessary for the timely and routine analysis of recorded earthquakes. On an average day Station personnel analyze fifteen to twenty events, ranging in size from small local earthquakes to major teleseisms.

The first section below describes the instrumentation chronology at Berkeley and Mt. Hamilton in detail, and the current instrumentation and recording at all stations in the network as an overview. The next section covers the evolution of broadband instruments in the Berkeley network, leading up to the current Berkeley Digital Seismograph Network (BDSN) instrumentation. The last section shows examples of records from the BDSN station at Mt. Hamilton and an example of a large teleseism recorded by one vertical-component and five three-component broadband stations in the Berkeley network.

OBSERVATORY INSTRUMENT CHRONOLOGY

The Seismographic Stations began operation in April 1887 with the installation of Ewing instruments at Mt. Hamilton and Ewing and Gray-Milne instruments at Berkeley (Louderback, 1942; Dewey and Byerly, 1969). These two stations have operated continuously since then, with improvements in

109

TABLE 1. Instrumentation at Berkeley

Dates of Operation	Type of Instrument	T_o s	T_g s	Component
Apr1887–1910	Ewing, three-Component	5		NS, EW, Z
	Ewing Duplex	5		Horizontal
	Gray-Milne Duplex			Horizontal
15Jun06–10Nov10	Omori Trono-meters	2		NS, EW
30Oct10–Sep61	Bosch-Omori 100 kg	15		NS, EW
	Wiechert 80 kg	6		Z
28Aug30–01Feb65	Wilip-Galitzin	12	12	NS, EW, Z
28Aug30 to date	Wood-Anderson	0.8		SN, WE
19Oct33–Sep62	Benioff 100 kg	1.0	0.4	Z
Jan47–Mar47	Sprengnether, DH	2.0	2.0	Z
21Jun47 to date	Benioff 100 kg	1.0	8.0	Z
Jan48 to 1950	Slichter	1.0		Z
Mar48 to 1950	Slichter	1.0		EW
Jan58 to date	100x torsion	0.8		NS, EW
01May59 to date	Benioff 100 kg	1.0	0.2	Z
01May59–29Aug62	Press-Ewing	30	90	NS, EW, Z
19Jan62–01Jan87	4x torsion	0.8		NS, EW
08Jun62 to date	Benioff 100 kg	1.0	0.75	NS, EW, Z[a]
	Sprengnether, S5007 10.7 kg	30[b]	100	NS, EW, Z
Mar64–30Mar71	Press-Ewing ULP[c]	45	300	N45°E
19Jun64–10Jun83	Press-Ewing[d]	30	Broad-band	N45°W, N45°E, Z
Aug64 to date	Press-Ewing	15	30	Z
9Dec69 to date	Sprengnether, ULP S5100H, 11 kg	100	300[e]	N45°E
30Mar71 to date	Sprengnether, ULP S5100H, 11 kg	100	300[e]	N45°W
04Oct73 to date	Sprengnether, ULP S5100V, 11 kg	100	300[e]	Z
01Nov68 to date	Willmot Seismo-scope SR-100	0.75		Duplex Horizontal
15Apr76 to date	SMA-1 #2500 with WWVB	0.038		N45°W, Down S45°W

TABLE 1. (*Continued*)

Dates of Operation	Type of Instrument	T_o s	T_g s	Component
29Apr76 to date	SMA-1 #2503 with WWVB	0.039		N45°W, Down S45°W
03Aug76 to date	CRA-1 #48 FBA-3	0.018		N, Down, E
09Mar78 to date	Telemetered Wood-Anderson	0.8		S, W
09Mar78 to date	Willmore MKII	1.0	0.2	Z
Jul78 to date	Weichert 160 kg	5		Horizontal

ᵃ Horizontals recording stopped on 01Nov85.
ᵇ Natural period was changed from 30 to 15 s on 12May65.
ᶜ Before 22Apr68 EW.
ᵈ Before 02Aug65 NS, EW, Z.
ᵉ 300-s galvanometer response effected electronically.
NOTE: This table was carefully checked against the original logbooks and supersedes all previously published tables.

TABLE 2. Instrumentation at Lick Observatory (Mount Hamilton)

Dates of Operation	Type of Instrument	T_o s	T_g s	Component
24Apr1887–23Mar11	Ewing, three-Component	5		NS, EW, Z
24Apr1887–23Mar11	Ewing Duplex	5		Horizontal
23Mar11–30Sep30	Wiechert Hor. 160 kg	4 to 8*		NS, EW
23Mar11–30Sep30	Wiechert Vert. 80 kg	4 to 8*		Z
08Apr28 to date	Wood-Anderson	0.8		SN, WE
12Feb48–Jun63	Benioff 100 kg	1.0	0.4	Z
May62 to date	Benioff 14.7 kg	1.0	0.2	Z
08Nov67–30May73	Willmore MK II	3.0	0.2	N45°E
12Mar85 to date	Streckeisen STS-1	20	0.2	Z, NS, EW

*During this period the free period was not constant. For precise information refer to the Bulletin of the Seismographic Stations.
NOTE: This table has been carefully checked against the original logbooks and it supersedes all previously published tables.

instrumental equipment from time to time (shown in tables 1 and 2) as development of the science and opportunity permitted. During the past century the instruments at Berkeley have been housed in vaults at the Students Observatory, Doe Library, Bacon Hall, Haviland Hall, Earth Sciences Building, Memorial Stadium, and the Byerly Vault (BKS). Currently, the Seismographic Stations operate instruments at eighteen stations in northern and central California, as shown in figure 1 and table 3. For details on the instrumental parameters and response curves, refer to Bolt and Miller (1975) and to the semiannual *Bulletin of the Seismographic Stations* (e.g., Darragh et al., 1986).

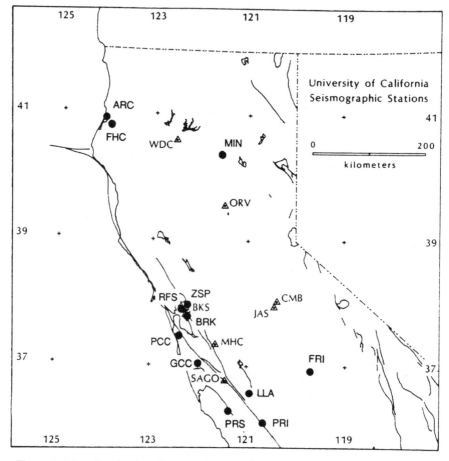

Figure 1. Map showing locations of seismographic stations in the University of California Berkeley network (1987). Broadband stations are indicated by triangles. BKS, CMB, and MHC are digitally recorded.

TABLE 3. Stations in operation: May 1987

Station (from N to S)	North Latitude	West Longitude	Elevation Meters	Code	Present Auspices and Date Established
Arcata	40°52.6'	124°04.5'	60	ARC	Humboldt State Univ. 1948
Fickle Hill	40°48.1'	123°59.1'	610	FHC	Humboldt State Univ. 1968
Whiskeytown	40°34.8'	122°32.4'	300	WDC	National Park Service 1948
Mineral	40°20.7'	121°36.3'	1495	MIN	National Park Service 1938
Oroville	39°33.3'	121°30.0'	360	ORV	Calif. Dept. of Water Resources 1963
Columbia	38°02.1'	120°23.1'	719	CMB	Columbia College 1986
San Pablo Dam	37°56.7'	122°15.4'	119	ZSP	East Bay M.U.D. 1978
Richmond Field Station	37°55.2'	122°19.8'	2	RFS	University of Calif. 1976
Berkeley (Byerly)	37°52.6'	122°14.1'	276	BKS	University of Calif. 1962
Berkeley	37°52.4'	122°15.6'	81	BRK	University of Calif. 1887
Pilarcitos Creek	37°30.0'	122°22.9'	91	PCC	Sare Ranch, 1965
Mt. Hamilton	37°20.5'	121°38.5'	1282	MHC	Lick Observatory 1887
Granite Creek	37°01.8'	121°59.8'	122	GCC	Richard E. Randolph, Santa Cruz 1965
Friant	36°59.5'	119°42.5'	119	FRI	Bureau of Reclamation 1971
San Andreas Geophysical Observatory	36°45.9'	121°26.7'	350	SAO	University of Calif. 1966
Llanada	36°37.0'	120°56.6'	475	LLA	Charles McCullough Ranch 1961
Paraiso	36°19.9'	121°22.2'	363	PRS	Paraiso Hot Springs 1961
Priest	36°08.5'	120°39.9'	1187	PRI	Federal Aviation Agency 1961

A wide range of instrumentation is operated at the stations, along with several methods of recording, as shown in table 4. Four of the stations (ARC, BKS, MHC, and MIN) house standard Wood-Anderson torsion seismographs, which have operated continuously for fifty to sixty years. Most of the stations have short-period vertical instruments. Five stations house three-component broadband instrumentation, discussed in detail in the next section. Whiskeytown has a vertical-component broadband seismometer with five signals telemetered to Berkeley. The Richmond Field Station houses a unique, continuously telemetered and recording nine-component borehole accelerometer array. The accelerometers are at the surface and at depths of 15 m and 47 m in the Bay mud, with the bottom instruments on the basement shale. They are recorded at 0.01 g and 0.5 g full scale with a 50-Hz bandwidth. Berkeley itself has the widest range of instrumentation, as indicated in table 1.

Several methods are used to record signals from the instruments (table 4). Eleven stations record on helicorders using heat-sensitive paper. These stations are used for the daily listing of events and for routine analysis. The Wood-Anderson, Worldwide Standardized Seismographic Network (WWSSN), and ultralong-period instruments record photographically on paper. The standard Wood-Anderson torsion seismograms are used to determine local magnitude. All analog telemetered signals are continuously recorded on analog tape that can be digitally sampled for analysis on microcomputers. Three stations (BKS, CMB, and MHC) house broadband instruments that are digitally telemetered and recorded. Analog tape and digital signals are dubbed onto tapes and cartridge disks for archiving. Most of the short-period vertical signals are also recorded on develocorder film, which is useful for rapidly timing phase onsets and locating events. In addition, Berkeley has instruments that record ink on paper (a Benioff vertical 100 kg) and on smoked paper (a Wiechert horizontal 160 kg). The Wiechert instrument was originally at MHC (1911–1930). Other instruments operated at Berkeley include a microbarograph (circa January 1963) and a creepmeter across the Hayward fault in Memorial Stadium (since October 7, 1965).

OBSERVATORY BROADBAND INSTRUMENT CHRONOLOGY

Beginning in 1963, a network of broadband seismographs evolved at the Seismographic Stations (University of California, Berkeley) in northern and central California (see semiannual *Station Bulletins* for response curves). By May 1987 the network of broadband seismographs had expanded to six stations, three with analog telemetry and recording (Oroville—ORV, San Andreas Geophysical Observatory—SAGO, and Whiskeytown—WDC) and three with digital telemetry and recording (Berkeley—BKS, Columbia College—CMB, and Mt. Hamilton—MHC).

TABLE 4. Instrumentation and Recording Media: May 1987.

Station (from N to S)	Instruments						No. Inst.	No. Channels	Recording Medium				
	SP	WA	BB	LP	ULP	SMA			H	P	AT	D	De
ARC		X					2	2		X			
FHC	X						1	1	X		X		X
WDC		X	X				1	5	X	X	X		X
MIN	X						3	3	X		X		X
ORV	X		X				4	4			X		X
CMB	X		X	X			4	7	X			X	X
ZSP	X						1	1	X		X		
RFS	X		X			X	9	18			X		
BKS	X	X	X	X	X	X	12	25	X	X	X	X	X
BRK	X			X	X	X	10	15	X				X
PCC	X						1	1			X		X
MHC	X	X	X				6	6	X	X	X	X	X
GCC	X						1	1			X		X
FRI	X						1	1	X		X		X
SAO	X		X			X	5	7	X		X		X
LLA	X						1	1			X		X
PRS	X						1	1			X		X
PRI	X						1	1	X		X		X

SP—Short period
WA—Wood-Anderson
BB—Broadband
LP—Long period
ULP—Ultralong period
SMA—Strong-motion accelerometer
H—Helicorder
P—Photographic paper
AT—Analog tape
D—Digital (tape and cartridge disk)
De—Develocorder

In 1973, installation of a three-component set of ultra-long period (ULP) seismometers in the Byerly Seismographic Vault (BKS) was completed. These Sprengnether S-5100 seismometers ($T_o = 100$ s) use electronic recentering feedback for long-term stability (plus temperature and barometric feedback for the vertical component). The response of ground-velocity records on photographic paper is equivalent to $T_o = 100$ s, $T_g = 300$ s, with a magnification of 500 at T_o.

Beginning in September 1975, low-gain (± 2 mm) and high-gain (± 0.02 mm) displacement signals from each of the three components at BKS were recorded on 0.03-inches-per-second, 0–10-Hz, FM magnetic tape. Since 1980, displacement signals from the three ULP seismometers have been digitized at ninety-nine samples per second with a resolution of 16 bits (96 dB), telemetered to the laboratory and recorded on magnetic tape at a density of 5,120 bits per inch. The least significant bit is equivalent to 0.25 micrometers of boom displacement, and the system response is flat to ground displacement from 0.01 Hz to 25 Hz.

The Whiskeytown (WDC) seismograph, installed in January 1973, consists of a Sprengnether S-5100 vertical seismometer in a sealed pressure vessel operating at $T_o = 40$ s, and with a damping ratio of 0.70. Five signals (low-gain and high-gain displacement and velocity and filtered short period) are FM telemetered to the Berkeley analog tape recorders.

Equipment was installed at Oroville (ORV) in 1979 to telemeter three-component broadband velocity signals from Geotech 7505 and 8700 seismometers ($T_o = 15$ s) to Berkeley. In February and March 1986 a three-component set of Streckeisen broadband seismometers was installed.

At the San Andreas Geophysical Observatory (SAGO or SAO), the central vault was instrumented in March 1968 with Sprengnether S-5000 (WWSSN type) three-component long-period ($T_o = 30$ s) seismometers. Displacement signals (0–10 Hz) were recorded on an on-site 0.06 inches per second magnetic tape recorder with a ± 10 mm full-scale range. The on-site tape recording was discontinued in October 1981. On November 20, 1985, (Z) and June 11, 1986, (NS, EW) Streckeisen broadband seismometers were installed, and their signals are now transmitted via FM telemetry to Berkeley.

A digital seismographic system (part of the USGS Digital Worldwide Standardized Seismographic Network system) was installed at Jamestown (JAS) in September 1980. The filtered outputs of Teledyne SL 210 and SL 200 seismometers are recorded with 16-bit resolution on 1,600-bit-per-inch magnetic tape. As a telemetry experiment on the use of commercial telephone lines, the USGS Albuquerque Seismological Laboratory designed hardware for a 2,400-bit-per-second telemetry link from JAS to Berkeley. In 1982, the control and recording part of the DWWSSN JAS station was installed at Berkeley (150 km west of JAS). In November 1986 the equipment was placed in a new permanent vault at Columbia College (CMB, 11 km NNE of JAS).

In spring 1985 a three-component set of Streckeisen broadband seismometers was installed at the Mt. Hamilton station (MHC) with FM telemetry to Berkeley. In October 1986 the MHC analog recording was converted to the PC-based broadband digital system described by Bolt et al. (1988), and in May 1987 an identical digital system at the BKS vault was connected. The BDSN system flow is shown in figures 2a and 2b. The BDSN was designed to meet a number of requirements. Each remote station provides broadband three-component and a short-period vertical component signals. The recording is continuous and on-scale for moderate local earthquakes ($M_L < 5$), large regional earthquakes ($M_L < 7$), and major teleseisms. Modular construction permits simple incorporation of new components into the system as technology advances. Automatic restart allows unattended operation of the remote station. Most of the hardware is commercially available and relatively inexpensive. The hardware components are integrated by a set of three machine language programs that provide the necessary common interface.

EXAMPLES OF BDSN SEISMOGRAMS

The dynamic-range and bandwidth capabilities of BDSN recordings are illustrated in figure 3 where a small ($M_L = 1.7$) local earthquake was recorded simultaneously with the surface waves from a large ($M_s = 6.8$) teleseism. The events have dominant periods of 0.37 s and 23 s respectively and are thus readily separable by convolution or filtering.

Figure 4 shows the spectrum of a local earthquake ($M_L = 3.1$, $\Delta = 12$ km) recorded by the MHC broadband digital seismograph. The inset waveform is the transverse-component (clockwise up) displacement time history (10-s record). Note the presence of the near-field ramp commonly observed on broadband displacement seismograms for Δ less than 20 km. The upper curve is the spectrum of the inset seismogram, and the lower curve is the spectrum of a 10-s noise sample immediately preceding the event. The signal-to-noise ratio is approximately 50 dB (a factor of about 300) in the 1–2-Hz frequency band. The steep slope at 5 Hz is due to the 10-pole low-pass anti-aliasing filter.

Calculation from the asymptotic low-frequency spectrum level of 6,500 nanometer-seconds yields a seismic moment of 1.7×10^{21} dyne-cm. This earthquake is a factor of five below full scale on the 16-bit telemetry system in the spectral domain at 1–2 Hz. It follows that the largest events that can be recorded on scale at 18 km are $M_L \simeq 3.8$ and $M_o \simeq 9 \times 10^{21}$ dyne-cm.

A strong regional earthquake, $M_L = 5.2$, recorded at MHC is shown in figure 5. This earthquake occurred adjacent to the Parkfield segment of the San Andreas fault and serves to indicate the seismic ground-motion ampli-

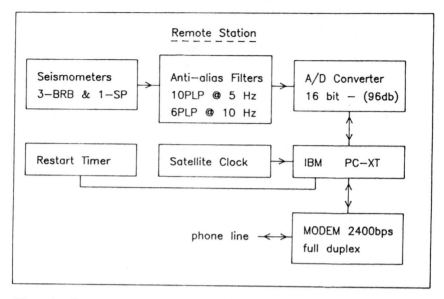

Figure 2a. Remote-station block diagrams showing principal hardware components. The A/D converter and the restart timer plug into the PC system bus, while the clock and modem connect to asynchronous serial ports.

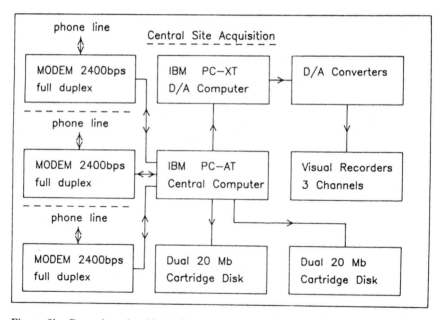

Figure 2b. Central-station block diagram showing principal hardware components. The D/A converters and the cartridge disk drives plug into the PC system bus, while the modems attach to asynchronous serial ports. All components are available commercially.

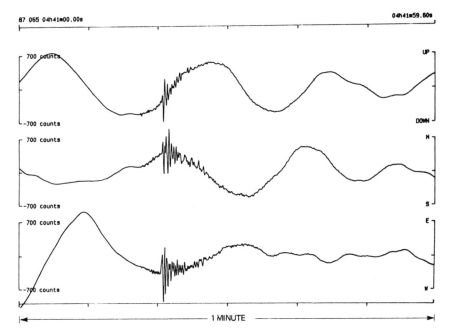

Figure 3. Bandwidth and dynamic range illustrated by a $M_L = 1.7$ local earthquake ($\Delta = 22$ km) superimposed on the surface waves from a $M_s = 6.8$ teleseism ($\Delta = 58°$). Full scale (700 counts) corresponds to 18.75 micrometers/second ground velocity.

tude expected in a characteristic Parkfield earthquake (Ellsworth et al., 1987). The MHC broadband system should remain on scale for earthquakes up to $M_L = 5.8$ in the Parkfield area.

Figure 6 shows the records from a large teleseism ($M_s = 7.1$) that occurred in the Santa Cruz Islands on July 6, 1987. This was the first major earthquake recorded by the Berkeley broadband network since the new BDSN digital equipment has been in operation at BKS and MHC. The MHC, ORV, and SAO traces are from Streckeisen STS-1 instruments (broadband velocity output), the WDC (vertical component only) and BKS traces are from Sprengnether S-5100 series instruments, and the CMB traces are from Teledyne SL 200 and SL 210 instruments. All traces are derived from velocity outputs except for BKS which has displacement outputs. Note the similarity in the body-wave traces and the differences in the surface wave envelopes.

ACKNOWLEDGMENT

The diligence of Seismographic Stations personnel in compiling the tables and preparing the figures is appreciated.

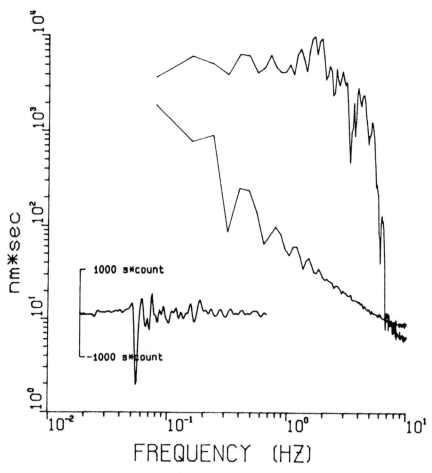

Figure 4. Example of digital waveform recorded at MHC and its associated spectra for a small local earthquake ($M_L = 3.1$, $\Delta = 12$ km). The noise spectrum (lower curve) is from the 10 seconds immediately preceding the event. Full scale (1000 count–seconds) corresponds to 0.54 millimeters ground displacement.

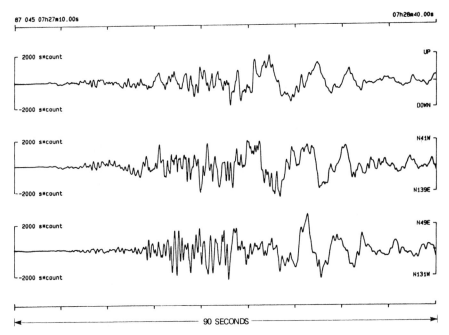

Figure 5. A strong regional earthquake ($M_L = 5.2$, Coalinga area, $\Delta = 194$ km, 14 Feb 1987) recorded at MHC. The time series has been integrated and is flat to ground displacement from 0.05 Hz to 5 Hz. Full scale (2000 count–seconds) corresponds to 1.07 millimeters ground displacement.

REFERENCES

Bolt, B. A., J. E. Friday, and R. A. Uhrhammer (1988). A PC-based broadband digital seismograph network. *Geophysical Journal*, 93: 565–573.

Bolt, B. A., and R. D. Miller (1975). *Catalog of Earthquakes in Northern California and Adjoining Areas: 1 January 1910-31 December 1972*. Seismographic Stations, University of California, 563 pp.

Darragh, R. B., M. R. McKenzie, and R. A. Uhrhammer (1986). *Bulletin of the Seismographic Stations, University of California*, 55, 1 & 2: 88.

Dewey, J., and P. Byerly (1969). The early history of seismometry (to 1900). *Bull. Seism. Soc. Am.*, 59: 183–227.

Ellsworth, W. L., L. D. Dietz, J. Frechet, and G. Poupinet (1987). Preliminary results of the temporal stability of coda waves in central California from high-resolution measurements of characteristic earthquakes. In Proceedings of Workshop XXVII, The Physical and Observational Basis for Intermediate-term Earthquake Prediction. *U.S. Geol. Surv. Open-file Report 87-591, 440-460*.

Louderback, G. D. (1942). History of the University of California Seismographic Stations and related activities. *Bull. Seism. Soc. Am.*, 32: 205–230.

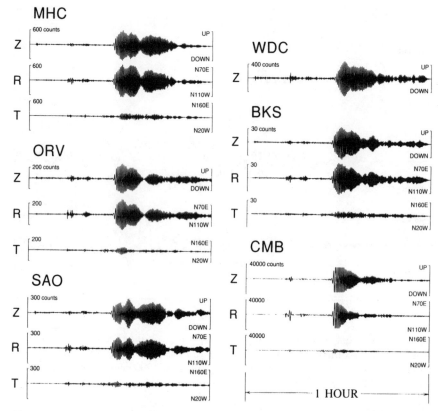

Figure 6. Example of a large teleseism ($M_s = 7.1$, Santa Cruz Islands, $\Delta = 82°$, 6 July 1987) recorded by one vertical-component and five three-component broadband stations in the Berkeley network. The horizontal components have been rotated to radial and transverse, and the traces are scaled to the maximum vertical amplitude.

EIGHT

Array Seismology—Past, Present and Future Developments

E. S. Husebye and B. O. Ruud

INTRODUCTION

Array seismology was born on September 19, 1957. On that day a nuclear explosion, code-named Rainier, was detonated under the Nevada desert principally to explore the ability of an underground test, unhampered by weather and concerns over radioactive fallout, to fulfill all the needs of a nuclear weapons test program. Rainier demonstrated this ability. The resulting seismological data were studied intensely in both scientific and political circles, setting a pattern that still prevails. Rainier and subsequent underground tests also demonstrated that the only effective way to detect such explosions was by seismic means. Thus, the science of seismology was given a rather prominent role in a political question: arms control. A specific aspect of the arms control issues was tied to banning all nuclear weapons testing. Such a ban was (and is) presumed to prevent (or at least severely curtail) the development of new, advanced nuclear weapons systems and also to prevent nuclear weapons proliferation. Note that first-generation bombs of the Nagasaki and Hiroshima types hardly require testing, while those of the third and fourth generation require twenty to thirty tests. In this case, successful evasion schemes would be exceedingly difficult (Massé, 1987).

The introduction of seismology to the political arena had, thus, already occurred by August 1958 when scientific experts from the United States, the Union of Soviet Socialist Republics, and the United Kingdom met in Geneva to design a seismic verification system as part of a Comprehensive Nuclear Test Ban Treaty. The outcome of this and subsequent Geneva Conferences was important to seismology on two accounts. First, they resulted in the recommendation of a global seismic monitoring system comprising 180 small array stations of ten SPZ (short-period vertical) seismographs complemented with three-component SP (short-period) and LP (long-period) instrumentation; ten of these arrays were for sea-floor deployment. Second, it was recognized that seismology per se was unable to meet political requirements for creating a reliable and acceptable verification system. Already at that time magnitude and yield estimates were the subject of expert controversy, adding to the political problems.

The outcome of the Geneva Conferences proved very beneficial for seismology. As a result of these conferences, several countries, notably the United States and the United Kingdom, launched large-scale research programs to modernize seismology and provide the technical means for monitoring compliance with treaties limiting or banning underground nuclear weapons tests (for example, see Kerr, 1985). The first concrete step toward establishing array seismology stemmed from the U.S. Berkner Panel's recommendation, in 1959, to construct large arrays with hundreds of sensors as a cost-efficient alternative to the "Geneva" concept of numerous small arrays of a few kilometers' aperture (see Bolt, 1976, chapter 6). This recommendation led to the only two large arrays ever built, namely, LASA (Montana) in 1964 (operational in 1971, closed down in 1978) and NORSAR (Norway) in 1971 (still in operation but with its size reduced). The United Kingdom's seismic monitoring program led to the construction in the 1960s of four medium-sized arrays at Eskdalemuir (Scotland), Yellowknife (Canada), Garibidinaur (India), and Warramunga (Australia), all of which are still in operation. Other major national array programs are those tied to the Gräfenberg array (West Germany) and the Hagfors array (Sweden). Array designs, developments, and deployments have now come almost full circle, as exemplified by the third-generation NORESS array (Norway) with an aperture of 3 km and twenty-five SPZ instruments, reasonably close to the original Geneva concept of 1958.

In this article, we address array development and operation over their current life span of nearly three decades. Particular emphasis is on operational principles and array performance in the context of earthquake surveillance and seismological research. We also consider future prospects of array operations in view of inexpensive mobile array deployments and innovative analysis techniques for three-component station records.

Above, we very briefly mentioned major political events and arms control issues leading to "forensic" (Thirlaway, 1985) and array seismology. These topics are adequately detailed in many books and will not be discussed further here. However, recommended references are Bolt (1976), Dahlman and Israelson (1977), Husebye and Mykkeltveit (1981), Press (1985), Kerr (1985), and Tsipis et al. (1986).

THE ARRAY CONCEPT

There is no strict definition of an array, although seismological arrays generally have three or more identical instruments properly spaced (spacing being governed by characteristic noise and signal correlation distances, which are naturally frequency dependent), centralized data acquisition, and integrated real-time processing. In this paper we will generally consider an array to have these properties.

An essential array capability is the locating of incoming signals in f-k (frequency–wave number) space, which in turn signifies a certain ray path in the Earth and/or the source location. Using the polarization characteristics of seismic waves, f-k locations of incoming signals can also be achieved on the basis of a single-site, three-component station (Christoffersson et al., 1988). In the extreme, such stations may be considered an array, albeit the requirement of a two-dimensional sensor layout is not met. Likewise, we may consider a small network used for monitoring local earthquake activities as an array, conditioned on real-time integrated signal processing, which is technically and economically feasible today. A remaining flaw would be poor to nonexistent signal correlation, which can be overcome by replacing individual signals by their envelopes (Hilbert transform), thus constituting the basis for so-called incoherent beamforming (Ringdal el al., 1975).

The major arrays noted above (like NORSAR, Yellowknife, Gräfenberg, and Hagfors) all comply with our definition of an array. Centralized data acquisition and integrated real-time processing are most important, if seismological networks are to be considered arrays, and are of economic interest as well. For example, if integrated signal processing is not feasible, why have real-time transfer of waveform data, which is rather costly? Alternatively, the relatively modest signal parameter data (like arrival time, amplitude, and slowness) from a single three-component station are extracted in situ or at a local center. Thus, off-line centralized processing of parametric data is feasible, and is essentially the way organizations like the National Earthquake Information Center (NEIC), the International Seismological Centre (ISC), and the European-Mediterranean Seismological Center (EMSC) operate.

ARRAY DEVELOPMENTS, DESIGN CRITERIA, AND DATA-PROCESSING SCHEMES

The concept of seismic arrays was first introduced to the seismological community by the conference of scientific experts convening in Geneva in 1958 as a principal means for monitoring compliance with a potential test-ban treaty barring or limiting yields of underground nuclear weapons tests. The scientific rationale for these recommendations was that properly summing the outputs from clusters of sensors would result in significant signal enhancement and at the same time provide estimates of signal direction. Although the array concept at that time was novel to seismologists, geophone clustering was widely used in seismic exploration. Furthermore, array usage was well established in other fields like radar, sonar, and radio astronomy, and the theoretical framework for associated signal processing or so-called anten-

na theory had been formulated. Ignoring the historical perspectives of the
theoretical developments, we proceed to give a brief presentation of common
array data-processing techniques as used in both operational and research
contexts. Simple schemes like delay-and-sum processing (beamforming) and
semblance are very popular, not only because they are easy to use but also
due to their robustness in a complex signal environment. A few article and
book references here are Capon (1969), Ingate et al. (1985), Aki and
Richards (1980), Haykin (1985), and Kanasewich (1981).

Phased-array beamforming

Real-time array data processing is usually based on this method. Denot-
ing the ith sensor output as $y_i(t)$ and its position vector r_i, the signal estimate
or beam $\hat{s}$ for N instruments is:

$$\hat{s}(t, u) = \sum_{i=1}^{N} w_i y_i(t - u \cdot r_i) \qquad (1)$$

where u is the horizontal (back azimuth) slowness vector, and w_i are weights.
An unbiased estimate of $\hat{s}$ is obtained by requiring the sum of the weights
over all N instruments to equal 1. With uniform weights, $w_i = 1/N$, the
beamforming is unweighted.

A simple power estimate for the beam signal in the time window $[T_1, T_2]$
for slowness u is:

$$P_b(u) = \frac{1}{T_2 - T_1} \int_{T_1}^{T_2} [\hat{s}(t, u)]^2 dt \qquad (2)$$

A more compact form is obtainable by introducing the data covariance matrix, namely:

$$C_{ij} = \frac{1}{T_2 - T_1} \int_{T_1}^{T_2} y_i(t - u \cdot r_i) y_j(t - u \cdot r_j) dt \qquad (3)$$

Equation (2) can be now written in matrix form as:

$$P_b(u) = w^* \mathbf{C}(u) w \qquad (4)$$

where the asterisk denotes transpose.

The so-called Nth root beamforming (Muirhead and Datt, 1976) is known
to have better directivity than conventional methods. Thus, it would be an
advantage to use the Nth root beam in equation (2) for slowness estimation.

f-k power spectrum

The conventional frequency-wavenumber power estimate, also called
classical beamforming, is defined as:

$$P(\omega, k) = d^*(k) \mathbf{C}(\omega) d(k) \qquad (5)$$

where $\mathbf{C}(\omega)$ is the spectra covariance matrix. d is a complex vector of phase delays and sensor weights defined as

$$d_i = w_i \exp(-i \, k \cdot r_i) \tag{6}$$

The relative advantage of the f-k signal power estimate, equation (5), is that the spectral covariance matrix is calculated just once for each frequency because the wavenumber dependence rests with the d-vector in equation (6). The disadvantage is that narrow-frequency-band estimates easily become unstable. Also, to ensure computational efficiency, the $\mathbf{C}(\omega)$ matrix is often estimated for a fixed time window, while time domain beamforming always accounts for move-out time across the array.

Broadband f-k power spectrum

The instability of conventional f-k analysis can be overcome by introducing its broadband variant. Using the relation $k = \omega u$ and integrating the f-k spectrum over the band $[\Omega_1, \Omega_2]$ we get:

$$P(u) = \frac{1}{\Omega_2 - \Omega_1} \int_{\Omega_1}^{\Omega_2} P(\omega, \omega u) d\omega \tag{7}$$

Note that this scheme is not computationally efficient as the spectral covariance matrix must be estimated for many frequencies. Also, time domain beamforming is broadband, in view of the prefiltering passband commonly used.

High-resolution beamforming methods

The best known of these methods is the maximum likelihood (ML) f-k estimator given by Capon (1969):

$$P_{\mathrm{ML}}(\omega, k) = [d^*(k)\mathbf{C}^{-1}(\omega)d(k)]^{-1} \tag{8}$$

A similar approach is applicable in the time domain using the so-called maximum-likelihood (ML) weights, $w = \dfrac{\mathbf{C}^{-1} \cdot l}{l^*\mathbf{C}l}$ (Aki and Richards, 1980, p. 616), where l is the N-dimensional unit vector $l^* = (1, \ldots, 1)$. With this substitution, we get from equation (4):

$$P_{\mathrm{ML}}(u) = [l^*\mathbf{C}^{-1}(u)l]^{-1} \tag{9}$$

Formally, the ML estimates are derived on the assumption that wavelets with different slownesses are statistically independent. For real signals this is seldom the case, hence the inability of high-resolution estimators to resolve correlating signals (for example, see Duckworth, 1983; Hsu and Baggeroer, 1986).

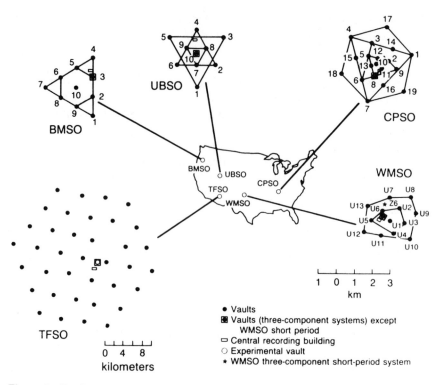

Figure 1. Configurations of various seismometer arrays at observatories constructed to evaluate detection capabilities of stations similar to those recommended by the Conference of Experts, Geneva (after Romney, 1985).

Semblance methods

Semblance is a simple coherency measure defined as $S = P_b/P_{av}$. Here P_b and P_{av} are, respectively, beam power and average single-channel power, which implies that semblance is in the interval $(0, 1)$. Because semblance is independent of signal power, it provides a convenient confidence measure in displays of wave-train time-varying properties like velocity spectra (see fig. 8 below).

The time-domain semblance estimate is defined as:

$$S(u) = \frac{1}{N^2} l^*\rho(u)l \qquad (10)$$

where ρ is the correlation matrix $[\rho_{ij} = C_{ij}/(C_{ii} \cdot C_{jj})^{1/2}]$. An ML variant of semblance is obtained using the ML weights discussed above, namely:

$$S_{ML}(u) = [l^*\rho^{-1}(u)l]^{-1} \qquad (11)$$

The semblance estimator is robust and thus works relatively well even for complex signals.

To summarize, most array data processing schemes were developed in the 1960s, so progress has been modest in this field in recent years. A potentially beneficial research avenue may be in adaptive signal processing, as used in radar and sonar for separately estimating interfering signals (see Bøhme, 1987; Monzingo and Miller, 1980; and Urban, 1985).

ARRAY DEPLOYMENT IN THE 1960s

The Geneva recommendations for small arrays as the principal seismological tool for comprehensive test ban (CTB) verification dominated the United States array research program in the ensuing years, although the Berkner Panel also recommended the use of large arrays (for a detailed account of these scientific-political discussions, see Bolt, 1976, chaps. 5 and 6). The first arrays to be deployed were the Wichita Mountain Observatory (WMSO), Unita Basin Observatory (UBSO), Blue Mountain Observatory (BMSO), and Cumberland Plateau Observatory (CPSO), while the Tonto Forest Observatory (TFSO) was significantly larger, as illustrated in figure 1. These arrays were operational for about ten years. Although having excellent site locations, with low noise and high signal sensitivity, these arrays seemingly did not contribute much toward array research. A major drawback was analog recording, which prevented integrated, real-time operation except for vertical stacking (no delay times used). In 1963 the first of the UK-type arrays was completed in Scotland which also used analog recording. The L-shaped configuration of these arrays (fig. 2) gave a rather skewed response pattern but did minimize costly ditching for cables.

The quantum leap in array development came with the construction of the LASA (Montana) array in 1964, achieved in the incredibly short time of just nine months (Anonymous, 1965). The LASA array remained unique on several accounts: its aperture of 200 km (fig. 2), its deployment of 630 short- and long-period seismometers, and, most important, its use of digital signal recording. The second large-aperture array to be constructed was NORSAR, a joint U.S.-Norway venture completed in 1970, with an aperture of 100 km and 196 seismometers (fig. 3). At about the same time, the Gräfenberg array was completed, unique in its use of broadband instruments (Buttkus, 1986).

In summary, the 1960s saw tremendous development in array technologies in terms of new, compact, and high-sensitivity seismometers, data transfer via links and cables over large distances, and ingenious recording systems including digital tapes. However, most of the array recordings were in analog form, thus limiting their use in broader seismological research. An integral part of array deployment was the development of schemes for handling the

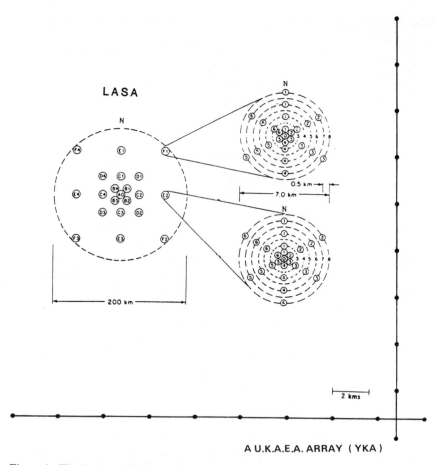

Figure 2. The L-shaped Yellowknife, Canada, array and the 200-km aperture LASA, Montana, array. Each of the twenty-one LASA subarrays initially comprised twenty-five short-period instruments (later reduced to sixteen) plus one three-component long-period seismometer.

multichannel data generated, and the theoretical foundation for array data processing as it is known today was laid in the 1960s.

SEISMIC ARRAY OPERATION IN THE 1970s

The 1960s were the decade of array deployment, while the 1970s were the decade of continuous real-time operation. For example, although LASA was completed in 1964, it did not become fully operational until 1971, coincident in time with NORSAR. The reason for this was simply that field instrumentation was commercially available, but an integrated computer

NORSAR

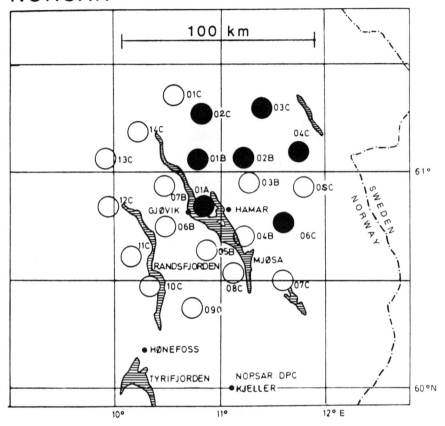

Figure 3. NORSAR. Each circle represents one subarray consisting of six short-period and one three-component long-period instruments. All twenty-two subarrays were in operation from 1971 to October 1, 1976, whereas only a subset of seven subarrays (filled circles) have been in operation since then.

hardware-software system had to be developed specifically for array operation. For example, IBM (Federal Systems Division) spent more than four years on this task before completing the LASA and NORSAR data-processing systems (see Bungum et al., 1971). After these arrays became operational, it took a year before the software was reasonably bug-free and, equally important, before the staffs at the respective array data centers in Alexandria, Virginia, and Kjeller, Norway, had mastered the automated array operations. For example, multiple-phase recordings like P and PP were initially featured as separate events simply because the analyst did not have a display of the complete wave record. Shortcomings of this kind were easy to detect because otherwise there would have been a marked increase of earth-quake activity in the North Atlantic well off the midoceanic ridges.

More subtle problems were tied to the apparently larger number of earth-quakes detected during local nighttime than during the day. With no scien-tific rationale for such a phenomenon, the alternative was that this was an artifact of array operation. The explanation turned out to be a diurnal change in noise characteristics, which were relatively broadband during the daytime, due to high-frequency cultural noise, and thus corresponded to a marked difference in detector false alarm rates for a fixed threshold. A few of the many nightly false alarms would inevitably be classed as "true" events, thus explaining the apparently higher earthquake activity. The solution to the problem was to keep the false-alarm rate flat by making the detector threshold a function of diurnal time (see Steinert et al., 1976). Also worth mentioning is that a "high-level" constraint was imposed on LASA not to report core phases, yet such events inevitably were recorded. In the array bulletin, such events were located at 105° distances. In due time, these arti-factual epicenter solutions "filtered" into NEIC and ISC files and, not too surprisingly, have been the subject of a few tectonic studies and modeling.

The LASA and NORSAR arrays were termed teleseismic arrays, stem-ming from the fact that their large apertures, and hence large station separa-tions, permitted operation only in essentially the 1.0–2.5-Hz band. This meant that local and regional event signals could not be handled properly due to poor signal correlation at higher frequencies (Ingate et al., 1985). This problem was further aggravated by the limited number of beams to be de-ployed due to limited computer capacity (IBM 360/40 computers of 1964). Poor detectability of regional events was to a large extent overcome by intro-ducing so-called incoherent or envelope beamforming. The signal envelopes were highly correlated—even though the "originals" were not—and were of relatively low frequency (see Ringdal et al., 1975). Although envelope beam-forming suppressed only the noise level variance (not the noise level per se) by a factor of $\sqrt{N}$, additional noise suppression was feasible by simple band-pass filtering. An added advantage of envelope beamforming was that due to relatively low "signal" frequencies, few beams were needed for adequate sur-veillance. In short, for NORSAR, envelope beamforming detected 85 per cent of the events detected by conventional signal beamforming techniques.

An interesting feature of array recordings is that sensor amplitudes for an individual event vary considerably and can be approximated by a log-normal probability distribution function (Husebye et al., 1974). Furthermore, any of the twenty-two NORSAR subarrays would, for one or more earthquake source regions within the teleseismic distance window, exhibit the largest signal amplitude. In other words, the amplitude "response" of the NORSAR siting structure is highly selective in terms of angle of incidence of the incom-ing wavefront (see figure 4).

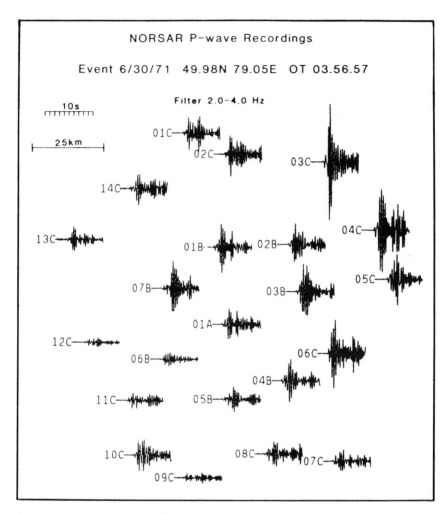

Figure 4. NORSAR. P-wave recordings from the center instruments of each subarray for an explosion in eastern Kazakhstan ($m_b = 5.4$, distance 38°). Note the large variations in signal amplitude and waveform complexity across the array. The signal frequency contents are similar for all instruments with the best signal-to-noise ratio in the band 2.0 to 4.0 Hz.

A practical aspect of the skewness in P-amplitude distributions across large arrays like LASA and NORSAR is that using only the four to six "best" subarrays for a given event results in signal-to-noise ratio enhancement, which is only marginally improved by including the remaining sixteen to eighteen subarrays in the beamforming process (Berteussen and Husebye, 1974). In the extreme, a single sensor may exhibit a signal-to-noise ratio roughly similar to that obtainable using the whole array. This, in turn, reflects a common observational fact regarding array monitoring of earthquake occurrence—almost all events (signals) detected by an array are visible on a subarray beam or single-channel record trace. This knowledge was once applied, but without much success, as an additional constraint to discriminate (nonparametric tests) between signal and noise wavelets for triggering close to the detector threshold (Fyen et al., 1975). The fundamental problem was that lowering detector threshold values causes the number of false alarms to increase more rapidly than the number of events expected from the log N recurrence relation (see fig. 5). In other words, even with elaborate processing schemes, there is little point in analyzing detections at and below thresholds at which the false alarm rate starts increasing rapidly. Besides, information extractable from small detections is not particularly useful in any context except generating "nocturnal" seismicity.

After a few years of practical experience in real-time operations of the LASA and NORSAR arrays, the work became rather routine and, moreover, expertly handled by analysts. At this time (around 1975) the more fundamental issue of large-array operation came into focus: could a limited number of large arrays manage the required seismic-event surveillance functions for monitoring compliance with a potential CTB? The performance of these arrays was relatively impressive; uptime on a monthly/yearly basis was 90–95 percent, and daily detections amounted to about twenty to twenty-five events, subject to seasonal variations and uncertainty in event locations of 50–200 km. However, the detection capability of these arrays, at body wave magnitude $(m_b) \sim 4.0$ at the 90 percent confidence level for favorable regions (see Ringdal et al. 1977), was not entirely superior to that of some ordinary stations at excellent quiet sites. In short, the problem of detecting weak signals is tied not only to suppressing ambient noise, but the site amplification factor also is important. In the extreme, a single instrument at NORSAR exhibited signal-to-noise ratios comparable to those of the best array beam, as hinted at above.

In the midseventies, after about five years of automated large-array operation, it became clear that even several large arrays of the LASA-NORSAR type would not be adequate for test-ban monitoring of nuclear weapons of yields down to 1 kiloton ($m_b \sim 4.0$ in granite). In particular, P-signals recorded in the teleseismic window would not provide a credible diagnostic

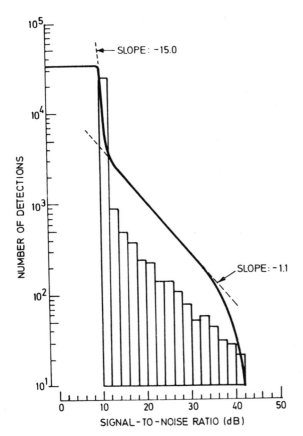

Figure 5. Number of detections by the automatic NORSAR detector as a function of STA/LTA (signal-to-noise) ratio for the period July to December 1972. The number of detections increases sharply below a signal-to-noise ratio of 12 dB where false alarms generated by noise fluctuation dominate detections triggered by real events.

for source identification. This realization, in combination with funding problems, regrettably resulted in curtailing the NORSAR operation to seven operative subarrays, while LASA was closed down in 1978.

In summary, it was demonstrated during the 1970s that automated array operation was technically feasible, but large arrays were not sufficient for test-ban monitoring. Furthermore, P-signals in the teleseismic window were adequately understood in terms of generation mechanisms and propagation path effects, while their diagnostic power for source identification remained doubtful.

ARRAY OPERATION IN THE 1980s

The hallmark of array seismology is the intimate link between research progress and easy access to data of superior quality. In the 1980s, with research emphasis on observations in the local (0–10°) and regional (10–30°) distance ranges, array observations from the 1960s and 1970s were not adequate in bandwidth or dynamic range. The very first step was, naturally, to reexamine the array concept vis-à-vis high-frequency seismic signals at relatively short distances. Basic data for this problem were easy to obtain, at least in the case of NORSAR, by using the existing cable infrastructure. That is, a subarray could easily be reconfigured to sensor spacings ranging from 100 to 1,200 m without costly field work. The analysis of these and similar observations focused upon parameters critical for array design, namely, noise and signal levels and spatial noise and signal correlations as functions of frequency. The most significant results were that the noise level outside the microseismic band of 0.5–2.5 Hz decreased at a rate of about f^{-4} up to about 10 Hz, and that the noise correlation function exhibited negative values of around 0.05 to 0.15 at certain station separations. Furthermore, for local and regional phases, the signal-to-noise ratios peaked in the 3–8 Hz band, while signal correlation decreased rapidly beyond 6–8 Hz. These noise and signal characteristics were built into the design of the new regional array NORESS (fig. 6) in that not all array elements were used because the close spacing of A- and B-ring elements would otherwise have entailed partly positive, that is, constructive, noise interference. For details see Mykkeltveit et al. (1983), Ingate et al. (1985), Bungum et al. (1985), and the NORSAR Semiannual Technical Summaries (editor L. B. Loughran, NORSAR).

As mentioned above, the NORESS design is aimed at optimizing signal-detection capabilities, but the penalty is a certain lack of spatial resolution, which naturally affects the array's event location capabilities (see Harris, 1982; Ruud et al., 1988). Even the much larger NORSAR and LASA arrays were not well suited for precise locations using standard epicenter estimation techniques. Using two arrays jointly for event locations would, of course, improve performance (Jordan and Sverdrup, 1981), but significant progress here would depend on the ability to extract more information from the array records. An interesting development in this context is the deployment of an additional regional array, ARCESS, in northern Norway (Karasjok, operational in October 1987), planned to be operated in tandem with NORESS for exploring expert system techniques to realize these goals.

The success of NORESS and the general availability of relatively cheap digital data technology have led to a revival of array research programs in several countries, notably Australia, Canada, Germany, UK, and Sweden. Such arrays, with apertures mostly 10 to 30 km, are somewhat larger than NORESS, but the research problems are much the same, with an emphasis on automated operation and interactive analysis workstation design.

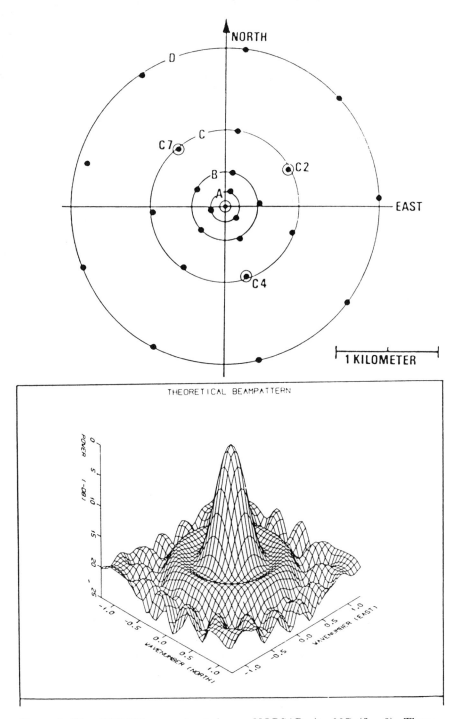

Figure 6. The NORESS array located near NORSAR site 06C (fig. 3). Three-component stations are marked by small circles. The center vault also contains a Geotech KS-36000-04 broadband bore-hole seismometer and a high-gain high-frequency (125-Hz) three-component seismometer. The array response in the f-k domain is also shown; contour levels are in dB down from the maximum.

Not only classical array seismology has benefited from recent advances in the fields of microcomputers and telecommunications. The same technology can easily be adapted to single-site three-component station operations, and of particular interest here is the development of flexible analysis techniques for handling this kind of data. For example, Christoffersson et al. (1988) have demonstrated a novel approach to decomposing three-component wavefield records using their phase information. A practical application of this technique to event location has been demonstrated by Ruud et al. (1988). In terms of performance, a single three-component station does not compare unfavorably with a small-aperture array, at least at local distances.

Detectors for picking P and S (Lg) phases at local distances have also been designed (see Magotra et al., 1987), thus supporting the feasibility of operating single-site three-component stations in ways similar to those of an array. Note that networks of such three-component stations with a centralized hub for joint analysis of data from many stations would indeed be a most powerful tool for monitoring compliance with a potential CTB.

To summarize, the 1980s have seen a revival of array seismology, particularly in developing new, small arrays and "digitally" upgrading previously deployed arrays. Most work has been aimed at automating array operation and designing interactive workstations for analyst screening of final results, tied mainly to bulletin preparation. Regarding data analysis, hardly any progress has taken place in the field of array processing and signal estimation techniques. Of some importance in this context is the novel analyzing technique of three-component recordings (Christoffersson et al., 1988; Magotra et al., 1987), which is likely to strongly upgrade the signal information retrievable from individual stations. Interestingly, the current U.S. Geological Survey (USGS) deployment of a national 150-station three-component broadband seismograph network, with near-real-time parameter and waveform event data transmitted by satellite to NEIC/USGS headquarters in Golden, Colorado, is providing a practical test of these developments (R. Massé, personal communication).

ARRAYS—FUTURE DEVELOPMENTS

Array deployments in the past decades demonstrated that the integrated operation of hundreds of seismometers is technically feasible in a real-time environment, but the potential monitoring performance in a CTB context has been less convincing. The main reason for this is a signal-amplitude decay in the 100-to-3,000-km range of between 1 and 2 magnitude units, which means that array surveillance performance in the teleseismic window is relatively inefficient. Another crucial factor is the significant decrease in noise level at frequencies above 2.5 Hz, thus giving an additional edge to surveillance at local and regional distances. With this realization, large array operations were regrettably curtailed at the end of the 1970s, and in the 1980s array seismology research interests have focused on monitoring at local and regional distances. Related problems are a need for improved physical understanding of wave propagation in the crustal waveguide, notably that of Lg waves. So far, most efforts have been in the design, deployment, and operation of small aperture arrays. NORESS may be considered a prototype of the joining of developments and operational experience over the past decades with general technological advances. Small-array event detection is relatively very good because of good signal-to-noise ratios above 2.5 Hz and the use of a sensor configuration that takes advantage of destructive noise interference during beamforming. Despite this, array seismology is at a crossroads. Considering the costs of array construction (about four million dollars for NORESS) and operation and demonstrated monitoring/surveillance performance, are arrays competitive with relatively dense networks of high-quality three-component stations that can be placed and run for a fraction of the cost? The problem is that arrays are still operated as superstations. The essential wave-field parameters extracted are onset time, amplitude, period, and the P-slowness vector. These are sufficient for producing fast bulletins but not much more. They are insufficient to identify source type at regional distances, which remains an unsolved problem despite much effort.

A single three-component station can now easily provide the same signal parameters, and a combination of several such observations yields a relatively comprehensive spatial view of the signal source. We implicitly refer to the way past and present earthquake surveillance has been performed, namely, by extracting few signal parameters from many stations. For an array, essentially one point of observation, to overcome this disadvantage it has to extract more information from the entire wave-field record. In other words, techniques for more extensive seismogram parameterization are required. Several approaches are feasible and will be briefly discussed below.

The Expert System Analog

This approach is currently exploited to ensure automated array operation in combination with interactive workstations for refinements of analysis results. A basic ingredient is an advanced data-management system that would have a "memory" of previous events in a given area, which in turn would ensure the "learning" aspect of operation. At the present stage of development, more extensive seismogram parameterization techniques have been given low priority. This system is not, strictly speaking, "expert," since there is no attempt to incorporate subtle analyst knowledge. The system is data driven, and refinements would be tied to identifying patterns in the records on the presumption that earthquake occurrence is somewhat stationary. This

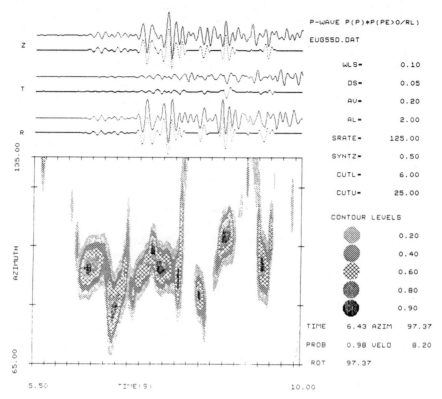

Figure 7. Three-component analysis of Shot 7, EUGENO-S Refraction Profile 4 in southern Sweden, distance 205 km. Signal processing parameters: SRATE = sample rate; WLS = window length; DS and AV = updating intervals for time and azimuth, respectively; AL = a smoothing parameter (see Christoffersson et al., 1988, for details on the method).

7a) χ^2 probabilities of P-wave particle motions. Original (solid) and filtered (dotted) records: lower probability (SYNTZ) for filtering/weighting = 0.50; lower (CUTL) and upper (CUTU) velocity passband of 6.5 km s^{-1} and 25.0 km s^{-1}. Lower right: cursor reading (+) off the screen.

7b) P-wave velocities instead of χ^2 probabilities. Original (solid) and filtered (dotted) records: lower probability (PROBLIM) for computing contours = 0.50; lower (CUTL) and upper (CUTU) velocities for filtering/weighting 6.0 km s^{-1} and 15.0 km s^{-1}. Lower right: cursor reading (+) off the screen.

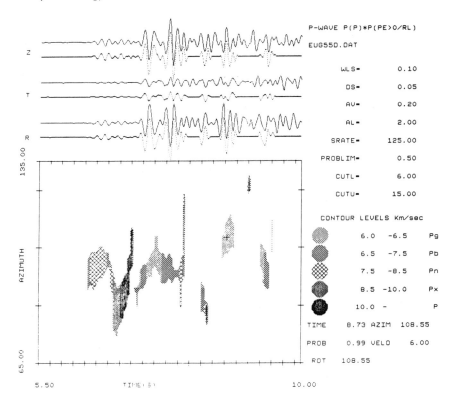

is the way a trained analyst works, recognizing characteristic waveforms of signals from specific areas; the tricky problem here is, naturally, to quantify the extent of similarity (T. Bache, personal communication).

Wave-field parameterization

This novel approach by Christoffersson et al. (1988) to three-component wave-field decomposition analysis is convenient for illustrating the problem involved (see fig. 7). The slowness vector variation along the P-wave train exhibits a distinct pattern that, at least, is stationary for NORESS three-component stations and repeated Semipalatinsk underground nuclear tests. More interesting here is that signal similarities are almost identical for one station and many explosions but disparate between two three-component NORESS stations for the same explosion (see Ruud et al., 1988). In other words, very localized siting structures appear to have a profound effect on the recorded wave field, hence the "correlation distance" of pattern similarities in the receiver area appears to be very small, of the order of 0.5–1.0 km. However, on the source side the corresponding correlation distance is of the order of tens of kilometers, at least as regards Semipalatinsk explosions.

These preliminary results from extensive wave-field parameterization may have important ramifications regarding vastly improved event location and source classification capabilities of small arrays and/or single three-component stations. Research in this field is well worth pursuing, including attribute processing as used in seismic prospecting (for example, see Vidale, 1986) and its recently introduced "ARMAG-Markov" variants (Tjøstheim, 1981; Karlsen and Tjøstheim, 1988).

Array signal processing

The theoretical groundwork of present-day array data processing schemes was formulated in the 1960s, and in this respect it suffices to refer to the many contributions from scientists at the Massachusetts Institute of Technology's (MIT) Lincoln Laboratory and Texas Instruments and Teledyne groups located at that time in Alexandria, Virginia. The analytic techniques developed were tied to processing P-waves in the teleseismic window, for which the implicit modeling of the P-signal as a single wavelet was quite adequate (Christoffersson and Husebye, 1974). For events at local and regional distances this assumption is less valid, in view of the more complex wave train of even the first-arriving P-wave. For example, narrow band f-k analysis may occasionally produce gross errors in slowness estimates due to either a corresponding weak signal coherency or interference. Broadband estimation techniques produce far more stable results, but the problem remains in the sense that slowness is a function of the frequency band used and of the window positioning in the signal (see fig. 8). This example illustrates both the strength and weakness of arrays. Even a small-aperture array like NORESS illuminates the complexities of the Earth, particularly the lithosphere, while our ability to quantify the structural heterogeneities as manifested in the seismogram remain relatively primitive. Not much progress in solving these kinds of problems has been made in the last decades. We consider such progress essential to justify operation and deployment of arrays in the next decade. Again, the reason is that networks of high-quality three-component stations will easily outperform array surveillance of global seismicity and CTB monitoring unless more precise signal and source information is extracted from the records.

SEISMOLOGICAL RESEARCH USING ARRAY DATA

The characteristic feature of an array is its ability to provide a two-dimensional, high-quality sampling of the wave field in a digital form. The sensor spacing is such that P-signal coherency is preserved while noise coherency is zero or slightly negative, as in the case of NORESS. Research applications of array data are in general aimed at exploiting the above characteristic features, and some major achievements, briefly presented in this section, have been accomplished.

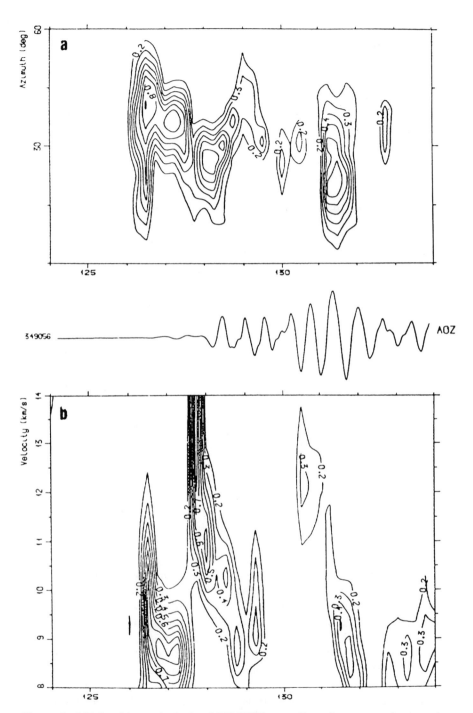

Figure 8. ML-Semblance analysis of NORESS recordings from an underground Novaya Zemlya explosion. Traces: that of AOZ displayed. Just as in case of three-component analysis, the slowness vector estimate varies considerably with window positioning in the P-wave train.

Microseisms and cultural noise studies

Some thirty years ago, microseismic studies were popular among seismologists, with a focus on generation mechanisms (coastal surf and low-pressure passage) and propagation efficiencies. Data from LASA and NORSAR in combination with the f-*k* analysis technique proved effective tools for demonstrating the relationship between low-pressure movements in, say, the North Atlantic and Norwegian seas and associated coastal surfs on the one hand, and the corresponding noise field variability at the array on the other (Bungum et al., 1971; Korhonen and Pirhonen, 1976).

Also, specific cultural noise studies have been undertaken, notably to explain a noise power spectra peak at 2.067 Hz, reflecting "energy" leakage from imperfectly balanced turbines at hydroelectric power plants (Hjortenberg and Risbo, 1975). The energy leakage may be considered a steady-state signal source and has been exploited as a means for monitoring tiny P- and S-velocity changes as a function of tidal crustal loads (Bungum et al., 1977). In the 1980s noise research has been tied to noise correlation as a function of sensor separation and its practical use for signal enhancement. New arrays like NORESS are equipped with instruments of high dynamic range (120 dB), which testifies to the relative importance of localized noise sources. For example, dam overflow in connection with spring flooding in the nearby Glomma River generated Rayleigh-type noise wavelets easily picked up by the NORESS detector. Incidently, this effect was first seen in the analysis of three-component records, as associated detections were initially attributed to instability in the analysis technique itself.

To summarize, noise-field analysis is important for optimizing array configuration and operation, while microseismic studies are definitely passé. However, an interesting avenue for future research may be the use of steady-state noise sources and even microseisms for imaging/tomographic mapping of structural heterogeneities. A work of interest on this topic is that of Troitskiy et al. (1981).

Gross Earth structures—p-τ inversion

The first use of array data for structural mapping was tied to "inverting" P-arrival times and associated $dT/d\Delta$ (or slowness) observations (see Chinnery and Toksöz, 1967; King and Calcagnile, 1976). The techniques used to analyze these data were initially Monte Carlo simulations and/or Abel's integral equation. The latter technique was later refined and is now generally known as p-τ inversion. It has found widespread application in refraction and wide-angle reflection data analysis (Stoffa et al., 1981). Due to the stationarity of both arrays and earthquake activities, only average information about earth structures can be provided in this way. However, due to the exceptionally good signal-to-noise ratios provided by array records, such data have provided detailed information on major secondary discontinuities

like those at 400 and 650 km (see Husebye et al., 1977). Travel-time triplica-
tions associated with these discontinuities are particularly visible in NOR-
SAR records of many western Russian underground explosions (King and
Calcagnile, 1976). Likewise, mapping and identifying various core phases
and associated travel-time branches have been demonstrated (Doornbos and
Husebye, 1972). Today, this kind of research is mainly history, in view of the
limited Earth sampling offered by an array. The trend is toward using the
comprehensive ISC data files and other seismological observations for generating laterally varying and partly anisotropic Earth models (see Anderson,
1985).

To summarize, array data analysis in the 1960–1970s provided relatively
detailed mapping of major discontinuities in the upper mantle and resolved
controversies regarding the generation mechanisms of so-called PKP precursor waves. There are still research avenues of interest in this context, such as
dynamic modeling of travel-time branches for the 400- and 650-km discontinuities. At NORSAR such recordings exhibit consistent and profound
changes in amplitude and frequency content between different phases, which
must reflect strong lateral variations across these boundaries.

Chernov media, three-dimensional mapping, and tomography

Perhaps the largest contribution of arrays to the science of seismology was
an early realization that the earth was distinctly inhomogeneous. This was
rather obvious from visual inspections of multisensor panels of P-wave array
records, since both time and amplitude anomalies were of nearly the same
order as those usually attributed to major regional structural differences (see
fig. 4). With the recognition of pronounced heterogeneities in the array
(LASA and NORSAR) siting areas and in the lithosphere, the next problem
was to develop tools for modeling this phenomenon. The first significant step
was by Aki (1973) who used the Chernov random-medium theory to model
P-wave time and amplitude variations. A variant of this same theory was
used by Clearly and Haddon (1972) to explain the scattering origin in the
lowermost mantle of the so-called PKP precursor waves. Studies similar to
those of Aki and others were undertaken at NORSAR, which also in this case
resulted in a reasonable fit to the observational data (Berteussen et al., 1975).
In another study, Husebye et al. (1974) demonstrated that P-wave amplitudes exhibit an approximately log-normal distribution, which subsequently
led to the development of maximum-likelihood magnitude estimation procedures (Ringdal, 1975; Christoffersson,1980). The common denominator for
these studies was the use of an essentially statistical description of earth
heterogeneities. In particular, the random-medium concept used for modeling Earth structures caused conceptual problems with many of our colleagues, and indeed we felt a bit uneasy ourselves. The lithosphere is definitely solid, hence deterministic approaches should be used for its mapping

and modeling. The solution to this fundamental seismological problem, a scientific breakthrough, came with a visit of Aki to NORSAR during the summer of 1974. The concept of block-inversion (the ACH-method), or three-dimensional imaging, was formulated after only a month, and this particular project was finalized at the Massachusetts Institute of Technology in 1975. The data first to be used in mapping lithosphere heterogeneities were P-travel-time anomalies from NORSAR, LASA, and the southern California network (Aki et al., 1976, 1977; Husebye et al., 1976). Dziewonski et al. (1977) extended the method to global mantle mapping, and others like Spencer and Gubbins (1980) introduced smart inversion schemes for joint estimation of source and structural parameters. The latter concept is particularly important in regional studies. The inversion technique initially offered by Aki, Christoffersson, and Husebye has now been extended to other seismological observations, including full waveform inversion, and is generally labeled Earth tomography. Instead of going into details here, we refer to recent major contributions on this topic by Carrion (1987), Goldin (1987), Nolet (1987), and Tarantola (1987).

As a curiosity, we should like to mention here that the development appears to have come full circle, as Flatté and Wu (1988) recently used scattering theory to provide a "scattering" three-dimensional image of the lithosphere beneath NORSAR based on essentially the same data as Aki et al. (1977) and Haddon and Husebye (1978), but using the correlation functions of these observations.

To summarize, the largest and most lasting contribution to seismology from arrays is that their observed puzzling P-wave time and amplitude anomalies led to the concept of Earth tomography, a major activity in Earth sciences today. However, the modeling of short-period P-amplitude anomalies remains problematic, although some success has been documented in this field as well (for example, see Haddon and Husebye, 1978; Thomson and Gubbins, 1982; Nowack and Aki, 1986).

Coda waves and associated scattering phenomena

In array seismology, wave-scattering phenomena have been, and still are, a major research topic. As mentioned previously, initial interests were focused on explaining and modeling precursory waves for PKP, PP, and other phases. A related, and by far more severe, problem is that of explaining and modeling the so-called coda waves (see Aki, 1969). Although many theoretical studies on this problem have been undertaken (see Wu and Aki, 1988), a remaining basic problem is that of decomposing the coda wave train. What we need to know, partly as a prerequisite for further theoretical investigations, is what wave types constitute the coda, say P and Lg waves. For such purposes, small-aperture arrays and single three-component stations are both eminently suited. Using maximum-likelihood variants of

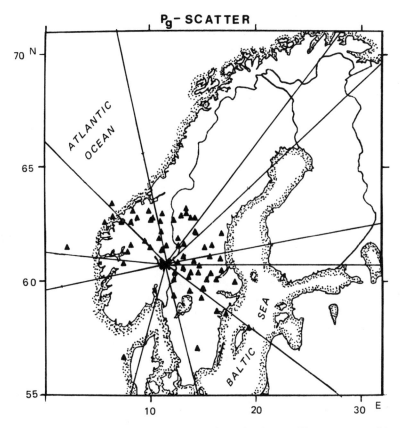

Figure 9. Locations of secondary "sources" for coda phases of P_g wave type subject to scattering at the receiver site. Thin lines represent azimuth of the events used in analysis. Note that scattering efficiency appears to be relatively weak to the south and west. The location of the scattering sources is based on three-component analysis.

broadband f-k analysis, Dainty (1988) has segmented the coda (usually within the 40–120-s window relative to the P-wave arrival) into scattering contributions from source and receiver sites. The outcome depends on source type, that is, earthquake or explosion, and focal depth. Since coherency is low in the coda, seldom exceeding 0.4 units for 3-s windows, relatively long windows of 10–20-s have to be used to ensure stable results. On the other hand, three-component records are less subject to severe interference, compared to a two-dimensional sensor deployment and permit time windows of one second in coda analysis. In other words, scattered P-wavelets are easy to identify and locate (see fig. 9) using the techniques mentioned in Christoffersson et al. (1988) and Ruud et al. (1988).

To summarize, small-aperture arrays have proved an important tool for decomposing the coda and hence providing an improved insight into the extent of mode-conversion and wave-propagation efficiencies in the heterogeneous lithosphere. Such problems are important in the context of extensive wavefield parameterization. Likewise, path-dependent coda excitation may provide a clue to earthquake prediction (Aki, 1988) and thus provide an additional rationale for coda-wave research. In parallel to the Chernov media-to-tomography development mentioned above, a statistical modeling approach may also be most fruitful here in the initial stages (see Karlsen and Tjøstheim, 1988).

DISCUSSIONS AND CONCLUSIONS

In this article we have presented an overview of array seismology as it has evolved over the past decades. Our viewpoints are to some extent colored by intimate familiarity with NORSAR, LASA, and NORESS design and operation. However, the operation and research tied to these arrays are representative of array seismology per se, although activities of other arrays are not so well cited in the scientific literature. Anyway, array seismology has contributed significantly to the development of our science, both on observational and theoretical bases, which reflects the two unique features of an array, namely, superior data quality paired with dense two-dimensional wave-field sampling. Today, the technical edge of arrays is mainly lost as networks of high-gain, digital, three-component stations, affordable even for academic institutions and consortia, can be operated in much the same way as an array. Naturally, conventional beamforming is not feasible, but incoherent (envelope) beamforming is (Ringdal et al., 1975); alternatively, individual station detectors may be used (Magotra et al., 1987). Added flexibility here would come from developments of mobile arrays which, within a few years, are likely to comprise many hundreds of high-quality field instruments.

So, what will likely be the future role of the mentioned stationary arrays now in operation and similar ones possibly yet to be deployed? First of all, their contribution to general seismological research will be modest in view of their small aperture, with the notable exception of coda studies. However, past NORSAR and LASA records remain unique and thus will still be of importance in research if they are generally available.

Arrays in future CTB monitoring roles are a "touchy" political/ seismological problem. For example, comprehensive simulation studies of seismic surveillance of both Russia and the United States have been undertaken by Evernden et al. (1986), while the same topic was covered in U.S. Congress hearings as part of the formulation of monitoring policies. In a technical note here by Bache, one conclusion was that a network of about forty three-component stations would have roughly the same capability for monitoring Russia as a net of twenty NORESS-type arrays. Such a conclusion is not entirely surprising, in view of the amplitude-distance dependence and the obvious need to view a seismic source from different angles to properly identify its mechanism. We do not consider this to be a "black/white" problem, but believe that a blend of small arrays and three-component stations will offer the best tool for CTB monitoring. This being said, the relative importance of arrays in this context will depend on our ability to extract far more information from the array records; the above-mentioned expert-system approach, in combination with ingenious coda-processing schemes, is a promising avenue.

Our concluding remark is that arrays, although conceived and deployed mainly for political purposes, have proved extremely beneficial for seismology. In the future, new breeds of arrays will be even more important as mobile arrays, now technically feasible, will permit scientific experiments aimed at the detailed mapping of specific parts of the lithosphere or the Earth's deep interior. Perhaps most important are recent advances in computing and data-storage technology that permit any seismologist to participate in these efforts (see Berry chap. 3 in this volume.) In short, today we have a global seismological community, while tomorrow we will have a global research brotherhood as well.

ACKNOWLEDGMENTS

With two decades of involvement in array seismology, we have had the opportunity and pleasure to meet many prominent scientists from many countries. I should like to mention specifically an acquaintance with K. Aki, who sees exciting research problems where others just see recordings, and A. Christoffersson, who has a knack for modeling both signal parameters and wave forms. Extensive monitoring discussions with GSE (Group of Scientific Experts) friends in Geneva, like R. Alewine, III, K. Muirhead, M. Henger, S. Lundbo, and others, are also much appreciated. Finally, the invitation to attend the Berkeley Seismograph Stations Centennial Symposia is acknowledged, and special thanks go to Prof. B. A. Bolt.

REFERENCES

Aki, K. (1969). Analysis of the seismic coda of local earthquakes: Source, attenuation and scattering effect. *J. Geophys. Res.*, 74: 615–631.

———— (1973). Scattering of P-waves under the Montana LASA. *J. Geophys. Res.*, 78: 1334–1346.

———— (1988). The impact of earthquake seismology to the geological community since the Benioff Zone Centennial. *Bull. Geol. Soc. Am.*, (submitted).

Aki, K., A. Christoffersson, and E. S. Husebye (1976). Three-dimensional structure of the lithosphere under Montana LASA. *Bull. Seism. Soc. Am.*, 66: 501–524.

——— (1977). Determination of the three-dimensional seismic structure of the lithosphere. *J. Geophys. Res.*, 82: 277–296.

Aki, K., and P. G. Richards (1980). *Quantitative Seismology: Theory and Methods.* Freeman, San Francisco, vols. I and II.

Anderson, D. L. (1985). Evolution of Earth structure and future directions of 3D modeling. In A. U. Kerr, ed., *The VELA Program; Twenty-five Years of Basic Research.* Executive Graphics Services, Defense Advanced Research Projects Agency, Rosslyn, Va., 399–418.

Anonymous (1965). *Large Aperture Seismic Array.* Advanced Research Projects Agency Technical Report, Washington, D.C.

Berteussen, K.-A., A. Christoffersson, E. S. Husebye, and A. Dahle (1975). Wave scattering theory in analysis of P-wave anomalies at NORSAR and LASA. *Geophys. J.*, 42: 403–417.

Berteussen, K.-A., and E. S. Husebye (1974). Amplitude pattern effects on NORSAR P-wave detectability. *Sci. Rep. 2-74/75*, NTNF/NORSAR, Kjeller, Norway.

Böhme, J. F. (1987). Array processing. In J. L. Lacoume et al., eds., *Signal Processing.* North Holland, Publ. 4, Amsterdam, 437–482.

Bolt, B. A. (1976). *Nuclear Explosions and Earthquakes: The Parted Veil.* W. H. Freeman, San Francisco, 309 pp.

Bungum, H., E. S. Husebye, and F. Ringdal (1971). The NORSAR array and preliminary results of data analysis. *Geophys. J.*, 25: 115–126.

Bungum, H., S. Mykkeltveit, and T. Kværna (1985). Seismic noise in Fennoscandia, with emphasis on high frequencies. *Bull. Seism. Soc. Am.*, 75: 1489–1514.

Bungum, H., T. Risbo, and E. Hjortenberg (1977). Precise continuous monitoring of seismic velocity variations and their possible connection to solid earth tides. *J. Geophys. Res.*, 82: 5365–5373.

Bungum, H., E. Rygg, and L. Bruland (1971). Short-period seismic noise structure at the Norwegian Seismic Array. *Bull. Seism. Soc. Am.*, 61: 357–373.

Buttkus, B. (1986). Ten years of the Gräfenberg array. *Geol. Jahrbuch Reihe E*, Heft 35, Hannover.

Capon, J. (1969). High-resolution frequency-wavenumber spectrum analysis. *Proc. IEEE*, 57: 1408–1418.

Carrion, P. (1987). *Inverse Problems and Tomography in Acoustics and Seismology.* Penn Publishing Co., Atlanta, Ga.

Chinnery, M. A., and M. N. Toksöz (1967). P-wave velocities in the mantle below 700 km. *Bull. Seism. Soc. Am.*, 57: 199–226.

Christoffersson, A. (1980). Statistical models for seismic magnitude. *Phys. Earth Planet. Inter.*, 21: 237–260.

Christoffersson, A., and E. S. Husebye (1974). Least square signal estimation techniques in analysis of seismic array recorded P-waves. *Geophys. J. R. Astr. Soc.*, 38: 525–552.

Christoffersson, A., E. S. Husebye, and S. F. Ingate (1988). Wavefield decomposition using ML-probabilities in modeling single-site three-component records. *Geophys. J.* 93: 197–213.

Cleary, J. R., and R. A. W. Haddon (1972). Seismic wave scattering near the core-mantle boundary: A new interpretation of precursors to PKP. *Nature*, 240: 549–51.

Dahlman, O., and H. Israelson (1977). *Monitoring Underground Nuclear Explosions*. Elsevier, Amsterdam, The Netherlands, 440 pp.

Dainty, A. M. (1988). Studies of coda using array and three-component processing. In R. S. Wu and K. Aki, eds., *PAGEOPH Special Issue on Scattering and Attenuation of Seismic Waves*.

Doornbos, D. J., and E. S. Husebye (1972). Array analysis of PKP phases and their precursors. *Phys. Earth Planet. Inter.*, 5: 387–399.

Duckworth, G. L. (1983). Processing and Inversion of Arctic Ocean Refraction Data. Sc.D. thesis, Massachusetts Institude of Technology and Woods Hole Oceanographic Institude, Cambridge, Mass.

Dziewonski, A. M., B. N. Hager, and R. J. O'Connell (1977). Large-scale heterogeneities in the lower mantle. *J. Geophys. Res.*, 82: 239–255.

Evernden, J. F., C. B. Archambeau, and E. Cranswick (1986). An evaluation of seismic decoupling and underground nuclear test monitoring using high-frequency seismic data. *Rev. Geophys.*, 24: 143–215.

Flatté, S. M., and R. S. Wu (1988). Small-scale structure in the lithosphere and asthenosphere deduced from arrival-time and amplitude fluctuations at NORSAR. In R. S. Wu and K. Aki, eds., *PAGEOPH Special Issue on Scattering and Attenuation of Seismic Waves*.

Fyen, J., E. S. Husebye, and A. Christoffersson (1975). Statistical classification of weak seismic signals and noise at the NORSAR array. *Geophys. J. R. Astr. Soc.*, 42: 529–546.

Goldin, S. V. (1987). *Seismic Travel Time Inversion*. SEG Bookmart, Tulsa, Okla.

Haddon, R. A. W., and E. S. Husebye (1978). Joint interpretation of P-wave travel time and amplitude anomalies in terms of lithospheric heterogeneities. *Geophys. J.*, 55: 263–288.

Harris, D. B. (1982). Uncertainty in direction estimation: A comparison of small arrays and three-component stations. *Lawrence Livermore National Lab., Tech. Rep. UCID-19589*, Livermore, Calif.

Haykin, S., ed. (1985). *Array Signal Processing*. Prentice-Hall, Englewood Cliffs, N. J., 433 pp.

Hjortenberg, E., and T. Risbo (1975). Monochromatic components of the seismic noise in the NORSAR area. *Geophys. J. R. Astr. Soc.*, 42: 547–554.

Hsu, K., and A. B. Baggeroer (1986). Application of the maximum likelihood method (MLM) for sonic velocity logging. *Geophys.*, 51: 780–787.

Husebye, E. S., A. Christoffersson, K. Aki, and C. Powell (1976). Preliminary results on the 3-dimensional seismic structure under the USGS Central California Seismic Array. *Geophys. J. R. Astr. Soc.*, 46: 319–340.

Husebye, E. S., A. Dahle, and K.-A. Berteussen (1974). Bias analysis of NORSAR and ISC reported seismic event m_b magnitudes. *J. Geophys. Res.*, 79: 2967–2978.

Husebye, E. S., R. A. W. Haddon, and D. W. King (1977). Precursors to P'P' and upper mantle discontinuities. *J. Geophys.*, 43: 535–543.

Husebye, E. S., and S. Mykkeltveit, eds. (1981). *Identification of Seismic Sources—Earthquakes or Underground Explosions*. NATO ASI Series, D. Reidel Publishing Co., Dordrecht, The Netherlands, 876 pp.

Ingate, S. F., E. S. Husebye, and A. Christoffersson (1985). Regional arrays and optimum data processing schemes. *Bull. Seism. Soc. Am.*, 75: 1155–1177.

Jordan, T. H., and K. A. Sverdrup (1981). Teleseismic location techniques and their application to earthquake clusters in the south-central Pacific. *Bull. Seism. Soc. Am.*, 71: 1105–1130.

Kanasewich, E. R. (1981). *Time Sequence Analysis in Geophysics*. University of Alberta Press, Alberta, Canada, 480 pp.

Karlsen, H., and D. Tjøstheim (1988). *Autoregressive segmentation of signal traces with applications to geological dipmeter measurements*. Dept. of Mathematics, Bergen University, Norway.

Kerr, A. U., ed. (1985). *The VELA Program. Twenty-five Years of Basic Research*. Executive Graphic Services, Defense Advanced Research Projects Agency (DARPA), Rosslyn, Va., 964 pp.

King, D. W., and G. Calcagnile (1976). P-wave velocities in the upper mantle beneath Fennoscandia and western Russia. *Geophys. J.*, 46: 407–432.

Korhonen, H., and S. Pirhonen (1976). Spectral properties and source areas of storm microseisms at NORSAR. *Sci. Rep. 2-75/76*, NTNF/NORSAR, Kjeller, Norway.

Magotra, N., N. Ahmed, and E. Chael (1987). Seismic event detection and source location. *Bull. Seism. Soc. Am.*, 77: 958–971.

Massé, R. P. (1987). *Seismic Verification of Nuclear Test Limitation Treaties: Workshop 2. Identification*. Office of Technical Assessment, Congress of the United States, Washington, D. C.

Monzingo, R. A., and T. W. Miller (1980). *Introduction to Adaptive Arrays*. Wiley, New York.

Muirhead, K. J., and R. Datt (1976). The N-th root process applied to seismic array data. *Geophys. J. R. Astr. Soc.*, 47: 197–210.

Mykkeltveit, S., K. Åstebøl, D. J. Doornbos, and E. S. Husebye (1983). Seismic array configuration optimization. *Bull. Seism. Soc. Am.*, 73: 173–186.

Nolet, G., ed. (1987). *Seismic Tomography, with Applications in Global Seismology and Exploration Geophysics*. D. Reidel, Dordrecht, The Netherlands.

Nowack, R. L., and K. Aki (1986). Iterative inversion for velocity using waveform data. *Geophys. J. R. Astr. Soc.*, 87: 701–730.

Press, F., ed. (1985). *Nuclear Arms Control: Background and Issues*. National Academy Press, Washington, D.C., 378 pp.

Ringdal, F. (1975). On the estimation of seismic detection thresholds. *Bull. Seism. Soc. Am.*, 65: 1631–1642.

Ringdal, F., E. S. Husebye, and A. Dahle (1975). P-wave envelope representation in event detection using array data. In K. G. Beauchamp, ed., *Exploitation of Seismograph Networks*. Nordhoff-Leiden, The Netherlands, 353–372.

Ringdal, F., E. S. Husebye, and J. Fyen (1977). Earthquake detectability estimates for 478 globally distributed seismograph stations. *Phys. Earth Planet. Inter.*, 15: 24–32.

Romney, C. F. (1985). VELA Overview: The early years of the seismic research program. In A. U. Kerr, ed., *The VELA Program. Twenty-five years of Basic Research*. Executive Graphics Services, Defense Advanced Research Projects Agency, Rosslyn, Va., 38–65.

Ruud, B. O., E. S. Husebye, S. F. Ingate, and A. Christoffersson (1988). Event location at any distance using seismic data from a single, three-component station. *Bull. Seism. Soc. Am.*, 78: 308–325.

Spencer, C., and D. Gubbins (1980). Travel-time inversion for simultaneous earthquake location and velocity structure determination in laterally varying media. *Geophys. J. R. Astr. Soc.*, 63: 95–116.

Steinert, O., E. S. Husebye, and H. Gjøystdal (1976). Noise variance fluctuations and earthquake detectability. *J. Geophys.*, 41: 289–302.

Stoffa, P. L., P. Buhl, J. B. Diebold, and F. Wentzel (1981). Direct mapping of seismic data to the domain of intercept time and ray parameter—A plane wave decomposition. *Geophys.*, 46: 255–267.

Tarantola, A. (1987). *Inverse Problem Theory*. Elsevier, Amsterdam, The Netherlands, 613 pp.

Thirlaway, H. I. S. (1985). Forensic seismology. In A. U. Kerr, ed., *The VELA Program. Twenty-five years of Basic Research*. Executive Graphics Services. Defense Advanced Research Projects Agency, Rosslyn, Va., 17–25.

Thomson, C. J., and D. Gubbins (1982). Three-dimensional lithospheric modeling at NORSAR: Linearity of the method and amplitude variations from the anomalies. *Geophys. J. R. Astr. Soc.*, 71: 1–36.

Tjøstheim, D. (1981). Multidimensional discrimination techniques—Theory and applications. In E. S. Husebye and S. Mykkeltveit, eds., *Identification of Seismic Sources—Earthquakes or Underground Explosions*. D. Reidel, Dordrecht, The Netherlands, 663–694.

Troitskiy, P., E. S. Husebye, and A. Nikolaev (1981). Lithospheric studies based on holographic principles. *Nature*, 294: 618–623.

Tsipis, K., D. W. Hafemeister, and P. Janeway (1986). *Arms Control Verification: The Technologies That Make It Possible*. Pergamon Brasey's International Defense Publications, Washington, D.C., 419 pp.

Urban, H. G., ed. (1985). *Adaptive Methods in Underwater Acoustics, NATO ASI Series C*. D. Reidel, Dordrecht, The Netherlands.

Vidale, J. F. (1986). Complex polarization analysis of particle motion. *Bull. Seism. Soc. Am.*, 76: 1393–1405.

Wu, R. S., and K. Aki, eds. (1988). Scattering and attenuation of seismic waves. *PAGEOPH Special Issue*. Vol. 128; no. 1/2.

PART THREE

Crustal Tectonics and the Distribution of Earthquake Foci

NINE

Seismicity Map of North America

E. R. Engdahl and W. A. Rinehart

INTRODUCTION

The Decade of North American Geology (DNAG) is a special project commemorating the 1988 centenary of the Geological Society of America (GSA). Publications resulting from the project will include the twenty-eight-volume *Geology of North America*, a six-volume Centennial Field Guide Set, four Centennial Special Volumes, twenty-three Continent-Ocean Transects, and seven Continent-Scale Maps of North America. The map set includes a Geological Map of North America, Gravity Anomaly Map, Magnetic Anomaly Map, Seismicity Map, Stress Map, Neotectonic Map, Thermal Aspects Map, and an accompanying volume, *Neotectonics of North America*. The maps will be wall size (four 42" × 55" sheets per map), in color, and made on a common base map at a scale of 1 : 5,000,000.

A GSA-sponsored workshop was held at the 1984 Seismological Society of America meeting in Anchorage, Alaska, to discuss construction of the seismicity map. The consensus goal of the seismicity map is to provide a useful resource on North American seismicity for seismologists, for Earth scientists at the graduate level, and for industry. The objective is to portray accurately North American seismotectonic features using the entire earthquake history from the early 1500s (pre-instrumental) through the modern period. Thus, construction of the map data base requires the rationalization of hundreds of thousands of earthquake hypocenters from global, national, regional, and local catalogs. Since modern data are more useful than historic data for resolving seismotectonic features, a scheme of data selection and representation must be devised that reveals details of the seismotectonic fabric of North America yet preserves a perspective of historical earthquake occurrence. The problem is further complicated by the highly variable monitoring capability of seismic networks and by the different types and rates of occurrence of earthquake activity throughout North America.

A scheme was developed at the workshop using regional magnitude-completeness thresholds that vary with time for data selection, and a system of symbols and colors to portray seismicity data on the map. Local seismotectonic features of the map can be addressed on a regional basis in contributions to the accompanying volume, which includes small-scale maps and cross sections.

The goal of this paper is to present further details of the rationale used to construct the seismicity map in general and to assess several interesting elements of earthquake monitoring in the western United States.

EARTHQUAKE DATA BASES

Catalog information on the occurrence of earthquakes usually includes parameters such as the origin time, location, focal depth, and magnitude or intensity of individual events. In the case of historic pre-instrumental earthquakes, these parameters must be determined entirely from intensity data and, hence, are less accurate than modern earthquake data. Presently, institutions around the world and in North America have varying degrees of responsibility for the collection and processing of earthquake data and for the catalog reporting of earthquake parameters on global, national, regional, and local scales.

On the global scale, the U.S. Geological Survey (USGS) and predecessor organizations (for example, the former U.S. Coast and Geodetic Survey) have been reporting the parameters of earthquakes worldwide within a few months of their occurrence through the Preliminary Determination of Epicenters (PDE) and earlier programs since 1928. The PDE program now routinely reports parameters for earthquakes as small as magnitude 4.5 worldwide and 3.5 within the conterminous United States. Two years after publication of the PDE reports, the International Seismological Centre (ISC)—prior to 1964, its predecessor the International Seismological Summary (ISS)—revises the PDE parameters and determines new events using a significantly larger data base. Global earthquake parameters have also been available from other sources such as the Bureau Central International de Séismologie (BCIS) and from special catalogs of larger earthquakes that often provide useful new information on the magnitudes of earlier events.

Prior to 1964, the global catalog of earthquake parameters is less complete, hypocenters are subject to greater uncertainty, and magnitude information is available for only the larger events. In 1964, with the advent of advanced computer processing of earthquake data and the installation of the Worldwide Standardized Seismograph Network (WWSSN), the reporting of earthquake parameters was sharply advanced. The data base for areas in North America not monitored by regional networks relies heavily on global earthquake parameters reported since 1964.

On the national level, the USGS has compiled data on earthquake occurrence through the publications *Earthquake History of the United States* and the annual *United States Earthquakes*, and through special compilations used to construct state seismicity maps and for hazard analysis. The Geological Survey of Canada has a similar and continuing effort.

On regional and local scales, the data bases are somewhat more complicated. With regional network coverage in California, the University of California at Berkeley has cataloged the seismicity of northern and central California since 1910, and the California Institute of Technology has cataloged the seismicity of southern and central California since 1932. It was not until the 1960s in Canada and the 1970s in the United States that other regional networks in other parts of North America started to routinely compute the parameters of smaller earthquakes. Many of the regional institutions started upgrading their historical catalogs in the 1960s and 1970s, and some groups such as the California Division of Mines and Geology, the Electric Power Research Institute, and private consulting firms have attempted to combine the data from several networks into a single catalog. These efforts have all had to overcome, with varying degrees of success, the kinds of problems addressed in the next section. To our knowledge, the data base assembled for the North American Seismicity Map is the first attempt to combine comprehensively the earthquake data from all sources in North America into a single catalog.

DATA BASE CONSTRUCTION

One of the most formidable problems in assembling the North American data base is the association of entries in different catalogs for the same earthquake. For example, we often find that the parameters of larger earthquakes based on globally distributed stations are significantly biased relative to parameters determined by regional data alone. It is also common to find an overlap in regional network coverage so that parameters for the same earthquake are independently estimated by different networks. In many instances, the earthquake locations have different biases or are less accurately determined by one of the networks. To further complicate the problem, the differences are not systematic, but may vary between regions and in time.

Resolution of this problem required the development of a catalog hierarchy and subjective estimates of probable errors in origin time, location, and magnitude on a region-by-region basis. In the most general sense, preferred parameters for individual earthquakes are ranked in the order of local, regional, national, and global estimates. Hierarchies in regions of overlap between networks are determined only after considerable discussion with regional experts.

In some cases, it is obvious that the same earthquake has been differently characterized in different catalogs. An origin-time error commonly found in data prior to 1964 is simply the difference between local and Greenwich mean time. There are also many one-hour errors due to changes between time zones, daylight savings time, and war time during World War II. One-minute errors in origin time are also common. Simple errors in origin time such as these are easy to identify, but other differences between catalogs require more careful individual attention. For example, locations for historical earthquakes are often quoted to only the nearest degree in some catalogs and to $0.25°$, $0.5°$, or $0.1°$ in others, resulting in large differences between locations. Even in modern catalogs, differences in regional location estimates for the same earthquake are sometimes found that are as large as 100 km because of regional network biases or poor determinations. Finally, very large magnitude differences, well beyond those that might be expected in the estimation of magnitudes by different methods, are often found between catalogs for earthquakes that appear to be the same.

The resolution of these difficulties had to be found by experimentation with origin time, location, and magnitude association windows that varied from one catalog to another and with region and time. For small windows, the association of earthquakes between catalogs for some previously determined hierarchy could be accomplished automatically. However, larger association windows were invariably needed to process historical data or to search for gross errors in modern data. In the latter case, the DNAG data base required the tedious examination of long lists of possible associations of earthquakes between catalogs on the basis of origin time, location, and magnitude. In this process, there are always some duplicate entries that cannot be resolved without the assistance of data contributors. This assistance was provided with varying degrees of thoroughness.

A number of different magnitude estimates are often reported for the same earthquake even in the same catalog. These magnitudes may be determined by using different methods and/or from different wave types not always easily related to one another. Frequently used magnitude scales include those based on estimates of the seismic moment (M_w), on the maximum amplitudes of teleseismic body waves (m_b) and surface waves (M_s), on the maximum amplitudes of local recordings (M_L), and on signal duration (M_D). As the earthquake size increases, many of these scales saturate, that is, reach a maximum value. For earlier, pre-instrumental earthquakes, only maximum intensities are known, which must be converted to magnitudes. Where necessary, we have converted maximum reported intensities to a magnitude (MI) using $MI = 1 + 2I_0/3$ for the western United States and Canada and

$MI = 0.5(I_0 + 3.5)$ east of the Rockies. To facilitate the assessment of reported magnitudes, we carry M_s, m_b, and up to five reported magnitudes for each event in the database. For data selection and plotting, we use the largest reported magnitude of each event unless some other hierarchy has been suggested by a regional contributor. Any errors introduced by this approach are not serious as we plot only in magnitude-interval classes of one unit and, although the larger events are reviewed very carefully, we are not attempting to produce definitive magnitude estimates for each event.

DATA SELECTION

It was recognized at the outset that plotting the entire historical record without accounting for changes in monitoring capability with time, or for the greater accuracy of modern data, would severely limit the usefulness of the seismicity map. For example, the expansion of regional networks and significant advances in processing of seismic data in the 1970s significantly lowered the magnitude threshold for seismicity data over large regions of the United States. On the other hand, we would like to know the locations, even though approximate, of larger-magnitude historic events relative to source zones that are well defined by low-magnitude modern seismicity data.

A solution to the problem was suggested by a seismic zonation of Canada for the purpose of seismic-risk estimation (Basham et al., 1985). The method requires the identification of spatially distinct earthquake source zones and the derivation of a magnitude-recurrence relation for each zone. A list of earthquakes can be selected for each zone on the basis of a magnitude-completeness test, that is, historical time periods over which earthquakes at different magnitude levels appear to be completely reported. We extend this concept to the case of regional network coverage as shown in figure 1, which displays generalized magnitude-completeness thresholds with time. This differs from the Basham et al. approach in that we are concerned with completeness of seismicity within regions now defined by regional network coverage and/or extensive cataloging of seismicity data, rather than within earthquake source zones that are spatially distinct. For a given time and region, only earthquakes with magnitudes large enough to be completely reported are selected for the DNAG seismicity map.

The benefits of such a scheme are numerous. It provides a natural selection of seismicity data that emphasizes larger earthquakes in the earlier historical period and smaller earthquakes in the more recent modern period. By a proper choice of symbol definition and scaling, as shown along the left margin of figure 1, we can see the relative levels of activity by scanning only the large symbols on the derived seismicity map, yet also see the fine detail provided by modern data. We further enhance the representation by using a darker shade for modern earthquake data. This enables viewers to easily

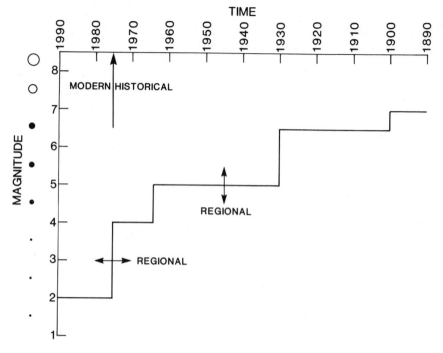

Figure 1. Generalized magnitude-completeness thresholds as a function of time. Actual magnitudes of completely reported earthquakes for a given time interval vary regionally (see figure 3). Symbol shading, definition, and scaling help to preserve the seismotectonic perspective of the map.

draw their own conclusions about the relationship of larger historical earthquakes to sources of modern earthquakes. The scheme dramatically reduces the effect of changes in the seismicity base with time, but preserves the seismotectonic character of the map.

REGIONAL NETWORK COVERAGE

Figure 2 displays approximate regional network boundaries or source regions in the western United States over which variations in magnitude-completeness thresholds with time have been estimated. Especially active source zones, such as Mammoth (MAM) and Yellowstone (YSTON), have been isolated because of the considerable overlap in network coverage, and this often appears to artificially partition the regional network coverage (as, for example, the coverage of YSTON by the MBMG network). However, in every case, more than one catalog has contributed to the data base for a particular source region. For regions not covered by regional networks, we

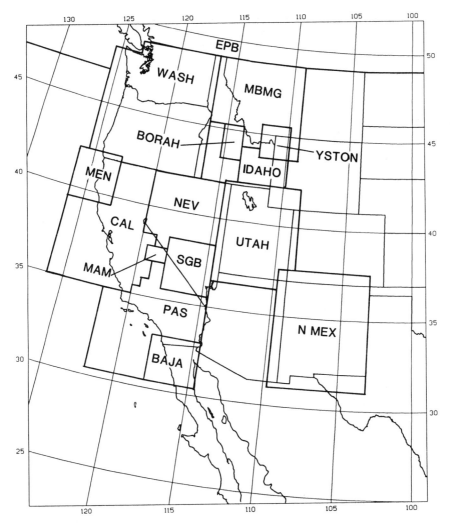

Figure 2. Definition of approximate regional network boundaries or source regions in western North America over which magnitude-completeness thresholds have been estimated. Abbreviations (for example, SGB: Southern Great Basin, MEN: Mendocino, and MAM: Mammoth Lake) are arbitrary since, in every case, more than one catalog contributed to the data base for a particular source region.

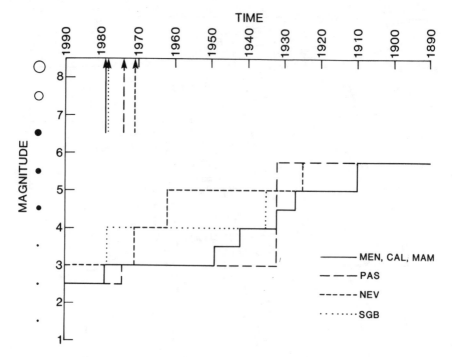

Figure 3. Magnitude-completeness thresholds versus time for selected western North America networks or source zones. The period prior to the 1920s is incomplete but includes all known earthquakes of maximum intensity seven or greater. The separation of modern and historical data (arrows) usually occurs in the 1970s.

used magnitude thresholds developed by Dewey et al. (1987) for a framework study. They use a uniform magnitude threshold of 3.5 for the conterminous United States since 1975, when regional network coverage expanded and the USGS initated a project to recover source parameters of all U.S. earthquakes to that level.

Variations in magnitude-threshold estimates with time are shown for selected western United States networks in figure 3. Some networks have produced rigorous analyses of their monitoring capability, but in most cases completeness thresholds with time are based entirely on the subjective judgment of regional experts. The period prior to the 1920s is known to be incomplete for all regional compilations. However, because of the importance of some of the moderate-size earlier earthquakes, we have, unless otherwise specified, set the magnitude threshold for the earlier period low enough to include all known earthquakes of maximum intensity 7 ($MI = 5.75$) or greater in the western United States. To provide some measure of homogeneity on the map, we plot only earthquakes of magnitude 2.5 or above in regions such as southern Nevada and central California, where the magnitude-completeness threshold might be as low as magnitude 2 in the modern period. The separation of modern and historical data usually occurs in the 1970s when magnitude-completeness thresholds were significantly lowered by the installation of regional networks.

SEISMICITY MAP

Figure 4 is a seismicity map for the western United States produced by the scheme previously described. Since detailed interpretations will be published elsewhere (for example, Dewey et al., 1987, and the volume accompanying the DNAG map set), we will attempt to describe only the highlights revealed by this map.

Regional patterns of seismicity in the part of the western United States shown in figure 4 can be interpreted within the context of plate-tectonic models. With modern high-resolution seismicity data, it is now possible to relate these patterns to local and global tectonic processes and to associate earthquakes with geologically mapped faults or other geologic structures. For example, in figure 4 northwest trending lineations of epicenters associated with right-lateral faults in California are superimposed on a background of more widely scattered epicenters and clusters of epicenters. Moreover, the rate of seismicity differs between zones that are approximately delineated by major structural provinces.

It is also quite evident that without the historical data the perspective of earthquake occurrence in time is lost or distorted. For example, sections of the San Andreas ruptured by major earthquakes in 1857 and 1906 are now relatively quiet, even at the lower magnitudes. On the other hand, some source zones, such as the region off Cape Mendocino and the Mammoth area, have clearly been highly seismic over the entire historical record. Larger historical earthquakes fold into the seismic patterns quite well, and inferences on their relationship to modern earthquake patterns (or lack thereof) are made possible.

Overall, the map achieves the desired objective. It displays fine details of the seismicity revealed by modern high-resolution data yet preserves information about historical earthquake occurrence. The result is an accurate portrayal of the seismotectonic fabric of the region over the period for which we have a recorded history.

DISCUSSION

Construction of the DNAG Seismicity Map of North America has revealed important facets about earthquake monitoring in the western United States.

For the most part, the western United States, including the Rocky Mountain region, is reasonably well monitored by present-day networks. Areas monitored to only about the magnitude 3.5 level include Oregon, large parts

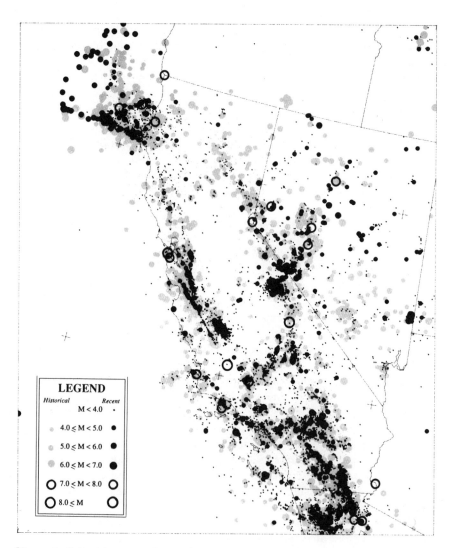

Figure 4. Seismicity map of part of western North America produced by the scheme described in the text. Relative symbol scaling is identical to that used for the DNAG Seismicity Map of North America. Historical data are more lightly shaded than modern data.

The legend of the figure reads:

LEGEND

Historical		Recent
	M < 4.0	•
	4.0 ≤ M < 5.0	•
	5.0 ≤ M < 6.0	●
	6.0 ≤ M < 7.0	●
	7.0 ≤ M < 8.0	○
	8.0 ≤ M	○

of Idaho, and Arizona. These are regions of low seismicity in which funding agencies have not been inclined to support the installation of permanent networks (although some short-term studies have been made). The offshore regions, especially west of about 126° near Cape Mendocino, obviously pose a special problem and are complete only to relatively high teleseismic magnitude thresholds.

There is considerable overlap in network coverage over large areas of the western United States. Networks in California and Nevada apparently share phase data, and in some cases the actual data stream, but individual catalogs often extend beyond their network boundaries, and there is considerable uncertainty in the choice of preferred hypocenters. To some extent, there is a duplication of effort, but this is probably desirable to insure continuity in the overall catalog. Somewhat better coordination exists between the United States and Canada in the Pacific Northwest, and Mexico in the Baja California region.

The users of regional network data in the western United States could certainly benefit through improved usage of magnitudes and better regional recurrence estimates. The types of magnitudes commonly used vary, and relationships between them are not well known. Some standardization seems essential. In most cases, network magnitude thresholds as a function of time are only subjective estimates. It is possible and necessary to perform a more careful analysis over well-defined regions.

Finally, a coordinated effort is needed to correct and update the DNAG data base for the western United States. This will require better definition of variations in network coverage with time, determination of more accurate regional magnitude-completeness thresholds, and some attempt to rationalize the differences between reported magnitudes.

ACKNOWLEDGMENTS

We thank G. Reagor for invaluable assistance in the preparation of catalog data for entry in the U.S. Geological Survey computer-based Earthquake Information System. J. W. Dewey, J. N. Taggart, and C. Stover are thanked for helpful reviews and suggestions.

REFERENCES

Basham, P. W., D. H. Wiechert, F. M. Anglin, and M. J. Berry (1985). New probabilistic strong seismic ground motion maps of Canada, *Bull. Seism. Soc. Am.*, 75: 563–595.

Dewey, J. W., D. P. Hill, W. L. Ellsworth, and E. R. Engdahl (1988). Earthquakes, faults, and the seismotectonic framework of the contiguous United States. In L. C. Pakiser, and W. D. Mooney, eds., *Geophysical Framework of the Continental United States, GSA Memoir.*

TEN

Seismicity of the Australian Plate and its Pacific Plate Margin

David Denham

INTRODUCTION

The patterns revealed in plots of earthquake hypocenters are crucial for interpreting tectonic processes within the Earth. At active plate boundaries, where a satisfactory model has been developed, hypocentral locations provide inportant information on tectonic details. Even in complicated areas, studies of the spatial distribution of earthquakes can provide considerable information on the geometries of the plate margins and the subduction zones. In the New Guinea region, for example, where the Australian and Pacific plates interact strongly, there is not one simple plate boundary but a cluster of small plates, each boundary accommodating a component of the total interaction. Furthermore, there is not one single subduction zone but several. For the Australian continent, however, which is an intraplate environment, there is no comparable tectonic model to successfully interpret the seismicity patterns. We know very little about the causes of this seismicity, except that the earthquakes are all shallow and caused by compressive forces, and that large earthquakes can and do occur in the Australian region. The task of developing a successful model to describe intraplate seismicity patterns is one of the most important seismological problems to be tackled in the next decade.

BACKGROUND

It is fitting, in this centennial anniversary symposium, that the first session is devoted to the mapping of earthquakes. For if one examines the advances associated with matters seismological, it is clear that these have, in many instances, depended on the available capability to locate and map earthquake hypocenters. Readers need hardly be reminded of the role played by seismology and seismologists in the development of plate tectonics, and how the delineation of plate boundaries was achieved by *interpreting* the spatial patterns of hypocenters. It was not enough to simply plot the hypocenters; it was necessary to *interpret* the patterns in terms of a meaningful model. Thus we have another example of the old adage that you see only what you know, and I suppose if any theme characterizes this paper, this is it. If you can fit the observations to a model, then all is well; if you can't, you have problems.

What I intend doing is to look at two regions associated with the Australian plate and demonstrate how, over the past eighty years or so, our improved capabilities to map earthquakes have led to an enhanced understanding of the tectonic processes in one region, where we have a model, and have led to little progress in the other region because we don't have a model. The two regions are the northern margin of the plate in the vicinity of New Guinea, and that part of the Australian plate occupied by the Australian continent (fig. 1).

PAPUA NEW GUINEA

The first publication on the seismicity of Papua New Guinea was probably Sieberg (1910), which was based largely on reports of earthquakes from the church missions established there close to the turn of the century. He listed twenty-four earthquakes that occurred in the period 1900–1906 (fig. 2). He even attempted to interpret the seismicity in terms of the tectonics of the region. However, apart from recognizing that "New Guinea and the Bismarck Archipelago form part of the innermost arc of young folded mountains which approach the rigid Australian platform," his general conclusion was that "our knowledge is very deficient in this respect, because only sporadic observations are available."

By the time Gutenberg and Richter's *Seismicity of the Earth* was published in 1954 the data set had improved considerably, and most epicenters were computed using arrival times recorded at seismographic stations. They used a time window from 1904 to 1952 and came close to relating earthquakes to a plate-tectonic type of activity. For example, they recognized (pp. 97–101) that "Most of the earth's surface is partitioned among a number of comparatively stable blocks, separated by active belts" and "the foci of deep shocks seem to be restricted to the vicinity of a nearly plane surface, which is probably related to a thrust surface between two different structures, usually dipping towards the continent." However, they mistakenly suggested that the midocean ridges "can hardly be young structures" even though they recognized that in the case of the mid-Atlantic ridge "Its parallelism with the continental coasts is so close that it practically demonstrates a mechanical connection with them." It is interesting to note that in the Papua New

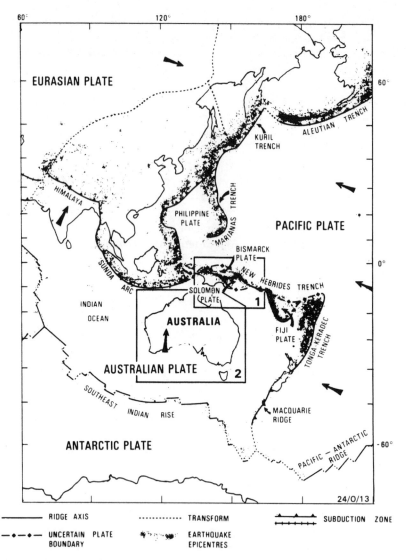

Figure 1. The Australian plate and its boundaries. Area 1 defines the New Guinea region and Area 2 the Australian continent, the two regions discussed in the text. Arrows indicate the directions of plate motion relative to the Antarctic plate.

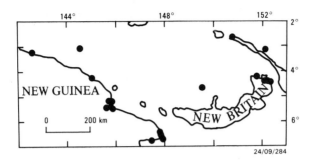

Figure 2. New Guinea epicenters for 1900–1906 (Sieberg, 1910).

Guinea region the main features of the shallow, intermediate (70–300 km), and deep (> 300 km) earthquakes had by then been determined, which is quite remarkable when one considers the extent of the global network in the pre-1950s, and also the absence of any regional stations at that time.

In Japan, meanwhile, Wadati (1934), using data from regional stations, had been able to define quite precisely the zone of earthquakes dipping beneath Honshu, and had also suggested that "This tendency seems to be observable in many volcanic regions in the world. Of course, we cannot say decisively but if the theory of continental drift suggested by A. Wegener be true, we may perhaps be able to see its traces of the continental displacement in the neighbourhood of Japan"—not bad for 1934.

In New Guinea, the next study after Gutenberg and Richter was made by Brooks (1965) who applied data from 1906 to 1962 to earthquake risk assessments. His results do not represent a significant improvement over Gutenberg and Richter's earlier work. However, Denham (1969) used data from the period 1958-1966 in an attempt to interpret the hypocentral patterns in terms of the fledgling plate-tectonic theories being developed at the time. Figure 3 shows his results. There is a significant improvement in the definition of the lineations, and it is clear that the northern boundary of the Australian plate is not a simple boundary. The reasons for the improvements in the data set were mainly due to the establishment of the Worldwide Standardized Seismographic Network (WWSSN) in the late 1950s and early 1960s and the computing facilities of the U.S. Coast and Geodetic Survey (USCGS). Some indication of the improvements may be gauged from the fact that only 256 events from the region were listed by Brooks (1965) for the period 1906–1962, whereas in 1966 alone 309 earthquakes were located in the same region by the USCGS.

Denham (1969) was able to identify the zones of deep and intermediate-depth earthquakes associated with the volcanic arcs and also the Bismarck Sea Seismic Zone (BSSZ). This is defined by the line of epicenters extending from 143° E to 152° E at 3° S. However, the northern boundary of the Aus-

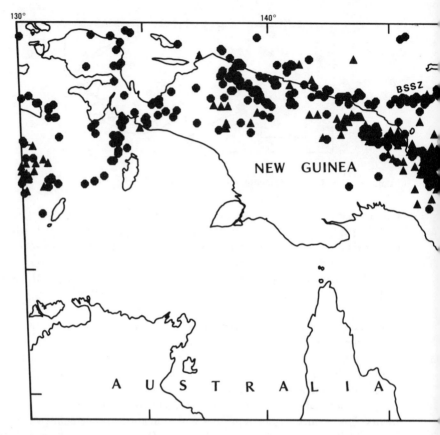

Figure 3. New Guinea epicenters for 1958–1966 earthquakes with $M \geqslant 5$ (Denham, 1969). BSSZ indicates the Bismarck Sea Seismic Zone, and SS indicates the Solomon Sea.

tralian plate was probably misidentified as being along the northern coast of the island of New Guinea and the northern margin of the Solomon Sea (SS).

As shown in figure 4, compiled from more recent data, this interpretation is probably not correct. The northern margin of the Australian plate is situated farther to the south. In figure 4 all epicenters located by twenty or more stations since 1970 have been plotted. The improved regional seismographic coverage since that date has revealed a zone of seismicity in the central part of the main island of New Guinea (A-A' in fig. 4a) and another zone near the East Papuan peninsula (see Ripper and McCue, 1983). These diagrams indicate the details that can be revealed with a good-quality data base. Each lineation can be interpreted in terms of plate tectonics and the interpreta-

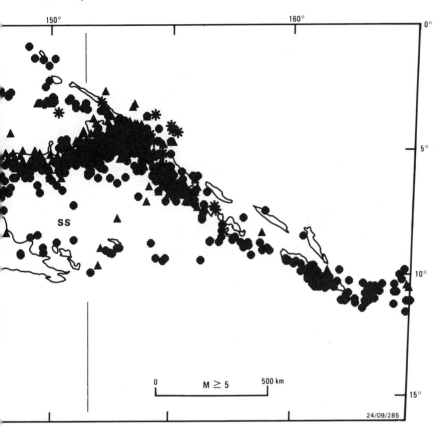

tions checked by analyzing fault-plane solutions and observations of recent crustal movements.

At depths between 70 and 300 km the hypocentral lineations are equally well determined and can be interpreted in terms of subducting lithosphere (fig. 4c). Similarly, for earthquakes deeper than 300 km (fig. 4d) the slabs (or what is left of them) are also clearly identified.

Therefore, in a plate margin situation, even though the tectonics are complicated it is possible to use the spatial distributions of earthquake hypocenters to unravel the current dynamics of the region. Such inferences are not possible in an intraplate environment where no suitable model for earthquake occurrences has as yet been developed.

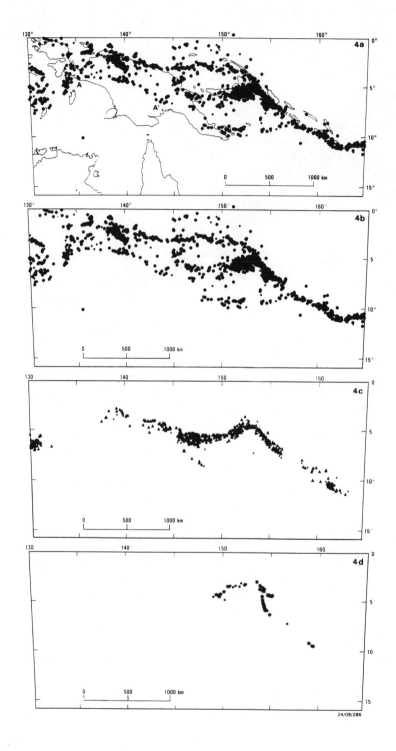

AUSTRALIAN CONTINENT

Earthquakes have been reported from the Australian continent since the First Fleet landed in 1788, but it was not until 1952 that a study of Australian seismicity was published (Burke-Gaffney, 1952). This was followed by Doyle et al. (1968), whose comprehensive study listed 165 earthquakes in the period 1897 through 1966. This data set is not large enough to determine any meaningful patterns.

If we examine a more recent data base including earthquakes through 1984, the situation is essentially unchanged (fig. 5). The epicentral patterns, or lack of them, are difficult to interpret in terms of a tectonic model. It is clear that most of the earthquakes occur within the continent, but the patterns of epicenters do not appear to correlate with any significant geological feature. Figure 5a shows the distribution of earthquakes and the main geological features, and figure 5b shows the earthquakes without visual distractors. Although there are several hundred epicenters, it is difficult to develop any continent-wide model that describes the occurrences. However, we can make the following statements.

1. The earthquakes in the Australian region appear, for the most part, to be restricted to areas of continental crust (Lambeck et al., 1984).
2. The patterns appear to define regions of comparatively high seismicity, which surround regions of lower seismicity.
3. All onshore earthquakes occur in the upper 20 km, and most are in the upper 10 km (Lambeck et al., 1984).
4. Although in some small areas the earthquakes appear to be associated with known faults (Bock and Denham, 1983), in many instances— particularly for large earthquakes—there is no apparent correlation between the earthquakes and pre-existing faults.
5. All reliable focal mechanisms obtained to date (thirty-eight) are consistent with the presence of compressive stress in the crust—confirmed by in-situ stress measurements and surface-faulting observations (Denham, 1986; Lambeck et al., 1984).

Figure 4. New Guinea epicenters for 1970–1984 where twenty or more stations have been used to locate the hypocenters.
(a) Shallow (0–50 km) earthquakes with coastlines. A-A' indicates the northern margin of the Australian plate in the center of New Guinea.
(b) Shallow earthquakes without coastlines.
(c) Intermediate Depth (70–300 km) earthquakes without coastlines.
(d) Deep (> 300 km) earthquakes without coastlines.
Notice how the shallow earthquakes define the plate and subplate boundaries, and the intermediate and deep earthquakes define the subducted slabs.

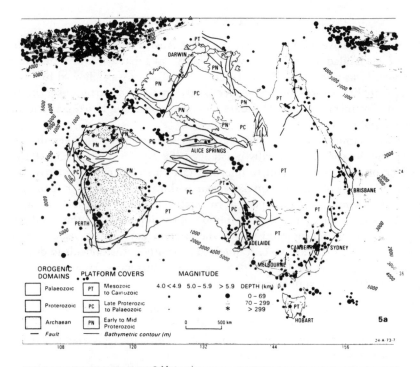

OROGENIC
DOMAINS

		PLATFORM COVERS	MAGNITUDE		

Palaeozoic

Proterozoic

Archaean

— Fault

PT	Mesozoic to Cainozoic
PC	Late Proterozoic to Palaeozoic
PN	Early to Mid Proterozoic

Bathymetric contour (m)

MAGNITUDE

4.0 < 4.9   5.0 – 5.9   > 5.9

·   ·   ●

·   *   *

DEPTH (km)

0 – 69
70 – 299
> 299

0   500 km

5a

24·A·73·7

108   120   132   144   156

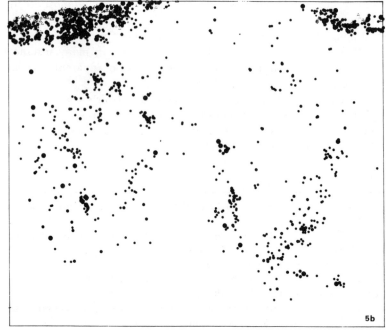

5b

Apart from these statements, which describe particular aspects of the seismicity in the Australian region, I would conclude that at present there is no reliable model to describe the overall space-time earthquake patterns.

DISCUSSION AND CONCLUSIONS

At the northern boundary of the Australian plate, in the Papua New Guinea region, even though the tectonics are complicated, detailed and accurate mapping of earthquake hypocenters can provide important information on the plate boundaries and subduction zones. This is because the patterns can be interpreted in terms of a known plate-tectonic model. However, for the Australian continent, which is an intraplate environment, there is no comparable model that can be used successfully to interpret the seismicity patterns. Thus, the development of a successful model to describe intraplate seismicity patterns is one of the most important seismological tasks to be tackled in the next decade, because large earthquakes can and do occur in intraplate regions.

ACKNOWLEDGMENT

I thank the Director, Bureau of Mineral Resources, Geology and Geophysics, for permission to publish.

REFERENCES

Bock, G., and D. Denham (1983). Recent earthquake activity in the Snowy Mountains region and its relationship to major faults. *J. Geol. Soc. Australia*, 30: 423–429.

Brooks, J. A. (1965). Earthquake activity and seismic risk in Papua and New Guinea. *Australian Bureau of Mineral Resources, Geology & Geophysics, Report No. 74.*

Burke-Gaffney, T. N. (1952). Seismicity of Australia. *Journal and Proceedings of the Royal Society of New South Wales*, 85: 47–52.

Denham, D. (1969). Distribution of earthquakes in the New Guinea-Solomon Islands region. *J. Geophys. Res.*, 74: 4290–4299.

—— (1986). Stress patterns in the Australian continent—Evidence from earthquakes, borehole deformations, and in-situ stress measurements, (abstract). In *Earthquake Notes* 57: 5.

Doyle, H. A., I. B. Everingham, and D. J. Sutton (1968). Seismicity of the Australian continent. *J. Geol. Soc. Australia*, 15: 295–312.

Figure 5. Australian epicenters of magnitude 4 or greater earthquakes, 1873–1985, (a) showing the main geological features and (b) without visual distractors. Notice how the epicenters appear to group around areas that have experienced no earthquakes.

Gutenberg, B., and C. F. Richter (1954). *Seismicity of the Earth and Associated Pheno-mena.* Princeton University Press, Princeton, N.J., 310 pp.

Lambeck, K., H. W. S. McQueen, R. A. Stephenson, and D. Denham (1984). The state of stress within the Australian continent. *Annales Geophysicae*, 2: 723–742.

Ripper, I. D., and K. F. McCue (1983). The seismic zone of the Papuan fold belt. *BMR J. Australian Geol. Geophys.*, 8: 147–156.

Sieberg, A. (1910) Die Erdbebentatigkeit in Deutsh-Neuguinea (Kaiser-Wilhelm-stand und Bismarck-archipel). *Petermanns Geographische Mitt., II, Heft* 2/3.

Wadati, K. (1934). On the activity of deep-focus earthquakes in the Japan Islands and neighborhoods. *Geophys. Mag.*, 8: 305–325, Tokyo.

ELEVEN

State of Stress in Seismic Gaps Along the San Jacinto Fault

Hiroo Kanamori and Harold Magistrale

INTRODUCTION

Data from the Southern California Seismic Network have been extensively used to map spatial and temporal variations of seismicity (for example, Hileman et al., 1973; Green, 1983; Webb and Kanamori, 1985; Doser and Kanamori 1986; Nicholson et al., 1986). A recent study by Sanders et al. (1986) clarified some of the important features of historical seismicity along the San Jacinto fault of southern California, one of the most prominent being the Anza seismic gap. Thatcher et al. (1975) investigated the spatial distribution of large earthquakes along the fault and indicated that a 40-km-long section from Anza to Coyote Mountain is deficient in seismic slip and can be considered a seismic gap (G1 in fig. 1). Sanders and Kanamori (1984) investigated the seismicity along an 18-km-long section (also often called the Anza seismic gap) centered near the town of Anza, and concluded that this section of the fault is locked and has the potential for a magnitude 6.5 event (G2 in fig. 1).

In this paper, we review the most recent activity along the San Jacinto fault and assess the seismic potential of this fault zone in light of an empirical relation between fault length, seismic moment, and repeat time obtained from earthquakes along active fault zones around the world.

RECENT SEISMICITY ALONG THE SAN JACINTO FAULT

Figure 1, a map of recent seismicity along the San Jacinto fault, does not clearly show the seismic gap. Figure 2 is a cross section of the seismicity along the strike of the fault and includes all the events between points A and A' in the narrow box shown in figure 1. A similar figure has been presented

179

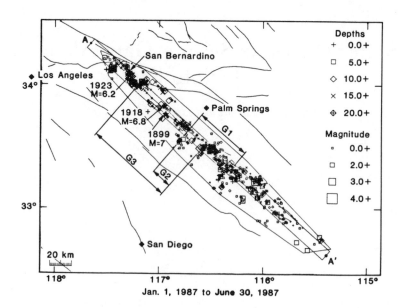

Jan. 1, 1987 to June 30, 1987

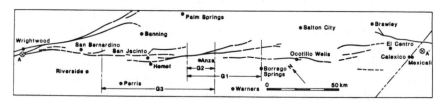

Figure 1. Seismicity along the San Jacinto fault, Southern California, for the period January 1, 1987, to June 30, 1987. The data are taken from the catalog of the Southern California Seismic Network. All the events in the polygon are shown. The narrow box A-A′ indicates the area used for the cross-sectional plot shown in figure 2. Geographical locations of the fault and the gaps are shown in the figure at the bottom.

by Sanders (1986) for an earlier time period. The most striking feature of these displays is the almost complete absence of seismic activity over an 80-km-long section (G3 in figs. 1 and 2) that includes the "Anza seismic gap." The only activity in this quiet zone is at a depth of about 13 km. Doser and Kanamori (1986) interpreted this activity to represent the bottom of the seismogenic zone along the San Jacinto fault.

We examined the seismicity in this zone for the period from July 1983 to December 1986 and found essentially the same seismicity pattern shown in figure 2.

The historical seismicity along this segment was reviewed by Thatcher et al. (1975), Sanders and Kanamori (1984), and Sanders et al. (1986).

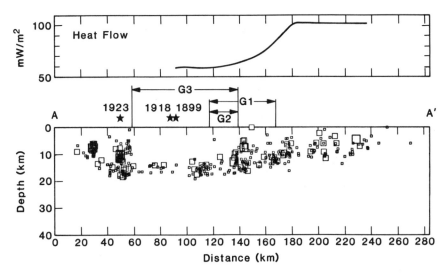

Figure 2. Seismicity cross section along the San Jacinto fault (lower figure). All the events in the box A-A' in figure 1 are shown. Three gaps, G1, G2, and G3, are indicated. The upper figure shows the variation of heat flow along the San Jacinto fault, taken from Lachenbruch et al. (1985).

Although the exact locations and sizes of the 1899, 1918, and 1923 events are uncertain, it is generally agreed that no large ($M_L > 6.5$) earthquake has occured in the 80-km quiet section at least since 1918.

Another notable feature in figure 2 is the steady increase in the depth of the seismogenic zone, as defined by the deepest activity, from the south to the north. Doser and Kanamori (1986) interpreted this trend in terms of a depression of the geotherm evidenced by a decreasing heat flow. The heat flow along the San Jacinto fault taken from Lachenbruch et al. (1985) is shown in figure 2.

INTERPRETATION

The seismicity pattern shown in figure 2 suggests that strain is building up in the locked fault zone at depths shallower than 13 km. The steady activity at the bottom of the seismogenic zone may be a manifestation of stress accumulation that will eventually cause failure of the overlying locked zone.

A similar seismicity pattern was observed before the 1979 Imperial Valley earthquake ($M_L > 6.5$). Doser and Kanamori (1986) relocated earthquakes along the Imperial fault. Figure 3 shows the cross section of seismicity along the strike of the Imperial fault for a period of about two years before the October 15, 1979, earthquake. The solid curve in the figure outlines the slip

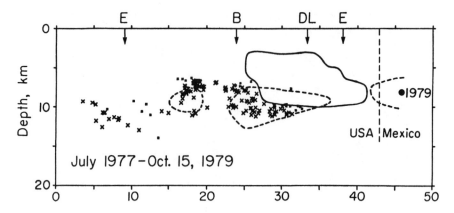

Figure 3. Cross section of seismicity along the strike of the Imperial fault for the period July 1977 to October 15, 1979. The hypocenters with A and B quality listed in the Southern California Network catalog, relocated by Doser and Kanamori (1986), are shown. The regions of the fault outlined by solid and dashed lines represent strike-slip offsets of one meter from the rupture models of Hartzell and Heaton (1983) and Archuleta (1984), respectively. E denotes the ends of the surface faulting and B the intersection of the Brawley fault with the Imperial fault.

zone of the main shock where the strike-slip displacement exceeded one meter (Hartzell and Heaton, 1983). Because of the limited station distribution of the network, the events between DL and the hypocenter, located to the south of the United States–Mexico border, could not be relocated and are not shown in figure 3. This pattern also suggests stress accumulation beneath the locked portion of the Imperial fault.

Given this loading mechanism, we can assess the state of stress in the seismic gaps along San Jacinto fault in the following manner. If we assume that the strain is accumulating on a fault of length L and width W, the accumulated seismic moment M_0 is given by

$$M_0 = \mu VWLT \tag{1}$$

where μ is the rigidity, taken to be 3×10^{11} dyne/cm^2, V is the slip rate, and T is the elapsed time since the last earthquake. If we take the entire 80-km quiet zone (G3) as a locked segment, then $W = 13$ km and $L = 80$ km.

Although the slip rate along the entire San Jacinto fault is not known accurately, Sharp (1981) indicates a minimum Quaternary long-term slip rate of about 8 to 12 mm/year for the segment in the vicinity of Anza. A slip rate of 1 cm/year seems to be a reasonable estimate.

Geodetic studies of King and Savage (1983) indicate an accumulation of

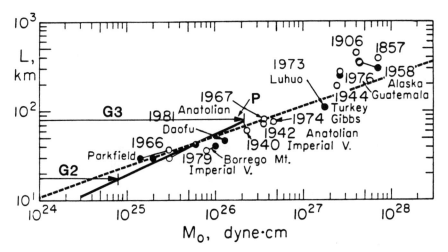

Figure 4. The relation between the fault length and seismic moment of shallow strike-slip earthquakes in active plate boundaries. The dashed line indicates a slope of 1/3 expected for the standard scaling relations. Closed and open circles are the data taken from Kanamori and Allen (1986) and Scholz et al. (1986), respectively. The horizontal lines indicate current strain accumulation in the seismic gaps along the San Jacinto fault.

right-lateral strain in this area at a rate of 0.3 μ strain/year. No surface fault creep has been measured for at least the last ten years along the San Jacinto fault near Anza (Louie et al., 1985; see also Sanders and Kanamori, 1984).

These observations suggest a steady strain accumulation in this gap for at least seventy years since the last large earthquake in 1918. Substituting $T = 70$ years into equation (1), we obtain $M_0 = 2.2 \times 10^{26}$ dyne-cm (corresponding to $M_w = 6.8$) as the minimum accumulated seismic moment along this segment. If the 1918 event did not break this segment, the cumulative moment could be even larger.

The next question is how close the presently accumulated strain is to the ultimate failure strain. We examine this problem on the basis of empirical data obtained from other earthquakes. Kanamori and Allen (1986) examined the relation between the fault length and seismic moment of shallow crustal earthquakes and found that, for a given fault length, earthquakes with longer repeat times have larger seismic moments than those with shorter repeat times. They interpreted this relation in terms of the difference in the strength of fault zones. Fault zones with longer repeat times are stronger than those with shorter repeat times. If we consider only the events with relatively short (less than 500 years) repeat times, a systematic relation can be obtained.

Figure 4 shows the relation between fault length L and seismic moment

M_0 of shallow strike-slip earthquakes with repeat times less than 500 years in the world. The open and closed circles indicate the data taken from Scholz et al. (1986) and Kanamori and Allen (1986), respectively.

The seismic moments accumulated in the two segments (G2 and G3) of the San Jacinto fault are indicated in the figure. As the time elapses, the accumulated moment increases along the horizontal line drawn for the given fault length. If the strength of the San Jacinto fault zone is comparable to that of other fault zones, the fault should break when the head of the arrow (point P) reaches the moment value defined by the average trend of the data. Since the seismic moment is generally considered to be proportional to the seismic-wave energy released in earthquakes, we use the term "energy" below in place of "moment."

Figure 4 shows that the strain energy presently accumulated along the longer gap (G3) is at least comparable to the average of the ultimate strain energy that can be stored in an 80-km fault segment. In this sense, one can conclude that this gap is close to failure. We note, however, that the empirical data indicate a factor-of-two spread in strain energy, suggesting that strain accumulation can continue for another seventy years or so without breaking this gap.

Another possibility is that the strain is not uniform along the gap because of varying slip histories, so that only a part of the gap may break in a smaller earthquake. We can estimate the accumulated strain for this case using equation (1), but some ambiguity exists in the width W. The empirical relation shown in figure 4 suggests that W is not constant, but is approximately proportional to L (see Scholz, 1982; Kanamori and Allen, 1986). Equation (1) then suggests that the accumulated energy is proportional to L^2. In figure 4 we show a straight line with a slope of $1/2$ passing through point P. This line determines the level of strain accumulation for gaps with different lengths. For example, for the shorter Anza gap (G2) $L = 18$ km, and the accumulated moment is about $M_0 = 1 \times 10^{25}$ dyne-cm ($M_w = 5.9$). If a gap with $L = 40$ km breaks, then $M_0 = 5 \times 10^{25}$ dyne-cm ($M_w = 6.4$).

CONCLUSION

A comparison of the size of the gap and the elapsed time since the last large earthquake with fault length-moment relations of shallow strike-slip earthquakes suggests that the strain energy accumulated in the 80-km seismic gap along the San Jacinto fault is comparable to the ultimate strain energy that can be stored there. However, the ultimate strain per unit volume of the earth's crust depends on the strength of the fault zone. The empirical relation indicates approximately a factor-of-two variation in the strength for faults in active plate boundaries. This range translates into a factor-of-two variation in repeat time. It is therefore possible that strain accumulation could continue for another seventy years or so without causing an earthquake.

Other possible scenarios include: 1) The present slip rate along the San Jacinto fault is much smaller than 1 cm/year, and it takes much longer than seventy years to accumulate enough strain to break the gap. 2) The depth of the seismogenic zone is significantly greater in this segment than elsewhere along the San Jacinto fault, as evidenced by the decrease in heat flow, resulting in an increase in the overall strength of the fault zone and in the repeat time. 3) The 1899 and 1918 earthquakes did not completely break this gap, and the accumulated strain is larger than indicated in figure 4. In this case, the gap is closer to failure than indicated by figure 4. 4) The 40-km-long gap may fail in several smaller earthquakes.

Despite this uncertainty inherent in the empirical methods, the information obtained from detailed analyses of seismicity and earthquake rupture processes provides an important clue to the state of stress in a seismic gap with respect to its ultimate strength.

Earthquake prediction on the basis of empirical methods like the one presented above, and many others currently used, is obviously of limited accuracy. Nevertheless, it provides a physical framework for further experiments. In the case of the seismic gaps along the San Jacinto fault, high-resolution seismicity studies have delineated the geometry of the gaps and the currently seismogenic zone, which has enabled us to determine the physical condition of the fault (Sanders and Kanamori, 1984; Doser and Kanamori, 1986). Detailed analysis of the rupture parameters of earthquakes in similar tectonic environments provides a tool to measure the level of strain accumulation relative to the ultimate strain.

Obvious next steps involve more physical measurements. Since earthquakes are ultimately caused by strain accumulation, continuous monitoring of the strain field in the gap area is crucial. Also, since fault ruptures appear to initiate from the bottom of the seismogenic zone, studies of spatial and temporal variations of source characteristics of the events near the bottom of the seismogenic zone are important.

ACKNOWLEDGMENTS

This research was partially supported by U.S. Geological Survey grant 14-08-0001-G1354. Contribution number 4505, Division of Geological and Planetary Sciences, California Institute of Technology, Pasadena, California 91125.

REFERENCES

Archuleta, R. J. (1984). A faulting model for the 1979 Imperial Valley earthquake. *J. Geophys. Res.*, 89: 4559–4585.

Doser, I. D., and H. Kanamori (1986). Depth of seismicity in the Imperial Valley region (1977–1983) and its relationship to heat flow, crustal structure, and the October 15, 1979, earthquake. *J. Geophys. Res.*, 91: 675–688.

Green, S. M. (1983). Seismotectonic study of the San Andreas, Mission Creek, and Banning fault system. Master's thesis, University of California, Los Angeles, 52 pp.

Hartzell, S. H., and T. H. Heaton (1983). Inversion of strong ground motion and teleseismic waveform data for the fault rupture history of the 1979 Imperial Valley, California, earthquake. *Bull. Seism. Soc. Am.*, 73: 1553–1584.

Hileman, J. A., C. R. Allen, and J. M. Nordquist (1973). *Seismicity of the South California Region, 1 January 1932 to 31 December 1972*. Seismological Laboratory, California Institute of Technology.

Kanamori, H., and C. R. Allen (1986). Earthquake repeat time and average stress drop. In S. Das, J. Boatwright, and C. H. Scholz, eds., Maurice Ewing volume 6, *Earthquake Source Mechanics*. American Geophysical Union, Washington D.C., 227–235.

King, N. E., and J. C. Savage (1983). Strain rate profile across the Elsinore, San Jacinto, and San Andreas faults near Palm Springs, California. *Geophys. Res. Lett.*, 10: 55–57.

Lachenbruch, A. H., J. H. Sass, and S. P. Galanis, Jr. (1985). Heat flow in southernmost California and the origin of the Salton Trough. *J. Geophys. Res.*, 90: 6709–6736.

Louie, J. N., C. R. Allen, D. C. Johnson, P. C. Haase, and S. N. Cohn (1985). Fault slip in southern California. *Bull. Seism. Soc. Am.*, 75: 811–833.

Nicholson, C., L. Seeber, P. Williams, and L. Sykes (1986). Seismicity and fault kinematics through the eastern Transverse Ranges, California: Block rotation, strike-slip faulting, and low-angle thrusts. *J. Geophys. Res.*, 91: 4891–4908.

Sanders, C. O. (1986). Seismotectonics of the San Jacinto fault zone and the Anza seismic gap. Ph.D thesis, California Institute of Technology, Pasadena, 180 pp.

Sanders, C. O., H. Magistrale, and H. Kanamori (1986). Rupture patterns and preshocks of large earthquakes in the southern San Jacinto fault zone. *Bull. Seism. Soc. Am.*, 76: 1187–1206.

Sanders, C. O., and H. Kanamori (1984). A seismotectonic analysis of the Anza seismic gap, San Jacinto fault zone, southern California. *J. Geophys. Res.*, 89: 5873–5890.

Scholz, C. H. (1982). Scaling relations for strong ground motion in large earthquakes. *Bull. Seism. Soc. Am.*, 72: 1903–1909.

Scholz, C. H., C. A. Aviles, and S. G. Wesnousky (1986). Scaling differences between large interplate and intraplate earthquakes. *Bull. Seism. Soc. Am.*, 76: 65–70.

Sharp, R. V. (1981). Variable rates of late Quaternary strike-slip on the San Jacinto fault zone, southern California. *J. Geophys. Res.*, 86: 1754–1762.

Thatcher, W., J. A. Hileman, and T. C. Hanks (1975). Seismic slip distribution along the San Jacinto fault zone, southern California and its implications. *Geol. Soc. Am. Bull.*, 86: 1140–1146.

Webb, T. H., and H. Kanamori (1985). Earthquake focal mechanisms in the eastern Transverse Ranges and San Emigdio Mountains, southern California, and evidence for a regional decollement. *Bull. Seism. Soc. Am.*, 75: 737–757.

TWELVE

The Need for Local Arrays in Mapping the Lithosphere

A. Eisenberg, D. Comte, and M. Pardo

INTRODUCTION

There has been a significant effort in recent years to establish global arrays of broadband seismographs. Although the benefit of this kind of instrumentation has become quite obvious, it is also important to improve local arrays.

In this chapter, data from aftershocks of the Chile earthquake of March 3, 1985, and some additional 1981 earthquakes are used to analyze some important details of the tectonics of central Chile.

Locations for the aftershocks of the 1985 earthquake are derived using only phase arrival times from local seismograph stations, and these are compared with locations for the same earthquakes determined using data recorded principally at teleseismic distances. It is shown that the local array hypocenters outline the central Chile Benioff zone much more clearly than solutions that depend on worldwide data, even when such useful algorithms as Joint Hypocenter Determination are used.

Some 1981 Chile earthquakes, too small to be recorded except by an array of local seismographs, yield focal mechanisms that suggest several breaks or flexures in the descending lithosphere south of 33°S latitude.

These features are not apparent when only larger teleseismically recorded events are considered.

EARTHQUAKE LOCATIONS

The Chile earthquake of March 3, 1985, provided an opportunity to study the tectonics of central Chile using local seismographic network data. Prior to the earthquake, a permanent network of ten stations, operated and maintained by the University of Chile, had been installed to study the Pocuro

187

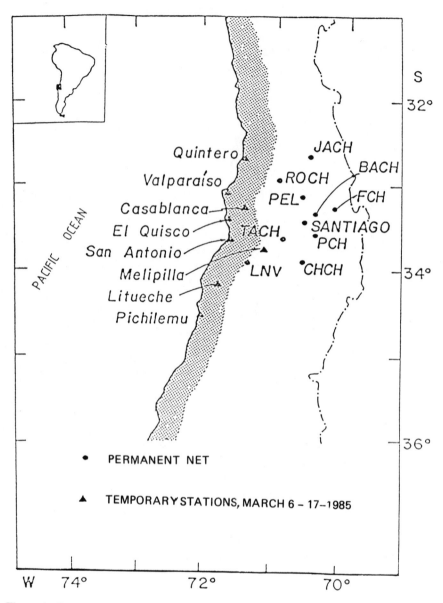

Figure 1. Permanent seismographic network of the University of Chile and temporary portable stations from UNAM installed after the March 3, 1985, central Chile earthquake.

fault that runs through the foothills of the Andes Cordillera. These stations are all east of the coastal region where the March earthquake occurred.

In order to better study the aftershock sequence of this event, the ten-station permanent array was supplemented by eight portable stations brought to the coast by scientists from the National Autonomous University of Mexico (UNAM). Both permanent and temporary station sites are shown in figure 1.

The 380 well-determined aftershock locations found from the data of this eighteen-station array are shown in figure 2. These epicenters were calculated using the flat layered crustal velocity model of Acevedo and Pardo (1985), with corrections in the form of P-wave and S-wave time delays at each array station, to compensate for the Earth's curvature. Only aftershocks with total recorded durations greater than 100 seconds and standard deviations in the final location of less than 0.5 seconds are plotted. S-wave arrival times were used in the locations of all 380 aftershocks.

A number of interesting features are shown by the 380 aftershocks of

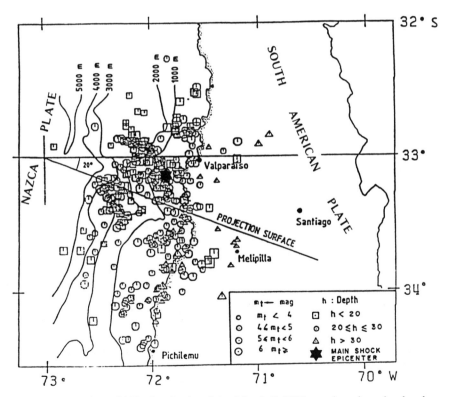

Figure 2. Location of 380 aftershocks of the March 3, 1985, earthquake using local-network data.

figure 2. First, earthquakes with depths less than 20 km are located mainly toward the deep marine trench that marks the margin between the Nazca and South American plates. Exceptions to this rule are a few shallow earthquakes occurring nearer the coast in the northernmost part of the aftershock zone.

Second, there is a concentration of inland earthquakes with focal depths greater than 30 km to the south of 33°S. These events could indicate a bending or breaking of the downgoing slab.

Third, there are regions relatively devoid of aftershocks to the south, north, and east of the epicenter of the main shock (shown in fig. 2 as a star). These possibly correspond to the zone of rupture of the main shock, or of the aftershocks during the first few hours after the main shock before the UNAM temporary seismographs could be installed. This conjecture is supported by several studies (Houston, 1987; Choy and Dewey, 1988) of the source main-shock using inversion of body wave amplitude data.

Finally, the aftershock hypocenters project with the least scatter onto a vertical plane striking S70°E. When projected onto this plane, the aftershocks define a fairly narrow zone dipping 10° to the east-southeast, as shown in the top panel of figure 3. The source zone so defined agrees well with one of the fault planes implied for many aftershock focal mechanism solutions (see fig. 4) and projects upward to the seafloor near the point where subduction of the Nazca plate begins. The preferred projection plane is approximately parallel to the direction of current Nazca–South American plate convergence as indicated by offshore fracture zones and paleomagnetic field-reversal data.

Many of the 380 aftershocks determined using local-array P-wave and S-wave phase-arrival information also appear in the standard earthquake catalog of NEIS (U.S. National Earthquake Information Service), which uses data from seismograph stations around the world to locate events. NEIS earthquakes, projected onto the same S70°E plane, are shown in the middle panel of figure 3. The most obvious feature of this plot is that almost all NEIS earthquakes have a standard (assigned)depth of 33 km.

It is well known that, without depth phases or phases from a few nearby seismograph stations, the depths of many events cannot be accurately determined and must be assigned. There are, however, also significant differences between the epicentral coordinates determined by NEIS and by this study for the March 3, 1985, earthquake aftershocks. These differences are summarized in the histograms of figure 5. The distance deviations of the NEIS locations relative to the local-array locations are shown in the upper panel of this figure. The mean of the distance deviations is 27 km, but almost ten percent of the earthquakes are more than 65 km apart. Azimuthal deviations appear to be bimodal, the poorest agreement occurring in the east-west direction. This observation agrees with the fact that most stations contributing data to

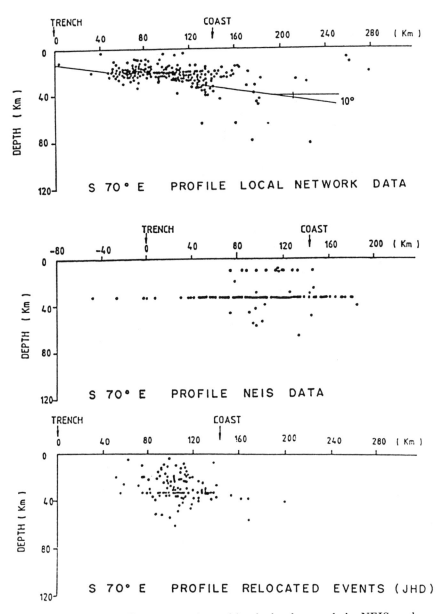

Figure 3. Projections of hypocenters located by the local network, by NEIS, and as relocated using JHD. The plane of projection is vertical and strikes S70°E.

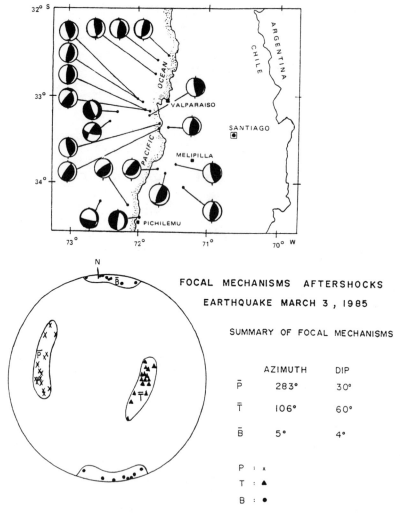

Figure 4. Fault-plane solutions of aftershocks of the March 3, 1985, earthquake.

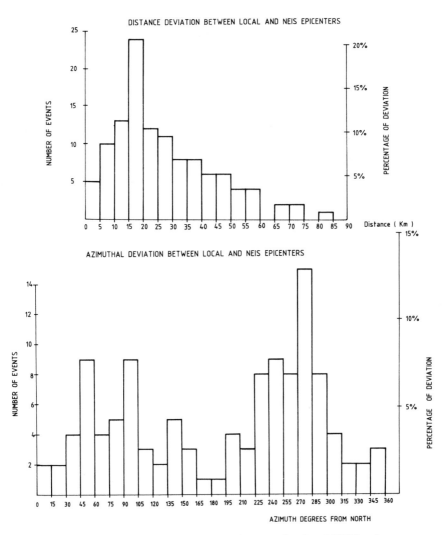

Figure 5. Distance and azimuthal deviations between local and NEIS epicenters.

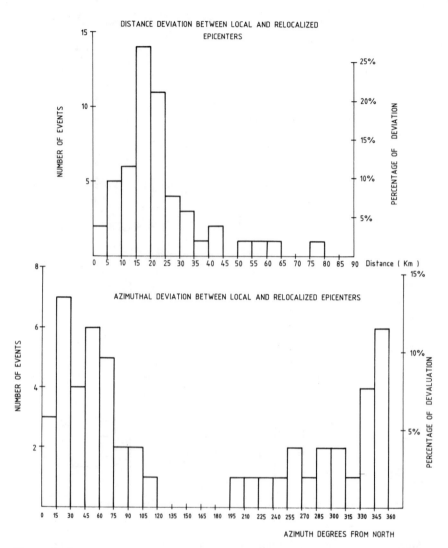

Figure 6. Distance and azimuthal deviations between local and relocated (JHD) epicenters.

NEIS are located north of central Chile, resulting in larger errors in longitude than in latitude.

The NEIS data using the Joint Hypocenter Determination algorithm (Dewey, 1970) have been reanalyzed by Choy and Dewey (1988). Results of this reanalysis are shown in the bottom panel of figure 3. It is clear that the depths of the aftershocks are still not well resolved, and that it is difficult to see the configuration of the subducted lithosphere from these hypocenters. Yet some improvement in agreement between these aftershock locations and the local-array locations is apparent from the comparisons provided by the histograms of figure 6. The mean of the distance deviations has been reduced to 22 km, and azimuthal deviations are now dominantly to the north, toward the NEIS stations.

FOCAL MECHANISMS

As has been discussed in several papers (for example, Stauder, 1973; Malgrange and Madariaga, 1983; Astiz and Kanamori, 1986), focal mechanisms developed for large earthquakes in Chile with worldwide data show the main features of the Nazca–South American plates convergence process. These are: the occurrence of low-angle thrust faulting at the interplate boundary, tensional normal faulting for intermediate depth earthquakes with occasional compressional thrust faulting after an event at this depth, and compressional reverse faulting for deep events. The data observed for the 1985 central Chile earthquake are consistent with this characterization (see fig. 4).

It will now be shown, however, that focal mechanisms for many small earthquakes in this same area show quite a different and more complex behavior, which may indicate discontinuities in the lithosphere. Using the central Chile seismograph network, Acevedo (1985) obtained 103 focal-mechanism solutions for 1981 earthquakes. The results of this work are summarized in figure 7. Many conclusions have been drawn from these data, but only two are discussed here.

The first conclusion is that, on the average, the slip direction during earthquakes north of 33°S latitude is east-west, while south of this latitude it is S70°E. It has been noted before (Eisenberg et al., 1972; Isacks and Barazangi, 1977; Comet et al., 1986; Pardo et al., 1986) that 33°S marks a latitude of discontinuity in Chilean tectonics as demonstrated by three related features: the absence of Quaternary volcanism between 33°S and 26.5°S latitudes, the beginning of Chile's central valley at 33°S, and the bending of the subducted Nazca plate between latitudes 26°S and 33°S. Recent work now indicates that south of 33°S the lithosphere seems to be moving in a different direction, which is also shown in the bending of the trench at that latitude. Again, both the east-west and the S70°E slip directions are different from the direction of Nazca–South American plate convergence (N70°E as shown in fig. 7) im-

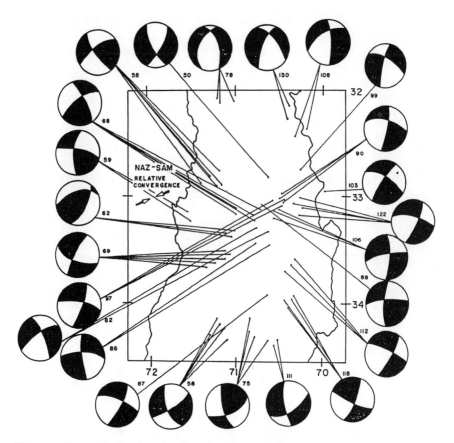

Figure 7. Composite focal mechanisms for events of 1981 with depths between 45 and 130 km located with the central Chile local network. Depth of focus is indicated for each set of earthquakes used in the composite solution. Direction of relative convergence of the Nazca and South American plates (N70°E) is obtained from the fossil magnetic reversals observed over the ocean floor.

plied by the pattern of paleomagnetic pole reversals observed over the ocean floor.

The second conclusion that can be drawn from the focal-mechanism data of figure 7 is that many of these small earthquakes (whose depths turn out to be in the 45–130 km range) show a strike-slip character. The preferred fault plane for these events can be assumed to be in the east-west direction. If these strike-slip mechanisms have been accurately determined, it means that the subducted Nazca plate is not only moving in a different direction south of 33°S but is also suffering internal breakage or flexure in a way implied by the rotation of the subduction trench at that latitude.

CONCLUSIONS

This paper indicates that data from local seismograph arrays are crucial in understanding details of local and regional tectonics, particularly in places remote from stations of the global network of standardized or broadband instruments.

In Chile it has been shown that the character of the Nazca plate subduction process can be adequately mapped only with data from local staions. This is because local stations are needed to accurately determine the hypocenters of local earthquakes and because the focal mechanisms of small local earthquakes are different from those of larger, globally recorded events. In particular, strike-slip mechanisms for small earthquakes recorded only by the central Chile network suggest plate breakage or flexure in the subducted Nazca plate south of 33°S latitude.

ACKNOWLEDGMENTS

This study was partially supported by projects FONDECYT 1115/86, 301/87, and DIB E-2244. We thank James Dewey for a preprint of the Choy and Dewey manuscript.

REFERENCES

Acevedo, P. (1985). Estructura Cortical y Estudio Sismotectónico de Chile Central entre las Latitudes 32.0 y 34.5 Sur. Masters thesis in geophysics, University of Chile, Santiago.

Acevedo, P., and M. Pardo (1985). Estructura cortical de Chile Central (32.5–34.5 S), utilizando el método de velocidad aparente minima de ondes P. *TRALKA* 2: 371–378.

Astiz, L., and H. Kanamori (1986). Interplate coupling and temporal variation of mechanisms of intermediate-depth earthquakes in Chile. *Bull. Seism. Soc. Am.*, 76: 1614–1622.

Choy, G., and J. Dewey (1988). Rupture process of an extended earthquake sequence: teleseismic analysis of the Chilean earthquake of 3 March 1985. *J. Geophys. Res.*, 93: 1103–1118.

Comte, D., A. Eisenberg, E. Lorca, M. Pardo, L. Ponce, R. Saragoni, S. K. Singh, and G. Suarez (1986). The central Chile earthquake of 3 March 1985. A repeat of previous great earthquakes in the region? *Science*, 233: 449–453.

Dewey, J. (1970). Seismicity Studies with the Method of Joint Hypocenter Determination. Ph.D. thesis, University of California, Berkeley.

Eisenberg, A., R. Husid, and J. Luco (1972). The July 8, 1971, Chilean earthquake. *Bull. Seism. Soc. Am.*, 62: 423–430.

Houston, H. (1987). Source Characteristics of Large Earthquakes at Short Periods. Ph.D. thesis, California Institute of Technology, Pasadena.

Isacks, B., and M. Barazangi (1977). Geometry of Benioff zones: Lateral segmentation and downward bending of the subducted lithosphere. In Island Arcs, Deep Sea Trenches, and Back Arc Basins, M. Talwani and W. C. Pitman III, eds., Maurice Ewing Series 1, American Geophysical Union, Washington, D.C.

Malgrange, M., and R. Madariaga (1983). Complex distribution of large and normal earthquakes in the Chilean subduction zone. *Geophys. J. R. Astr. Soc.*, 73: 489–505.

Pardo, M., D. Compte, and A. Eisenberg (1986). Secuencia sismica de Marzo en Chile Central. *Proc. 4th Jornadas Chileas de Sismologia e Ingenieria Antisismica and International Seminar on the Chilean March 3 Earthquake*, 1: A1–A15.

Stauder, W. (1973). Mechanism and spatial distribution of Chilean earthquakes with relation to subduction of the oceanic plate. *J. Geophys. Res.*, 78: 5033–5061.

THIRTEEN

Dense Microearthquake Network Study of Northern California Earthquakes

J. P. Eaton

INTRODUCTION

Over the last twenty years, large-scale networks of telemetered short-period seismographs have emerged as an important new tool in seismology. Much of the development and testing of such networks has been carried out in central California by the U.S. Geological Survey (USGS). The goal of this work has been to improve the sensitivity and hypocentral resolution of such networks to permit the detailed mapping of seismogenic structures within the crust. Such mapping, in conjunction with traditional geologic mapping and analysis, should help to clarify the internal processes that shape the Earth's crust and produce earthquakes.

The dedicated work of the UC Berkeley seismographic station and its staff had laid the groundwork for much of the expanded effort described below. Particularly important was the work of Perry Byerly in establishing the northern California seismic network and training students to study the earthquakes it recorded. The catalog of northern California earthquakes based on that network remains one of the primary accomplishments of California seismology (Bolt and Miller, 1975). This catalog was the basis for an excellent analysis of the tectonics of central and northern California by Bolt et al. (1968).

This summary of the development and results of the telemetered USGS northern California network includes:

1. A recapitulation of the origin and growth of the network,
2. a description of the standard USGS seismograph system and the characteristics of earthquake records it produces,
3. a presentation of the principal network results in the form of regional seismicity maps and cross sections, and

4. a discussion of those results in terms of the underlying processes that
generate the earthquakes.

THE USGS NORTHERN CALIFORNIA SEISMIC NETWORK

Origin and development

The development of the USGS telemetered network was preceded by exploratory studies, employing dense networks of portable seismographs, of
aftershocks of the Parkfield earthquake in 1966 and of earthquakes along the
creeping section of the San Andreas fault in 1967. Experimental eight-station
telemetered network clusters along the San Andreas near Palo Alto (1966)
and San Juan Bautista (1967) were augmented by telemetered stations along
the San Andreas, Hayward, and Calaveras faults to form an irregular fifty-
station network by the end of 1969. Early results of these experiments (Eaton
et al., 1970) showed that a dense network of simple seismographs permitted
mapping of microearthquakes with sufficient precision to delineate the causative faults within the crust and to determine the style of faulting associated
with them.

To provide such network coverage for the entire San Andreas fault system, which seemed essential for any serious attempt to predict earthquakes on
the San Andreas, would require hundreds of stations. Considering likely constraints on funding and manpower, it was clear that stations of the network
would have to be very simple and inexpensive to install, maintain, and operate. The commercial equipment employed in the experimental telemetered
network appeared to be generally satisfactory, so the basic parameters it
embodied were adopted for the larger network. Efforts to improve the system
components in terms of power consumption, internal noise, and overall reliability have continued until the present.

A typical station consists of a 1-Hz moving-coil vertical component
seismometer and a small, low-power amplifier/VCO package to prepare the
seismometer signal for transmission to Menlo Park via telephone line or
radio link. Both the seismometer and electronic package are sealed in short
sections of plastic pipe and buried directly in the ground. Power is supplied
by lithium batteries for telephone-line sites or by either air-cell batteries or
solar-cell power supplies for radio sites. The constant-bandwidth frequency-
division FM multiplex system used for data transmission accommodates up
to eight seismic channels on one voice-grade telephone circuit, and signals
from separate components or sites can be combined on a single transmission
circuit by simple addition of their carriers in a summing amplifier.

Methods of recording and analyzing telemetered seismic data have
evolved gradually to accommodate the growing network. Initially, incoming
signals were discriminated and recorded on 16-mm film-strip recorders (Develocorders) for hand analysis. Later, backup for the network was provided

by recording the incoming multiplexed signals in direct record mode on 14-track magnetic tape. At present, primary recording and analysis of the discriminated and digitized signals are carried out by computer, although the entire network is recorded on magnetic tape, and selected stations are recorded on Develocorders for backup (Lee and Stewart, this volume, chap. 5).

The distribution of USGS stations telemetered to Menlo Park is shown in figure 1. Most stations contain only one high-gain vertical component seismograph (dots). Others contain one or more low-gain horizontal and/or vertical components as well (triangles). Stations of the UC Berkeley network in operation in 1965 before the USGS net was installed are indicated by stars.

Although the USGS network grew at an average rate of about fifteen stations per year after 1966, there were important spurts in growth in the years 1968–1970, 1975–1976, and 1979–1983. The last two spurts were in response to substantial increases in funding for the earthquake program in 1973 and 1976.

The early network was concentrated along the San Andreas fault between San Francisco and Parkfield. The present areal coverage was attained by 1980, and subsequent increases have mostly filled in and reinforced the sparser parts of the network. By the mid-1980s data from more than 400 seismographs at more than 350 USGS stations were being telemetered to Menlo Park for recording and analysis.

Frequency Response of the Seismic System and Character of its Records

The response of the standard USGS seismic system can be described as broadband intermediate frequency range. It is flat (to constant peak ground velocity) from about 1 to about 25 Hz. The lower frequency cutoff corresponds to the seismometer free period, and the upper frequency cutoff is accomplished electronically in the discriminators to suppress system noise, including cross modulation from adjacent telemetry channels. The most serious limitation of the system is its relatively low dynamic range, about 40 dB. Overall system performance also depends on the mode of recording: poorest for Helicorders and Develocorders, better for compensated tape playbacks, and best for on-line digitization at the discriminator outputs. Overall responses of the high- and low-gain USGS systems are compared with those of the big Benioff (JAS) and the standard Wood-Anderson in fig. 2.

Between frequencies of 0.2 and 30 Hz the shape of the USGS system response curve is approximately the inverse of the spectral amplitude of quiet-site Earth noise (QSN, fig. 3a). This relationship insures that the amplitude of recorded Earth noise is relatively independent of frequency within that range (QSN, fig. 3b) and that the detection of signals that are only slightly larger than background noise is independent of frequency. Earthquake signals are also transformed spectrally in the recording process. Logarithmic

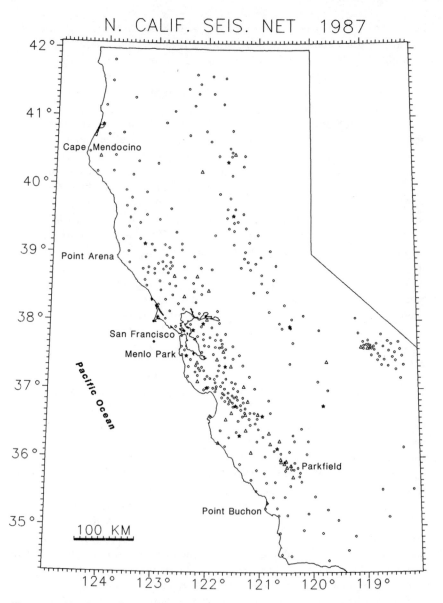

Figure 1. Northern California Seismic Net. Star = 1965 UC Berkeley station. Triangle = Telemetered USGS station, vertical plus horizontal. Dot = Telemetered USGS station, vertical only.

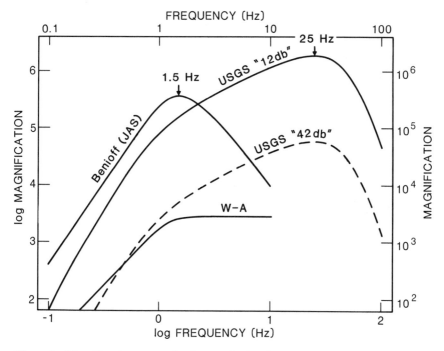

Figure 2. Magnification curves for the standard and low-gain USGS seismic systems, the standard Wood-Anderson seismograph, and the 100-kg Benioff seismograph.

spectral ground displacement curves for magnitude 2 and 4 earthquakes, according to the Brune source model with an average stress drop of 5 bars, are compared with that of quiet-site Earth noise and with the USGS system magnification curve in figure 3a. Such curves for magnitude 1 through magnitude 7 earthquakes, for a recording distance of 100 km, were combined with the magnification curve to produce the logarithmic spectral record amplitude curves in figure 3b. The peaks in these curves should correspond to the dominant frequencies in the records. For earthquakes between magnitude 1 and just over magnitude 4, these peaks also correspond to the respective corner frequencies in the ground displacement spectral amplitude curves. For quakes of magnitude 5 and larger, the record spectral peak and predominant frequency remain constant at 1 Hz and correspond to the natural frequency of the seismometers.

As a specific example, the predominant frequency in the record of a magnitude 3.0 earthquake should be about 4 Hz, and record amplitudes should decrease at a rate of about 6 dB/octave toward both higher and lower frequencies. Records obtained from tape playbacks of the low-gain vertical and north-south components of a magnitude 3.0 earthquake, recorded at station

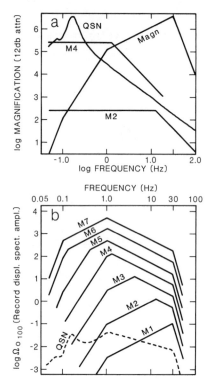

Figure 3. a) Comparison of USGS system response curve with quiet-site ground noise displacement spectrum (QSN) and Brune earthquake ground displacement spectrum curves (at 5-bar stress drop) for magnitudes 2 and 4 earthquakes.
b) Comparison of USGS system record spectral amplitude curves for magnitude 1 through 7 earthquakes (at 100 km distance and for a 5-bar stress drop) and for quiet-site noise.

HQR from a source 3 km deep and 22 km away, are shown in figure 4. In accordance with the expectation discussed above, the peak record amplitudes of this magnitude 3.0 earthquake fall in the 2.5–5.0-Hz band, and amplitudes fall off gently within the range 1–20 Hz and more abruptly at higher and lower frequencies.

NORTHERN CALIFORNIA SEISMICITY: 1980–1986

The distribution of earthquakes in northern California for the seven years 1980–1986 is shown in figure 5. Only earthquakes of magnitude 1.3 and larger with data from seven or more stations in their hypocentral determinations are included. This time period was chosen because network coverage

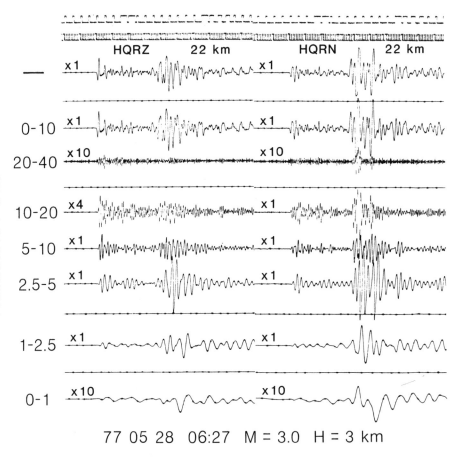

Figure 4. Low-gain vertical (HQRZ) and north-south (HQRN) component records of a 3-km-deep magnitude-3 earthquake 22 km from station HQR. Top traces are without filters. Second through seventh traces were played back through 24 dB/octave bandpass filters. Filter corner frequencies and relative playback gains are indicated on the individual traces.

has not changed substantially since 1980. Even for these years, however, the catalog is believed to approach completeness at magnitude 1.3 only in the core of the network between Cholame and Laytonville. In the northern and northeastern parts of the net, the catalog is incomplete below magnitude 2.0.

Several broad zones of seismicity dominate the map. The most prominent coincides with the Coast Ranges between Cholame and Laytonville. Another prominent zone is associated with the Mendocino fracture zone and triple junction, within about 100 km of Cape Mendocino. A third, somewhat less well-defined zone runs along the east side of the Sierra Nevada from near

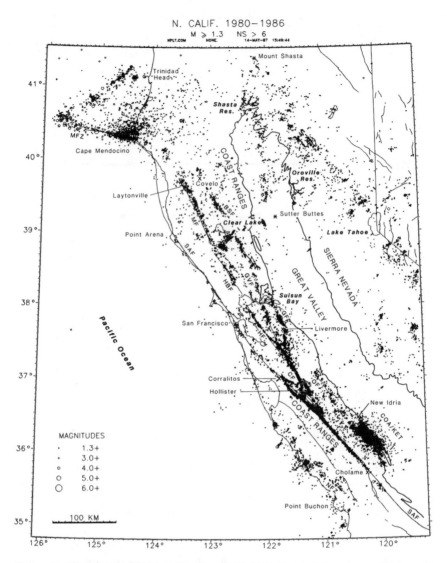

Figure 5. Northern California seismicity: 1980–1986. Symbol sizes are scaled according to magnitudes. Only events with magnitudes greater than or equal to 1.3 and with
seven or more stations in the hypocentral solution were included in the plot. Abbreviations: SAF = San Andreas fault, NFZ = Nacimiento fault zone, OF = Ortigalita
fault, CF = Calaveras fault, HF = Hayward fault, GF = Greenville fault,
GVF = Green Valley fault, BSF = Bartlett Springs fault, HBF = Healdsburg fault,
MF = Maacama fault, MFZ = Mendocino fracture zone, COA/KET = Coalinga/
Kettleman aftershocks region.

Mount Shasta on the northwest to Mono Lake on the southeast. A fourth zone appears to run along the western foothills of the Sierra Nevada from Shasta reservoir to Oroville, with a branch that deflects southward to the center of the valley north of the Sutter Buttes. Other small concentrations of earthquakes are scattered beneath the western Sierra Nevada and beneath the Great Valley, but these do not form a continuous zone like those described above.

We shall explore the distribution of earthquakes around Cape Mendocino and in the Coast Ranges in more detail in search of an explanation for the contrasting styles of seismicity in these principal regions of northern California.

Mendocino seismic zone

An expanded map of the Mendocino seismic zone is shown in figure 6, which also outlines the subregions for which cross sections are presented below. The Gorda/Juan de Fuca, Pacific, and North American plates meet at a common point, the Mendocino Triple Junction, where the Mendocino fracture zone meets the coastline. Global analysis of relative plate motions (Atwater, 1970) suggests that the relative motion between the Gorda/Juan de Fuca plate and the Pacific plate can be resolved into about 5.1 cm/year right-lateral displacement along the Mendocino fracture zone and about 2.7 cm/year convergence across it (fig. 7). The same analysis suggests that the Gorda/Juan de Fuca plate is subducting obliquely (in about a N52°E direction) beneath the North American plate at about 2.5 cm/year if the motion between the Pacific and North American plates is 5.8 cm/year right-lateral strike-slip along the San Andreas. For somewhat smaller San Andreas slip rates, the direction of subduction is more easterly, but the rate of subduction is almost unchanged.

Just how the San Andreas ties into the triple junction is not clear. The trace of the San Andreas is very poorly defined between Cape Mendocino and Point Arena, a distance of about 150 km. Moreover, the region between the end of the Coast Ranges seismic zone and the Mendocino seismic zone appears to be almost aseismic. These problems, as well as the basic framework of plate motions (fig. 7), should be kept in mind as we examine the pattern of seismicity around Cape Mendocino in more detail.

The highest concentration of epicenters in the Mendocino seismic zone (fig. 6) is in a 50-km-long band extending about N75°W from the shoreline at Punta Gorda, just south Cape Mendocino, to about longitude 125°W. This zone lies beneath the north-facing Gorda escarpment at the eastern end of the Mendocino fracture zone (Bolt et al., 1968). A more diffuse zone of epicenters extends this band 80 km farther west to about 126°W longitude. The overall trend of this zone is 10° to 15° more northerly than the near-west trend of the Mendocino fracture zone west of 126°W longitude.

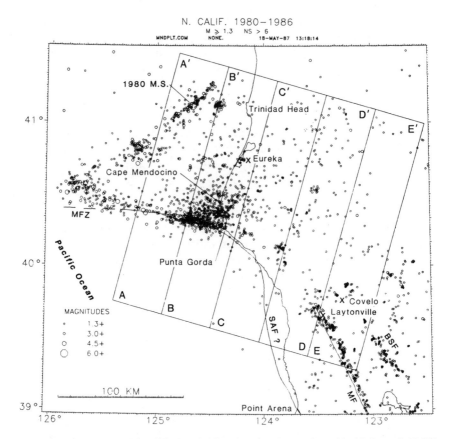

Figure 6. Map of the Mendocino seismic zone showing regions (A-A′ through E-E′) for which cross sections were prepared. Abbreviations: SAF = San Andreas fault, MF = Maacama fault, BSF = Bartlett Springs fault, MFZ = Mendocino fracture zone, 1980 M. S. = epicenter of the November 8, 1980, Eureka earthquake.

The second prominent linear zone of epicenters was entirely defined by aftershocks within the first month after the November 8, 1980, Eureka earthquake. This zone extends from about 40.5°N, 126°W, where it joins the west end of the zone of epicenters described above, for a distance of about 140 km along a N53°E trend to a point about 30 km northwest of Trinidad Head. The trend of this zone agrees with the strike of the fault deduced from the fault-plane solution of the November 8 earthquake. It appears to mark the principal zone of faulting (left-lateral strike-slip) associated with that earthquake (Eaton, 1981).

A third group of earthquakes in the Mendocino region shows little tendency to concentrate in linear zones. Events of this group spread over a sub-

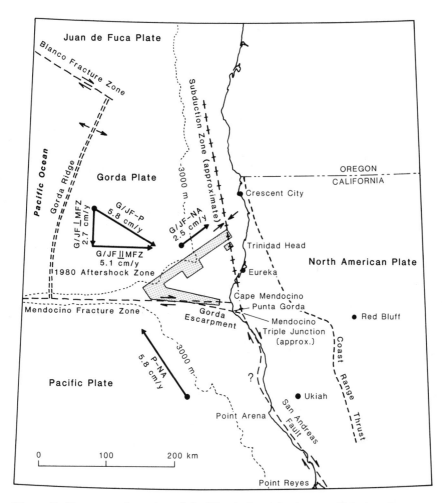

Figure 7. Plate tectonic setting of the Mendocino seismic zone. Relative plate motions are from Atwater (1970). G/JF = Gorda/Juan de Fuca, P = Pacific, and NA = North American plates. The G/JF-P motion is resolved into its components parallel to (G/JF $\parallel$ MFZ) and perpendicular to (G/JF $\perp$ MFZ), the Mendocino fracture zone. The location (if not the definition) of the Mendocino triple junction, the subduction zone north of Cape Mendocino, and the San Andreas fault north of Point Arena are uncertain.

rectangular zone defined by the shoreward projection, parallel to a line trending S75°E, of the 1980 aftershock zone. These events are most concentrated near Cape Mendocino and die off gradually with increasing distance from that point. Their concentration also diminishes abruptly about 100 km inland from the coastline.

To explore the three-diminsional aspects of the distribution of Mendocino earthquakes we have plotted a sequence of five cross sections in which vertical projection planes are perpendicular to the N75°W trend of earthquakes associated with the Mendocino fracture zone and approximately parallel to the trend of the coastline between Cape Mendocino and Trinidad Head. The sections A-A' through E-E' depict earthquakes in five contiguous 40 by 200-km rectangles that span the range from 60 km offshore to 140 km onshore. Vertical lines on the sections at 75 km show the position of the southern edge of the band of earthquakes west of Cape Mendocino or its landward projection. Just offshore, this line (fig. 6) coincides with the inferred fault that Jennings (1975) shows branching southeastward from the Mendocino fault zone. Horizontal lines at 20- and 30-km depths are shown to ease comparison of the sections. Sections west of A-A' were not included because focal depths are unreliable. All five sections are shown in figure 8, with A-A' (westernmost) at the top and E-E' (easternmost) at the bottom. This sequence of sections should be viewed like sequential transverse sections of a biological specimen, which can be used to trace longitudinal variations in complex structures. The principal mapped features on figure 6 that we wish to trace and compare are: (1) events on the Mendocino fracture zone, (2) aftershocks of the 1980 Eureka earthquake, (3) events in the diffuse swarm centered on the triple junction and lying north of the fracture zone and its landward projection, and (4) events in the linear zones of epicenters in the northern Coast Ranges that terminate south of the Mendocino seismic zone.

Events along the Mendocino fracture zone are very prominent in sections A-A' and B-B', where they are concentrated in a dense, vertically elongated zone of hypocenters at depths of 10 to 35 km that dips 70° to 75° toward the north (that is, to the right in fig. 8). Seismicity appears to terminate abruptly south of the fracture zone. The concentration of hypocenters at depths of 10 to 25 km and at distances of 80 to 85 km on section B-B' corresponds to the cluster of events on figure 6 where the Mendocino fault zone (Jennings, 1975) approaches the shoreline at Cape Mendocino. On section C-C', 20 to 60 km inland from the shoreline, the trend of the fracture zone is represented

Figure 8. Transverse cross sections of the Mendocino seismic zone. Regions corresponding to sections A-A' through E-E' are outlined in figure 6. Only earthquakes with magnitudes greater than or equal to 1.5 ($M \geq 1.5$) and with seven or more stations in the hypocentral solution ($NS > 6$) were included.

MENDOCINO SEISMIC SECTIONS
TRANSVERSE
M ≥ 1.5   NS > 6

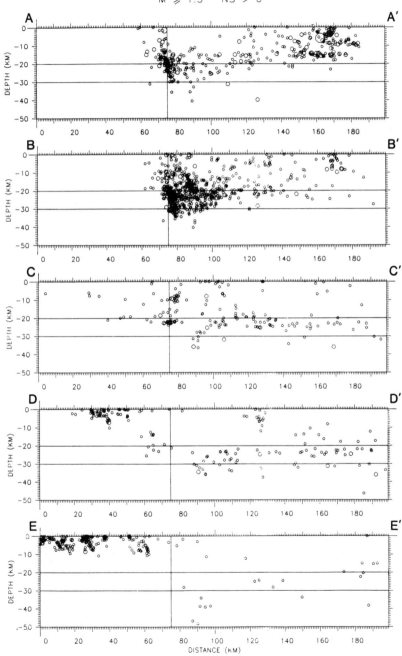

only by modest clusters of events at 10- and 25-km depths, and farther east is unmarked by earthquakes.

The aftershocks of the 1980 Eureka earthquake are prominent on section A-A' at depths from the surface to about 20 km and at distances of 120 km to 180 km on the profile. The 1980 aftershock zone runs diagonally across region A-A' and passes out of it to the west at about 120 km on the profile. On section B-B' the 1980 aftershocks are represented by the shallow cluster at 170 km. This cluster occurred about 20 km southeast of the eastern end of the principal 1980 fault break during the 1980 aftershock sequence (fig. 6).

The character of the scattered events north of the fracture zone and east of the 1980 aftershock zone appears simplest in sections C-C' and D-D', from 20 to 100 km east of the shoreline. On C-C' these earthquakes appear to occur largely in a 10-km-thick zone between 20 and 30 km deep. This zone is horizontal between about 130 and 190 km on the profile. It appears to bow upward between 95 and 130 km and to bend downward sharply south of 95 km just before an abrupt cutoff at 85 km. In section D-D' the zone is slightly thicker and more uniform in depth, although it does bend downward at its south end between 90 and 100 km on the profile. In section E-E' events of this group are sparser than farther west and appear primarily in three patches: 80 to 100 km, 120 to 150 km, and 170 to 190 km. The patch on the south, at about 90 km, descends to a depth of about 50 km. A west-northwest to east-southeast profile through the zone of scattered earthquakes suggests that the zone dips very gently eastward for about 70 km from the coastline and then more steeply farther east. However, the number of events defining the steeply dipping part of the zone is very small (Cockerham, 1984).

The group of earthquakes discussed above is more difficult to isolate on sections A-A' and B-B' because it merges with events along the fracture zone on the south and along the 1980 aftershocks zone on the north. On section A-A' these events appear in a horizontal band 10 to 20 km deep between 110 and 180 km on the profile. This band appears to thicken south of 110 km and to merge with events along the fracture zone at depths of 15 km to at least 30 km. On section B-B' these events define a band 15–25 km deep between 110 and about 180 km. South of 110 km the zone thickens and appears to blend into the concentrated zone of hypocenters just north of the fracture zone. Heavier concentrations of events just north of the fracture zone suggest that the earthquakes may be related to disrupted seismogenic slab fragments. The scattered events on C-C' at distances less than about 75 km mostly lie offshore, west of the inferred trace of the San Andreas fault. They suggest that earthquakes occur as deep as 20 km, but the network coverage is poor, and hypocentral locations are uncertain in this region.

The northern ends of the Maacama and Bartlett Springs faults appear as the shallow zones of earthquakes (0–10 km deep) between 20 and 50 km on section D-D' and 0 and 65 km on section E-E'. The sharp change in maximum depth of earthquakes marks the boundary between the Mendocino and Coast Ranges seismic zones.

Coast Ranges Seismic Zone

An expanded map of the Coast Ranges seismic zone, with outlines of regions for which cross sections were constructed, is shown in figure 9. The pattern of seismicity and its relationship to the San Andreas fault, as well as the position of the fault within the Coast Ranges, vary greatly from southeast to northwest. The most extensive feature of the seismicity is a nearly continuous band of earthquakes near the midline of the Coast Ranges, extending from Cholame on the southeast to Laytonville on the northwest. This line coincides with the creeping section of the San Andreas fault where it runs diagonally across the Coast Ranges between Cholame and Corralitos. Seismicity along the San Andreas is weak where it approaches the Coast northwest of the actively creeping section, between Corralitos and San Francisco along the southern end of the 1906 earthquake rupture zone. Northwest of San Francisco, where the 1906 offsets were largest, the San Andreas lies along the western edge of the Coast Ranges and is almost aseismic. Southeast of Cholame, in the region of the 1857 earthquake rupture zone, the San Andreas lies along the eastern edge of the Coast Ranges and, as northwest of San Francisco, is virtually aseismic.

In the region of complex faulting southeast of Hollister, adjacent to the section where creep dies out along the San Andreas, both the dense line of earthquakes and fault creep branch northward off the San Andreas fault onto the Calaveras fault farther east. The line of earthquakes follows the Calaveras, Hayward, Healdsburg, and Maacama faults, in order, past the east side of San Francisco Bay and on northwestward to Laytonville. A second, less continuous line of earthquakes branches eastward from the Calaveras fault south of Livermore. The second line can be followed northwestward from Livermore along the Greenville, Concord, Green Valley, and Bartlett Springs faults as far as Covelo. This line lies 30 to 40 km east of the principal Calaveras/Maacama line, and along its southern half it lies near the eastern edge of the Coast Ranges.

An apparent southeastward continuation of the line of earthquakes near the east edge of the Coast Ranges follows the Ortigalita fault from San Luis Reservoir to New Idria, east of the northern part of the creeping section of the San Andreas fault. An ill-defined linear zone of earthquakes west of the Coalinga/Kettleman aftershock zone suggests that the Ortigalita trend may extend even southeast of New Idria.

Additional, more prominent features of the southern part of the Coast Ranges seismic zone, however, are the broad bands of scattered earthquakes that lie along the flanks of the Coast Ranges, particularly on the eastern flank southeast of New Idria. There, the 20-km-wide by 50-km-long aftershock

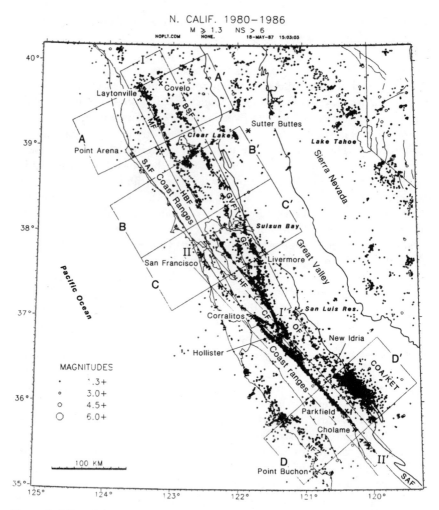

Figure 9. Map of the Coast Ranges seismic zone showing regions (I-I′, A-A′, etc.) for which cross sections were prepared. Abbreviations: SAF = San Andreas fault, NFZ = Nacimiento fault zone, OF = Ortigalita fault, CF = Calaveras fault, HF = Hayward fault, GF = Greenville fault, GVF = Green Valley fault, BSF = Bartlett Springs fault, HBF = Healdsburg fault, MF = Maacama fault, COA/ KET = Coalinga/Kettleman aftershock region.

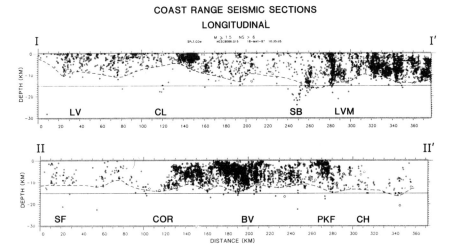

Figure 10. Longitudinal cross sections along the Maacama/Calaveras fault zone (I-I') and the San Andreas fault (II-II'). Only earthquakes with magnitudes greater than, or equal to 1.5 ($M \geq 1.5$) and with seven or more stations in the hypocentral solutions ($NS > 6$) were included. The dashed lines mark the apparent lower limit of the zone of continuous seismicity along the faults. The widths of the zones of earthquakes included on the plots are 60 km for I-I' and 30 km for II-II'. Vertical exaggeration of these sections is two times. Abbreviations: LV = Laytonville, CL = Clear Lake, SB = Suisun Bay, LVM = Livermore, SF = San Francisco, COR = Corralitos, BV = Bear Valley, PKF = Parkfield, CH = Cholame.

zone of the 1983 Coalinga and 1985 Kettleman Hills earthquakes, is the dominant feature on the map for 1980–1986. Both these large earthquakes, as well as almost all of their larger aftershocks, had thrust or reverse fault sources on planes with strikes nearly parallel to the San Andreas (Eaton, in press). The aftershock zone shows the extent of the zone of crustal shortening near Coalinga. Its large width contrasts sharply with the narrow lines of epicenters that mark creeping sections of the major near-vertical strike-slip faults and of the aftershocks of the large earthquakes that occur along them (Eaton et al., 1970; Cockerham and Eaton, 1987).

To examine the Coast Ranges seismicity in more detail, we have constructed cross sections for each of the boxes outlined on figure 9. Events within each box were projected onto a vertical plane parallel to the long axis of the box. Sections I-I' and II-II' (fig. 10) are longitudinal sections parallel to the dense lines of earthquakes in the northern Coast Ranges (Maacama, Bartlett Springs to Calaveras faults) and the southern Coast Ranges (San Andreas fault), respectively. The northern box (I-I') is 60 km wide in order to include both the central and eastern lines of earthquakes, while the south-

ern box (II-II') is only 30 km wide in order to separate activity on the San
Andreas from that on its major branches north of Hollister.

The longitudinal profiles illustrate two principal aspects of seismicity
along the faults: (1) the intensity of seismic activity along the fault and (2)
the depth to the bottom of the continuous seismogenic zone along the fault.
Two reference lines are drawn on the longitudinal sections. The first is a
straight line at 15-km depth. The second (dashed) line marks the depth of the
abrupt decrease in the abundance of earthquakes at the apparent base of the
continuous seismogenic zone. Some of the scattered hypocenters below this
line are reliably located and deserve special note. Others are possibly poorly
located events that occurred at shallower depths.

Earthquakes on profile I-I' are moderate in number and rather evenly
distributed along the fault from Laytonville to Suisun Bay (0 to 250 km)
except for the dense shallow cluster of events in the Geysers/Clear Lake
region (135 to 155 km). The depth to the bottom of the continuous seismogenic zone averages about 10 km over this region. It descends to about 12–13
km south of the Geysers/Clear Lake region and rises to only 5 km beneath,
and just north of, that region. A small deeper cluster of well-located events,
however, lies at 13–18 km beneath the shallow continuous seismogenic zone
near Clear Lake. Near Suisun Bay the eastern line of seismicity lies at the
eastern edge of the Coast Ranges, and earthquakes beneath Suisun Bay
occur as deep as 15–25 km. Farther southeast along profile I-I' the bottom of
the seismogenic zone ranges between 10 and 15 km and averages 12 to 13 km
deep. The heavy concentration of events along this southern section of the
profile reflects both an increased level of background seismicity and aftershocks of several large earthquakes.

The most prominent feature on section II-II' is concentration of earthquakes along the creeping section of the San Andreas fault, between Corralitos (120 km) and Parkfield (280 km). The base of the continuous seismogenic
zone ranges from 10 to 15 km and averages 12 to 13 km deep along this
section. Northwest of Corralitos, between 90 and 120 km on the profile,
earthquakes shallower than 10 km are virtually absent, although weak seismicity between 10 and 15 km deep continues beneath the quiet zone. Farther
northwest, patches of small, infrequent earthquakes occur between the surface and about 12 km deep in the distance ranges 55 to 90 km and 5 to 35 km.
The northernmost of these earthquakes are on the San Andreas fault adjacent to San Francisco.

Seismicity along most of the southern half of the actively creeping section
of the San Andreas, between about 210 and 256 km on the profile, is less
intense than along the northern half (120 to 210 km) and at the extreme
southern end just north of Parkfield. Most events in this section of less
intense seismicity are between 2 and 12 km deep. The section of the fault that

broke in the 1966 Parkfield earthquake, between about 280 and 320 km on the profile, is less seismic than the section northwest of Parkfield, and earthquakes along this section die out southeastward. Southeast of Cholame (320 km) there is a 10-km gap in seismicity followed by weak seismicity between 330 and 360 km. This southeasternmost patch of earthquakes on the profile is mostly between 8 and 15 km deep.

The transverse sections A-A' to D-D' in figure 11 were positioned to illustrate how the pattern of seismicity transverse to the Coast Ranges varies along their length. Each section is 200 km long and shows earthquakes from an 80-km wide box across the Coast Ranges projected onto a vertical plane that is perpendicular to the dense line of earthquakes traversing the box. On these sections, strike-slip faults perpendicular to the boxes appear as narrow, near-vertical linear concentrations of events. On all four sections the vertical line of events near 100 km on the profile represents the most prominent line of epicenters (fig. 9) near the midline of the Coast Ranges. It represents the San Andreas fault on D-D', the Hayward fault on C-C', the Healdsburg fault on B-B', and the Maacama fault on A-A'. The vertical lines of events at 130 to 140 km on profiles A-A', B-B', and C-C' represent the line of epicenters, about 35 km east of the midline, along the eastern edge of the Coast Ranges. In section D-D' the great mass of events between about 125 and 145 km represents the aftershocks of the 1983 Coalinga and 1985 Kettleman Hills earthquakes athwart the boundary between the Coast Ranges and the Great Valley.

South-to-north variations in seismicity of the San Andreas are demonstrated dramatically by the cross sections. Earthquakes along the southern 80 km of the creeping section of the San Andreas are densely clustered in a vertical line from the surface to a depth of about 13 km (D-D'). Earthquakes on the San Andreas near San Francisco are few in number and scattered over a somewhat broader zone than farther south (C-C'). Section B-B' north of San Francisco shows the San Andreas to be virtually aseismic. Section A-A' from Point Arena northward shows only minor seismicity along the San Andreas.

Most of the deeper earthquakes on the cross sections occur beneath the Great Valley or near the eastern boundary of the Coast Ranges. On section B-B' the events 10 to 20 km deep near 190 km on the profile occurred about 10 km east of the Coast Ranges boundary, 20 km southwest of the Sutter Buttes. On section C-C' the sparse, vertically elongated zone of earthquakes 15 to 25 km deep between 130 and 140 km on the profile is beneath Suisun Bay where the Valley indents the eastern edge of the Coast Ranges. On section D-D' the earthquakes deeper than 15 km mostly lie beneath and east of the Coalinga/Kettleman aftershock zone. Although relatively few in number (about one percent as many as the Coalinga/Kettleman aftershocks), these

COAST RANGE SEISMIC SECTIONS
TRANSVERSE

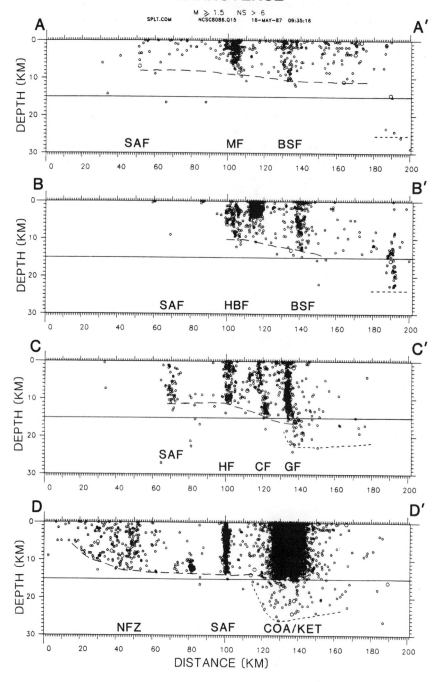

events cannot be ascribed to poor locations, and they reveal a broad zone of mild seismicity in the lower crust beneath the eastern edge of the Coast Ranges and adjacent Great Valley.

On sections A-A' to C-C' the San Andreas fault lies near the coastline and the continental margin. On D-D' it is about 70 km inland, and seismicity in the Coast Ranges west of the fault is remarkably different from that west of the fault, offshore on the northern cross sections. A landward-thickening zone of diffuse seismicity extends inland from the west end of the profile to near 60 km on the profile. The zone of modest concentration of events near 50 km corresponds approximately to the Nacimiento fault. Except for a concentrated cluster of events 10 to 13 km deep near 80 km on the profile (San Ardo), there is little seismicity between about 65 and about 100 km (San Andreas fault). The lower limit of the seismic zone is very sharp from about 10 km, where it is about 5 km deep, to the San Andreas, where it is about 13 km deep. Crustal seismicity is weak for about 15 km northeast of the San Andreas. Farther east, but still west of the Coalinga/Kettleman aftershocks, the density of earthquakes in the upper crust increases moderately, and earthquakes appear in the lower crust. Focal mechanisms of large earthquakes in the bands of seismicity along the coast, as well as in the Coalinga/Kettleman region, show that both flanks of the Coast Ranges in box D-D' are under compression normal to the San Andreas fault, and that the predominant mode of failure is along thrust and reverse faults on planes with strikes parallel to the San Andreas (Eaton, 1985; Eaton and Rymer, in press).

TECTONIC IMPLICATIONS

Global plate tectonics provides an overview of the relative motion of the North American, Pacific, and Gorda/Juan de Fucca plates along their common boundaries in northern California: the San Andreas fault, the Mendocino fracture zone, and the coastal subduction zone north of Cape Mendocino. Plate tectonics studies, however, tell us little about the structure of the boundaries. Detailed local observations are needed to define particular

---

Figure 11. Tranverse cross sections of the Coast Ranges seismic zone. The regions projected onto profiles A-A' through D-D' are outlined in figure 9. Each profile is centered on, and perpendicular to, the continuous line of earthquakes near the Coast Ranges midline. Dashed lines indicate the approximate bottom of the seismogenic zone beneath the Coast Ranges. The events deeper than 15 km on the right end of the profiles are beneath the eastern edge of the Coast Ranges or the adjacent Great Valley. The dotted line indicates the approximate bottom of the seismogenic zone beneath the Coast Ranges/Great Valley boundary region. Two times vertical exaggeration. Abbreviations as for figure 9.

boundaries more precisely and to study the processes in the crust and upper mantle through which they operate.

Contemporary seismicity provides a snapshot of the number, location, size, and style of faulting associated with the plate boundaries and the triple junction. The record of seismicity based on instrumental studies is incomplete because of its short duration, but it can be supplemented by the longer-term historical seismic record. Earthquakes are important symptoms of deformation of the Earth's crust and mantle, but tell only part of the story. Much deformation occurs silently, particularly in the mantle and lower crust. This limitation must be kept in mind when we use seismicity to infer processes in the crust. Nonetheless, the northern California seismicity data do document the generation of earthquakes by plate boundary processes over a very large region with remarkable uniformity and sensitivity. The mechanical implications of the seismicity data, as well as their sensitivity and areal extent, invite their use to compare and contrast crustal processes in the two major seismic regions of northern California, the Mendocino and Coast Ranges seismic zones.

Mendocino

The pattern of earthquakes in the Mendocino seismic zone suggests that the southeastern corner of the relatively young and weak Gorda plate is being crushed against the northeastern corner of the older, stronger Pacific plate in consequence of the convergent component of relative motion in the region. The larger right-lateral strike-slip component of relative motion should carry the disrupted remnants of the south edge of the Gorda plate eastward beyond the east edge of the Pacific plate, where these remnants appear to be obducted onto (or against) the western edge of the North American plate. Subsequent northwestward motion of the Pacific plate relative to the North American plate should entrain the Gorda-plate debris in the boundary zone between those plates in the northern Coast Ranges.

The continuity of the grossly furrowed topography onshore between Cape Mendocino and Trinidad Head with that east of the Maacama fault farther south suggests that these regions share important features of origin and internal structure. The Franciscan Complex, which largely coincides with that topography, contains much material that appears to have been crushed and mixed by a process like that now affecting the southeastern corner of the Gorda plate (Fox, 1983a).

The present geometry of the Gorda ridge relative to the Blanco fracture zone on the north and the Mendocino fracture zone on the south suggests that the southern quarter of the ridge, where it curves to remain perpendicular to the Mendocino fracture zone, is becoming inactive and is requiring an adjustment in the location of the Mendocino fracture zone between the Gorda ridge and the Mendocino triple junction. Such a readjustment is also suggested by the trend of the band of earthquakes along the fracture zone just west of Cape Mendocino. The torque required to rotate the Gorda/Juan de Fuca plate in a clockwise direction and to maintain the plate-crushing contact between the Gorda and Pacific plates just west of Cape Mendocino, may be produced by the southeastward drag along the eastern edge of the Gorda plate caused by its oblique subduction beneath the North American plate. Left-lateral faulting on northeast striking faults across the southeastern corner of the Gorda plate (Silver, 1971), such as occurred during the November 8, 1980, earthquake, is a consequence of the strong normal forces developed across the eastern end of the Mendocino fracture zone by the process outlined above.

Coast Ranges

The driving force behind earthquakes in the Coast Ranges seismic zone is the transform (boundary) between the North American and Pacific plates. Details of the gross physical properties of this boundary and how it works are lacking. Some outstanding questions are: (1) How wide is the transform in the upper mantle, and where is it located relative to the San Andreas fault and the midline of the Coast Ranges? (2) Is displacement across the transform in the mantle abrupt and discontinuous, as at a fault, or distributed in some manner across a broad zone? (3) Is the upper crust decoupled from the lower crust and upper mantle over the transform? (4) Do rigid sections of the upper crust resist internal deformation and "integrate" distributed displacement across their bases and concentrate it in faults along their edges?

The principal observations from contemporary seismicity and the historical seismic record can be summarized by the following statements: (1) The maps and cross sections presented above show that the Coast Ranges seismic zone is complex and that its most prominent features vary from northwest to southeast within it. (2) Most of the displacement between the Pacific and North American plates at the Earth's surface occurs on the San Andreas fault. (3) Where the San Andreas crosses the center of the Coast Ranges, between Cholame and Corralitos, most of the displacement occurs as creep accompanied by countless small earthquakes; where it lies along the edges of the Coast Ranges most of the offset occurs during infrequent, very large earthquakes. (4) Long-term offset rates (over hundreds of years) across the Calaveras/Maacama and Greenville/Bartlett Springs fault zones, which are marked by linear concentrations of small earthquakes like that along the rapidly creeping section of the San Andreas, are small compared to that on the San Andreas (now locked) farther west. (5) The trace of the San Andreas fault between Point Arena and Cape Mendocino lies offshore and is difficult to identify. It is believed to deflect about 40 km to the east and generally to follow the coast north of Point Arena. Macroseismic effects of the 1906 earthquake indicate that this northernmost section of the fault broke in 1906. The long-term offset rate on this section should be the same as that south of Point Arena, but the total offset across it should decrease to zero as it approaches the triple junction, which is its point of origin. (6) The depth to the base of the seismogenic zone along the principal strike-slip faults in the Coast Ranges averages about 10 km north and 12 to 13 km south of Clear Lake. The depth to the base of the seismogenic zone appears to increase gradually from west to east across the Coast Ranges. This effect is most pronounced along the eastern margin of the Coast Ranges and the adjacent Great Valley, where focal depths are as great as 15 to 25 km. Earthquakes deeper than 15 km (in the lower crust) are extremely rare elsewhere in the Coast Ranges but common beneath the Great Valley. (7) Both flanks of the Coast Ranges southeast of Hollister are marked by scattered patches and broad zones of earthquakes whose sources indicate crustal compression normal to the San Andreas fault. These earthquakes may be caused by lateral spreading of the southern Coast Ranges resulting from misalignment between the San Andreas fault in the upper crust and a more northerly trending transform in the mantle below. Such a misalignment is suggested by recent studies of global plate-motion directions (Minster and Jordan, 1984).

From the distribution of current seismicity and the position of the San Andreas fault, it appears that the entire Coast Ranges is underlain by a broad zone of right-lateral shear deformation. The restriction of earthquakes to the upper crust beneath the Coast Ranges, but not beneath the contiguous portions of the Great Valley on the east or the Mendocino seismic zone on the north, suggests that the lower crust deforms plastically beneath at least the central part of the Coast Ranges. The branching and spacing of major strike-slip faults in the upper crust north of Hollister suggest some sort of decoupling between the brittle upper crust and the plastic lower crust. The parallel, subequally spaced traces of the three major branches northwest of Livermore suggest that sections of the brittle upper crust resist internal deformation and concentrate distributed displacements beneath them onto their fault boundaries.

Decoupling of the upper and lower crust in the southern Coast Ranges can also account for the relatively aseismic zones lying between the actively creeping San Andreas fault and the zones of compression and reverse-fault earthquakes along both the east and west flanks of the Ranges. Horizontal decoupling horizons 12 to 15 km deep beneath the center of the Ranges curve upward through the brittle upper crust where it is driven beyond the margins of the plastic zone (over the transform) in the lower crust (Eaton and Rymer, in press).

Evidence for tracing the San Andreas between Point Arena and the triple junction is very weak. The principal zone of displacement between the Pacific and North American plates most likely lies near the coastline just southeast of the triple junction: the intense zone of seismicity between the

Gorda and Pacific plates terminates abruptly where the Mendocino fracture zone intersects the coastline. Farther south, the trace of the San Andreas is well defined where it strikes northwestward out to sea just north of Point Arena. Here, its trace is subparallel to, but offset about 40 km to the southwest of, the coastline southeast of Cape Mendocino. The most prominent feature of the rather weak seismicity linking these two sections of the fault is the diffuse north-south trending band of small earthquakes between Point Arena and the northern end of the line of earthquakes along the Maacama fault (fig. 5). The offset of the San Andreas may be associated with this band of earthquakes.

The sliver of crust between the Calaveras/Hayward/Maacama and San Andreas faults is an enigma. Its eastern boundary is marked by the line of frequent small earthquakes along the Coast Ranges midline, and its western boundary is the virtually aseismic section of the San Andreas that produced the 1906 earthquakes. South of Clear Lake it is nearly aseismic, but north of Clear Lake it contains diffuse clusters of small earthquakes. Topographically, this region is much simpler and more homogeneous than the region just east of the Calaveras/Maacama fault zone, which is characterized by bold northwest trending ridges of such relief and length as to suggest a tectonic origin (Fox, 1983b). These relationships suggest a marked difference in the response of the upper crust west and east of the Calaveras/Maacama fault zone to the right-lateral strain across the Coast Ranges. West of that zone, the upper crust stores accumulating strain, without internal disruption, for eventual release along the San Andreas in a major earthquake. Along and east of that zone, it appears to yield gradually by internal deformation and slip along boundaries within it in a manner that may limit the size of earthquakes it can produce and enhance the grossly ridged topography that characterizes it.

REFERENCES

Atwater, Tanya (1970). Implications of plate tectonics for the Cenozoic tectonic evolution of western North America. *Geol. Soc. Am. Bull.*, 81: 3513–3536.

Bolt, B. A., C. Lomnitz, and T. V. McEvilly (1968). Seismological evidence on the tectonics of central and northern California and the Mendocino Escarpment. *Bull. Seism. Soc. Am.*, 58: 1725–1767.

Bolt, B. A., and Roy D. Miller (1975). *Catalog of Earthquakes in Northern California and Adjoining Areas*: 1 January 1910–31 December 1972. Seismographic Stations, University of California, Berkeley, 1–567.

Cockerham, R. S. (1984). Evidence for a 180-km-long subducted slab beneath northern California. *Bull. Seism. Soc. Am.*, 74: 569–576.

Cockerham. R. S., and J. P. Eaton (1987). The earthquake and its aftershocks, April 24 through September 30, 1984. In Seena N. Hoose, ed., The Morgan Hill, California, earthquake of April 24, 1984. *U.S. Geol. Surv. Bull. 1639*, 15–28.

Eaton, J. P. (1981). Detailed study of the November 8, 1980 Eureka, California, earthquake and its aftershocks (abs.). *EOS*, 62: 959.

——— (1985). The May 2, 1983 Coalinga earthquake and its aftershocks: A detailed study of the hypocentral distribution and of the focal mechanisms of the larger aftershocks. In M. J. Rymer and W. L. Ellsworth, eds., Mechanics of the May 2, 1983 Coalinga Earthquake. *U.S. Geol. Surv. Open-file Report 85-44*, 132–201. Menlo Park, California. Regional seismic background of the May 2, 1983 Coalinga earthquake. Op. cit., 44–60.

Eaton, J. P., W. H. K. Lee, and L. C. Pakiser (1970). Use of microearthquakes in the study of the mechanics of earthquake generation along the San Andreas fault in central California. *Tectonophysics*, 9: 259–282.

Eaton, J. P., and M. J. Rymer (in press). Regional seismotectonic model for the southern Coast Ranges. In M. J. Rymer and W. L. Ellsworth, eds., Mechanics of the May 2, 1983, Coalinga earthquake. *U.S. Geol. Surv. Professional Paper 1487*.

Fox, K. F., Jr. (1983a). Melanges and their bearing on late Mesozoic and Tertiary subduction and interplate translation of the west edge of the North American plate. *U.S. Geol. Surv. Professional Paper 1198*, 1–40.

——— (1983b). Tectonic setting of late Miocene, Pliocene, and Pleistocene rocks in part of the Coast Ranges north of San Francisco, California. *U.S. Geol. Surv. Professional Paper 1239*, 1–33.

Jennings, C. W., compiler (1975). *California Data Map No. 1: Faults, Volcanoes, and Thermal Springs and Wells*. California Divisior of Mines and Geology.

Minster, J. B., and T. H. Jordan (1984). Vector constraints on Quaternary deformation of the western United States east and west of the San Andreas fault. *Pacific Section Soc. Econ. Paleontology and Mineralogy*, 38: 1–16.

Silver, E. A. (1971). Tectonics of the Mendocino triple junction. *Geol. Soc. Am. Bull.* 82: 2965–2978.

FOURTEEN

Hypocenter Mapping and the Extensibility of Seismotectonic Paradigms

James W. Dewey

INTRODUCTION

This paper will consider earthquake mapping from the viewpoint of scientific "paradigms," in the context of Kuhn's (1970) theory of the structure of scientific revolutions. Paradigms are "universally recognized scientific achievements that for a time provide model problems and solutions to a community of users" (Kuhn, 1970, p. *viii*). A paradigm is a framework within which the community identifies and solves the puzzles of its discipline. It provides both a basis for interpreting old data and, more important in the long run, a rationale for acquiring new data. A paradigm may be gradually modified in order to account for new results of ongoing observations. From time to time, the community may face observations that either contradict the paradigm in a fundamental way or that are both inexplicable by the paradigm and too important for the community to ignore. The community ultimately resolves such a crisis by adopting a radically new paradigm that accounts for the observations that led to the old paradigm and that also explains the observations that could not be accounted for by the old paradigm. This radical change of paradigm, in Kuhn's model, constitutes a scientific revolution.

For the past two decades, most research in seismotectonics has been based on two paradigms. On a local scale, we have the earthquake/fault paradigm: societally and tectonically significant crustal earthquakes commonly occur as the result of shear displacement on preexisting geologic faults that are big enough to, in principle, be imaged by appropriate geologic or geophysical data. On a broad scale, there is what I will call the earthquake/plate-tectonics paradigm: the locations and focal mechanisms of many earthquakes are predictable from a knowledge of the relative motions of tectonic plates on the Earth's surface and by application of a few simple constitutive rules governing plate behavior. Seismotectonic research is commonly based on both paradigms, but this is not always so. I find it convenient from an expository standpoint to consider the two paradigms separately.

At present, neither the earthquake/fault nor earthquake/plate-tectonics paradigm faces anomalies of the sort that imply an imminent revolution throughout seismotectonics. There are, however, some earthquake source regions that have been studied from the viewpoints of the two paradigms and that nevertheless remain poorly understood. Seismicity data from these regions do not strongly suggest slip on preexisting faults when interpreted by the current fault paradigm, or the working of a particular plate-tectonics process when interpreted by the current plate-tectonics paradigm. Moreover, there is a precedent for proposing locally applicable models that are essentially independent of the current earthquake/fault and earthquake/plate-tectonics paradigms. Individual earthquakes have, for example, been modeled as consequences of large landslides (Kanamori et al., 1984; Eissler and Kanamori, 1987) or of tensile failure under high fluid pressure (Julian, 1983). Seismologists who work in puzzling source regions therefore face three options. They can continue to apply current plate-tectonics and fault paradigms, hoping that more and higher quality data will reveal the nature of the source regions. Alternatively, they can try to explain the existing observations by modifying the current paradigms without abandoning the fundamental assumptions upon which the paradigms are based. Finally, they can abandon the paradigms altogether and, hoping to precipitate a scientific revolution in a subfield of seismotectonics, search for locally applicable seismotectonic models that do not involve plate-tectonics processes or slip on preexisting faults.

This paper will attempt to demonstrate the value of the two conservative options for solving local puzzles—the collection of more data in the framework of existing paradigms and the elaboration of existing paradigms. My intent is not to belittle the importance of contemplating radically new paradigms but rather to convey the extent to which recent observational studies and recent elaborations have strengthened the existing paradigms. A wide range of phenomena is already at least partially accounted for by the paradigms; the solution to some local puzzles may lie in a few more data points plus the application of hypotheses developed in other seismic zones. Furthermore, the paradigms have continued to be extensible to cover previously unexplained observations and are therefore likely to be extensible in the future to cover still more observations.

THE EARTHQUAKE/FAULT PARADIGM

The hypothesis that earthquakes result from faulting developed near the turn of the century (Dutton, 1904; Reid, 1910) and evolved with contributions from many scientific disciplines. Although different communities of earth scientists have different studies of seismogenic faulting as models, and their paradigms accordingly differ somewhat, I would suggest that the basic earthquake/fault paradigm for mapping crustal shocks comprises the following theses: (1) most crustal earthquakes result from the release of tectonic strain energy by sudden shear fracture along preexisting faults; (2) high-quality seismicity data from an active crustal source region will define two-dimensional planar or slightly curved zones of hypocenters, corresponding to faults, and focal mechanisms will have nodal planes parallel to the local orientations of the hypocentral surfaces; and (3) large crustal earthquakes occur on large faults, which therefore may extend from seismogenic depths to the near-surface and be mappable with geologic or geophysical data. The preceding theses are hypotheses and expectations that appear inherent in the ways in which observational seismologists design seismicity studies and in the ways in which they seem most naturally to interpret the resulting hypocenters and focal mechanisms.

A suite of observations that exemplify each of the theses in the basic earthquake/fault paradigm is found in the Parkfield, California, section of the San Andreas fault (fig. 1). Five earthquakes of magnitude about 6 have taken place since 1857 on apparently the same segment of the fault; the coseismic displacement seismologically inferred for each shock appears equal to the displacement that would be expected to accumulate elastically across the fault between shocks (Bakun and McEvilly, 1984). The most recent such shock occurred in 1966; geodetic data are consistent with the segment of fault that ruptured in 1966 being currently locked at depth and accumulating strain (Harris and Segall, 1987). Small and moderate earthquakes occur on a nearly vertical plane beneath the surface trace of the fault and have mechanisms consistent with slip on the fault. The fault zone is conspicuous in regional geology and geomorphology.

In a region in which seismogenic faults are not revealed in seismographic or geologic data as directly as the San Andreas fault is revealed near Parkfield, the earthquake/fault paradigm may be elaborated as in studies of the Coalinga earthquake of 2 May 1983 (fig. 1). Hypocenters and focal mechanisms in the Coalinga region do not define a single plane, and the causative fault of the main shock of 2 May 1983 does not outcrop at the surface. The hypocenters and focal mechanisms are, however, well accounted for in terms of slip on intersecting faults (Eaton, 1985b). Stein and King (1984) have shown that the seismogenic reverse or thrust faulting that occurred at depth appears to manifest itself as folding in the weak near-surface sedimentary rock. They suggest that, in regions in which surface rock is sedimentary, the presence of reverse faulting at depth may often be found more easily by searching for associated folds rather than outcrops of fault planes. In this case, the apparent failure of the Coalinga earthquake to conform to the third thesis of the earthquake/fault paradigm led to a richer version of the para-

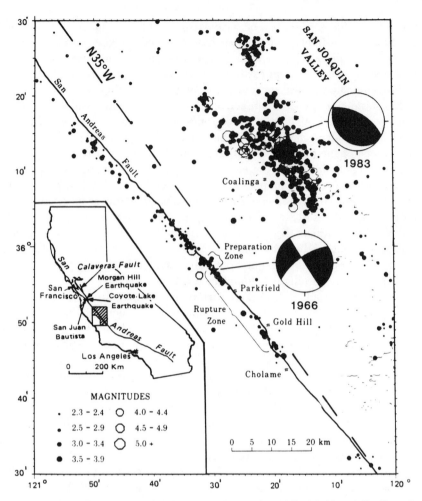

Figure 1. Seismicity of central California in the region of Parkfield and Coalinga for the period 1975–1984 (from Dewey et al., in press, after Bakun and Lindh, 1985). Focal mechanisms of the 1966 Parkfield and 1983 Coalinga earthquakes are shown. N35° W is the direction of pure transform motion between the Pacific and North American plates.

digm, in which active surface folds are added to active fault traces as possible indicators of potentially dangerous earthquake sources.

The seismicity of central Idaho (fig. 2) provides examples of several phenomena not yet, but probably soon to be, incorporated into the earthquake/ fault paradigm. These phenomena are the quiescence of major faults at the small magnitude level for long periods between the generation of large earthquakes, the occurrence of small and moderate earthquakes away from major faults, and the occurrence of aftershocks on faults other than those of the corresponding main shocks.

Central Idaho was the site of the magnitude (M_s) 7.3 Borah Peak earthquake of 28 October 1983. The cause of that earthquake was slip on a major preexisting fault, the Lost River fault (Crone et al., 1987), most of which had been quiescent down to magnitude 3.5 during the previous two decades (fig. 2). From 1963 until the 1983 Borah Peak main shock, small and moderate earthquakes in central Idaho had occurred most frequently several tens of kilometers west and north of the Borah Peak source. Although aftershocks in the first ten days following the main shock were located close to the coseismic fault surface defined from geologic and geodetic data, later aftershocks occurred in a zone twice as long as the main-shock rupture (fig. 2).

Such observations might be viewed as already accounted for in an extended earthquake/fault paradigm, because they are considered possible outcomes of seismicity studies premised on the seismogenic-fault model. But I am not aware of an independently defined community of users that has reached consensus about the seismotectonic environments in which these phenomena should be considered expected outcomes of seismicity studies.

The phenomenon of fault quiescence is currently being studied using the hypothesis that individual segments of seismogenic faults slip by characteristic amounts in the coseismic phase of each seismic cycle, and that the characteristic displacement and interval between displacements of a given fault segment tend to increase with segment length (Allen, 1968, Sieh, 1978; Schwartz and Coppersmith, 1984). Faults that comprise many segments are most likely to experience frequent small and moderate shocks; faults that comprise a few large segments are most prone to long periods of quiescence separated by large earthquakes. This characteristic-displacement hypothesis would lead to an elaboration of thesis 2 of the earthquake/fault paradigm. Although seismographic recording in active source regions would still be expected to define planar faults, the largest faults in the region might not be revealed in a time period much shorter than the durations of the seismic cycles on the faults. Quiescence at small and moderate magnitudes would be expected in a short period of seismographic monitoring of a fault if geologic studies showed the fault to be geometrically simple with a recent history of large, episodic displacements.

The characteristic-displacement hypothesis also explains the observation

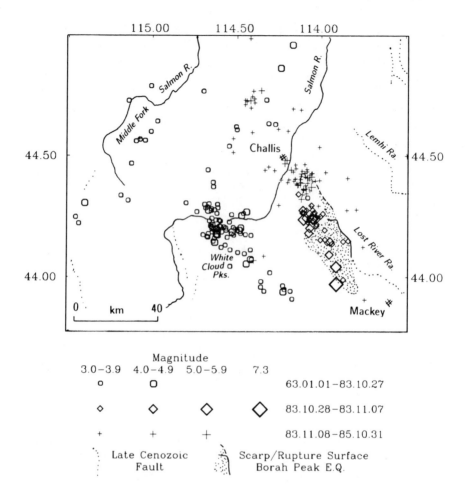

Figure 2. Seismicity of central Idaho in the vicinity of the Borah Peak earthquake of 28 October 1983. Epicenters are distinguished according to whether the shocks occurred before, within ten days after, or between ten days and two years after the Borah Peak main shock. Epicenters were computed by Dewey (1987). Borah Peak fault scarps are from Crone et al. (1987), and the rupture surface is from Ward and Barrientos (1986).

that some large earthquakes are followed by aftershocks near, but not on, the main-shock rupture surface. Stress is effectively relaxed on the simple main-shock source by the occurrence of the main shock, and most of the main-shock surface will not rupture again until sufficient strain energy has accumulated to again produce the characteristic displacement. Aftershocks occur on the margins of the main-shock rupture, due perhaps to slip on smaller branch faults, which must accommodate some of the displacement of the main fault (King, 1983), or to slip on preexisting faults on which effective shear stress has increased as a consequence of main-shock faulting (Chinnery, 1966; Nur and Booker, 1972). Many aftershock studies are conducted on the assumption that aftershock hypocenters are distributed on the surface that slipped in the main shock. Under the characteristic-displacement hypothesis applied to aftershock sequences, the location of aftershocks of a major earthquake would be expected to define fault surfaces secondary to the fault surfaces on which most of the main-shock seismic moment was released.

Small earthquakes occurring kilometers to tens of kilometers away from major regional faults have traditionally been interpreted as due to minor faults slipping under the same regional tectonic stress causing slip on the major faults (Richter, 1958). Substantial elaboration of this interpretation has come with studies showing the wide range of preexisting fault orientations that may be favorable to slip under a given stress field (McKenzie, 1969; Angelier, 1984). It is also commonly accepted that some small earthquakes may reflect local stress fields that are either independent of the regional stress field or second-order consequences of large tectonic displacements induced by the regional stress field. Algorithms have been developed that permit extraction of several significantly different orientations of focal mechanisms from a suite of first motion data for a group of earthquakes (Brillinger et al., 1980) and that enable a search for a single orientation of the tectonic stress field that may be consistent with differently oriented focal mechanisms (Gephart and Forsyth, 1984).

Midplate regions, located far from the belts of earthquakes and late-Cenozoic deformation that define plate boundaries in the earthquake/plate-tectonic paradigm (see next section), pose special problems for the earthquake/fault paradigm. In most midplate areas monitored by regional or local networks of seismographs, the resulting hypocenters and focal mechanisms do not define planes of shear displacement coinciding with mapped crustal faults (for example, see Bollinger and Sibol, 1985; Wetmiller et al., 1984). It is possible that, in some of these areas, midplate earthquakes do not occur on preexisting faults but rather represent fractures of previously intact rock, being thereby natural analogs of some mine rockbursts (Evernden, 1975). In that case, the distribution of microcracks or the rheological properties of the unfractured rock, rather than the presence of geologically mappable faults, might determine the positions of earthquakes (McGarr et al.,

1975). Even if the resulting earthquakes involved the development of faults in previously intact rock, such earthquakes would not fulfill all of the expectations of the earthquake/fault paradigm. Earth scientists would lose one of the most important pratical consequences of the paradigm, that sites of future earthquakes are in principle identifiable by mapping of the faults on which they will occur. The apparent ineffectiveness of the paradigm in many midplate regions may, however, be due to the small sizes of the shocks for which the paradigm is being called upon to account. As just noted, even in areas with well-documented seismogenic faulting in the western United States, it may be difficult to associate many small earthquakes with individual faults. But in the active parts of the western United States, seismologists' confidence in the earthquake/fault paradigm does not depend on its making sense of the small shocks.

An observation that supports the appropriateness of the earthquake/fault paradigm for at least some midplate regions is that late Cenozoic reactivation of pre-Cenozoic faults has been identified at a number of sites in the central and eastern United States (Wentworth and Mergner-Keefer, 1983; Donovan et al., 1983). Most of these faults have been quiescent during the time period in which earthquakes might have been reliably located in their vicinities, but, as noted earlier in this section, quiescence of potentially seismogenic faults is quite commonly observed in regions of high Cenozoic tectonism. The crucial implication of the reactivation is that crustal faults can persist as sites of shear failure in tectonic environments that are far different from the environments in which the faults originally formed.

Results from a multidisciplinary investigation of the Mississippi Embayment seismic zone (fig. 3) have shown the value of the earthquake/fault paradigm in an important midplate seismic region. In addition, the Mississippi Embayment studies must be viewed as justifying the patience-trying accumulation of seismographic, geophysical, and geologic observations to solve a seismotectonic puzzle. The Mississippi Embayment source produced the New Madrid earthquakes of 1811 and 1812, the largest in the history of the central and eastern United States. The status of our knowledge of the distribution of earthquake epicenters in the Mississippi Embayment prior to mid-1974 is shown in the left panel of figure 3; the distribution does not suggest the presence of faults. In mid-1974, Saint Louis University installed a regional network in the Mississippi Embayment region (Stauder et al., 1976). This network greatly increased the number and accuracy of earthquake hypocenters in the Mississippi Embayment (right panel, fig. 3); the 1975–1985 data also permitted more accurate determination of hypocenters of pre-1975 shocks (Gordon, 1983). Geophysical studies conducted in the late 1970s and early 1980s suggested that the Mississippi Embayment is underlain by a late Precambrian–early Paleozoic rift (Hildenbrand, 1985), and geologic studies identified the late-Holocene Lake County uplift above the

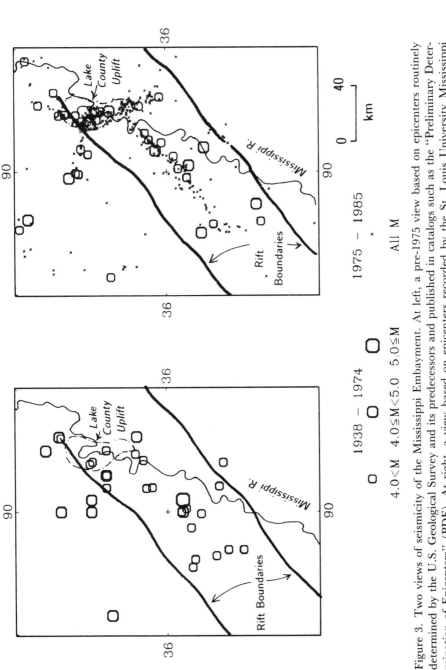

Figure 3. Two views of seismicity of the Mississippi Embayment. At left, a pre-1975 view based on epicenters routinely determined by the U.S. Geological Survey and its predecessors and published in catalogs such as the "Preliminary Determination of Epicenters" (PDE). At right, a view based on epicenters recorded by the St. Louis University Mississippi Embayment Network for 1975–1985 (small diagonal crosses) and on pre-1975 earthquakes whose locations have been recomputed using calibration events from the post-1975 era (Gordon, 1983). The rift boundaries and outline of the Lake County Uplift, though plotted in the left frame, are taken from the post-1975 work of Hildenbrand (1985) and Russ (1982).

most active part of the seismic zone. Epicenters, Paleozoic structure, and Quaternary data now fit a fault model quite nicely. The lineations suggested by recently recorded epicenters would correspond to individual faults being reactivated under a uniform stress system (Russ, 1982); focal mechanisms of the larger shocks of the past decade are consistent with this interpretation (Herrmann and Canas, 1978). The Lake County uplift probably represents the surface expression of a basement reverse fault (Russ, 1982; Nicholson et al., 1984) similar to the anticline that represents the surface effect of the reverse-slip fault at Coalinga, California.

THE EARTHQUAKE/PLATE-TECTONICS PARADIGM

The earthquake/plate-tectonics paradigm emerged as one aspect of the global-tectonics revolution of the 1960s (Isacks et al., 1968). According to the paradigm, the Earth's crust and upper mantle comprise continent-sized slabs, or plates, of lithosphere that move with respect to each other and that are separated by boundaries along which their relative motions are accommodated. Over geologic time, the motions of the plates relative to each other are so much greater than their internal deformations that the plates are treated as rigid in global kinematic analysis of lithospheric displacements. Earthquakes occur on the plate boundaries. The type of displacement— normal, reverse, or strike-slip—producing the earthquakes on a given boundary depends on whether the relative motion of the adjacent plates is away from, toward, or parallel to the boundary.

An example of one type of refinement of the earthquake/plate-tectonics paradigm is given by ongoing studies of the ratio of seismic to aseismic slip across a plate boundary. Plate-tectonics models can predict the amount of relative motion between two plates that must be accommodated by some kind of slip on their mutual boundary, but the original earthquake/plate-tectonics paradigm did not provide a basis for estimating the percentage of relative plate motion across a particular boundary that would be accommodated by seismic slip. Recent studies have searched for systematic dependencies of this ratio on such plate-tectonics parameters as plate age and convergence rate (for example, Kanamori, 1986).

In the United States, the dependence of the seismic/aseismic ratio on plate age is at the heart of a controversy on the likelihood of great earthquakes in the Pacific Northwest subduction zone. The kinematics of global plate motions implies a convergence of 30 to 40 mm/year across the Pacific Northwest subduction zone. The thrust interface between the Juan de Fuca and North American plates has not, however, been seismogenic during the period in which it has been instrumentally monitored. Because the Pacific Northwest subduction zone involves the subduction of young oceanic plate, and because there is a worldwide tendency for the seismic/aseismic ratio to increase as the age of subducting lithosphere decreases, it has been suggested that the plate interface is only temporarily quiescent and is storing energy for a future great earthquake (Heaton and Kanamori, 1984). But it is not clear if the tendency for seismogenic subduction of young lithosphere can be extrapolated to imply that the very young sediment-covered lithosphere of the Juan de Fuca plate should be seismogenic. Possibly underthrusting in the Pacific Northwest is accommodated aseismically, as would be suggested by extrapolation from the recent lack of plate interface earthquakes there. Both aseismic and seismic underthrusting seem consistent with the earthquake/plate-tectonics paradigm in its present form; resolution of the Pacific Northwest controversy is likely, however, to lead to the paradigm being modified or extended to more completely account for the behavior of young lithosphere in subduction zones.

The first versions of the earthquake/plate-tectonics paradigm did not account for the occurrence of earthquakes in plate interiors. Further development of the earthquake/plate-tectonics paradigm has relaxed the assumption of quasi-rigidity for broad regions of late-Cenozoic deformation in continental lithosphere adjacent to plate boundaries. However, the assumption of quasi-rigidity for the cratonic interiors of continental plates and for oceanic plates has been retained. Plate-tectonics kinematics rules are now applied to compute the motion of tectonically stable plate interiors from the orientations of and rates of slip along boundaries of oceanic plates (Minster and Jordan, 1978). The tectonically active belts on the margins of continental plates are modeled as buoyant lithosphere that deforms in response to the quasi-rigid motion of the plate interiors (Atwater, 1970; McKenzie, 1978).

An example of how modified plate tectonics principles may be applied to a region of deformed continental lithosphere adjacent to a major plate boundary is given by recent studies of the Coalinga, California, earthquake of 2 May 1983 (figure 1). The slip vector of the earthquakes is nearly orthogonal to the direction of relative motion between the North American and Pacific plates, so the shock cannot be viewed as accommodating slip between essentially rigid plates. This apparently places the earthquake outside the paradigm. However, Eaton (1985a) and Minster and Jordan (1987) have noted that the strike of the San Andreas fault in central California is rotated several degrees counterclockwise from the trend of pure transform motion between the North American and Pacific plates predicted by assuming that oceanic plates and the interiors of continental plates are undeformed. In addition, the North American plate east of the San Andreas fault is experiencing west-northwest, east-southeast extension in the Basin and Range province. With relative motion between the undeformed interiors of the plates of about 56 mm/year, the strike of the fault and extension in the Basin and Range would result in about 10 mm/year of convergent plate motion orthogonal to the strike of the San Andreas fault, which must therefore be accommodated by slip on some structure other than the San Andreas itself (Minster and Jordan, 1987). Some of this long-term motion would have been accommodated by slip on the fault that caused the Coalinga earthquake. Thus, the apparent failure of a crude application of the paradigm becomes a success with more sophisticated application, more data, and a broader context.

Many of the quantitative applications of the plate-tectonics paradigm cannot be used in the study of midplate earthquakes. For example, even the modified form of the paradigm applied to the study of the Coalinga earthquake cannot be used to account for the rake and rate of displacement on a fault in the interior of a plate experiencing negligible long-term deformation. Plate-tectonics models have been used, however, to account for midplate stress fields as due principally to plate-driving or plate-resisting forces on the boundaries of elastic lithospheric plates (Richardson et al., 1979). In addition, many students of midplate earthquakes see a correlation between midplate source regions and plate-boundary regions that were last active in the Paleozoic or Mesozoic.

Several characteristics of the midplate Mississippi Embayment seismic zone (figure 3) may be explainable by current or ancient plate-tectonics processes. The late Precambrian–early Paleozoic rift structure beneath the Embayment is thought to have developed at the edge of the North American craton at the opening of the proto–Atlantic Ocean but to have failed to develop into an oceanic spreading center (Hildenbrand, 1985). The focal mechanisms of most earthquakes in the Embayment imply an axis of maximum compressive stress approximately parallel to axes of maximum compressive stress throughout the interior of the North American plate. The source is viewed in the earthquake/plate-tectonics paradigm as an old plate-boundary structure now reactivated in a stress regime that, because it is platewide, is probably due to the forces that move plates or resist plate motion.

DISCUSSION

The extensions of the earthquake/plate-tectonics and earthquake/fault paradigms cited in this paper frequently do more than enable the paradigms to cover, one by one, individual unexplained observations. Commonly, an extension to one paradigm aimed at explaining one observation resolves other puzzles in that paradigm or puzzles in the other paradigm. The interpretation of the Coalinga earthquake as accommodating plate motion normal to the San Andreas fault, for example, both explains the orientation of the slip vector in the earthquake and suggests that the systematic small discrepancy between the regional strike of the fault and the calculated direction of pure transform motion between the North American and Pacific plates is not due to errors in the plate-kinematics modeling. The fact that it is still possible to clear up several puzzles with one hypothesis must be counted as evidence of the continuing vigor of the two paradigms.

Although the two paradigms have been most successful in regions of intense late-Cenozoic tectonism, one must be impressed that they also account for some of the most significant observations made over the past two decades in midplate regions. These observations include the nearly uniform orientation of the stress tensor across large areas of midplate North America, the evidence for seismogenic slip on preexisting faults in the Mississippi Embayment, and the discovery of late-Cenozoic slip on faults formed before the Cenozoic.

ACKNOWLEDGMENTS

This paper is an outgrowth of a review of the seismicity of the contiguous United States that I have written with D. P. Hill, W. L. Ellsworth, and E. R. Engdahl (Dewey et al., in press). The reader is encouraged to consult Dewey et al., (in press) for more complete references to studies of the source regions and for a treatment of U.S. seismicity that does not once mention "paradigm."

I thank Bob Engdahl and Dave Perkins for their helpful reviews. Dave suggested a number of sentence rewrites, whose use I gratefully acknowledge.

REFERENCES

Allen, C. R. (1986). The tectonic environments of seismically active and inactive areas along the San Andreas fault system. *Stanford Univ. Publ., Geol. Sci.*, 11: 70–82.

Angelier, J. (1984). Tectonic analysis of fault slip data sets. *J. Geophys. Res.*, 89: 5835–5848.

Atwater, T. (1970). Implications of plate tectonics for the Cenozoic tectonic evolution of western North America. *Geol. Soc. Am. Bull.*, 81: 3513–3536.

Bakun, W. H., and A. G. Lindh (1985). The Parkfield, California, earthquake prediction experiment. *Science*, 229: 619–623.

Bakun, W. H., and T. V. McEvilly (1984). Recurrence models and Parkfield, California, earthquakes. *J. Geophys. Res.*, 89: 3051–3058.

Bollinger, G. A., and M. S. Sibol (1985). Seismicity, seismic reflection studies, gravity and geology of the central Virginia seismic zone: Part I. Seismicity. *Geol. Soc. Am. Bull.*, 96: 49–57.

Brillinger, D. R., A. Udías, and B. A. Bolt (1980). A probability model for regional focal mechanism solutions. *Bull. Seism. Soc. Am.*, 70: 149–170.

Chinnery, M. A. (1966). Secondary faulting: I. Theoretical aspects. *Can. J. Earth Sciences*, 3: 163–174.

Crone, A. J., M. N. Machette, M. G. Bonilla, J. J. Lienkaemper, K. L. Pierce, W. E. Scott, and R. C. Bucknam (1987). Surface faulting accompanying the Borah Peak earthquake and segmentation of the Lost River fault, central Idaho. *Bull. Seism. Soc. Am.*, 77: 739–770.

Dewey, J. W. (1987). Instrumental seismicity of central Idaho. *Bull. Seism. Soc. Am.*, 77: 819–836.

Dewey, J. W., D. P. Hill, W. L. Ellsworth, and E. R. Engdahl (in press). Earthquakes, faults, and the seismotectonic framework of the contiguous United States. In L. C. Pakiser and W. D. Mooney, eds., *Geophysical Framework of the Continental United States*, to be published as a Memoir of the Geological Society of America.

Donovan, R. N., M. C. Gilbert, K. V. Luza, D. Marchini, and D. Sanderson (1983). Possible Quaternary movement on the Meers fault in southwestern Oklahoma. *Oklahoma Geology Notes*, 43: 124–133.

Dutton, C. E. (1904). *Earthquakes*. Putnam, New York, 314 pp.

Eaton, J. P. (1985a). Regional seismic background of the May 2, 1983, Coalinga earthquake. In Mechanics of the May 2, 1983, Coalinga earthquake. *U.S. Geol. Surv. Open-file Report 85–44*, 44–60.

———. (1985b). The May 2, 1983, Coalinga earthquake and its aftershocks: A detailed study of the hypocenter distribution and of the focal mechanisms of the larger aftershocks. In Mechanics of the May 2, 1983, Coalinga earthquake. *U.S. Geol. Surv. Open-file Report 85–44*, 132–201.

Eissler, H. K., and H. Kanamori (1987). A single-force model for the 1975 Kalapana, Hawaii, earthquake. *J. Geophys. Res.*, 92: 4827–4836.

Evernden, J. F. (1975). Seismic intensities, "size" of earthquakes and related parameters. *Bull. Seism. Soc. Am.*, 65: 1287–1313.

Gephart, J. W., and D. W. Forsyth (1984). An improved method for determining the regional stress tensor using earthquake focal mechanism data: Application to the San Fernando earthquake sequence. *J. Geophys. Res.*, 89: 9305–9320.

Gordon, D. W. (1983). Revised hypocenters and correlation of seismicity and tectonics in the central United States. Ph.D. thesis, St. Louis University, 199 pp.

Harrris, R. A., and P. Segall (1987). Detection of a locked zone at depth on the Parkfield, California, segment of the San Andreas fault. *J. Geophys. Res.*, 92: 7945–7962.

Heaton, T. H., and H. Kanamori (1984). Seismic potential associated with subduction in the northwestern United States. *Bull. Seism. Soc. Am.*, 74: 933–941.

Herrmann, R. B., and J. -A. Canas (1978). Focal mechanism studies in the New Madrid seismic zone. *Bull. Seism. Soc. Am.*, 68: 1095–1100.

Hildenbrand, T. H. (1985). Rift structure of the northern Mississippi Embayment from the analysis of gravity and magnetic data. *J. Geophys. Res.*, 90: 12607–12622.

Isacks, B., J. Oliver, and L. R. Sykes (1968). Seismology and the new global tectonics. *J. Geophys. Res.*, 73: 5855–5899.

Julian, B. R. (1983). Evidence for dyke intrusion earthquake mechanisms near Long Valley, California. *Nature*, 303: 323–325.

Kanamori, H. (1986). Rupture process of subduction-zone earthquakes. *Ann. Rev. Earth Planet. Sci.*, 14: 293–322.

Kanamori, H., J. W. Given, and T. Lay (1984). Analysis of seismic body waves excited by the Mt. St. Helens eruption of May 18, 1980. *J. Geophys. Res.*, 89: 1856–1866.

King, G. (1983). The accommodation of large strains in the upper lithosphere of the

earth and other solids by self-similar fault system: The geometrical origin of
b-value. *PAGEOPH*, 121: 761–815.

Kuhn, T. S. (1970). *The Structure of Scientific Revolutions (2d ed.)*. University of Chicago
Press, Chicago, 210 pp.

McGarr, A., S. M. Spottiswoode, and N. C. Gay (1975). Relationship of mine
tremors to induced stresses and to rock properties in the focal region. *Bull. Seism.
Soc. Am.*, 65: 981–993.

McKenzie, D. P. (1969). The relation between fault plane solutions for earthquakes
and the direction of the principal stresses. *Bull. Seism. Soc. Am.*, 59: 591–601

———. (1978). Active tectonics of the Alpine-Himalayan belt: The Aegean Sea and
surrounding regions. *Geophys. J. R. Astr. Soc.*, 55: 217–254.

Minster, J. B., and T. H. Jordan (1978). Present-day plate motions. *J. Geophys. Res.*,
83: 5331–5354.

———. (1987). Vector constraints on western U.S. deformation from space geodesy,
neotectonics, and plate motions. *J. Geophys. Res.*, 92: 4798–4804.

Nicholson, C., D. W. Simpson, S. Singh, and J. E. Zollweg (1984). Crustal studies,
velocity inversions, and fault tectonics: Results from a microearthquake survey in
the New Madrid seismic zone. *J. Geophys. Res.*, 89: 4545–4558.

Nur, A., and J. R. Booker (1972). Aftershocks caused by pore fluid flow? *Science*. 175:
885–887.

Reid, H. F. (1910). The mechanics of the earthquake. *Report of the State Earthquake
Investigation Commission*, vol. 2. Carnegie Institution of Washington, Washington,
D.C., 192 pp.

Richardson, R. M., S. C. Solomon, and N. H. Sleep (1979). Tectonic stress in the
plates. *Rev. Geophys. Space Phys.*, 17: 981–1019.

Richter, C. F. (1958). *Elementary Seismology*. Freeman, San Francisco, 768 pp.

Russ, D. P. (1982). Style and significance of surface deformation in the vicinity of
New Madrid, Missouri. *U.S. Geol. Surv. Professional Paper 1236*, 95–114.

Schwartz, D. P., and K. J. Coppersmith (1984). Fault behavior and characteristic
earthquakes: Examples from the Wasatch and San Andreas fault zones. *J. Geophys.
Res.*, 89: 5681–5698.

Sieh, K. E. (1978). Slip along the San Andreas fault associated with the great 1857
earthquake. *Bull. Seism. Soc. Am.*, 68: 1421–1448.

Stauder, W., M. Kramer, G. Fischer, S. Schaefer, and S. T. Morrissey (1976). Seismic characteristics of southeast Missouri as indicated by a regional telemetered
microearthquake array. *Bull. Seism. Soc. Am.*. 66: 1953–1964.

Stein, R. S., and G. C. P. King (1984). Seismic potential revealed by surface faulting:
1983 Coalinga, California, earthquake. *Science*, 224: 869–871.

Ward, S. N., and S. E. Barrientos (1986). An inversion for slip distribution and fault
shape from geodetic observations of the 1983, Borah Peak, Idaho, earthquake.
J. Geophys. Res., 91: 4909–4919.

Wentworth, C. M., and M. Mergner-Keefer. (1983). Regenerate faults of small Cenozoic offset—Probable earthquake sources in the southeastern United States. *U.S.
Geol. Surv. Professional Paper 1313*, S1–S20.

Wetmiller, R. J., J. Adams, F. M. Anglin, H. S. Hasegawa, and A. E. Stevens (1984).
Aftershock sequences of the 1982 Miramichi, New Brunswick, earthquakes. *Bull.
Seism. Soc. Am.*, 74: 621–653.

PART FOUR

Analysis and Interpretation of Observatory Data

FIFTEEN

Development of Fault-Plane Studies for the Mechanism of Earthquakes

Agustín Udías

OBSERVATIONS OF THE SIGNS OF P-WAVE FIRST MOTIONS

The first methods to study the source mechanism of earthquakes were based on observations of the compressional or dilatational nature of the first impulse of the P-waves. Because of the simplicity of this type of data, these methods are still widely used. Provided instrumental polarities are not reversed, the methods do not require homogeneous or well-calibrated seismographs. Basically, these methods compare the observed distribution of signs of the P-wave first impulses with those expected from some theoretical model of the earthquake source.

Interest in the compressional or dilatational character of the first motion of P-waves arose from the early analysis of seismograms. Among the first authors to discuss this character were Omori (1905) and Galitzin (1909). One of the first indications that there may be a connection between this type of observations and the mechanism of the earthquakes was made by Walker (1913). The first studies used observations at a single station of the signs of the first motions from many earthquakes. Somville (1925) carried out a global study using observations at the Uccle station from earthquakes in the period 1910 to 1924. The results were plotted on a world map with a polarity assigned to each epicenter. The same type of analysis was done by Rothé and Peterschmitt (1938) using observations at Strasbourg for the period 1924 to 1931, and by Di Filippo and Marcelli (1949) using observations at Rome from 1938 to 1943. In all cases observations were represented on a map, and regularity patterns were sought for the different seismic regions.

In North America, similar work was performed by Gutenberg (1941), who used 4,207 observations at nine stations from 1960 local earthquakes in southern California. For each station he plotted on a map the distribution of

243

244 Analysis and Interpretation of Data

compressions and dilatations. Gutenberg took Reid's elastic rebound theory for the mechanism of earthquakes and assumed two simple models of vertical faults with either purely horizontal or purely vertical motion. Under these conditions the pattern of the compressions and dilatations at a near station on the surface of the earth is relatively simple. He observed a quadrant distribution compatible with a strike-slip mechanism on a vertical fault of similar trend for all shocks in the region. He also plotted, on the same map, data from all the stations in the form of small arrows at each epicenter in the direction of the stations. This analysis can be considered as the first precursor of the method of joint fault-plane solutions. Byerly and Evernden (1950) used observations from the Berkeley station of earthquakes in the circum-Pacific belt, separating them according to depth. Their conclusion was that the distribution of compressions and dilatations depends on the orientation of the faults and the direction of movement along them; one can expect a consistent pattern over a wide zone only when the tectonics are fairly simple and the direction to the observing station bears a consistent relation to all faulting in the area.

It was soon realized that this type of analysis was not very successful, and it was replaced by the study of observations by many stations for one earthquake.

BYERLY'S METHOD

Studies using many observations of the polarities of P-wave first motion from one earthquake encounter serious difficulties at first. In some cases, as in Japan due to the dense network of stations, it was possible to study the distribution on the surface of the Earth of the directions of first motions from local earthquakes. For some simple mechanisms, the patterns can be easily identified. After some attempts by Gutenberg in 1915 and Labozzeta in 1916, it was Shida, in 1917, who first identified the quadrant distribution of compressions and dilatations (Kawasumi, 1937). However, this is not possible for teleseismic distances, and a method must be found to compensate for the effects on ray propagation of the variation of the velocity with depth in the Earth. Byerly was the first to solve this problem, introducing, in 1928, the concept of extended positions in his study of the mechanism of the Chile earthquake of November 11, 1922.

For the mechanism of earthquakes, Byerly accepted Reid's elastic rebound theory. The motion of the two sides of the fault was identified with the mathematical model of a couple of forces in the direction of the motion. According to the theoretical work of Nakano (1923), this type of source for a homogeneous medium gives rise to P-waves with a quadrant distribution of compressions and dilatations separated by two orthogonal nodal planes. If the observations in the Earth are reduced to an equivalent homogeneous medium, the problem can be solved by separating them by two orthogonal planes, one of which will be the fault plane. Byerly's identification of the fling motion of the two sides of a fault with a single force couple was not correct, because the appropiate equivalent force model for a shear dislocation is a double couple with no net moment, but both force models give the same quadrant distribution of signs of P-wave first motions. The single- versus double-couple controversy for the mechanism of earthquakes was debated well into the 1960s.

Byerly succeeded in reducing the observations to a homogeneous medium by substituting an "extended" position for the actual position of the stations on the surface of the Earth. These extended positions are those that correspond to each observation, assuming that the ray path is a straight line, that is, if the Earth is a homogeneous medium. After replacing the actual observation points by their extended positions, the results from theory can be applied.

The extended positions are plotted on a stereographic projection, with the anticenter as the pole (fig. 1a). On this projection the nodal planes passing through the focus project as circles. The method consists of plotting the observations (compressions and dilatations) on the projected extended positions of the stations and separating them into four alternating regions by means of two circles passing through the center of the projection. From this representation, the strikes and dips of the two nodal planes are determined. One of the first published solutions by Byerly (1938) is for the earthquake of July 6, 1934, off the coast of northern California (fig. 2). From the solution, he concluded that the distribution of compressions and dilatations was consistent with motion along a N40.5°W plane, with the Pacific side moving northwesterly and the continental side southeasterly, in agreement with the observed displacement in 1906 on the San Andreas fault.

Byerly's method was rapidly adopted as a standard method for the study of earthquake mechanisms. He and his coworkers at the University of California, Berkeley, developed the method further, introducing other types of projections and observations of the polarization of S-waves (Byerly and Stauder, 1958; Stauder, 1962). An ambitious program, the "Fault-Plane Project," was started in 1951 in the Dominion Observatory (Canada) by Hodgson, who published tables of extended distances for P-waves and different focal depths based on the Jeffreys-Bullen travel-time tables (Hodgson and Storey, 1953).

THE FOCAL SPHERE

Independent of Byerly's work, studies of the mechanisms of earthquakes using first-motion data were pursued in Japan and Europe. In Japan, after the seminal work of Shida, a method was used that was based on the separa-

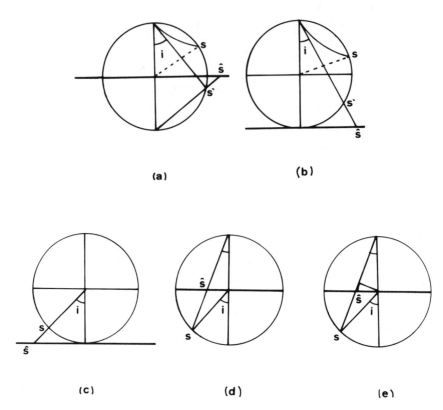

Figure 1. Projections of the Earth and the focal sphere: a) Extended positions and Byerly's projection. b) Extended positions and central projection used by Knopoff (1961a). c) Central projection. d) Wulff-net stereographic projection. e) Equal-area (Schmidt) stereographic projection.

tion of compressions and dilatations plotted on a geographical map and that took advantage of the dense network of seismographic stations. For simple source models, such as strike-slip faults, the pattern for near stations is four quadrants separated by straight lines, independent of the velocity distribution. Early Japanese work already used a variety of source models, in general, combinations of forces and couples with and without moments (Honda, 1962). The limitations of using the distribution of data on a geographical map, even for local earthquakes, was soon evident, and the method was not applicable to teleseismic distances. To obviate this problem, the concept of the focal sphere was developed, that is, a small sphere of homogeneous material and unit radius around the focus. Rays leaving the focus and arriving at a particular station intersect the surface of the sphere at points located by their azimuth and take-off angles i. Stations at any dis-

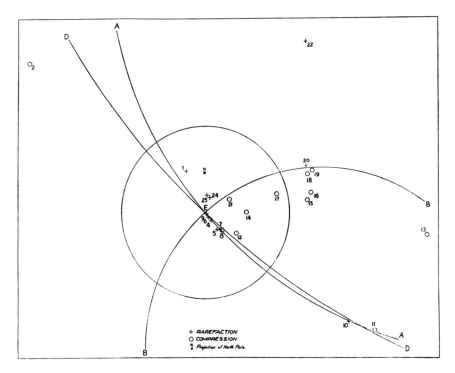

Figure 2. Fault-plane solution of the earthquake of July 6, 1934, off the coast of northern California using Byerly's method (Byerly, 1938).

tance, Δ, can then be projected back, along the ray, to the surface of the focal sphere. The take-off angles for either local or teleseismic distances can be calculated if the distribution of velocity in the Earth is known.

Early work in Europe, such as that of Hiller in 1934, followed the same method as in Japan, using local stations. Koning (1942), in Holland, called attention to the use of the focal sphere; he was the first to use the Wulff stereographic projection, to project not the focal sphere but rather the surface of the Earth. This approach was fully developed by Ritsema (1952), who was the first to carry out the complete determination of the fault-plane solution using the Wulff-net projection of the focal sphere. The use of the Wulff net permits an easy separation of compressions and dilatations by two orthogonal planes (Ritsema, 1955). Ritsema (1958) calculated a useful set of (i, Δ) curves for foci of different depth and applied this method to a number of earthquakes, mainly in southeast Asia and in Europe.

In Japan the focal sphere, called by Honda the "model sphere," was initially used to represent the results of the mechanism performed on geographical maps, in what was called the "mechanism diagram," by means of

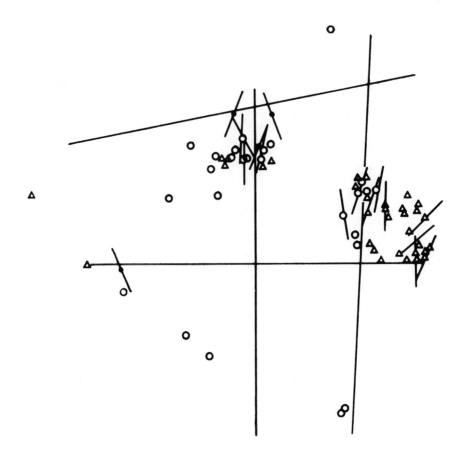

MARCH 19, 1957, 12h

NO. 13

Figure 3. Fault-plane solution of the earthquake of March 11, 1957, in the Aleutian islands based on the first motion polarities of P-waves and S-wave polarization directions (Stauder and Udías, 1963).

an equal-area or Schmidt stereographic projection (fig. 1e). Honda's early work since 1931 followed this procedure. In 1958, Honda and Emura made the first use of this type of projection of the focal sphere to plot the data and separate compressions and dilatations by two orthogonal planes (Honda, 1962).

Focal-mechanism studies have been carried out in the Soviet Union since 1948. Russian seismologists used observations of first motions of P-, SV-, and SH-waves, plotting them on a Wulff-net projection of the focal sphere, which also represented the nodal lines for these waves (Keilis-Borok, 1956).

Another representation of the focal sphere on a plane is achieved by means of the central projection on which the nodal planes project as straight lines, but which inconveniently projects near stations at large distances from the center of the projection (fig. 1c). This projection was used by Stauder to represent (fig. 3) P-wave first motions and S-wave polarization data (Stauder and Udías, 1963). The equivalence of the different representations and projections of the focal sphere was shown by Scheidegger (1957). The different projections of the focal sphere are shown in figure 1. Today, the equal-area projection is more generally used since it has a better definition near the center of the projection (fig. 4). For local earthquakes, ray-tracing techniques are applied with layered or variable velocity models of the Earth crust to project the observation points onto the focal sphere. In these cases values of the take-off angles depend strongly on the models used and the focal depth. For teleseismic distances the angles are derived from travel-time curves and depend on the assumed value of velocity at the focal depth.

NUMERICAL METHODS AND COMPUTER PROGRAMS

With the advent of computers, the question soon arose of applying numerical methods to the fault-plane problem. The earliest attempt seems to be that of Homma (1941) who tried unsuccessfully to apply the method of least squares. Knopoff (1961a,b) presented the first workable formulation of the problem. He considered that the probability that a station reading is correct depends on the signal-to-noise ratio (S_i/N_i). If R_i are the observed readings, the probability is given by

$$\pi_i = \frac{1}{2}\left[1 + \mathrm{erf}\left(\frac{S_i}{N_i}\right)\mathrm{sgn}\, S_i\, \mathrm{sgn}\, R_i\right] \tag{1}$$

Substituting a constant α for the noise and putting the theoretical expressions for the normalized amplitudes in terms of the orientation of the source, the problem is to find the orientation that corresponds to a maximum probability of correct readings. The function to be maximized is given by

$$\phi = \sum_{i=1}^{N} \log \frac{1}{2}\left[1 + \mathrm{erf}\left(\frac{U_{ri}}{\alpha}\right)\mathrm{sgn}\, U_{ri}\, \mathrm{sgn}\, R_i\right] \tag{2}$$

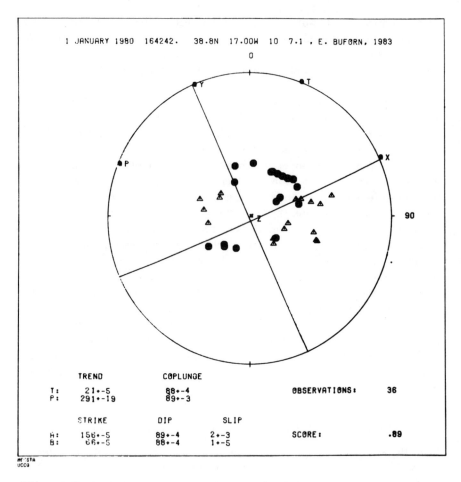

Figure 4. Fault-plane solution of the earthquake of January 1, 1980, in the Azores islands using the equal-area projection. Numerical values and errors have been obtained by means of the algorithm of Brillinger et al. (1980).

where sgn R_i and sgn U_{ri} are the observed and calculated signs of P-wave motion. The problem was solved using a projection of the observations into an antipodal plane of the epicenter (fig. 1b). On this projection the nodal planes project as straight lines. The problem was expressed and solved in Cartesian coordinates for the three parameters that defined the two nodal lines and the noise parameter α. The maximization of ϕ was done by an iterative procedure, starting with some initial values, until convergence was achieved. Assuming the function ϕ to be approximately Gaussian in the vicinity of its maximum, standard errors of the solution could be determined.

The main drawback of this method was the projection adopted, which exaggerates the weight of near stations.

The problem was reformulated by Kasahara (1963) using spherical coordinates in the focal sphere. He used the above expression for the function ϕ but rewrote the expressions for the theoretical amplitudes of P-waves in terms of the strikes and dips of the two planes. (Because of the orthogonality condition only three angles are independent). Maximization of the function ϕ was achieved, after approximating it in the vicinity of its maximum, by a quadratic and the use of successive approximations from an initial solution. Kasahara also considered the use of weights for the stations based on their past performance.

The basic ideas of Knopoff and Kasahara were used in the computer program developed by Wickens and Hodgson (1967) in which the function to be maximized was the "score," defined as

$$S = \left| \frac{\sum\limits_{i=1}^{n} W_{pi} \, \text{sgn} \, \phi_{pi} \, \text{sgn} \, R_i \pm D}{\sum\limits_{i=1}^{n} W_{pi}} \right| \tag{3}$$

where sgn ϕ_{pi} are the signs of the theoretical amplitudes, and sgn R_i the signs of the observed polarities. W_{pi} are weighting functions that depend on the expected amplitudes (modified from Knopoff's)

$$W_{pi} = \left| 2\phi_{pi} \, (1 - |\phi_{pi}|) + 0.3 \, \text{sgn} \, \phi_{pi} \right| \tag{4}$$

D is a parameter based on the sign changes between successive trials. The maximization process was performed by a systematic rotation of the two orthogonal nodal planes through all their possible values in a search for the orientation that maximized the score. The procedure was carried out first with a coarse grid and then with a finer subgrid around the best twenty trials. A variability measurement, first proposed by Ritsema (1964), is given by the angular rotation of the planes around the solution allowing two additional observations to be inconsistent. The program could also use weights of the stations based on their past performance. It plotted the solutions using Byerly's projection. This program was used extensively in the Dominion Observatory (Canada) in a reevaluation of the fault-plane solutions for the period 1922 to 1962.

Udías and Baumann (1969) developed a mixed method that combined signs of first motions of P- and S-wave polarization angles. The source used was a double couple, and the program searched for a minimum combined error of the two types of data

$$E = \left[\frac{1}{N} \sum_{i=1}^{N} (\epsilon_i - \epsilon_{c_i})^2 \right]^{1/2} + 100 \sum_{i=1}^{N} \left| \text{sgn} \, U_{pi} - \text{sgn} \, U_{pci} \right| \tag{5}$$

where ϵ_i and ϵ_{ci} are the observed and calculated polarization angles of the S-wave, and sgn U_{pi} and sgn U_{pci} are the observed and calculated signs of first motion of the P-wave. In this expression E is a sum of the standard error of the residuals of the polarization angles of S-waves plus the number of inconsistencies of P-wave data multiplied by 100. This scheme is equivalent to using the P-wave data as a constraint. The program searched for the orientation of the source that best satisfied the S-wave data, only within the region of those solutions with a minimum error in P-wave data. The problem was expressed in spherical coordinates on the focal sphere, representing the source by the X and Y axes defining the orientation of the two couples of forces. The solution was obtained by a systematic change of these two axes in small increments of the polar angles. Solutions depend greatly on having a sufficient number of good S-wave polarization measurements. This method was improved by Chandra (1971), who introduced a weighting procedure to give P- and S-wave data similar weight. A minimum of the combined P- and S-wave errors was again found by a systematic search that varied the orientation of the X and Y axes. Chandra gives error contours for P- and S-wave data that are smoother than those presented by Udías and Baumann.

The problem of combining signs of P-wave first motion and S-wave polarization angles in a fault-plane solution was considered again by Pope (1972) and Dillinger et al. (1972) with a more rigorous statistical approach. A likelihood function for the combined solution was proposed as the product of the P and S likelihood functions so that,

$$L = k \exp\left[-\ln\left(\frac{p}{1-p}\right)\bar{R}_p - \frac{1}{2\sigma^2}R_s\right] \tag{6}$$

where p is the probability of agreement for a P-wave observation, $\bar{R}_p$ is the number of incorrect P-wave readings, R_s is the sum of the squares of S-wave residuals, and σ^2 is the variance of the observed S-wave data. p and σ were obtained from separate P- and S-wave solutions or from previous experience. The program used discrete incremental rotations of the X and Y axes of the solution over half the focal sphere to find the values where L was greatest. The authors do not give confidence limits for the combined solution, but calculate fiducial regions (regions of equal value of L) that give an indication of the variability of the solution.

A probabilistic formulation of the problem was proposed by Keilis-Borok et al. (1972) using a maximum likelihood method. They proposed three problems: to check the hypothesis that the observations agree with a given type of model; given two types of models, to select the one that better agrees with the observations; and to find a confidence region for the axes of the focal model. In the first case, if a_k are the observed signs of P-wave motion and α_k the theoretical signs, the maximum likelihood function is given by

$$L = \sum_{k=1}^{N} \pi_k{}^{(a_k+1)/2} (1 - \pi_k)^{(a_k-1)/2} \qquad (7)$$

where π_k, the probability of a correct reading with respect to the model at station k, is given by

$$\pi_k = p \frac{1 + \alpha_k}{2} + (1 - p) \frac{1 - \alpha_k}{2} \qquad (8)$$

p is the probability of reading a compression and α_k is a function of I_x, Q_x, I_y, the angles (trend and plunge) of the X and Y axes that define the model. Maximum likelihood estimates of these parameters are found as usual by maximization of the function L by means of a search process. In a similar way the appropriate confidence regions for these parameters can be obtained.

An extension of the problem to consider fault-plane solutions for groups of earthquakes in the same region was presented by Brillinger et al. (1980). This joint treatment endeavors to answer a wider series of question, such as whether for a given region the principal axes of stress have the same orientation for all earthquakes, and whether earthquakes are separable into clusters of different predominant mechanisms. The method simultaneously handles data from many earthquakes, with individual solutions treated as particular cases of the general problem. The probability of reading a compression at station j from shock i is written as

$$\pi_{ij} = \gamma + (1 - 2\gamma) \, \phi(\rho_i A_{ij}(\bar{\theta})) \qquad (9)$$

where γ is a small constant that accounts for reading errors, ϕ is the normal cumulative distribution function, $A_{ij}(\bar{\theta})$ are the normalized expected amplitudes due to a particular orientation of the source $\bar{\theta}$ (ϕ_x, θ_x, ϕ_y) and ρ_i is a parameter that weights all observations of a shock with respect to the regional solution. The maximum likelihood estimates of the parameters of the source orientation (X and Y or T and P axes) are obtained by maximizing the function

$$L = \sum_{i=1}^{M} \sum_{j=1}^{N_i} \log \frac{1}{2} | 1 - (2\pi_{ij} - 1) \, Y_{ij}| \qquad (10)$$

where Y_{ij} are the P-wave observations, M is the number of earthquakes, and N_i is the number of observations for each of them. Because L is a differentiable function of the parameters of the problem (ϕ_x, θ_x, ϕ_y, ρ_i), available efficient routines can be used for its maximization. The program uses an iterative process from a given initial solution. Standard errors of the estimates are determined, and methods for testing the hypothesis concerning the parameter values are applied. In joint solutions the values of ρ_i versus p_i (the

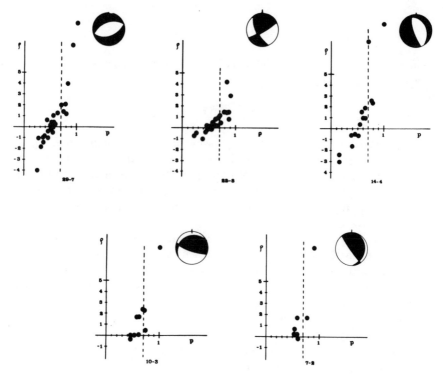

Figure 5. Example of separation of joint solutions into groups according to Udías et al. (1982). Plots are of p_i (scores) versus ρ_i (event parameters) for twenty-nine Pyrenean microearthquakes. Joint solutions and separations into groups are shown. Numbers refer to the events in each run and those separated to form each group.

scores) are used as discriminants to divide the shocks into groups, each with the same regional mechanism (fig. 5). This method has been extended by Buforn and Udías (1984) to handle also signs of SH- and SV-wave first motions.

Although many other methods have been developed for the study of source mechanisms, such as waveform analysis and moment-tensor inversion, the fault-plane method is still widely used due to its simplicity. Since late 1950, fault-plane solutions have been used in the tectonic interpretation of seismically active regions, and their study later had an important role in the establishment of the global theory of plate tectonics. A series of studies in the later 1960s and early 1970s has shown the agreement between the results of fault-plane solutions and plate motions predicted from theory along the different plate boundaries. Fault-plane solutions are used today as standard information in seismotectonic studies, and many agencies calculate and publish them on a routine basis.

ACKNOWLEDGMENT

The author wishes to thank Prof. B. A. Bolt of the University of California, Berkeley, for critically reading the manuscript, and Dr. A. R. Ritsema of the Royal Netherlands Observatory, De Bilt, for his comments. Research was partially supported by the Direccion General de Investigacíon Científica y Tècnica, project PB 86-0431-Co501 and by the United States-Spain Joint Committee for Scientific and Technological Cooperation, project CCA-83009.

REFERENCES

Brillinger, D. R., A. Udías, and B. A. Bolt (1980). A probability model for regional focal mechanism solutions. *Bull. Seism. Soc. Am.*, 70: 149–170.

Buforn, E., and A. Udías (1984). An algorithm for focal mechanism determination using signs of first motion of P, SV, and SH waves. *Rev. de Geofisica*, 40: 11–26.

Byerly, P. (1928). The nature of the first motion in the Chilean earthquake of November 11, 1922. *Am. J. Sci. (Series 5)*, 16: 232–236.

——— (1938). The earthquake of July 6, 1934: Amplitudes and first motion. *Bull. Seism. Soc. Am.*, 28: 1–13.

Byerly, P., and J. F. Evernden (1950). First motion in earthquakes recorded at Berkeley. *Bull. Seism. Soc. Am.*, 40: 291–298.

Byerly, P., and W. Stauder (1958). Mechanism at the focus of an earthquake. *Earthquake Notes*, 24: 17–23.

Chandra, U. (1971). Combination of P and S data for the determination of earthquake focal mechanisms. *Bull. Seism. Soc. Am.*, 61: 1655–1673.

Di Filippo, D., and L. Marcelli (1949). Sul movimento iniziale delle onde sismiche registrate a Roma durante il periodo 1939–1943. *Ann. Geofisica*, 2: 589–606.

Dillinger, W. H., S. T. Harding, and A. J. Pope (1972). Determining maximum likelihood body wave focal plane solutions. *Geophys. J. R. Astr. Soc.*, 30: 315–329.

Galitzin, B. (1909). Zur frage der bestimmung des azimuts der epizentrums eines beben. *C. R. des Seances de l'Assoc. Int. Seism. Zermatt*, 132–141.

Gutenberg, B. (1941). Mechanism of faulting in southern California indicated by seismograms. *Bull. Seism. Soc. Am.*, 31: 263–302.

Hodgson, J. H., and R. S. Storey (1953). Tables extending Byerly's fault-plane techniques to earthquakes of any focal depth. *Bull. Seism. Soc. Am.*, 43: 49–61.

——— (1954). Direction of faulting in some larger earthquakes of 1949. *Bull. Seism. Soc. Am.*, 44: 57–83.

Homma, S. (1941). Calculation of the focal mechanism of deep-focus earthquakes by the least square method. *Kenshin-Ziho*, 11: 365–378.

Honda, H. (1962). Earthquake mechanism and seismic waves. *J. Phys. of the Earth*, 10: 1–97.

Kasahara, K. (1963). Computer program for a fault-plane solution. *Bull. Seism. Soc. Am.*, 53: 1–13.

Kawasumi, H. (1937). An historical sketch of the development of knowledge concerning the initial motion of an earthquake. Bureau Central Séismologique International, Ser. A, *Travaux Scientifiques*, Strasbourg, 15: 1–76.

Keilis-Borok, V. I. (1956). Methods and results of the investigations of earthquake mechanism. Bureau Central Séismologique International, Ser. A, *Travaux Scientifiques*, Strasbourg, 19: 383–394.

Keilis-Borok, V. I., V. F. Pisarenko, J. I. Pyatetskii-Shapiro, and T. S. Zhelankina (1972). Computer determination of earthquake mechanism. In V. I. Keilis-Borok, ed., *Computational Seismology*. Plenum, New York, 32–45.

Knopoff, L. (1961a). Analytical calculation of the fault-plane problem. *Publ. Dominion Obs.*, 24: 309–315.

——— (1961b). Statistical accuracy of the fault-plane problem. *Publ. Dominion Obs.*, 24: 317–319.

Koning, L. P. G. (1942). On the mechanism of deep-focus earthquakes. *Gerl. Beitr. Geophys.*, 58: 159–197.

Nakano, H. (1923). Notes on the nature of the forces which give rise to the earthquake motions. *Seism. Bull. Centr. Met. Obs. Japan*, 1: 92–120.

Omori, F. (1905). Similarity of seismic motions originating at neighboring centers. *Earthquake Invest. Com. Publ. (Tokyo)*, 21: 9–52.

Pope, A. J. (1972). Fiducial regions for body wave focal plane solutions. *Geophys. J. R. Astr. Soc.*, 30: 331–342.

Ritsema, A. R. (1952). Over diepe aardbevingen in de Indische Archipel. Doctoral thesis, Rijks, Universiteit Utrecht, Utrecht, 1–132.

——— (1955). The fault-plane technique and the mechanism in the focus of the Hindu-Kush earthquakes. *Indian J. Meteorol. Geophys.*, 6: 41–50.

——— (1958). (*i*, Δ)-curves for bodily seismic waves of any focal depth. *Verhandl. 54, Inst. Meteor. Geofis., Djakarta.*

——— (1964). Some reliable fault-plane solutions. *Pure and Appl. Geophys.*, 59: 58–74.

Rothé, E., and E. Peterschmitt (1938). Nature des sécusses séismiques: Compressions et dilations. *71 Congrès des Soc. Savantes*, 113–117.

Scheidegger, A. E. (1957). The geometrical representation of fault-plane solutions of earthquakes. *Bull. Seism. Soc. Am.*, 47: 89–110.

Somville, O. (1925). Sur la natur de l'onde initiale des téléséismes en registrés a Uccle de 1910 à 1924. Bureau Central Séismologique International, Ser. A, *Travaux Scientifiques*, Strasbourg, 2: 65–76.

Stauder, W. (1962). The focal mechanism of earthquakes. *Advances in Geophysics*, 9: 1–76.

Stauder, W., and A. Udías (1963). S-wave studies of earthquakes of the north Pacific, Part II: Aleutian Islands. *Bull. Seism. Soc. Am.*, 53: 59–77.

Udías, A., and D. Baumann (1969). A computer program for focal mechanism determination combining P and S wave data. *Bull. Seism. Soc. Am.*, 59: 503–519.

Udías, A., E. Buforn, D. R. Brillinger, and B. A. Bolt (1982). Joint statistical determination of fault plane parameters. *Phys. Earth Planet. Inter.*, 30: 178–184.

Walker, G. W. (1913). *Modern Seismology*. Longmans, Green, London.

Wickens, A. J., and J. H. Hodgson (1967). Computer re-evaluation of earthquake mechanism solutions (1922–1962). *Publ. Dominion Obs.*, 33: 1–560.

SIXTEEN

Deterministic and Stochastic Approaches in Seismogram Analysis

Keiiti Aki

INTRODUCTION

Looking back on the last 100 years of modern seismology, one is most impressed by the great contrast between the complexity of the first observed seismogram, obtained in 1881 (fig. 1), and the simplicity of the first synthetic seismogram, calculated by Lamb in 1904 for a point source in a homogeneous half space (fig. 2). The observed seismogram is much richer in complexity, and therefore in information, than the calculated one. This complexity has made seismology a vital branch of the earth sciences. If Lamb's synthetic seismogram had well explained the observed seismogram, we would probably not be celebrating the centennial anniversary of the University of California, Berkeley, Seismographic Stations.

There have been two successful approaches in investigating observed complex seismograms. One is based on a deterministic model and the other on a stochastic model. Let us first briefly review some successful applications of both approaches.

SUCCESSFUL DETERMINISTIC APPROACHES

An example of a successful deterministic approach in seismology is long-period seismology, in which the complex effect of small-scale heterogeneity is smoothed out by low-pass filtering in the time domain.

Another example is CDP (or CMP) stacking combined with wave-equation migration used in analyzing reflection seismograms obtained by a dense array of sensors placed on the surface of the Earth. The migration procedure is based on the wave equation for a smooth Earth model, usually a homogeneous medium, and its success is due to the elimination of complex

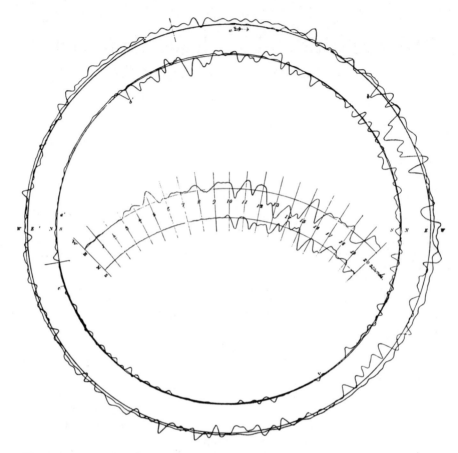

Figure 1. A record, obtained with Ewing's horizontal pendulum seismograph, of a strong local earthquake on March 8, 1881 (reproduced from 1884 issue of *Nature*, 30: 174). Two of the pendulums write on the same surface. The recording plate revolves continuously and is stopped after an earthquake. The beginning of the earthquake is marked as *a*, *a'* (about 90° apart), respectively, on the EW and NS traces. In the center, the traces have been aligned on a common time scale.

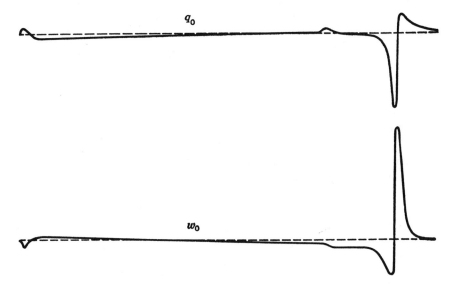

Figure 2. The first synthetic seismogram due to Lamb (1904) for a point force in a homogeneous half-space. Upper and lower curves are horizontal and vertical displacements, respectively.

effects of small-scale heterogeneities by suppressing high-slowness waves using low-pass filtering in the space domain.

A dangerous consequence of successes in long-period seismology and reflection seismology is that they tend to makes us believe that *the Earth is smooth*, when actually we are smoothing the observed data. The stochastic modeling approach, on the other hand, tries to accept the Earth as rough.

SUCCESSFUL STOCHASTIC APPROACHES

A successful example of the stochastic approach is the Wiener-Robinson deconvolution used in the processing of reflection seismograms for many years.

Another example is the ω-square scaling law used for predicting strong ground motion for a wide range of magnitude.

The backscattering model of local earthquake coda waves is yet another example of the stochastic modeling approach recently gaining wide acceptance in the seismological community.

A problem with these stochastic modeling approaches is the extremely simple assumptions underlying them. For Wiener-Robinson deconvolution, the reflection seismogram is assumed to be the convolution of white noise and minimum-phase (or minimum-delay) wavelets. For ω-square scaling, the strong-motion accelerogram is assumed to be band-limited white noise, and large and small earthquakes are self-similar. For coda waves, the coda is assumed to be due to S-wave to S-wave backscattering from randomly distributed weak scatterers throughout the local lithosphere.

NEED FOR BOTH APPROACHES

Thus, in both the deterministic and stochastic approaches, we simplify nature. In the former, we smooth out the complexity in observed data by low-pass filtering in time and/or space, and in the latter, we make simplified assumptions about the nature of small-scale heterogeneities in our Earth model.

I have been involved with many students and colleagues in studies using both approaches and feel strongly that both are needed for a healthy future development of seismology. The deterministic approach gives more definitive results when applied to properly filtered data but tends to give unreliable and unstable results when applied to data containing the effects of factors not included in the model. The stochastic approach is more robust, and can always give some useful results, but leaves us with the feeling that the results are not final, but temporary, awaiting the ultimate deterministic analysis.

Interestingly, text books on seismology, including my own with Paul Richards (Aki and Richards, 1980), are mostly concerned with the deterministic approach and very little with the stochastic approach. I feel that there is a general belief in the seismological community that the deterministic approach is superior to the stochastic approach.

My main proposition in the present paper is that both deterministic and stochastic approaches equally represent respectable efforts by seismologists to understand complex natural phenomena. I believe the stochastic approach should receive more attention from seismologists, especially young and bright ones (who tend to dislike this approach perhaps because the community as a whole tends to place it below the deterministic approach).

In order to illustrate the points made so far, I shall use the example of coda waves.

SOME RECENT RESULTS FROM CODA WAVE ANALYSIS

The coda waves of local earthquakes have been studied extensively by a stochastic modeling approach, as summarized in a recent review by Herraiz and Espinosa (1986). The most remarkable feature of coda waves is their independence of the source-receiver path, as demonstrated by Aki (1969), Aki and Chouet (1975), Rautian and Khalturin (1978), and Tsujiura (1978), among others, for various parts of the Earth. To illustrate this independence, figure 3 shows the records of a local earthquake recorded by the NORSAR

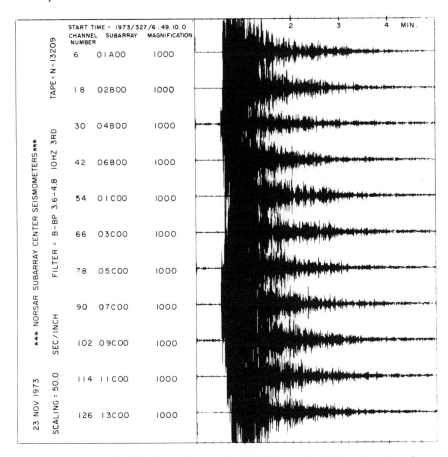

Figure 3. Short-period (band pass from 3.6 to 4.8 Hz) records of a local earthquake at various subarray centers of the NORSAR array. The epicentral distance is a few kilometers to the closest subarray and more than 100 km to the farthest. The decay of coda amplitude shows no dependence on the distance between the earthquake source and seismograph station.

array with an aperture of about 100 km. The epicentral distance is a few kilometers from the closest subarray and more than 100 km from the farthest. The direct P- and S-waves (not recognizable in fig. 3) do, of course, vary strongly among the subarrays, but the amplitudes of the coda waves and the manner of their decay are roughly the same for all subarrays, despite the great differences in source-receiver distance.

The above simple and clear observation demands explanations. A deterministic modeling of coda waves, however, is impossible because we don't know the details of small-scale heterogeneity in the Earth that may be affecting observed coda waves.

The above observation can be explained if coda waves are backscattered waves from heterogeneities distributed randomly throughout the lithosphere. Assuming further that they are due to single S-to-S backscattering, Aki and Chouet (1975) obtained the power spectrum of coda waves at a lapse time t (measured from the origin time) for the case of coincident source and receiver

$$P(\omega|t) = \frac{\beta}{2} g(\pi) |\phi_o\left(\omega, \frac{\beta t}{2}\right)|^2 \exp(-\omega t/Q_c) \qquad (1)$$

where β is the S-wave velocity, $g(\pi)$ is the backscattering coefficient, $\phi_0(\omega, r)$ is the Fourier transform of primary S-waves observed at a distance r from the source location, and Q_c is the apparent quality factor obtained by fitting equation (1) to the observed envelope of coda waves. If the assumption of S-to-S single scattering is correct, Q_c should be equal to Q_β of direct shear waves, which was confirmed, at least for Japan, by Aki (1980).

Singh and Herrmann (1983) estimated Q_c at 1 Hz in the continental United States and found a very strong positive correlation between Q_c^{-1} and regional tectonic activity. Their spatial resolution for the Q_c^{-1} measurement, however, was limited to about 1,000 km because they used the time window from about 100 s to 1,000 s due to the great distance between the epicenter and the station. Because of this poor spatial resolution, areas, such as New Madrid and Charleston, with historic seismicity could not be identified as low-Q areas.

To study the relationship between Q^{-1} and historic seismicity, we need higher spatial resolution than 1,000 km for the Q^{-1} measurement, as well as better seismicity records. China has one of the most complete catalogs of historic earthquakes and relatively uniform and dense distribution of local seismic stations.

Jin and Aki (1987) applied Herrmann's (1980) method of determining Q_c to more than 1,000 seismograms from local earthquakes near eighty-two stations distributed throughout China. The resultant Q_c value at 1 Hz is plotted at each station in figure 4, where contours of constant Q_c are drawn for $Q_c = 100, 200, 400, 600,$ and $1,000$. The resultant contour map of Q_c divides the mainland of China into several high-Q and low-Q regions. This map shows much more detailed variation of Q_c than that obtained by Singh and Herrmann (1983) for the United States, because the latter is based on the coda data for the lapse-time window from 100 s to 1,000 s, while the map for China is based on the coda data for the lapse-time window up to about 100 s.

The contour map of Q_c is compared with epicenters of major earthquakes ($M>7$) in figure 5. We find a very strong correlation between them: seismically active regions such as Tibet, western Yunnan, and northern North China correspond to low-Q regions, and stable regions such as the Ordos plateau, middle-east China, and the desert in southern Xinjiang have very high Q.

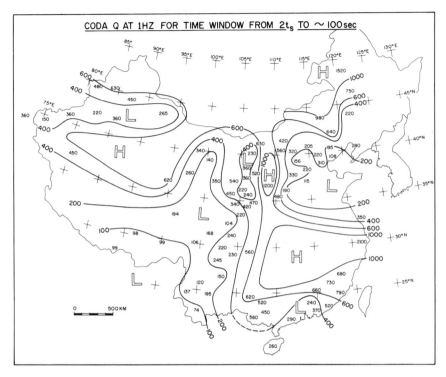

Figure 4. The values of Q_c in mainland China at 1 Hz from the time window from twice the S travel time to about 100 s, and the contours of constant Q_c for $Q_c = 100$, 200, 400, 600, and 1,000.

Two different symbols are used to distinguish earthquakes that occurred before 1700 from those that occurred after 1700. As is well known among Chinese seismologists, there has been a migration of epicenters from west to east during the last 300 years in North China. It is interesting to note that current Q values for the region active before 1700 are about twice as high as those for the region currently active. This result suggests that the low-Q region might have migrated together with the high seismicity. This suggestion has been confirmed by the Q value estimated by Chen and Nuttli (1984) using the map of intensity decay. Jin and Aki (1987) found that the Q value measured from the intensity decay for an earthquake that occurred before 1700 in the northern North China area was indeed about half the current Q value measured by the coda method.

Thus, the analysis of coda waves by a stochastic modeling approach leads to an extraordinary finding that the Q value changed by a factor of two in about three hundred years.

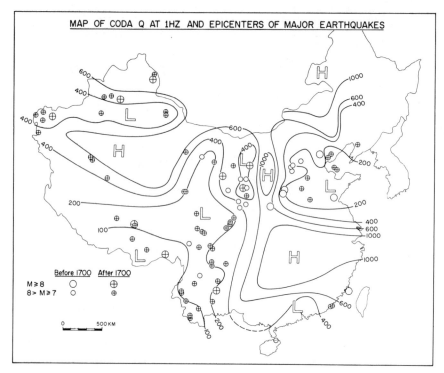

Figure 5. Map of Q_c at 1 Hz and epicenters of major earthquakes with $M>7$. Different symbols are used for earthquakes that occurred before and after 1700.

DISCUSSION AND CONCLUSIONS

The above example of coda wave analysis illustrates both strong and weak points of the stochastic modeling approach. First, these results, which are of tremendous importance for long-term earthquake hazard mitigation planning, could not be obtained by a deterministic approach without a major experimental and analysis program requiring great time and manpower. With stochastic modeling, the map of Q values was obtained by one person (Anshu Jin) in a year or so using existing data. This quickness and relative ease (by no means easy for Anshu Jin who had to analyze records at each of the eighty-two stations), make people suspicious of the results. If the same map was constructed by a ten-year effort of 100 scientists using a deterministic approach, more people would believe the result. This is the frustration with the stochastic modeling approach. It must await the broad acceptance of its results until the deterministic approach proves them.

In the meantime, however, this quick and easy approach may find solutions for difficult problems, such as earthquake prediction, much sooner than a deterministic approach alone. Life is short, and when you get older you tend to become more appreciative of the stochastic modeling approach.

ACKNOWLEDGMENT

This work was supported in part by the U.S. Geological Survey under grant 14-08-0001-G1381.

REFERENCES

Aki, K. (1969). Analysis of the seismic coda of local earthquakes as scattered waves. *J. Geophys. Res.*, 74: 615–631.

——— (1980). Attenuation of shear waves in the lithosphere for frequencies from 0.05 to 25 Hz. *Phys. Earth Plan. Inter.*, 21: 50–60.

Aki, K., and B. Chouet (1975). Origin of coda waves: Source, attenuation and scattering effects. *J. Geophys. Res.*, 80: 3322–3342.

Aki, K., and P. G. Richards (1980). *Quantitative Seismology, Theory and Methods.* W. H. Freeman, San Francisco.

Chen, P., and O. W. Nuttli (1984). Estimates of magnitudes and short-period wave attenuation of Chinese earthquakes from modified Mercalli Intensity data. *Bull. Seism. Soc. Am.*, 74: 957–968.

Herraiz, M., and A. F. Espinosa (1986). Scattering and attenuation of high-frequency seismic waves: Development of the theory of coda waves. *U.S. Geol. Surv. Open-file Report 86-455*, 1–92.

Herrmann, R. E. (1980). Q estimates using the coda of local earthquakes. *Bull. Seism. Soc. Am.*, 70: 447–468.

Jin, A., and K. Aki (1987). Spatial correlation of coda Q with the long-term seismicity in China: Implication to the eastern and central U.S. long-term seismicity. Presented at the annual meeting of the Seismological Society of America, Santa Barbara, California, March 24–27, 1987.

Lamb, H. (1904). On the propagation of tremors over the surface of an elastic solid. *Phil. Trans. R. Soc. London*, A203: 1–42.

Rautian, T. G., and V. I. Khalturin (1978). The use of coda for determination of the earthquake source spectrum. *Bull. Seism. Soc. Am.*, 68: 923–948.

Singh, S. K., and R. B. Herrmann (1983). Regionalization of crustal coda Q in the continental United States. *J. Geophys. Res.*, 88: 527–538.

Tsujiura, M. (1978). Spectral analysis of the coda waves from local earthquakes. *Bull. Earth. Res. Inst.*, Tokyo University, 53: 1–48.

SEVENTEEN

Some Examples of the Statistical Analysis of Seismological Data

David R. Brillinger

"Data! data! data!" he cried impatiently, "I can't make bricks without clay."
Sherlock Holmes
—*A. Conan Doyle,* The Adventure of the Copper Beeches *(1892)*

"Mr. . . . has joined the society, and, like many engineers, is interested in the possible effects of earthquakes. . . . These men want to know the seismicity of given places. The Lord help them!"

If the engineers of the county will cooperate with the Seismological Society of America in the effort to gather and publish data regarding earthquakes, the Seismological Society of America will gladly undertake to get them some help here on this earth.
—Seismological Notes *(1911, p. 185)*

INTRODUCTION

A subject that has been called statistical seismology has too few researchers but a number of success stories to its credit. Vere-Jones and Smith (1981) reviewed much of the work in the subject up to 1980. This presentation concentrates on some themes of contemporary statistics that seem of some relevance to the seismological circumstance. The examples of their use are based principally on the work of my students and myself.

That statistics is important in seismology seems self-evident. This was recognized very early on. Rothé (1981) recorded that part of the program of the 1891 Tokyo Earthquake Investigation Committee was

To draw up a list of shocks with dates and times for each phase; to study the distribution of earthquakes in space and time; to study possible relations with the seasons, the phases of the moon, meteorological conditions, etc.

These are all data sets ripe for statistical analysis. It may be mentioned generally that there are massive seismological data sets, that uncertainty abounds, and that there are floods of hypotheses and inferences. Earthquake prediction is in the public mind. Seismology is also important to statistics. This results in part from the field's remarkable generosity in making data sets available and from the intriguing formal problems it raises.

The foremost researcher in statistical seismology has to be Harold Jeffreys. His research altered the field of both seismology and statistics in major fashions. His working attitude is illustrated by the remarks: ". . . I have been insisting for about twenty years that the claim of finality for any scientific inference is absurd" (Jeffreys, 1939) and "The uncertainty is as important a part of the result as the estimate itself. . . . An estimate without a standard error is practically meaningless" (Jeffreys, 1967).

Of Jeffreys's work, Hudson (1981) has written: "The success of the Jeffreys-Bullen travel time tables was due in large part to Jeffreys's consistent use of sound statistical methods."

The part of Jeffreys's work that has perhaps affected statistics the most is his development of robust/resistant techniques for handling nonnormal and bad data. Other scientists whose work has had major impact on seismological statistics include: Keiiti Aki, Bruce Bolt, Allin Cornell, Yan Kagan, Vladimir Keilis-Borok, Leon Knopoff, Bob Shumway, John Tukey, and David Vere-Jones. More recent contributors include Daniele Veneziano and Yosihiko Ogata.

LIKELIHOOD-BASED PROCEDURES

In the statistical approach to data analysis it is usual to view observations as realizations of random variables. Important to that approach is the notion of likelihood. If the (multivariate) observation $(Y_1, \ldots, Y_n)$ is assumed to come from a random variable with probability function $p(y_1, \ldots, y_n | \theta)$, depending on the unknown parameter θ, then the likelihood function of θ given the observation is defined to be

$$L(\theta) = p(Y_1, \ldots, Y_n | \theta)$$

Employing likelihood-based inference procedures handles and unifies a variety of problems. The procedures are often highly efficient. There are corresponding estimation, testing, and confidence procedures, (referring back to the second Jeffreys's quote). Results derived from different data sets may be combined routinely.

In applications, the approach is to set down a likelihood based on a conceptual model of the situation at hand. As an example of employing a likelihood procedure, consider the problem of estimating the seismic moment and stress drop of a particular event given a particular seismogram. For a variety of source models, researchers have related the seismic moment and stress drop to characteristics of the amplitude spectrum, $|\Omega(\omega)|$, (that is, the modulus of the Fourier transform of the signal). Suppose that the seismogram is written

$$Y(t) = u(t;\theta) + \epsilon(t) \tag{1}$$

where u is the signal, θ is an unknown parameter and ϵ is the "noise." If $\Omega(\omega;\theta)$ denotes the Fourier transform of $u(t;\theta)$, then what is given, from the source model, is the functional form of $|\Omega(\omega;\theta)|$. Following Brune (1970), common forms (for displacement measurements) include

$$|\Omega(\omega;\theta)| = a / \sqrt{1 + (\omega/\omega_0)^b} \text{ and } a/[1 + (\omega/\omega_0)^2]$$

where $\theta = \{a, b, \omega_0\}$, are the parameters to be estimated. Estimates of the seismic moment and stress drop may be determined once estimates of a and ω_0 are available. The practice has been to estimate the unknowns graphically from a plot of the modulus of the empirical Fourier transform, $|d_Y^T(\omega)|$, where

$$d_Y^T(\omega) = \sum_{t=0}^{T-1} Y(t) \, e^{-i\omega}$$

$0 \le \omega \le \pi$. The following likelihood-based procedure was suggested in Brillinger and Ihaka (1982) and developed in detail in Ihaka (1985).

When the asymptotic distribution of $|d_Y^T(\omega)|$ is evaluated for the case of stationary mixing $\epsilon(t)$, it is found to depend on $|\Omega(\omega;\theta)|$ and $f_{\epsilon\epsilon}(\omega)$ alone, where $f_{\epsilon\epsilon}(\omega)$ is the power spectrum of the noise. Hence, given an expression only for the modulus of Ω, one can proceed to estimate θ. For the model (1), and small noise, one has

$$|d_Y^T(\omega)| = |\Omega(\omega;\theta)| + (d_\epsilon^T(\omega) + d_\epsilon^T(-\omega))/2 + \ldots$$

showing variation around $|\Omega|$ independent of $|\Omega|$. However, when deviations of $|d_Y^T|$ from a fitted version of itself are plotted versus the fitted values, dependence of the error on $|\Omega|$ is apparent. An example is provided in figure 1. This is the result of computations for an earthquake of magnitude 6.7 that occurred in Taiwan on 29 January 1981. The data were recorded by one of the instruments of the SMART 1 array (Bolt et al., 1982). The top graph of the figure provides the transverse S-wave portion of the recorded accelerations. The lower graph provides the deviations plot just referred to. This plot suggests that the noise is in part "signal generated."

Various physical phenomena can lead to signal-generated noise. These include multipath transmission, reflection, and scattering. The following is an example of a model that includes signal-generated noise.

$$Y(t) = u(t) + \sum_k [\gamma_k u(t - \tau_k) + \delta_k u^H(t - \tau_k)] + \epsilon(t)$$

where τ_k are time delays, u^H is the Hilbert transform of u, γ_k, δ_k like a and b above, are parameters to be estimated reflecting the vagaries of the transmission process, and $\epsilon(t)$ is unrelated noise. The inclusion of the Hilbert transform allows the possibility of phase shifts. Assuming γ_k, δ_k, τ_k are random, and evaluating the large sample variance, one is led to approximate the distribution of the discrete Fourier transform values, $Y_j = d_Y^T(\omega_j)$ by a complex normal with mean $\Omega(\omega_j;\theta)$ and variance $\Gamma_j = 2\pi T[\rho^2|\Omega(\omega_j;\theta)|^2 + \sigma^2]$, $\omega_j = 2\pi j/T$. Here it has also been assumed that ϵ is white noise (of variance σ^2),

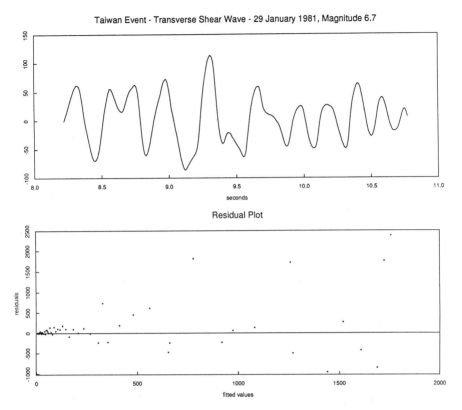

Figure 1. The top graph provides the computed transverse shear wave component derived from data recorded by the SMART 1 array. The bottom graph provides residuals, that is, the difference between the absolute values of the empirical Fourier transform values and their mean values determined from the final fitted values. These are plotted against the fitted values. Wedging is apparent.

that the expectations of γ_k and δ_k are zero, and that the process τ_k is Poisson. The ratio ρ^2/σ^2 measures the relative importance of signal-generated noise. In the likelihood approach one proceeds to estimate θ by deriving the marginal distribution of the $|Y_j|$ and then setting down the likelihood. This likelihood when evaluated is found to be approximately

$$\prod_j \left\{ \exp\left[-\frac{|Y_j|^2 + |\Omega|^2}{\Gamma_j} \right] I_0 \left[\frac{2|Y_j|\,|\Omega_j|}{\Gamma_j} \right] \frac{1}{\Gamma_j} \right\}$$

where I_0 denotes a modified Bessel function. Figure 2 shows a fit of the model $|\Omega(\omega)| = a|\omega| / [1 + (\omega/\omega_0)^4]$ to the data of figure 1. The fit is good.

Once estimates of a, ω_0 are at hand, they may be converted to estimates of

Taiwan Event - Amplitude Spectrum

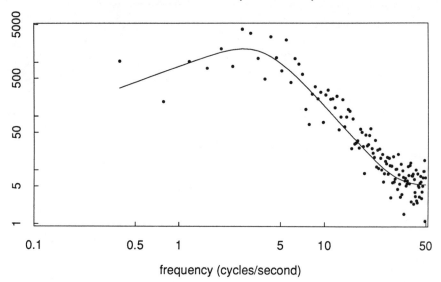

frequency (cycles/second)

Figure 2. The plotted points are the absolute values of the discrete Fourier transform of the data of figure 1. The smooth curve is the result of fitting the Brune-type model $|\omega| / [1 + (\omega/\omega_0)^4]$.

the seismic moment and stress drop via the theoretical relationships that have been developed. Uncertainty measures are directly available for the estimates. Details of this technique and a study of its theoretical properties may be found in the thesis of Ihaka (1985).

BORROWING STRENGTH

"Borrowing strength" is the colorful term John Tukey has introduced for the class of statistical procedures that seek to improve on naive estimates by incorporating data from parallel but formally distinct circumstances. These procedures also go under other names, such as pooling, random effects, James-Stein, shrinkage, empirical Bayes, and Bayes. The technique of damped regression provides an example most known to seismologists. Of the notion generally, Mallows and Tukey (1982) have remarked: "Knowing when to borrow and when not to borrow is one of the key aspects of statistical practice." A popular account of "improved" estimates is given in Efron and Morris (1977). The case of the linear model is developed, with examples, in Dempster et al. (1981).

To begin with a simple example, suppose that one wishes to estimate the mean μ_i of a population i, and one has available the mean $\overline{Y}_i$ of a sample of values from that population. Then the naive estimate of μ_i is $\bar{Y}_i$. Suppose, however, that other populations beyond the ith, and corresponding sample means, are available. Suppose that these populations are all somewhat similar. Let $\bar{Y}$ denote the mean of all the sample means of the populations. Consider borrowing strength, in the estimation of μ_i, from the other populations; specifically consider forming an estimate

$$q\bar{Y}_i + (1 - q)\bar{Y} \tag{2}$$

for some q lying between 0 and 1. One would like to choose q to be near 1 if $\bar{Y}_i$ can almost stand on its own, but q to be near 0 if the $\bar{Y}_i$ are highly variable. This problem may be formalized via a random effects model, specifically by setting down a model

$$Y_{ij} = \mu + \epsilon_i + \epsilon_{ij}$$

with the ϵ_i, say, independent variates with mean 1 and variance τ^2, and the ϵ_{ij} independent variates with means 0 and variance σ^2. Then, for the case of samples all the same size, J, the "best" linear unbiased estimate of $\mu_i = \mu + \epsilon_i$ is given by expression (2) with

$$q = J\tau^2/(J\tau^2 + \sigma^2)$$

In the case that τ is zero, q is 0, and the estimate is $\bar{Y}$. In the case that τ is infinity, q is 1, and the estimate is $\bar{Y}_i$.

As an example of what is involved here, consider the problem of developing attenuation relationships. Quite a variety of specific functional forms, involving a finite number of real-valued parameters, have been set down. For example, Joyner and Boore (1981) develop the relationship

$$\log A = -1.02 + 0.249M - \log \sqrt{d^2 + 7.3^2} - 0.00255 \sqrt{d^2 + 7.3^2} \tag{3A}$$

for (mainly) western United States earthquakes with A peak horizontal acceleration, with M moment magnitude, and with d closest distance to the surface fault rupture in kilometers. To prevent earthquakes with many recordings from dominating the estimates, Joyner and Boore carried out the fitting in two stages. First magnitude was not included in the model, but an event constant was. Then the event constant estimates were regressed on magnitude to obtain the term $-1.02 + 0.249M$. There were 23 events and 182 records in all.

One may obtain "improved" estimates as follows. The Joyner-Boore functional form will be retained. Let the subscript i index the event, and j index the record within the event. Consider the (random effects) model

$$\log A_{ij} = \alpha_i + \beta_i M_i - \log\sqrt{d_{ij}^2 + \delta_i^2} - \gamma_i \sqrt{d_{ij}^2 + \delta_i^2} + \epsilon_{ij} \tag{3B}$$

where α_i, β_i, γ_i, $\delta_i = 1, \ldots, I$, are independent realizations of random variables with means μ_α, μ_β, μ_γ, μ_δ and variance σ_α^2, σ_β^2, σ_γ^2, σ_δ^2, respectively.

TABLE 1

Parameter	Estimate	Standard Error
μ_α	-0.969	0.210
μ_β	0.239	0.034
μ_γ	0.00187	0.00091
μ_δ	6.99	2.29
σ_α	0.0617	0.0700
σ_β	0.148	0.066
σ_γ	0.00193	0.00127
σ_δ	0.0294	132.
σ	0.213	0.014

The ϵ_{ij} are independent noises with mean 0 and variance σ^2. This model ties together the events, but each event has its own α, β, γ, δ. (The usual non-linear regression model corresponds to σ_α, σ_β, σ_γ, σ_δ identically 0.) Implications of this model are that records for the same event are correlated and that the disparate numbers of records for the events are handled automatically. Assuming that the random variables involved are normal, the model can be fit by maximum likelihood (employing numerical quadrature as needed). The results are provided in table 1. In some cases, for example σ_α, σ_δ, there is a clear suggestion that the corresponding population parameter may be 0.

Once fit, model (3B) may be used, for example, for obtaining "improved" estimates of the attenuation behavior of the individual events. Consider for example the 1979 Imperial Valley aftershock. The data for this event are the points plotted in figure 3. Also plotted, as the curve of short dashes, is the result of fitting the Joyner-Boore functional form to the data for this event alone. Clearly, this curve is not too useful away from the cluster of observations. It has high uncertainty as well.

The solid curve graphed is the estimate of

$$E\{\alpha_0 + \beta_0 M_0 - \log(\sqrt{d^2 + \delta_0^2}) - \gamma_0 \sqrt{d_2 + \delta_0^2} + \epsilon_0 \mid \text{all the data}\} \qquad (4)$$

with subscript 0 referring to this particular event. One has obtained a much more reasonable curve. This curve would be of use if one wished to estimate, a posteriori, an acceleration experienced in the Imperial Valley aftershock at a specified distance from the epicenter, for example to relate it to damage experienced at that distance.

The curve of long dashes in figure 3 is the Joyner-Boore curve, equation

Imperial Valley, 1979 Aftershock

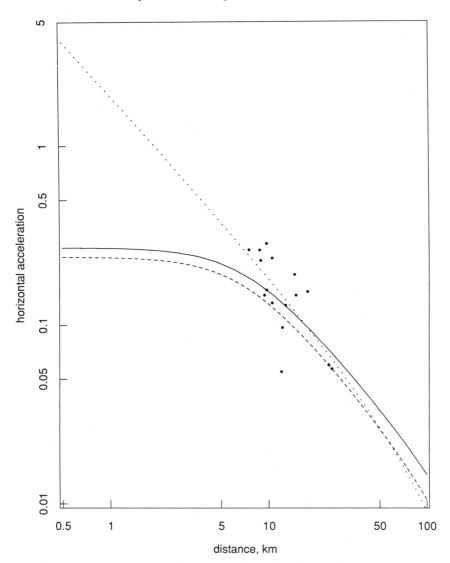

Figure 3. Points plotted are observed accelerations at the indicated distances. The curve of short dashes is the result of fitting the Joyner-Boore functional form to these data points only. The curve of long dashes is the curve developed by Joyner and Boore using the data set of twenty-three events. The solid curve is the "improved" estimate developed from expression (4) and the model (3B).

(3A). It is not inappropriate. A thing to note however is that the Joyner-Boore curve is the same for all events of the same magnitude, here $M_o = 5.0$. It does not take special note of the actual data for the event.

Figure 4 provides "improved" estimates for three other events. In each case, the improved estimates (solid curves) are plotted, as well as the Joyner-Boore (dashed) curves given by equation (3A). The general effect of borrowing strength here, and typically, has been to provide a curve lying nearer to the mass center of the points observed in the particular event of concern. Of particular note is the case of the 1957 Daly City event where but one observation was available. One could not sensibly fit a curve to that data point alone. The Joyner-Boore curve has some validity. The "improved" curve pulls the Joyner-Boore shape nearer to the available observation. In the case of the 1979 Imperial Valley event the two curves are very close to each other. This is the case with the most observations (38).

NONPARAMETRIC AND SEMIPARAMETRIC ESTIMATION

Traditionally, the formal theories of statistical estimation were directed at cases involving a finite dimensional parameter. Exceptions consisted mainly of the cases of histograms and power spectral density estimates. Another exception was provided by the various curve estimates developed by seismologists, particularly Jeffreys, to deal with travel-time data (which correspond to a problem of infinite dimensional regression analysis, albeit one with a multivalued regression function). Recently, statisticians have turned to the problem of curve estimation in broad general situations. Problems studied include: estimation of a nonparametric transformation of the dependent variable, transformations of variates involved in quantal models, and (semiparametric) situations involving both finite and infinite dimensional parameters. In some cases the estimates are based on likelihoods, are adaptive, and may be anticipated to be highly efficient. References, with discussion, to statistical aspects of this work, are Breiman and Friedman (1985) and Hastie and Tibshirani (1986). Wegman (1984) is a survey article on some aspects.

As an example of what is involved here, return to the problem of developing attenuation relationships. Above, the Joyner-Boore functional form

$$\log A = \alpha + \beta M - \log \sqrt{d^2 + \delta^2} - \gamma \sqrt{d^2 + \delta^2} \tag{5}$$

was employed. Some theory suggests the use of the log and square root transformations in such a relationship; however, the theory is not definitive, and variants of equation (5) have been proposed.

These days one can often turn to a nonparametric analysis, estimating general transformations from the data. In Brillinger and Preisler (1984), monotonic functions θ, ϕ, and ψ were estimated for a relationship

$$\theta(A) \approx \phi(M) + \psi(d)$$

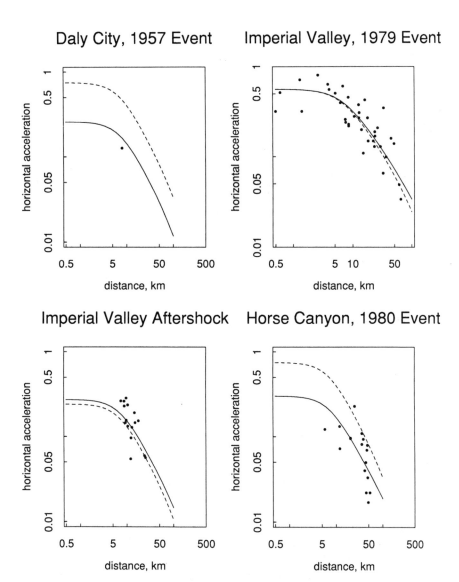

Figure 4. Observed accelerations are plotted for the four indicated events. The solid curve is the "improved" estimate, while the dashed curve is that of Joyner and Boore.

In determining such functions, critical assumptions were that the functions were smooth and the relationship additive. The formal model fit was

$$\theta(A_{ij}) = \phi(M_i) + \psi(d_{ij}) + \epsilon_i + \epsilon_{ij}$$

with i indexing an event and j a record within an event. The model was fit by a variant of the ACE procedure of Breiman and Friedman (1985). Figure 5 presents the results, namely the estimated functional transformations, θ, ϕ, ψ, for the Joyner-Boore data. The transformation of magnitude is essentially linear. The general transformation of amplitude found is nearer to a cube root than a logarithm. The transformation of distance decays in a steady manner, as might have been anticipated.

From these curves one can obtain broadly applicable, predicted values of acceleration corresponding to specified magnitudes and distances.

OTHER TOPICS

Had time and space allowed, other topics that would have been reviewed include: general procedures for uncertainty estimation (such as the jackknife and the bootstrap), dimensionality estimation procedures (such as Akaike's information criterion), adaptive techniques, modeling incomplete data (or biased sampling), regression diagnostics, influence measures, and techniques for analyzing quantal data.

A CONCLUDING REMARK

I end with a personal comment, based on a "noncollaboration" with a seismic researcher. A year or so ago, a young geologist came to see me because he had been advised that I might be able to help in computing uncertainties attached to some risk figures he had prepared. Happy to oblige was my feeling; however, as we talked, it became a highly frustrating business for both of us. As we tried to establish a common language it turned out that we really did not have an operational one. He had never taken any sort of statistics course. His problem was a hard one, so subtle techniques were called for. Sadly that is where the matter ended. Had he been at Berkeley, steady contact would have allowed a continuation, but he was not. There is no denying that there is much material that earth scientists have to be expert in. However, I would hope that statistics could be more routinely included in the list.

ACKNOWLEDGMENTS

This research was carried out with the partial support of NSF Grant MCS-8316634. It has benefited substantially from many discussions on the statis-

Estimated Transformations for Attenuation

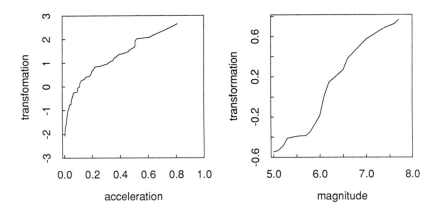

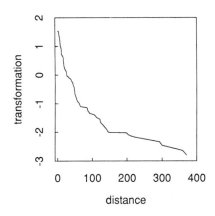

Figure 5. Estimated monotonic transformations of acceleration, magnitude, and distance providing the "best" additive relationship of acceleration in terms of magnitude and distance for the Joyner-Boore data set.

tical analysis of seismological data with Bruce Bolt and David Vere-Jones through the years. I thank them for all the help and encouragement they have provided.

I thank Bob Darragh for preparing the Smart 1 data record for analysis.

REFERENCES

Bolt, B. A., Y. B. Tsai, K. Yeh, and M. K. Hsu (1982). Earthquake strong motions recorded by a large near-source array of digital seismographs. *Earthquake Engin. Structural Dynamics*, 10: 561–573.

Breiman, L., and J. H. Friedman (1985). Estimating optimal transformations for multiple regression and correlation. *J. Am. Statist. Assoc.*, 80: 580–597.

Brillinger, D. R., and G. R. Ihaka (1982). Maximum likelihood estimation of source parameters. *Earthquake Notes*, 53: 39–40.

Brillinger, D. R., and H. K. Preisler (1984). An exploratory analysis of the Joyner-Boore attenuation data. *Bull. Seism. Soc. Amer.*, 74: 1441–1450.

Brune, J. N. (1970). Tectonic stress and the spectra of seismic shear waves from earthquakes. *J. Geophys. Res.*, 75: 4997–5009.

Dempster, A. P., D. B. Rubin, and R. K. Tsutakawa (1981). Estimation in covariance components models. *J. Am. Statist. Assoc.* 76: 341–353.

Efron, B., and C. Morris (1977). Stein's paradox in statistics. *Scientific American*, 236: 119–127.

Hastie, T., and R. Tibshirani (1986). Generalized additive models. *Statistical Sci.*, 3: 297–309.

Hudson, J. A. (1981). Mathematics for seismology. *J. Inst. Math. Appl.*, 17: 34–39.

Ihaka, G. R. (1985). Ruaumoko. Ph.D. Diss., Statistics Dept., University of California, Berkeley.

Jeffreys, H. (1939). The times of P, S and SKS, and the velocities of P and S. *Mon. Not. R. Astr. Soc. Geophys.*, Suppl. 4: 498–547.

——— (1967). Statistical methods in seismology. In K. Runcorn, ed., *International Dictionary of Geophysics*. Pergamon, London, 1398–1401.

Joyner, W. B., and D. M. Boore (1981). Peak horizontal acceleration and velocity from strong-motion records including records from the 1979 Imperial Valley, California, earthquake. *Bull. Seism. Soc. Am.*, 71: 2011–2038.

Mallows, C. M., and J. W. Tukey (1982). An overview of techniques of data analysis emphasizing its exploratory aspects. pp. 111–172 In J. Tiago de Oliveira and B. Epstein, eds., *Some Recent Advances in Statistics*. Publicacoes do II Centenario da Academia das Ciencias de Lisboa, Portugal.

Rothé, J-P. (1981). Fifty years of history of the International Association of Seismology (1901–1951). *Bull. Seism. Soc. Am.*, 71: 905–923.

Vere-Jones, D., and E. G. C. Smith (1981). Statistics in seismology. *Commun. Statist. Theor. Meth.*, A10(15): 1559–1585.

Wegman, E. J. (1984). Optimal nonparametric function estimation. *J. Statistical Planning and Inference*, 9: 375–387.

EIGHTEEN

Seismic Energy, Spectrum, and the Savage and Wood Inequality for Complex Earthquakes

Kenneth D. Smith, James N. Brune, and Keith F. Priestley

INTRODUCTION

As a result of calculations of energy radiation from a deterministic fault model, Haskell (1966), introduced a statistical model of fault rupture to better represent the irregular motions observed on strong-motion records (Housner, 1947, 1955; Thompson, 1959) and the observed generation of high-frequency energy from earthquakes with large source dimensions. An extension of this model was introduced by Aki (1967). In his model, Haskell (1966) visualized the actual faulting process as a swarm of acceleration and deceleration pulses arising from the variations in the elastic properties along the fault. These pulses propagate along the fault with some mean velocity but are highly chaotic in detail. Depending on the spatial and temporal correlation length of these pulses, this model can have a far-field displacement amplitude spectral falloff, beyond the corner frequency, proportional to ω^{-1} (spatial correlation length much larger than time correlation wavelength) or to ω^{-3} (spatial correlation length comparable to time correlation wavelength).

Approaching the problem from a different point of view, Brune (1970) introduced a fractional-stress-drop model to represent abrupt fault locking or healing, or nonuniform stress drop like a series of multiple events with parts of the fault remaining locked, in either case causing the fault to have less slip than if a uniform static stress drop over the whole fault equaled the dynamic stress drop. Aki (1972) characterized this process as a series of "rapid slips and sudden stops." In the Brune model the fractional stress drop introduces an ω^{-1} slope in the displacement amplitude spectrum beyond the corner frequency, and thus leads to considerably more high-frequency energy than for an ω^{-2} falloff model with the same seismic moment and source dimension. This effect is of great importance in determining the level of strong

279

ground motion during large earthquakes. Some more recent models of earthquakes have incorporated similar features, for example, the asperity models
of Hartzell and Brune (1977) and McGarr (1981), the barrier model of
Papageorgiou and Aki (1983), and the complex multiple-event models of
Joyner and Boore (1986) and Boatwright (1988).

The shape of the spectrum beyond the corner frequency is obviously important to calculations of the total radiated energy. The total radiated energy
is given by an integral of the square of the far-field velocity spectrum over
frequency. On the one hand, if the displacement amplitude spectrum falls off
as ω^{-2}, the velocity spectrum falls off as ω^{-1}, and the velocity-squared spectrum (proportional to energy) falls off as ω^{-2}, so that there is relatively little
contribution to the total energy beyond the corner frequency. On the other
hand, if the displacement amplitude spectrum falls off as ω^{-1}, the velocity
spectrum (and velocity-squared spectrum) is constant, and the contribution
to the total radiated energy is proportional to the bandwidth of that portion
of the spectrum.

The shape of the spectrum beyond the corner frequency is of crucial
importance to the Savage and Wood (1971) hypothesis, or inequality, in
which the apparent stress is always less than half the stress drop. Since the
apparent stress is proportional to the total radiated energy, it is obviously
directly related to the existence of an ω^{-1} band in the displacement amplitude spectrum. In fact, we show in the next section that the Savage and
Wood (1971) hypothesis is violated directly in proportion to the width of the
ω^{-1} section of the amplitude spectrum for equidimensional faults.

The empirical evidence for an ω^{-1} band in far-field earthquake displacement spectra remains subjective, but more data from high dynamic range,
broadband digital seismographs may soon provide more objective evidence.
In a recent article, Brune et al. (1986) gave some preliminary evidence from
the Anza, California, seismic array (Berger et al., 1984) that displacement
spectra from small, low-stress-drop earthquakes behave in this way, thus
offering some support for the partial-stress-drop model for small-stress-drop
events. However, the critical frequencies involved were so high that uncertainties in attenuation leave the results in question (Anderson, 1986). Similar
weak support for an ω^{-1} band is reported by Anderson and Reichle (1987) in
a study of small aftershocks of the Coalinga earthquake recorded on the Parkfield strong-motion array. One study (Tucker and Brune, 1974) of the displacement of larger earthquakes (M_L equal 4 to 5) provides evidence for a
band of ω^{-1} spectral falloff that does not suffer from the uncertainties that
affect studies of smaller earthquakes. Unfortunately Tucker and Brune had
only two observing stations so that their results are not as reliable as, for
example, would be the case for similar larger events recorded on the Anza
array, with ten high-quality digital stations.

Vassiliou and Kanamori (1982) have published results from a study of energy estimates based primarily on teleseismic body-wave pulse shapes recorded on long-period WWSSN instruments, which could not give reliable estimates of high-frequency radiated energy. However, on the basis of strong-motion records from four earthquakes they argued that most of the radiated energy in the near field was adequately represented in the far-field long-period pulse shapes. In this paper we reconsider two of these earthquakes from a different point of view and conclude that significant energy is radiated at frequencies higher than the Haskell corner frequency for the overall dimensions.

In a recent study of the 1978 Tabas, Iran, earthquake, Shoja-Taheri and Anderson (1988) estimated the radiated energy on the basis of near-field strong-motion records. They obtained results one to two orders of magnitude higher than corresponding teleseismic energy estimates based on a procedure developed by Boatwright and Choy (1986). This dramatically illustrates the importance of reconciling near-field and far-field energy estimates. Boatwright (personal communication) has questioned the Shoja-Taheri and Anderson results, in part because of this large discrepancy.

Most recently Priestley and Brune (1987) and Priestley et al. (1988) found strong evidence for the existence of ω^{-1} spectral falloffs for the Mammoth Lakes and Round Valley, California, earthquakes. It was this new evidence from the Mammoth Lakes earthquakes, and the results of a class exercise in estimating the radiated energy for various spectral shapes, that stimulated the present study.

SEISMIC ENERGY

Gutenberg and Richter (1942, 1956) proposed the first dynamic measure of the energy radiated by fault rupture. They related the radiated energy to the earthquake magnitude. Magnitude measures are usually based on information from a limited frequency band and do not adequately represent the contributions of all frequencies to the radiated energy. However, integration of the velocity-squared seismogram, in the determination of the radiated seismic energy, does incorporate the entire frequency band.

Wu (1966) derived a simple expression for determining the radiated S-wave energy, which incorporated the S-wave radiation pattern

$$E_S = \frac{24\pi}{15}\, \rho\beta R^2 (4\pi^2) \int_0^\infty |\Omega(f)\cdot f|^2 df \qquad (1)$$

where ρ is density, β is the shear wave velocity, R is the hypocentral distance, and $\Omega\,(f)$ is the spectral displacement amplitude according to Brune (1970). Hanks and Thatcher (1972) obtained an analytic solution to the integration of the velocity-squared spectrum in equation (1) for a simple displacement spectrum in which the asymptotes of the constant-amplitude, long-period level and an ω^{-2} (or f^{-2}) high-frequency falloff meet at some (sharp) corner frequency, f_0. The analytic solution of equation (1) for this approximate model is

$$E_S = \frac{256\pi^3}{15} \rho\beta R^2\Omega_0^2 f_0^3 \qquad (2)$$

where Ω_0 is the zero frequency displacement spectral amplitude. Hanks and Thatcher decreased E_S by a factor of two in order to be consistent with the energy of the Brune (1970) model. The actual difference is a factor of 1.67, resulting from the fact that the Brune displacement spectrum is rounded at the corner frequency. This illustrates the dependence of the calculation of the seismic energy on the shape of the spectrum near the corner frequency.

Using the following definition of seismic moment M_0 (Keilis-Borok, 1957)

$$M_0 = 4\pi\rho\beta^3 R\Omega_0$$

and an apparent stress (Wyss, 1970) equal to $\mu E_s/M_0$, where μ is the rigidity of the faulted crust, an expression for apparent stress for the Hanks and Thatcher (1972) asymptotic approximation to the Brune (1970) model displacement amplitude spectrum can be developed from equation (2). This expression is

$$\frac{64\pi^2}{15}\rho R\Omega_0 f_0^3 \simeq 42.1\rho R\Omega_0 f_0^3 \qquad (3)$$

Similarly, the Hanks and Thatcher energy approximation can be recast in terms of seismic moment as

$$E_S = \frac{16\pi}{15}\frac{M_0^2 f_0^3}{\mu\beta^3} \simeq 3.35\frac{M_0^2 f_0^3}{\mu\beta^3} \qquad (4)$$

These expressions are of interest because there is some evidence that actual earthquake spectra have a sharper corner than for the Brune (1970) model (Brune et al., 1979). We will discuss the relationship between spectral shape and radiated energy and the reason for selecting a sharp corner model in a later section.

Note that equation (4) was arrived at making no assumptions concerning the relationship of the corner frequency to the source geometry, and the R dependence is now only in the definition of the seismic moment. Equation (4) is similar in form to derivations of Randall (1973) and Vassiliou and Kanamori (1982).

ENERGY RESULTS FOR THE SAVAGE AND WOOD, OROWAN, AND BRUNE MODELS

Savage and Wood (1971) propose a faulting model in which the final stress level (S_0 in their terminology) is lower than the dynamic frictional stress,

S_f. This results in a static stress drop, $S - S_0$ (where S is the initial stress), greater than the dynamic stress drop, $S - S_f$. They suggest this "overshoot" results from the momentum of the moving fault block. Savage and Wood (1971) express their model in terms of energy and stress drop, specifically in the ratio of twice the apparent stress to the stress drop. In other words, if

$$\frac{\mu E_S}{M_0} < \frac{S - S_0}{2} \tag{5}$$

holds, then the final stress, S_0, is less than the frictional stress, and there is, through their argument, "overshoot" (Savage and Wood, 1971 provide a complete derivation). The apparent stress and the static stress drop are measured quantities. Evaluation of (5) depends on reliable measures of stress drop and radiated energy.

Relationship (5) is the Savage and Wood inequality. Savage and Wood determined E_S primarily using the Gutenberg-Richter magnitude-energy ($M_L - E_S$) relationship (with few exceptions) and static stress drops reported in the literature. They concluded that in most cases the apparent stress was significantly less than half the stress drop, in support of an "overshoot" model. We believe that recent, more accurate measures of energy and stress drop, as described later, do not support this conclusion.

Orowan (1960) proposed a faulting model in which the final stress, S_0, is equal to the frictional stress, S_f. In this case, the effective stress is equal to the stress drop, and the radiated seismic energy reduces to

$$E_S = \frac{S - S_0}{2} \bar{u} A \tag{6}$$

where $\bar{u}$ is the average slip, and A is the fault area. For the Orowan model (5) becomes an equality.

In the Brune (1970) model the far-field shear-wave pulse shape is determined by the effective stress, but the spectrum for the far-field pulse accounts for only forty-four percent of the Orowan energy. Most of this difference can be accounted for by the shape of the Brune spectra at the corner frequency, and this leads to a discussion of energy as a function of spectral shapes.

ENERGY AND SPECTRAL SHAPE

The radiated energy is a function of spectral shape. In particular, the shape of the spectra near the corner frequency and the high frequency spectral falloff control the measure of the radiated energy, since the displacement amplitude spectrum is multiplied by ω and then squared. As discussed earlier, Hanks and Thatcher (1972) integrated the ω^{-2} spectral shape, with a sharp corner frequency, to calculate the radiated energy. If we assume a Brune (1970, 1971) relationship between corner frequency and source dimension, do not decrease the integral by a factor of two (that is, depart from Hanks and Thatcher, 1972, in this respect), and include P-wave energy (one-eighteenth that in the S-wave; Wu, 1966), then eighty-three percent of the Orowan dislocation energy of equation (6) is accounted for. Thus, the ω^{-2} spectral shape, with a sharp corner and a Brune (1970, 1971) relationship between the corner frequency and the source dimension, accounts for nearly all of the dislocation energy.

It is clear that if the spectral falloff at high frequency is steeper than ω^{-2} there will be less radiated energy. For example, average high-frequency spectral falloffs of ω^{-3} account for only forty-eight percent of the Orowan energy, if the corner frequency and source dimension are given by the Brune (1970, 1971) model.

For circular fault rupture and a Brune (1970, 1971) relationship between corner frequency and source dimension, intermediate spectral slopes, ω^{-1} (or $\omega^{-1.5}$), beyond the inital corner frequency result in higher radiated energies than would be the case for the Orowan model, the amount depending on the bandwidth of this portion of the spectrum. Of course, high-frequency spectral falloffs of ω^{-1} cannot extend to infinite frequencies, since this would imply infinite energies.

In the Brune (1970) model, the bandwidth of the ω^{-1} portion of the spectrum is proportional to the fractional-stress-drop parameter ϵ, and thus for $\epsilon = 0.1$ the total radiated energy is about ten times as great as for $\epsilon = 1$. Similarly, if the parameter $\dfrac{K_L \beta}{K_T}$ in the Haskell (1966) model is 0.007 (spatial correlation length much longer than the time correlation wavelength; see his figure 2), then there is a broad section of the energy spectrum that contributes linearly to the total radiated energy.

For large strike-slip earthquakes, a rectangular source model is usually more appropriate, since rupture is constrained at depth and extends only in length. The spectrum for a Haskell-type rectangular rupture theoretically results in two corner frequencies (Haskell, 1966; Savage and Wood, 1971), one associated with the length and another with the width of the rupture surface, with the spectrum falling off as ω^{-1} in between. For a constant-stress-drop model, the width controls the amount of slip for a given stress drop. Energies determined by integrating the spectral shape resulting from the rectangular source geometry of the Haskell model are consistent with radiated energies that would result from the Orowan assumption. Thus, if the second (higher) corner frequency is higher than expected for the width of the fault in the Haskell (1966) spectrum, that is, the intermediate slope is longer, then the radiated energy is clearly higher than for the Orowan case, and again the Savage and Wood inequality is violated. Thus, for rectangular sources we will test whether the second corner frequency is higher than predicted for the Haskell model, and for equidimensional sources we will test whether there is any ω^{-1} section in the spectrum.

DATA

We have attempted to construct the attenuation-corrected far-field radiated energy spectrum for a number of moderate to large earthquakes. At high frequencies, we have used near-source recordings to minimize the effects of uncertainty in attenuation. At low frequencies, we have used moment constraints based on long-period seismic waves.

Although there have been great improvements in understanding the various factors that affect high-frequency near-source recordings, large uncertainties remain. Recent advances in observing high-frequency weak and strong motions, including down-hole recordings, have opened the possibility of resolving many of these questions. Although vigorous debate continues about the effects of, for example, near-site attenuation and surface-layer amplification, we attempt in this study to present preliminary evidence relating to the question of total radiated energy.

Composite acceleration spectra have been constructed for the following earthquakes: 1940 Imperial Valley (fig. 1a), 1971 San Fernando, California (fig. 1b), 1978 Tabas, Iran (fig. 2a), 1979 Coyote Lake(fig. 2b), 1979 Imperial Valley, California (fig. 3a), 1980 Mexicali Valley (fig. 3b), 1984 Morgan Hill, California (fig. 4a), 1984 Round Valley, California (fig. 4b), and 1985 Michoacan, Mexico (fig. 5). The figure captions include references to the specific acceleration records used in constructing the spectra. Although the discussion of the calculation of radiated energy has been in terms of velocity spectra, acceleration spectra are plotted in figures 1–5. This helps to emphasize the high-frequency component.

These acceleration spectra have been corrected for free-surface effects (a factor of 2), and, for the Imperial Valley events, an additional correction factor of 3.4 has been applied to account for amplification within the thick sedimentary layer (Mungia and Brune, 1984a). For the acceleration records from other sedimentary sites, a correction factor of 2 has been applied along with the free-surface correction.

For recordings very near to the source, the scaling of the energy with distance, equation (1), has to be modified. The nearest part of the ruptured area may be only several kilometers from the recording site, and the station can be considered to be in the near field. For the Michoacan event we are faced with such a source-receiver geometry and have attempted to account for it by scaling the high-frequency energy contribution appropriately. We have multiplied the integration of the velocity-squared spectrum of the near-field acceleration record by the ratio of twice the rupture area (to account for both sides of the fault) to that of a sphere of radius 10 km, and then assumed that this was the true amount of energy radiated from a point source. We then applied the R^2 distance scaling in equation (1) with respect to the distance between the recording site and the fault. The long-period level is not

1940 Imperial Valley, CA

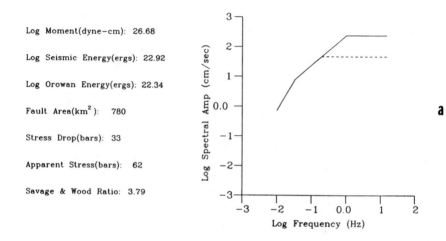

Log Moment(dyne-cm): 26.68

Log Seismic Energy(ergs): 22.92

Log Orowan Energy(ergs): 22.34

Fault Area(km^2): 780

Stress Drop(bars): 33

Apparent Stress(bars): 62

Savage & Wood Ratio: 3.79

1971 San Fernando, CA

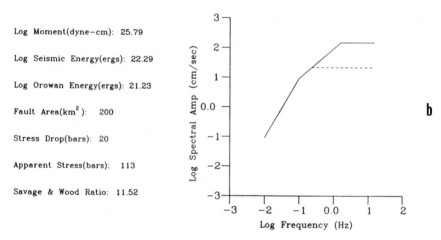

Log Moment(dyne-cm): 25.79

Log Seismic Energy(ergs): 22.29

Log Orowan Energy(ergs): 21.23

Fault Area(km^2): 200

Stress Drop(bars): 20

Apparent Stress(bars): 113

Savage & Wood Ratio: 11.52

Figure 1. (a) 1940 Imperial Valley, California. High-frequency level is determined from the corrected El Centro acceleration spectra; N-S component (Mungia and Brune, 1984b). (b) 1971 San Fernando, California. High-frequency level is determined by the corrected spectra of the transverse component of the Pacoima Dam accelerogram (Trifunac, 1972). The dashed line represents the high-frequency level that would result from a corner frequency determined from the fault width (table 1) for a Haskell (1966) model (Savage and Wood, 1971).

TABLE 1   Source Parameters for Figure 1 Earthquakes

1940 Imperial Valley, California

Origin time:	May 19, 1940	04:36:41 UTC
Epicenter:	32.7°N	115.5°W
Magnitude:	M_L 6.7	
Focal mechanism:		

Moment:		
Field observations	8.4×10^{26}	
Surface waves	4.8×10^{26}	(Reilinger, 1984)
Long-period body waves		(Doser and Kanamori, 1987)

Fault dimensions: A fault plane of length 65 km and width 12 km has been estimated from geologic information (Richter, 1958; Trifunac and Brune, 1970).

Average slip: 205 cm

Stress drop: 33 bars

1971 San Fernando, California

Origin time:	February 9, 1971	14:00:42 UTC	
Epicenter:	34.43°N	118.23.7°E	13.0 km
Magnitude:	M_L 6.4	m_b 6.2	M_S 6.5
Focal mechanism:	strike N67°W	dip 52°NE	

Moment:		
Field observations	1.5×10^{26}	(Trifunac, 1972)
Surface waves	6.3×10^{25}	(from M_S)
Long-period body waves		

Fault dimensions: From the aftershock locations and the relocation of the main shock (Allen et al., 1971; Hanks, 1974) the fault has an initial dip of 23° and steepens at depth to 52°. The dimension of the aftershock zone is approximately 23 by 14 km^2.

Average slip: 175 cm

Stress drop: 25 bars

1978 Tabas, Iran

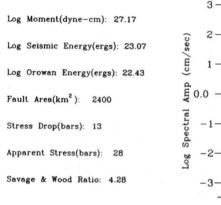

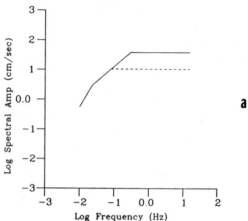

Log Moment(dyne–cm): 27.17

Log Seismic Energy(ergs): 23.07

Log Orowan Energy(ergs): 22.43

Fault Area(km^2): 2400

Stress Drop(bars): 13

Apparent Stress(bars): 28

Savage & Wood Ratio: 4.28

a

1979 Coyote Lake, CA

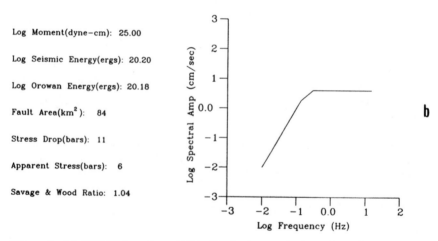

Log Moment(dyne–cm): 25.00

Log Seismic Energy(ergs): 20.20

Log Orowan Energy(ergs): 20.18

Fault Area(km^2): 84

Stress Drop(bars): 11

Apparent Stress(bars): 6

Savage & Wood Ratio: 1.04

b

Figure 2. (a) 1978 Tabas, Iran. High-frequency level is determined from the corrected Tabas acceleration spectra; transverse component (Shoja-Taheri and Anderson, 1987). (b) 1979 Coyote Lake, California. High-frequency level is determined from the corrected spectra of the Gilroy Array No. 1 accelerogram; N40°W horizontal component (Brady et al., 1980a). The dashed line represents the high-frequency level that would result from a corner frequency determined from the fault width (table 2) for a Haskell (1966) model (Savage and Wood, 1971).

TABLE 2   Source Parameters for Figure 2 Earthquakes

1978 Tabas, Iran

Origin time:	September 16, 1978	15:35:56.6 UTC	
Epicenter:	33.342°N	57.400°E	5 km
Magnitude:	M_L 7.7	m_b 6.5	M_S 7.4
Focal mechanism:	strike N28°W	dip 31°NE	

Moment:
Field observations		
Surface waves	1.5×10^{27}	(Niazi and Kanamori, 1981)
Long-period body waves	8.2×10^{26}	(Niazi and Kanamori, 1981)

Fault dimenstions: This event was associated with 85 km of discontinuous surface faulting. Extensive zones of bedding-plane slip with thrust mechanism developed in the hanging-wall block, indicating an extensive hanging-wall deformation. The width of the slip surface, based on early aftershock locations, was about 30 km (Berberian, et al., 1979; Berberian, 1982)

Average slip: 196 cm

Stress drop: 14 bars

1979 Coyote Lake, California

Origin time:	August 6, 1979	17:05:22.7 UTC	
Epicenter:	37.102°N	121.503°E	6.3 km
Magnitude:	M_L 5.9	m_b 5.4	M_S 5.7
Focal mechanism:	Strike N30°W	dip 80°NE	

Moment:
Field observations	1.6×10^{25}	(King et al., 1981)
Surface waves	1.0×10^{25}	(from M_S)
Long-period body waves		

Fault dimenstions: The fault surface outlined by aftershock locations principally consists of two right stepping *en echelon*, northwest trending, partially overlapping, nearly vertical sheets. The overlap occurs near a prominent bend in the surface trace of the Calaveras fault. Reasenberg and Ellsworth (1982) infer from the distribution of early aftershocks that slip during the main shock was confined to a 14-km-long portion of the northwest sheet between 4- and 10-km depth. Focal mechanisms and hypocentral distributions of aftershocks suggest that the main rupture surface itself is geometrically complex, with left stepping imbricate structures.

Average slip: 40 cm

Stress drop: 13 bars

1979 Imperial Valley, CA

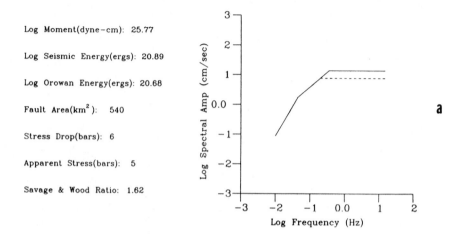

Log Moment(dyne-cm): 25.77

Log Seismic Energy(ergs): 20.89

Log Orowan Energy(ergs): 20.68

Fault Area(km^2):   540

Stress Drop(bars): 6

Apparent Stress(bars):   5

Savage & Wood Ratio: 1.62

1980 Mexicali Valley

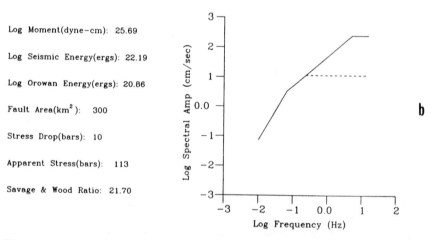

Log Moment(dyne-cm): 25.69

Log Seismic Energy(ergs): 22.19

Log Orowan Energy(ergs): 20.86

Fault Area(km^2):   300

Stress Drop(bars): 10

Apparent Stress(bars):   113

Savage & Wood Ratio: 21.70

Figure 3. (a) 1979 Imperial Valley, California. The high-frequency level is determined from the corrected spectra of the Keystone Road El Centro Array accelerogram; N140°E horizontal component (Brady et al., 1980*b*). (b) 1980 Mexicali Valley, Mexico. The high-frequency level is determined from the corrected spectra of the Victoria, Mexico accelerogram; N40°W horizontal component (Mungia and Brune, 1984*a*). The dashed line represents the high-frequency level that would result from a corner frequency determined from the fault width (table 3) for a Haskell (1966) model (Savage and Wood, 1971).

TABLE 3   Source Parameters for Figure 3 Earthquakes

1979 Imperial Valley, California

Origin time:	October 15, 1979	23:16:54.3 UTC	
Epicenter:	32.644°N	115.309°W	10 km
Magnitude:	M_L 6.6	m_b 5.7	M_S 6.9
Focal mechanism:	strike N28°W	dip 31°NE	

Moment:
  Field observations
  Surface waves 6.0×10^{25} (Kanamori and Regan, 1982)
  Long-period body waves

Fault dimenstions: Surface breaks were limited to a zone from approximately 10 to 40 km northwest of the epicenter. Aftershock epicenters occurred within an area 110 km long, from the Cerro Prieto geothermal area to the Salton Sea. During the first eight hours of the aftershock sequence, activity was concentrated in a zone approximately 45 km northwest of the epicenter (Johnson and Hutton, 1982). Aftershocks extended to approximately 12-km depth.

Average slip: 37 cm

Stress drop: 6 bars

1980 Mexicali Valley, Mexico

Origin time:	June 9, 1980	3:28:18.9 UTC	
Epicenter:	32.220°N	114.985°E	5 km
Magnitude:	M_L 6.1	m_b 5.6	M_S 6.4
Focal mechanism:			

Moment:
  Field observations
  Surface waves 5.0×10^{26} (from M_S)
  Long-period body waves

Fault dimensions: The earthquake did not cause surface rupture. The epicenter was 10 km southeast of the city of Victoria, and the most intense aftershock activity was centered 20 km northwest of Victoria, implying a rupture length of 30 km. The width of the fault is assumed to be 10 km (Anderson et al., 1987, submitted for publication).

Average slip: 56 cm

Stress drop: 11 bars

1984 Morgan Hill, CA

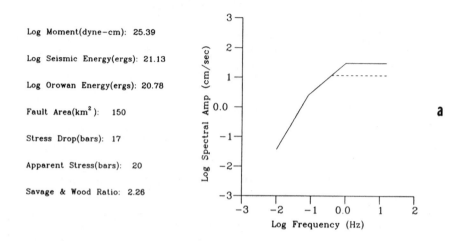

Log Moment(dyne–cm): 25.39

Log Seismic Energy(ergs): 21.13

Log Orowan Energy(ergs): 20.78

Fault Area(km^2): 150

Stress Drop(bars): 17

Apparent Stress(bars): 20

Savage & Wood Ratio: 2.26

1984 Round Valley, CA

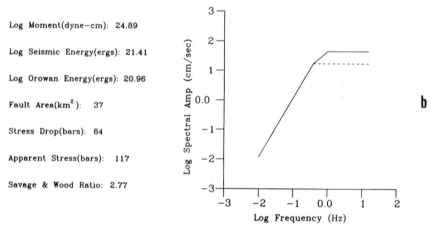

Log Moment(dyne–cm): 24.89

Log Seismic Energy(ergs): 21.41

Log Orowan Energy(ergs): 20.96

Fault Area(km^2): 37

Stress Drop(bars): 84

Apparent Stress(bars): 117

Savage & Wood Ratio: 2.77

Figure 4. (a) 1984 Morgan Hill, California. The high-frequency level is determined from the corrected spectra of the Anderson Dam–Downstream accelerogram; N40°W component (Brady et al., 1984). (b) 1984 Round Valley, California. The high-frequency level is controlled by the corrected spectra of the Paradise Lodge accelera-tion record, and the intermediate slope is determined from long-period body waves; transverse component of the acceleration record (Priestley et al., 1988). The dashed line represents the high-frequency level that would result from a corner frequency determined from the fault width (table 4) for a Haskell (1966) model (Savage and Wood, 1971).

TABLE 4   Source Parameters for the Figure 4 Earthquakes

1984 Morgan Hill, California

Origin time:	April 24, 1984	21:15:18.8 UTC	
Epicenter:	37.309°N	121.768°E	8.4 km
Magnitude:	M_L 6.2	m_b 5.7	M_S 6.1
Focal mechanism:	strike N34°W	dip 84°SE	

Moment:
Field observations		
Surface waves	2.5×10^{25}	(from M_S)
Long-period body waves	2.0×10^{25}	(Ekstrom, 1985)

Fault dimensions: From detailed aftershock locations during the early hours of the sequence with dimensions approximately 24 km by 5 km which was surrounded by aftershocks (Cockerham and Eaton, 1984). They inferred this to represent the slip surface of the main shock.

Average slip: 70 cm

Stress drop: 22 bars

1984 Round Valley, California

Origin time:	November 23, 1984	18:08:25.5 UTC	
Epicenter:	37.455°N	118.603°E	13.4 km
Magnitude:	M_L 5.8	m_b 5.4	M_S 5.7
Focal mechanism:	strike N35°E	dip 80°SE	

Moment:
Field observations	3.8×10^{24}	(Gross and Savage, 1985)
Surface waves	7.9×10^{24}	(Priesley and Smith, 1987)
Long-period body waves	6.6×10^{24}	(Priestley and Smith, 1987)

Fault dimensions: During the six hours following the main shock, aftershocks outlined approximately a 7×7 km^2 vertical plane, the center section of which was nearly free of activity. This region, which was approximately 36 km^2, was inferred to be the slip surface during the main shock by Priestley et al. (1988).

Average slip: 73 cm

Stress drop: 23 bars

1985 Michoacan, Mexico

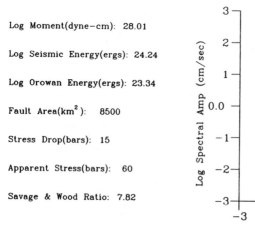

Log Moment(dyne−cm): 28.01

Log Seismic Energy(ergs): 24.24

Log Orowan Energy(ergs): 23.34

Fault Area(km^2): 8500

Stress Drop(bars): 15

Apparent Stress(bars): 60

Savage & Wood Ratio: 7.82

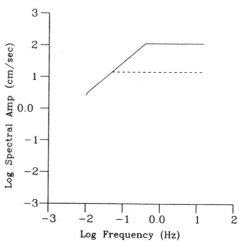

Figure 5. 1985 Michoacan, Mexico. High-frequency level controlled by the average spectra (corrected for surface amplification) of the Michoacan acceleration array; transverse components (Anderson et al., 1986). The dashed line represents the high-frequency level that would result from a corner frequency determined from the fault width (table 5) for a Haskell (1966) model (Savage and Wood, 1971).

affected, since it is determined from the seismic moment, but the high-frequency level is increased.

For all but the 1984 Round Valley, California, earthquake, a rectangular source geometry is a good approximation to the fault geometry suggested by aftershock patterns. The Coyote Lake and Morgan Hill, California, earthquakes have particularly well-recorded aftershock sequences, which allow a good constraint on the rupture extent. Tables 1−5 include references for source dimensions for all events. Note that table numbers correspond to figure numbers. In constructing the spectra, the intersection of the long-period level as determined from the seismic moment and the trend of the acceleration spectra was in all cases approximately equal to or consistent with the lowest corner frequency (representing fault length) expected for a Haskell rectangular model (Savage 1974a). Plotted in figures 1−5 is the second (higher) corner frequency for the theoretical Haskell model, which is fixed by the depth extent (width) of rupture (dashed line). This corner is fixed by the depth of fault rupture for each event as referenced in corresponding tables 1−5. The composite spectrum of the Coyote Lake earthquake indicates a second corner frequency very nearly equal to that expected for a Haskell-type rupture and is the only event in our study where this is true.

TABLE 5 Source Parameters for the Earthquake of Figure 5

1985 Michoacan, Mexico

Origin time:	September 19, 1985	13:17:49.1 UTC	
Epicenter:	18.14°N	102.71°E	16 km
Magnitude:		m_b 6.8	M_S 8.1
Focal mechanism:			

Moment:		
Field observations		
Surface waves	10.3×10^{27}	(Priestley and Masters, 1986)
Long-period body waves	3.0×10^{27}	(Priestley and Masters, 1986)

Fault dimensions: Early aftershocks located by Singh (written communications) outlined a surface area approximately 170×50 km^2 and dipping about 15° beneath the coast.

Average slip: 230 cm

Stress drop: 19 bars

The 1984 $M_L = 5.8$ Round Valley, California, earthquake is the only event for which we have created a composite spectrum that shows a circular or equidimensional rupture area. The Round Valley spectrum also has the additional constraint, at intermediate frequencies, of teleseismic body-wave amplitudes recorded at GDSN (Global Digital Seismic Network) stations, as well as long-period surface-wave information (20 s) and a near-source (<5 km epicentral distance) acceleration recording (Priestley et. al., 1988).

Also provided in figures 1–5 are the calculations of the radiated energy from equation (1), the energy from equation (6) that would result for an Orowan-type event, the stress drop as determined from the spectra, seismic moment, apparent stress, and fault area. The "Savage and Wood ratio" (that is, the ratio of twice the apparent stress to the stress drop, as shown below) is also included:

$$2\frac{\mu E_S}{M_0} / (S - S_0) \qquad (7)$$

If this number is less than 1, then by the Savage and Wood argument there would be "overshoot," the final stress level being less than the frictional stress. This number is greater than or equal to 1 for all events studied.

LARGE EARTHQUAKES AS COMPOSITES OF SMALLER EVENTS AND ENERGY IMPLICATIONS

A Savage and Wood ratio greater than 1 (violating the Savage and Wood inequality) implies that the static stress drop, $S - S_0$, is relatively low, or that a significant amount of extra energy is being radiated at intermediate and high frequencies. Individual subevents, small with respect to the total fault dimensions but with high dynamic stress drops, would contribute more to the high-frequency energy (Boatwright, 1982). For the acceleration spectra of the Michoacan earthquake, Anderson et al. (1986) termed this the "roughness" portion of the spectra, after Gusev (1983), and clearly this "roughness," or high-frequency detail, can be seen on their near-field displacement pulses (figure 6 of Anderson et al., 1986). The high velocity pulse observed on the Pacoima Dam record for the 1971 San Fernando, California, earthqauke was interpreted by Hanks (1974) as being due to an initial high-stress-drop subevent with a much higher stress drop than determined for the entire faulting event. This in part contributed to the extended intermediate slope in the spectrum of the Pacoima Dam accelerogram, but most of the energy in this range comes from later high-frequency complexities in the record.

Hartzell (1982), Papageorgiou and Aki (1983), Mungia and Brune (1984b), Joyner and Boore (1986), and Boatwright (1988), among others, have simulated the ground motion of large earthquakes using a summation of small events. Spectral shapes generated by these models relate directly to the calculation of radiated energy and apparent stress, and therefore evaluation of the Savage and Wood inequality (5). For instance, the asperity model of Boatwright (1988) incorporates an intermediate slope of ω^{-1} to $\omega^{-1.5}$ and is similar in principle, as stated by Boatwright, to the "partial stress drop model" of Brune (1970). In this model a high-stress-drop event occurs within a larger source area of lower stress drop and gives rise to a relative increase in high-frequency energy. For this case the Savage and Wood inequality is violated.

FREQUENCY-BAND LIMITATIONS AND THE CALCULATION OF RADIATED ENERGY

Vassiliou and Kanamori (1982) calculated the seismic energy radiated by large earthquakes using teleseismic body waves. They determined that most of the energy radiated by large earthquakes is below 1 to 2 Hz, therefore within the bandwidth of GDSN stations, and that this frequency band was sufficent for energy calculations. This method can be applied if the displacement spectrum falls off as ω^{-2} at frequencies higher than 1 to 2 Hz. However, for several of the events we have studied there are important energy contributions at frequencies greater than 1 Hz (spectra with extended intermediate slopes). This can be seen especially in the spectra of the 1971 San Fernando (fig. 1) and 1980 Mexicali Valley (fig. 3) earthquakes where the second (higher) corner frequencies are greater than 1 Hz.

Band limitations can also be a problem at long periods. The integration of velocity-squared time series from the acceleration record would return less reliable estimates of radiated energy if the bandwidth of the instrument is at a higher frequency than the lowest corner frequency of the far-field spectra. Therefore, composite spectra or wideband instrumentation would be required to incorporate all the details of the spectral shape, particularly for larger events with significant intermediate slopes.

DISCUSSION

We have constructed estimates of the spectra of several large to moderate size earthquakes and integrated the velocity-squared spectra to determine the radiated seismic energy. Seismic moments have been used to constrain the long-period level (flat portion of the far-field displacement spectrum), and near-source acceleration spectra have been used to constrain the high-frequency amplitudes. Approximate corrections for free-surface and sediment amplification have been made. Significant intermediate slopes of ω^{-1} apparently exist in the spectra, with consequent increases in the calculated radiated energy. These intermediate slopes extend to higher frequencies than those predicted for the Haskell (1966) model (Savage, 1974a, b). Interpreted in terms of apparent stress and static stress drop, these earthquakes violate the Savage and Wood inequality (5) and provide evidence against "overshoot" as a source model in these cases. The $M_L = 5.8$ 1984 Round Valley, California, earthquake, the only event considered here that has a more or less equidimensional rupture surface (Priestley et al., 1988), has a composite spectrum with an intermediate slope of ω^{-1}. The initial corner frequency in the Round Valley spectrum is a good approximation to the source dimension, as determined from the aftershock pattern, for a Brune (1970) type source model. This event is a good example of the calculated energy being greater than that predicted for an Orowan rupture in equation (6).

On the basis of their data, Savage and Wood (1971) suggested a ratio of twice the apparent stress to static stress drop of 0.3 as a typical value (that is, accounting for only thirty percent of the Orowan energy), and they used this result as evidence for the "overshoot" model of equation (7). Assuming a Brune (1970, 1971) model and a sharp corner frequency, we have shown that such a ratio would require steeper ($\approx \omega^{-2}$) high-frequency spectral falloffs, beginning at the corner frequency, than are generally accepted. Hanks (1979) argued against ω^{-3} high-frequency spectral falloffs. In terms of rupture models, focusing due to rupture velocity and the angle with respect to the fault normal affect the shape of the spectra over the focal sphere. However, average high-frequency spectral falloffs of ω^{-3} do not exist in the spectra of far-field S-waves for these models (Joyner and Boore, 1986; Joyner, 1984; Boatwright, 1980; Madariaga, 1973; Sato and Hirasawa, 1973).

Our spectra have typically been constructed from one acceleration record, and we have necessarily made some assumptions about the location of the station with respect to the fault, radiation pattern effects, average spectral shape, and site effects; thus, there remains considerable uncertainty in our results. The ideal situation would be to have many stations surrounding the source and be able to account for focusing, site effects, and radiation pattern to a much greater degrees.

Our purpose in this study has been to show how spectral shape relates to estimates of apparent stress, to further pursue the idea of integration of the entire spectral shape as a method of determining radiated energy, to document cases of intermediate slopes in the spectra of moderate to large earthquakes, and to use energy considerations to show that for many earthquakes the Savage and Wood (1971) inequality is violated. There is no strong evidence that the overshoot mechanism is ever operative.

ACKNOWLEGMENTS

This research was partially funded by U.S. Geological Survey research grant 14–0007–G1326.

REFERENCES

Aki, K. (1967). Scaling law of seismic spectrums. *J. Geophys. Res.*, 72: 1217–1231.

——— (1972). Scaling law of earthquake source time function. *Geophys. J. R. Astr. Soc.*, 31: 3–25.

Allen, C. R., G. R. Engen, T. C. Hanks, J. M. Nordquist, and W. R. Thatcher (1971). Main shock and larger aftershocks of the San Fernando earthquake, February 9, through March 1971. *U.S. Geol. Surv. Professional Paper 733*, 17–20.

Anderson, J. G. (1986). Implication of attenuation for studies of the earthquake source. In *Earthquake Source Mechanics*, Geophysics Monograph 37, Maurice Ewing vol. 6. American Geophysical Union, 311–318.

Anderson, J. G., P. Bodin, J. N. Brune, J. Prince, S. K. Singh, R. Quaas, and M. Onate (1986). Strong ground motion from the Michoacan, Mexico, earthquake. *Science*, 233: 1043–1049.

Anderson, J. G., J . N. Brune, and R. S. Simons (1987). The Victoria accelerogram from the June 9, 1980 Mexicali Valley, Mexico earthquake (Submitted to *Bull. Seism. Soc. Am.*).

Anderson, J. G., and M. S. Reichle (1987). Study of spectra and site effects from Coalinga aftershocks recorded near Parkfield, California (Submitted to *Bull. Seism. Soc. Am.*).

Berberian, M. (1982). Aftershock tectonics of the 1978 Tabas-e-Golshan (Iran) earthquake sequence: A documented active thin and thick skinned tectonic case. *Geophys. J. R. Astr. Soc.*, 68: 499–530.

Berberian, M., I. Asudeh, R. G. Bilham, C. H. Scholz, and C. Soufleris (1979). Mechanism of the main shock and the aftershock study of the Tabas-e-Golsham (Iran) earthquake of September 16, 1978: A preliminary report. *Bull. Seism. Soc. Am.*, 69: 1851–1859.

Berger, J., L. M. Baker, J. N. Brune, J. B. Fletcher, T. C. Hanks, and F. L. Vernon (1984). The Anza array: A high dynamic-range, broadband, digitally radiotelemetered seismic array. *Bull. Seism. Soc. Am.*, 74: 1469–1481.

Boatwright, J. (1980). A spectral theory for circular seismic sources: Simple estimates of source dimension, dynamic stress drop, and radiated energy. *Bull. Seism. Soc. Am.*, 70: 1–26.

———— (1982). A dynamic model for far field acceleration. *Bull. Seism. Soc. Am.*, 72: 1049–1068.

———— (1988). The seismic radiation from composite models of faulting. *Bull. Seism. Soc. Am.*, 78: 489–508.

Boatwright, J., and B. Choy (1986). The acceleration spectra of subduction zone earthquakes. *EOS*, 76: 310.

Brady, A. G., P. N. Mork, V. Perez, and L. D. Porter (1980*a*). Processed data from the Gilroy array and Coyote Creek records, Coyote Lake, California earthquake 6 August 1979. *U.S. Geol. Survey Open-file Report 81–42.*

Brady, A. G., V. Perez, and P. N. Mork (1980*b*). The Imperial Valley earthquake, October 15, 1979. Digitization and processing of accelerograph records. *U.S. Geol. Surv. Open-file Report 80–703*, 197–209.

Brady, A. G., R. L. Porcella, G. N. Bycroft, E. C. Etheredge, P. N. Mork, B. Silverstein, and A. F. Shakal (1984). Strong-motion results from the main shock (Morgan Hill, California) of April 24, 1984. *U.S. Geol. Surv. Open-file Report 84–498*, 18–26.

Brune, J. N. (1970). Tectonic stress and spectra of seismic shear waves from earthquakes. *J. Geophys. Res.*, 75: 4997–5009.

———— (1971). Correction. *J. Geophy. Res.*,76: 5002.

———— (1976). The physics of strong ground motion. In C. Lomnitz and E. Rosenblueth, eds., *Seismic Risk and Engineering Decisions.* 141–177, Elsevier Sci. Publ. Co., New York.

Bruen, J. N., R. J. Archuleta, and S. Hartzell (1979). Far-field S-wave spectra, corner frequencies, and pulse shapes. *J. Geophys. Res.* 84: 2262–2272.

Bruen, J. N., J. Fletcher, F. L. Vernon, L. Harr, T. Hanks, and J. Berger (1986). Low stress-drop earthquakes in light of new data from the Anza, California telemetered digital array. In *Earthquake Source Mechanics*, Geophysics Monograph 37, Maurice Ewing vol. 6. American Geophysical Union, 269–274.

Cockerham, R. S. and J. P. Eaton (1984). The April 24, 1984 Morgan Hill earthquake and its aftershocks, *California Division of Mines and Geology Special Publication 68*, 215–236.

Doser, D. I., and H. Kanamori (1987). Long-period surface waves of four western United States earthquakes recorded by the Pasadena strain meter. *Bull. Seism. Soc. Am.*, 77: 236–244.

Ekstrom, G. (1985). Centroid-moment tensor solution for the April 24, 1984, Morgan Hill, California, earthquake. *California Division of Mines and Geology Special Publication 68*, 209–214.

Gross, W. K., and J. C. Savage (1985). Deformation near the vicinity of the 1984 Round Valley, California, earthquake. *Bull. Seism. Soc. Am.*, 75: 1339–1347.

Gusev, A. A. (1983). Descriptive statistical model of earthquake source radiation and its application to an estimation of short-period strong ground motion. *Geophys. J. R. Astr. Soc.* 74: 787–808.

Gutenberg, B., and C. F. Richter (1942). Earthquake magnitude, intensity, energy, and acceleration. *Bull. Seism. Soc. Am.*, 32: 163–191.

―――― (1956). Earthquake magnitude, intensity, energy, and acceleration (second paper). *Bull. Seism. Soc. Am.*, 46: 105–145.

Hanks, T. (1974). The faulting mechanism of the San Fernando earthquake. *J. Geophys. Res.* 79: 1215–1229.

―――― (1979). b values and $\omega^{-\gamma}$ seismic source models: Implications for tectonic stress variations along active crustal fault zones and the estimation of high-frequency ground motion. *J. Geophs. Res.*, 84: 2235–2242.

Hanks, T., and W. Thatcher (1972). A graphical representation of seismic source parameters. *J. Geophys. Res.*, 77: 4393–4405.

Hartzell, S. H. (1982). Simulation of ground accelerations for the May 1980 Mammoth Lakes, California, earthquakes. *Bull. Seism. Soc. Am.*, 72: 2381–2387.

Hartzell, S. H., and J. N. Brune (1977). The Horse Canyon earthquake of August 2, 1975: Two-stage stress-release process in a strike-slip earthquake. *Bull. Seism. Soc. Am.*, 69: 1161–1173.

Haskell, N. A. (1966). Total energy spectral density of elastic wave radiation from propagating faults: Part II. A statistical source model. *Bull. Seism. Soc. Am.*, 56: 125–140.

Housner, G. W. (1947). Ground displacement computed from strong-motion accelerograms. *Bull. Seism. Soc. Am.*, 37: 299–305.

―――― (1955). Properties of strong ground motion earthquakes. *Bull. Seism. Soc. Am.*, 45: 197–218.

Johnson, C. E., and L. K. Hutton (1982). Aftershocks and preearthquake seismicity: In The Imperial Valley California, earthquake of October 15, 1979. *U.S. Geol. Survey Professional Paper 1254*, 51–54.

Joyner, W. B. (1984). A scaling law for the spectra of large earthquakes. *Bull. Seism. Soc. Am.*, 74: 1167–1188.

Joyner, W., and D. M. Boore (1986). On simulating large earthquakes by Green's function addition of smaller earthquakes. In *Earthquake Source Mechanics*, Geophysics Monograph 37, Maurice Ewing vol. 6. American Geophysical Union, 269–274.

Kanamori, H., and J. Regan (1982). Long-period surface waves: In The Imperial Valley California, earthquake of October 15, 1979. *U.S. Geol. Surv. Professional Paper 1254*, 55–58.

King, N. E., J. C. Savage, M. Lisowski, and W. H. Prescott (1981). Preseismic and coseismic deformation associated with the Coyote Lake, California, earthquake. *J. Geophys. Res.*, 86: 892–898.

Keilis-Borok, V. I. (1957). Investigation of the mechanism of earthquakes. *Tr. Inst.*

Geofis. Akad. Nauk, SSSR, 40 (in Russian). (Engl. transl., *Sov. Res. Geophys. Ser.,* 4, 1960).

Madariaga, R. (1976). Dynamics of an expanding circular fault. *Bull. Seism. Soc. Am.,* 66: 639–666.

McGarr, A. (1981). Analysis of peak ground motion in terms of a model of inhomogeneous faulting. *J. Geophys. Res.,* 86: 3901–3912.

Mungia, L., and J. N. Brune (1984a). High stress drop events in the Victoria, Baja California, earthquake swarm of March 1978. *Geophys. J. R. Astr. Soc.* 79: 725–752. 752.

———. (1984b). Simulations of strong ground motion for earthquakes in the Mexicali-Imperial Valley region. *Geophys. J. R. Astr. Soc.,* 79: 747–771.

Niazi, M., and H. Kanamori (1981). Source parameters of the 1978 Tabas and 1979 Qainat, Iran, earthquakes from long-period surface waves. *Bull. Seism. Soc. Am.,* 71: 1201–1213.

Orowan, E. (1960). Mechanism of seismic faulting. *Geol. Soc. Am. Memoir,* 79: 323–345.

Papageorgiou, A. S., and Aki (1983). A specific barrier model for the quantitative description of inhomogeneous faulting and the prediction of strong ground motion. Part. I. Description of the model. Part II. Applications of the model. *Bull. Seism. Soc. Am.,* 73: 693–722, 953–978.

Priestley, K. F., and J. N. Brune (1987). Spectral scaling for the Mammoth Lakes, California, earthquakes (submitted to *Bull. Seism. Soc. Am.*).

Priestley, K. F., and T. G. Masters (1986). Source mechanism of the September 19, 1985, Michoacan earthquake and its implications. *Geophysical Research Letters,* 13: 601–604.

Priestley, K. F., K. D. Smith, and R. S. Cockerham (1988). The 1984 Round Valley, California earthquake sequence (accepted by *Geophys. J. R. Astro. Soc.*).

Randall, M. J. (1973). The spectral theory of seismic sources. *Bull. Seism. Soc. Am.,* 63: 1133–1144.

Reasenberg, P., and W. L. Ellsworth (1982). Aftershocks of the Coyote Lake, California, earthquake of August 6, 1979: A detailed study. *J. Geophys. Res.,* 87: 10, 637–10, 655.

Reilinger, R. (1984). Coseismic and post seismic vertical movements associated with the 1940 M 7.1 Imperial Valley, California, earthquake. *J. Geophys. Res.,* 89: 4531–4538.

Richter, C. H. (1958). *Elementary Seismology.* W. H. Freeman, San Francisco, California.

Sato, T., and T. Hirasawa (1973). Body wave spectra from propagating shear cracks. *J. Physics Earth,* 21: 415–431.

Savage, J. C. (1974a). Relation of corner frequency to fault dimensions. *J. Geophys. Res.* 77: 3788–3795.

———. (1974b). Relation between P- and S-wave corner frequencies in the seismic spectrum. *Bull. Seism. Soc. Am.,* 64: 1621–1627.

Savage, J. C., and M. D. Wood (1971). The relation between apparent stress and stress drop. *Bull. Seism. Soc. Am.,* 61: 1381–1386.

Shoja-Taheri, J., and J. G. Anderson (1988). The 1978 Tabas, Iran, earthquake: An interpretation of strong motion records. *Bull. Seism. Soc. Am.,* 78: 142–171.

Thompson, W. T. (1959). Spectral aspects of earthquakes. *Bull. Seism. Soc. Am.*, 49: 91–98.

Trifunac, M. D. (1972). Stress estimates for the San Fernando, California, earthquake of February 9, 1971: Main event and thirteen aftershocks. *Bull. Seism. Soc. Am.*, 62: 721–749.

Trifunac, M. D., and J. N. Brune (1970). Complexity of energy release during the Imperial Valley, California earthquake of 1940. *Bull. Seism. Soc. Am.*, 60: 137–160.

Tucker, B. E., and J. N. Brune (1974). Source mechanisms and $m_b - M_S$ of aftershocks of the San Fernando earthquake. *Geophys. J. R. Astro. Soc.*, 49: 371–426.

Vassiliou, M. S., and H. Kanamori (1982). The energy released in earthquakes. *Bull. Seism. Soc. Am.*, 72: 371–387.

Wu, F. T. (1966). Lower limit of the total energy of earthquakes and partitioning of energy among seismic waves. Ph.D. Diss., California Institute of Technology.

Wyss, M. (1970). Stress estimates of South American shallow and deep earthquakes. *J. Geophys. Res.*, 75: 1529–1544.

NINETEEN

Constraints from Seismograms on the Physical Characteristics of Explosions

Brian W. Stump

INTRODUCTION

The waveforms generated by explosions contain information about both the physical properties of the explosion and the surrounding geologic material (Minster, 1985; Bache, 1982; Massé, 1981; Rodean, 1981). This paper presents a short review of these waveforms and some of their implications. The particular subjects discussed are: (1) the physical characterization of contained explosions; (2) the effect of source depth on characterization, in particular relating the motion from a near-surface burst to a fully contained explosion; (3) the relative importance and separation of stochastic and deterministic wave propagation effects; and (4) some simple experiments to check linear superposition.

Ground motions from explosions have been recorded from the very near nonlinear regime out to teleseismic distances (figure 1). At the closest ranges the material surrounding the explosion responds nonlinearly, with accelerations of hundreds or thousands of gs and rise times on the order of milliseconds (Rodean, 1981). In the near-field linear region one observes fairly simple seismograms, with durations on the order of seconds and accelerations generally less than 1 g (Stump and Johnson, 1984; Stump and Reinke, 1987; Vidale and Helmberger, 1987). Typical ranges for the near-field linear region of small chemical explosions (tens of pounds) are tens of meters, while for large nuclear explosions they are on the order of several kilometers. At regional distances the seismogram duration is tens to hundreds of seconds and characterized by P_n, P_g, S, R_g, and L_g phases (Pomeroy et al., 1982). Finally, at teleseismic distances the body waves have frequencies under 1 Hz, while long-period surface waves are also observed (Massé, 1981, Bache, 1982).

WAVEFORMS FROM CONTAINED EXPLOSIONS

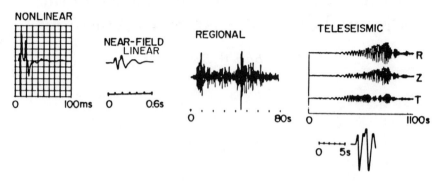

Figure 1. Schematic representation of explosion waveforms ranging from the close-in nonlinear regime out to teleseismic distances.

The work discussed in this paper focuses upon the near-field linear region. There are three reasons for this emphasis: (1) propagation path effects can be minimized; (2) a broadband characterization of the source can be attempted; and (3) the length scale of the problem allows the formulation and implementation of carefully designed experiments.

CONTAINED EXPLOSIONS

Two sets of data from contained explosions are investigated. The first is from a small-scale chemical explosion (256 lb) detonated at a depth of 11.5 m in alluvium (acronym CHEAT). The second is from a nuclear explosion with an announced yield of less than 20 kton, also detonated in alluvium, at a depth of 273 m (acronym COALORA). The physical processes that accompany these events include: (1) initial cavity formation and subsequent simple Sharpe (1942) pressure-pulse generation dependent on material type; (2) tensile failure of near-surface layers (spallation), which repartitions the initial spherical energy radiation from the source (Viecelli, 1973; Day et al., 1983); (3) tectonic strain release or motion driven along planes of weakness, which leads to complex radiation and transverse motions (Massé, 1981); and (4) cavity collapse (McEvilly and Peppin, 1972).

The vertical and radial accelerograms recorded at 50 m from the chemical explosion are shown in figure 2. The amplitudes and waveshapes as a function of azimuth around the source support a fair amount of azimuthal symmetry. Such data are replicated by simple isotropic cavity models. In contrast, transverse motions from the same source are as displayed in figure 3. Although these waveforms have peak amplitudes on the order of only four-

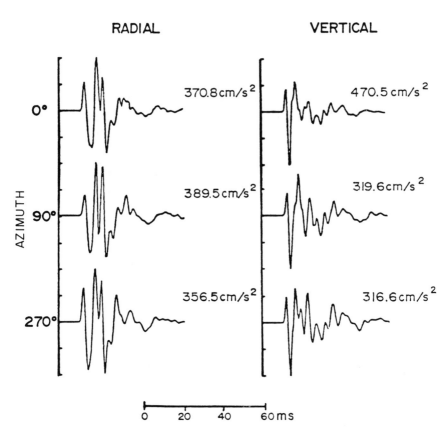

Figure 2. Vertical and radial accelerations from the chemical explosion CHEAT at azimuths ranging from 0 to 270°.

teen to forty-seven percent of the radial acceleration at 50 m, they indicate a source or propagation effect that leads to azimuthally variable radiation.

Similar observations are made for the nuclear explosion as indicated in figure 4 where the vertical, radial, and transverse displacements from COALORA are displayed. Even though the observation range is an order of magnitude greater than that from the chemical explosion (549 m compared to 50 m), the radial and vertical motions are similar in shape and amplitude. The transverse motions are generally smaller in amplitude, have higher frequency, and exhibit considerable azimuthal variation. Spectral estimates of these same data illustrate further azmuthal differences in the motions (fig. 5).

CHEAT TRANSVERSE

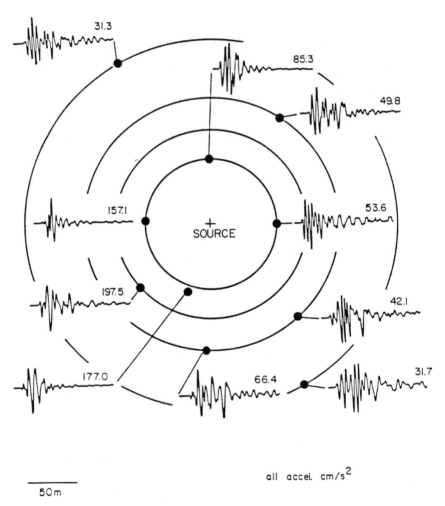

all accel. cm/s^2

50m

Figure 3. Transverse accelerations from the chemical explosion CHEAT.

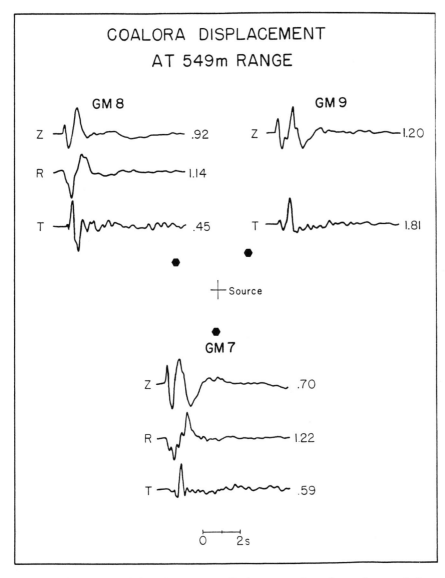

Figure 4. Vertical, radial, and transverse displacements from the nuclear explosion COALORA.

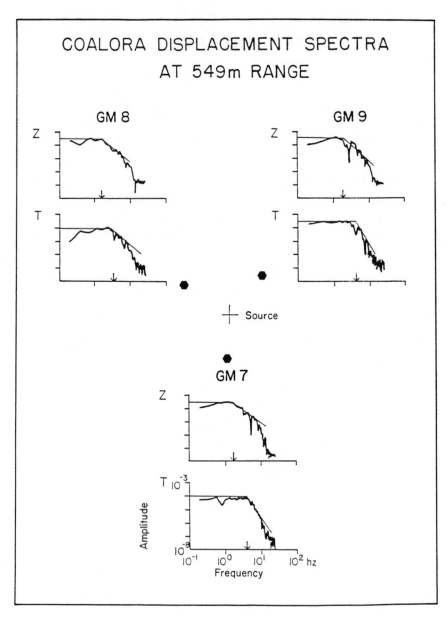

Figure 5. Displacement spectra from COALORA. Arrows indicate approximate spectral corner frequency.

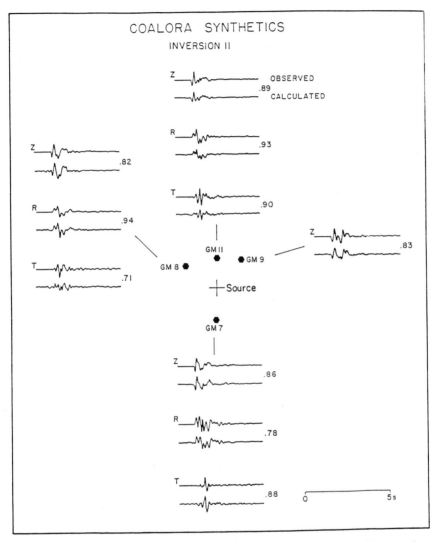

Figure 6. Observed and modeled velocity waveforms from COALORA. The correlation coefficents are given to the right of each waveform pair.

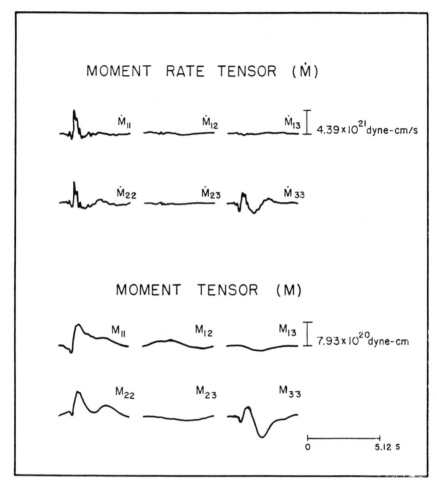

Figure 7. The moment and moment rate tensors for COALORA. Only six elements of the moment tensor are given since the second rank tensor is symmetric.

The vertical spectra are characterized by a 1.5-Hz corner frequency, f^{-2} high-frequency decay, and a long-period level at least three times greater than the transverse long-period level. The transverse motions also have a considerably higher-corner frequency (4 Hz) and f^{-3} high-frequency decay.

In order to separate the source and propagation effects, an inverse modeling exercise was undertaken in which the source is represented as a set of force-moments, M_{ij}, while the propagation effects are accounted for by a set of Green's functions appropriate to the medium, $G_{ni,j}$. Then,

$$U_n = G_{ni,j}\, M_{ij}$$

an equation that holds in the frequency domain. The modeling exercise consists of computing a set of Green's functions and then solving for the source, given an observational data set. In matrix form this result becomes

$$\mathbf{M} = \mathbf{G}^{-1} \, U$$

The ability of this procedure to model the observations from the nuclear explosion COALORA is summarized in figure 6. Both peak amplitudes and waveshapes are well replicated as indicated by the average radial correlation coefficent of 0.88, vertical correlation coefficent of 0.85, and transverse correlation coefficent of 0.83.

The force-moment and force-moment rate tensor from this modeling exercise are summarized in figure 7 (COALORA), in which the 1 and 2 indices represent the horizontal coordinates, and the 3 index represents the vertical coordinate. Three attributes are noted: (1) the diagonal elements of the force-moment tensor, the isotropic source, dominate; (2) the deviatoric components are an order of magnitude smaller than the diagonal elements; and (3) the M_{33} component, which represents the force couple in the vertical direction, has a secondary long-period component attributable to spallation, the tensile failure of near-surface layers.

A similar result came from the inverse modeling of CHEAT (figure 8). The source is primarily isotropic, followed by the longer-period spallation contribution as indicated on the M_{33} component. The source time functions for the COALORA and CHEAT explosions are remarkably similar except for the order of magnitude change in time scale.

The resulting source of the radiated near-field waveforms is dominated by the isotropic component followed by spallation that repartitions the energy. The relative importance of spallation on the M_{33} component is further supported by studies of synthetic data that include spallation contributions (Stump, 1987). The deviatoric moments are a factor of ten smaller, with indication of a higher-frequency content.

SOURCE DEPTH EFFECTS AND ENERGY COUPLING

Taking advantage of the small-scale characteristic of the near-field experiments, a set of chemical explosion tests were designed to quantify the effect of source depth on radiated seismic energy. Sources (256-lb TNT spheres) were placed at depths varying from 1.84 to 11.5 m in alluvium. Waveforms were recorded in the 17–228-m range.

Radial and vertical velocity records for all source depths at the 228-m range are shown in figure 9. The initial body waves are identified by the rectilinear motion. Surface waves yield clear retrograde elliptical motion, with the vertical (dashed line) following the radial (solid line) motion. Qual-

NEAR-FIELD MOMENT TENSORS

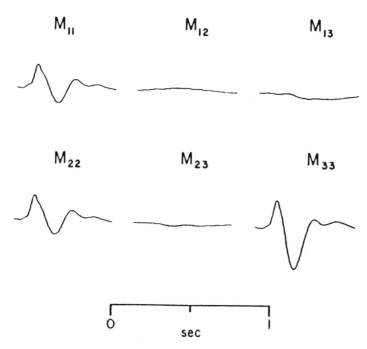

Figure 8. The moment tensor for CHEAT. All moments are relative to the M_{33} component, which has a peak of 5.10×10^{16} dyne-cm.

itatively, one can observe the rise in body-wave amplitudes relative to the surface waves with increasing source depth.

The particle motions are used to separate the body and surface waves, as discussed above. Once this separation is completed, the data are used to quantify the relative and absolute coupling of seismic energy into body and surface waves (Flynn and Stump, 1987). The body and surface waves are corrected for geometrical spreading and attenuation. Once this process is completed, the energy flux is calculated in the time or frequency domain

$$F = \rho C \int [v(t)]^2 dt$$

where F is the energy flux (ergs/cm^2), ρ is density (g/cm^3), C is the propagation velocity (cm/s), and $v(t)$ is the recorded particle velocity (cm/s). The total energy in the body waves observed at the range, R, becomes

$$E = 4\pi R^2 F$$

RADIAL and VERTICAL VELOCITY
at 228 meters

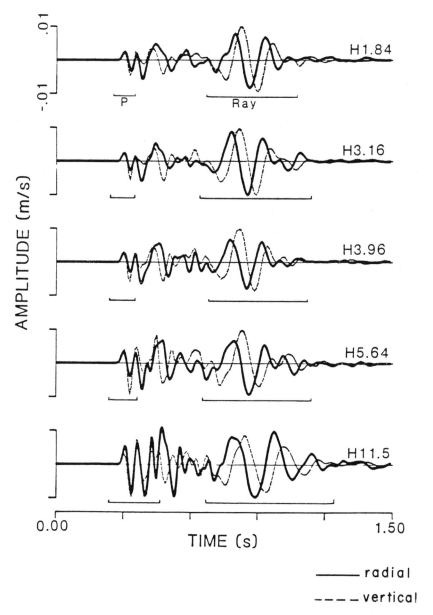

Figure 9. Velocity waveforms observed at 228 m from 256-lb explosions at 1.84 to 11.5 m depth. Solid lines are the radial motion, dashed lines the vertical. *H* is the source depth.

Similarly, the total energy in the surface wave becomes

$$E = 2\pi RhF$$

where h is the effective depth of penetration for the surface wave.

These procedures are used to develop the percent total energy in body and surface waves for all source depths (fig. 10). These estimates were made for observation ranges of 17, 37, 73, and 228 m, yielding consistent results. For the shallowest source, 1.84 m, sixty percent of the energy is in the Rayleigh wave, while forty percent is in the P-wave. The percentage of energy in the P-wave increases with increasing source depth until, at 11.5 m, eighty percent of the seismic energy is in the body (P-)waves and twenty percent in the

P and RAYLEIGH PERCENT OF TOTAL ENERGY vs DEPTH

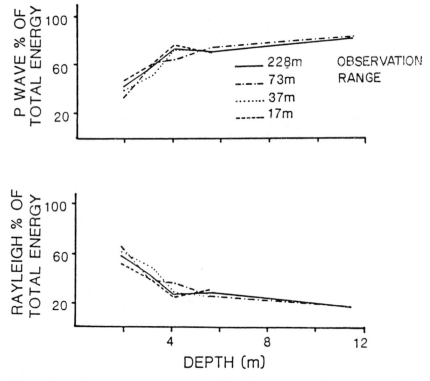

Figure 10. Percent P- and Rayleigh energy as a function of source depth at four ranges. All charges are 256 lb.

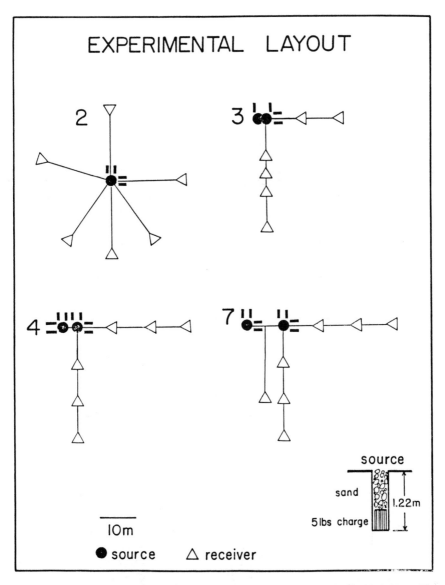

Figure 11. The experimental layout for a series of 5-lb sources designed to quantify stochastic and deterministic propagation effects and check superposition between sources (acronym ARTS). Solid lines represent the edges of the crater following the explosion.

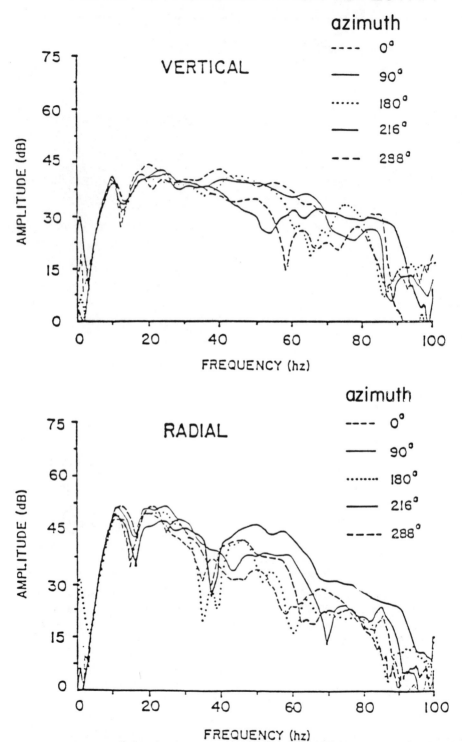

Figure 12. Acceleration spectra from ARTS 2.

EVENT 4 VERTICAL

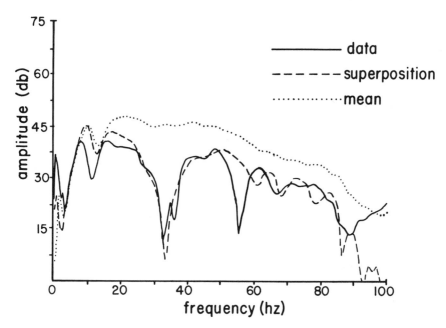

Figure 13. Data and single-burst predictions from the two-burst ARTS 4. The two 5-lb charges were 4 m apart. The superposition waveform represents the results for two single-burst waveforms delayed in time to simulate the 4-m separation between charges. The mean estimate is for two charges no time delay.

surface (Rayleigh) waves. Since the chemical energy in the explosion is known, absolute estimates of seismic energy are obtainable. The efficiency of energy coupling varies from 0.7 percent for the 1.84-m source to three percent for the 11.5-m source.

STOCHASTIC AND DETERMINISTIC PROPAGATION

All propagation-path effects cannot be modeled deterministically. The random nature of geological media makes a statistical characterization more appropriate for some studies. A final set of experiments was designed to separate deterministic and stochastic propagation effects and to test for linear superposition of motions from multiple sources.

Figure 11 gives the experimental layout for a series of 5-lb sources designed to characterized the single-burst environment (event 2) and check for superposition in the plane of symmetry between the two charges and in the plane of the two charges (events 3, 4, 7). The radial and vertical acceleration spectra from event 2 (all gauges at 20 m) are given in figure 12. The wave-forms themselves, their spectra, and coherence estimates all indicate little variation in waveforms for frequences between 3 and 35 Hz. Above 35 Hz as much as a 15-dB variation in spectral levels is observed. The alluvial test site where these experiments were conducted has intermittent caliche beds. These caliche lenses are 0.5 to 1.5 m in length and have twice the P-wave velocity of the surrounding alluvium. Simple single-scattering calculations indicate that the large variation in amplitude above 35 Hz can be explained by wave-field interactions with the caliche beds.

Taking the 3–35-Hz band as deterministic, one can use the ensemble single-source estimate to check superposition in the two-burst data. Figure 13 gives the observed and predicted spectra from event 4 (4-m source separa-tion) in the plane of the two sources. The observations and predictions sup-port linear superposition to about 40 Hz, including the interference hole at 32 Hz.

CONCLUSIONS

A number of physical models of explosive sources have been shown, along with the supporting observational data. These representations include par-tially and fully contained explosions. Both chemical and nuclear sources are shown to generate waveforms by similar mechanisms, including spallation. Energy partitioning between body and surface waves is found to be strongly influenced by source depth. Absolute coupling values for a suite of chemical explosions in alluvium range from 0.7 to 3.0 percent. Finally, it is found that the deterministic and stochastic wave-propagation effects must be quantified prior to in-situ experimental superposition checks.

REFERENCES

Bache, T. C. (1982). Estimating the yield of underground nuclear explosion. *Bull. Seism. Soc. Am.*, 72: S131–S168.

Day, S. M., N. Rimer, and J. T. Cherry (1983). Surface waves from underground explosions with spall: Analysis of elastic and nonlinear source models. *Bull. Seism. Soc. Am.*, 73: 247–264.

Flynn, E. C., and B. W. Stump (1987). Effects of source depth on near source seismo-grams. *J. Geophys. Res.* (to appear).

Massé, R. P. (1981). Review of seismic source models for underground nuclear explo-sions. *Bull. Seism. Soc. Am.*, 71: 1249–1268.

McEvilly, T. V., and W. A. Peppin (1972). Source characteristics of earthquakes, explosions, and afterevents. *Geophys. J. R. Astr. Soc.*, 31: 67–82.

Minster, B. J. (1985). Twenty-five years of source theory. In Ann U. Kerr, ed., *The Vela Program—A Twenty-five Year Review of Basic Research.* Executive Graphic Ser-vices, Defense Advanced Research Projects Agency, Rosslyn, Virginia, 67–116.

Pomeroy, P. W., W. J. Best, and T. V. McEvilly (1982). Test ban treaty verification with regional data—A review. *Bull. Seism. Soc. Am.*, 72: S829–S129.

Rodean, H. C. (1981). Inelastic processes in seismic wave generation by underground explosions. In E. S. Husebye and S. Mykkeltveit, eds., *Identification of Seismic Sources—Earthquake or Underground Explosion*. D. Reidel, Dordrecht, The Netherlands, 97–190.

Sharpe, J. A. (1942). The production of elastic waves by explosive pressures. I. Theory and empirical field observations. *Geophysics*, 7: 144–154.

Stump. B. W. (1987). Resolution of complex explosive source functions in the frequency domain. *Geophys. J. R. Astr. Soc.* (to appear).

Stump, B. W., and L. R. Johnson (1984). Near-field source characterization of contained nuclear explosion in tuff. *Bull. Seism. Soc. Am.*, 74: 1–26.

Stump, B. W., and R. E. Reinke (1987). Experimental seismology: In situ source experiments. *Bull. Seism. Soc. Am.*, 77: 1295–1311.

Vidale, J. E., and D. V. Helmberger (1987). Path effects in strong motion seismology. In Bruce A. Bolt, ed., *Seismic Strong Motion Synthesis*. Academic Press, Orlando, Florida.

Viecelli, J. A. (1973). Spallation and the generation of surface waves by an underground explosion. *J. Geophys. Res.*, 78: 2475–2487.

TWENTY

Studies Using Global Seismological Networks

Lane R. Johnson

INTRODUCTION

The primary purpose of this paper is to show how data collected by a network of seismographic stations can be used to make inferences about the velocity structure of the Earth. The structure of the entire Earth is considered, requiring the use of a global network of seismographic stations. Seismic travel times provide the basic observational data for the study. The reasons for this choice include the fact that large amounts of such data are readily available, so that a reasonably complete sampling of the Earth can be achieved, and the fact that short-period body waves sample the Earth in a localized manner and have relatively high resolution compared to other types of seismic waves.

GLOBAL NETWORKS

Almost from the beginning of seismology as a science, seismologists have been aware of the advantages of using networks of stations to acquire information about the Earth. The basic concept is that when ground-motion data acquired from a number of different sampling points on the surface of the Earth are processed collectively, a variety of analysis procedures can be used, which is not possible when the data from the different sampling points are processed individually. In general, the dimensions of the network should span the region of study, and the resolution that can be achieved is directly related to the spacing between individual stations of the network. Thus, a study of the velocity structure of the entire Earth requires a global network of seismological stations. Fortunately, such a network is available. Over 1,000 seismographic stations scattered over the surface of the Earth are in continuous operation.

A number of organization, such as the National Earthquake Information Center (NEIC) of the U.S. Geological Survey and the International Seismological Centre (ISC) in Newbury, England, provide the very important services of collecting, organizing, and distributing the information recorded by individual seismographic stations around the globe. These organizations perform a variety of functions, including the collection of basic readings taken from seismograms at most of the world's seismographic stations, the association of these data with individual earthquakes, the location of the earthquakes, the determination of magnitudes, and the publication of the raw data and the results of the analysis. Because of the data management services provided by these organizations it is possible to treat all the seismographic stations on the Earth as a single network.

THE TAU METHOD OF ANALYSIS

The objective of tau analysis is to extract information about the velocity structure of the Earth from travel-time data gathered by a global network. For an Earth in which the velocity $v(r)$ depends only upon the radial coordinate r, the time and distance along a ray path from source to receiver are given by the parametric equations

$$T(p) = 2 \int_{r_p}^{R} r^2 v^{-2} (r^2 v^{-2} - p^2)^{-1/2} \frac{dr}{r} \tag{1}$$

$$\Delta(p) = 2 \int_{r_p}^{R} p(r^2 v^{-2} - p^2)^{-1/2} \frac{dr}{r} \tag{2}$$

where p is the horizontal slowness of the ray, R is the radius of the Earth, and r_p is the radius of the deepest point of the ray. Equations (1) and (2) can be combined through a Legendre transformation to obtain the quantity known as tau in seismology:

$$\tau(p) = T(p) - p\Delta(p) = 2 \int_{r_p}^{R} (r^2 v^{-2} - p^2)^{1/2} \frac{dr}{r} \tag{3}$$

A simple geometrical interpretation of $\tau(p)$ is that it represents the zero-distance intercept time of the tangent to the travel-time curve having slope p. The function $\tau(p)$ has some special properties that have always been useful in the forward problem of seismic travel times (see for example Rudzki, 1898), but these special properties took on added importance when the uniqueness of the inverse problem was analyzed in detail (Gerver and Markushevitch, 1966, 1967; Johnson and Gilbert, 1972; McMechan and Wiggins, 1972; Bessonova et al., 1974, 1976).

The pair of variables $T(p)$ and $\Delta(p)$ are the ones most commonly used in seismology to characterize travel-time data because this information can be extracted directly from seismograms at a single station, although the information is available in the form $T(\Delta)$, which leaves the slowness p unspecified. The single variable $\tau(p)$ contains all the information of $T(p)$ and $\Delta(p)$ but cannot be estimated directly from seismograms at a single station. However, given data from a network of stations, the situation is quite different. It can be shown directly from equation (3) that

$$\tau' \equiv \frac{d}{dp}\tau(p) = -\Delta(p) \tag{4}$$

This leads to a Clairaut-type differential equation for τ

$$p\tau' - \tau + T(-\tau') = 0 \tag{5}$$

whose solutions have been thoroughly studied (Courant and Hilbert, 1962). Bessonova et al. (1974, 1976) show how the singular solution of this equation can be obtained by graphical means and also point out that, even when observational errors are present in both T and Δ, the uncertaintly in τ has a simple statistical interpretation. Thus, given $T(\Delta)$ observations from a network of stations, there exists a stable and simple process for obtaining direct estimates of $\tau(p)$ and its statistical uncertainty. The quatity $\tau(p)$ has several other advantages that are useful in the analysis of travel-time data. For instance, it is a monotonic function of p, which is not true of either $T(p)$ or $\Delta(p)$, and is continous except at values of p corresponding to low-velocity zones. In addition, the inverse problem of converting $\tau(p)$ into $v(r)$ has been solved by Bessonova et al. (1976) in such a way that uncertainties in $\tau(p)$ can be mapped directly into uncertainties in $v(r)$.

DATA

The travel times for this study were obtained from the ISC *Bulletins*. This is a large and homogeneous catalog that has been used in a wide variety of different seismological studies. In their raw form these data can contain a variety of errors, including errors in source location, errors in association, errors in phase identification, errors in clocks, errors in reading times, and errors in recording times. While the existence of these errors does complicate the analysis procedure, it does not preclude the extraction of valuable information about the Earth from these catalogs. In a series of studies (Lee and Johnson, 1984a, 1984b; Johnson and Lee, 1985; Tralli and Johnson, 1986a, b, c) a fairly comprehensive set of techniques has been developed for dealing with the problems associated with this type of bulletin data. An important part of the analysis is the application of the uniform reduction method (Jeffreys, 1961; Buland, 1986) to separate a primary central distribution of the data from a background of anomalous outliers. The primary distribution is then checked for normality with both the chi-squared and Kolmogorov-

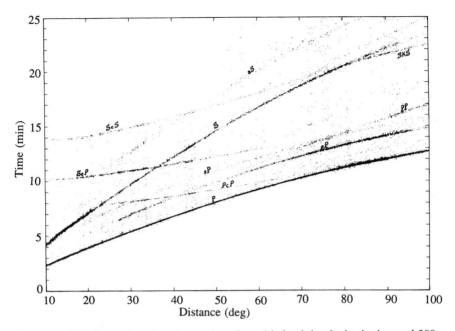

Figure 1. ISC travel-time data for earthquakes with focal depths in the interval 500 to 550 km. An approximate depth correction has been applied to place all of the focal depths at 525 km. About 38,000 data points are contained in this plot.

Smirnoff tests. With the careful application of such procedures, it is possible to routinely obtain sample standard errors for a single observation of less than 1 s for P-waves and 3 s for S-waves. Given the large amount of data available in these catalogs, this degree of scatter is definitely small enough to allow meaningful inferences about Earth structure. So far, the ISC *Bulletin* data for the time interval 1971–1981 have been analyzed, and both quantity and quality of the data have been found to improve with time.

In a typical year close to a million different phases are reported to the ISC, so several million travel-time observations are available for the 1971–1981 period. An indication of the quality of these data can be found in figure 1, a plot of travel times from sources in a 50-km depth interval centered at a depth of 525 km. The scale of this plot does not do justice to the details contained in these data, but a large number of body-wave phases are well defined and have been labeled. There is no difficulty in constructing tau functions for most of the phases shown on this plot.

Another example of the raw travel-time data is shown in figure 2. This shows travel times of P-waves that have sampled the Earth's core. The conversion of these travel times to tau estimates using the method of Bessonova et al. (1976) is shown in figure 3. Values of tau and its uncertainty are

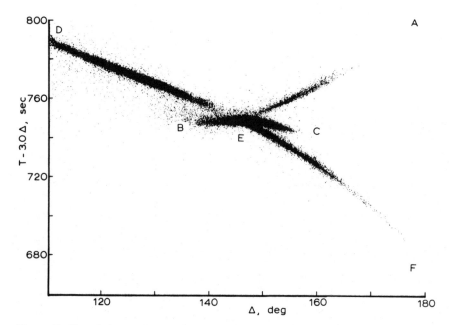

Figure 2. Travel times of approximately 60,000 P-waves from shallow sources that have penetrated the Earth's core. Letters denote the end points of the various branches of the travel-time curve according to conventional notation.

obtained simply by estimating the mean value of the reduced travel times and its standard error at the extremums. In this example, the extremums are maximums for the prograde BC and EF branches of the core travel-time curve and a minimum for the AB retrograde branch. The 99.9-percent confidence intervals for these tau estimates were about 0.1 s, which represents a precision approaching 1 part in 10^4.

AVERAGE STRUCTURE

The travel-time data for direct P- and S-waves in the mantle and PKP- and SKS-waves in the core were analyzed according to the method described in the previous two sections. The resulting tau estimates were then inverted using the method of Bessonova et al. (1976) to obtain velocity models for P- and S-waves in the mantle and P-waves in the core. Details of the analysis procedures can be found in Lee and Johnson (1984b), Tralli and Johnson (1986a), and Johnson and Lee (1985). In this part of the study, travel times from the entire Earth were lumped together and treated as one homogeneous data set, so the velocity models are a function only of the radial dimension and represent lateral averages of the Earth at any given radius. A more expli-

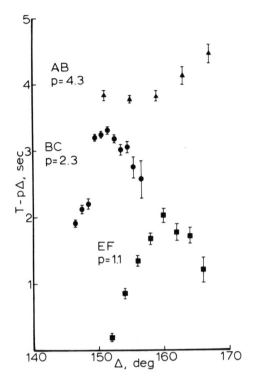

Figure 3. Reduced travel times obtained from the data of figure 2. Three different values of slowness are shown for three different branches of the travel-time curve in the core. The time scale is relative, and the error bars represent 95-percent confidence intervals.

cit type of lateral averaging is described in Tralli and Johnson (1986a) where a weighting function proportional to the fractional surface area was used in computing the average.

Figure 4 shows the laterally averaged P- and S-wave velocities for the mantle. As can be seen in the figure, the results agree very well with the PREM model (Dziewonski and Anderson, 1981). The primary difference involves the low-velocity zone, which cannot be resolved by the travel-time data used in this type of study. Figure 5 shows similar results for the Earth's core, and the agreement with the PREM model is again quite good. These results seem to justify the conclusion that meaningful information about laterally averaged velocities within the Earth can be extracted from *Bulletin* travel-time data collected from a global network.

Although not shown in figures 4 and 5, confidence intervals for the velocities were also estimated. At the 95-percent confidence level the widths of these confidence intervals are about 0.5 km/s in the upper mantle, 0.2 km/s in the

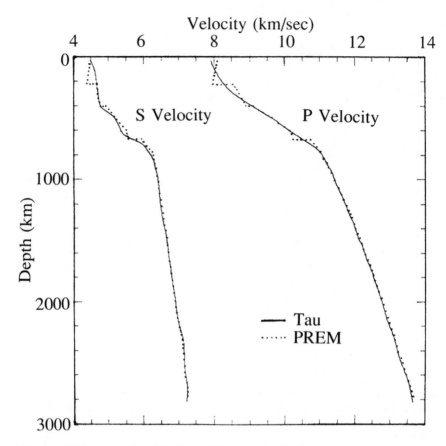

Figure 4. Global averages of the P- and S-wave velocities in the mantle derived from the tau analysis. The PREM model (Dziewonski and Anderson, 1981) is shown for comparison.

lower mantle, and 0.5 km/s in the core. The resolution in depth is about 75 km in both the mantle and core.

LATERAL VARIATIONS

In the last few years the study of the three-dimensional properties of the Earth's internal structure has become an area of intense interest. Network travel times can provide an effective means of investigating these more complicated variations within the Earth, provided that the ray paths define a reasonably complete sampling of the Earth's interior. This last point requires careful consideration in a global study because of the nonuniform sampling inherent in natural seismicity patterns and the distribution of seismographic

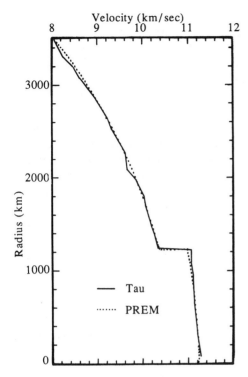

Figure 5. Global averages of P-wave velocities in the core derived from the tau analysis. The PREM model (Dziewonski and Anderson, 1981) is shown for comparsion.

stations. In the initial part of the study it was decided to avoid some of the problems of this nonuniform sampling by taking advantage of the lateral variations known to exist in the crust and shallow mantle and by determining how deeply these could be traced into the mantle. This was achieved by analyzing the data in terms of a tectonic regionalization. The ray paths were characterized in terms of the type of tectonic region present at the source, midpoint, and receiver. Initially, the global tectonic regionalization of Jordan (1981) was used, which consists of three oceanic regions and three continental regions divided primarily according to geologic age. However, in analyzing the statistics of the travel times it was apparent that a seventh region containing the oceanic trenches was needed, so the regionalization of Jordan was modified accordingly.

Once the travel-time data had been characterized by tectonic regions, they were converted to estimates of $\tau(p)$ according to the method outlined above in the section on tau method. Then, following a fairly straightforward method developed in Tralli and Johnson (1986a), it was possible to obtain equivalent "single-region" tau functions for each of the tectonic regions. In addition, end-point correction functions were obtained for both sources and receivers in each of the tectonic regions. The statistics of all these estimates were carried through the entire analysis procedure so the significance of differences in tau estimates for different regions could be tested. Furthermore, the methods of Bessonova et al. (1976) allows one to convert confidence intervals in tau to confidence intervals in velocity, which is a further aid in assessing the validity of suggested lateral variations.

The single-region tau functions and their uncertainties were converted directly to velocity models with confidence intervals for each of the tectonic regions. The significant differences between the various regions are confined primarily to the upper 1,000 km of the mantle, which is what one would expect from a method designed to extract that part of the lateral variations correlated with surface tectonics. The lateral variations in the upper 1,000 km of the mantle for the P-wave velocity are shown in figure 6 and those for the S-wave velocity are shown in figure 7. Anomalies in velocity are typically less than 1 percent. In both oceans and continents the velocities at the top of the mantle correlate well with geologic age, with velocities increasing from young to old oceans and similarly from young active continental regions to old shields. In general, the lateral variations in P- and S-wave velocities in the upper 200 km of the mantle are consistent with each other and also consistent with modern models of plate tectonics. There are also interesting lateral variations at greater depths, but the reliability of these features is more questionable. For instance, there is a definite suggestion in the S-wave velocities that the 400- and 650-km discontinuities are deeper under continents than under oceans, which would be an important result if it could be firmly established. However, this pattern is not duplicated in the P-wave velocities, an inconsistency that must be explained before one is willing to place much confidence in velocity anomalies of this type.

End-point corrections for both source and receiver were analyzed separately to learn more about laterally varying velocity anomalies in the crust and shallow mantle, and the details of this analysis are presented in Tralli and Johnson (1986b). These end-point corrections are similar to the time terms of refraction seismology but are estimated as a function of slowness, which makes it possible to make inferences about the causative velocity anomalies. Furthermore, they are estimated separately for sources and receivers in the same region, so information about systematic errors in hypocentral parameters can be extracted from the data. A very systematic picture emerged from this type of analysis for P-waves that is generally consistent with modern concepts of plate tectonics and crustal evolution. The corrections are all less than 1 s. Oceanic regions have negative velocity anomalies in the shallow mantle, while continental regions have positive anomalies, with the size of the anomaly correlating with increasing crustal age in both cases. Furthermore, interpretations in terms of variations in crustal thickness

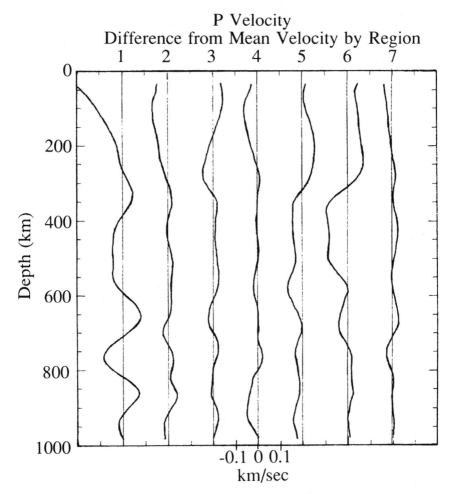

Figure 6. Differences between the P-wave velocities for each tectonic region and the reference velocity model obtained by averaging all the regions with a weighting proportional to surface area. The regions are: (1) young oceans, (2) intermediate-age oceans, (3) old oceans, (4) active continents, (5) continental platforms, (6) continental shields, and (7) oceanic trenches.

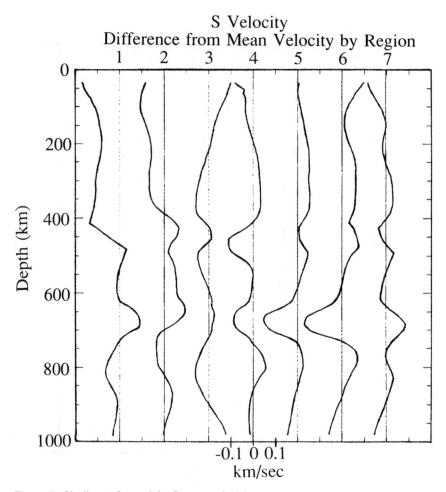

Figure 7. Similar to figure 6 for S-wave velocities.

also indicate a thickening of the crust with age in both oceans and continents. Evidence for systematic regional biases in hypocentral parameters were also extracted from these data and indicate that oceanic sources are systematically mislocated, with origin times that are too late and/or focal depths that are too shallow, while continental sources have origin times that are too early and/or focal depths that are too deep.

In order to determine what fraction of lateral variations in mantle velocities is actually being explained by results such as those shown in figures 6 and 7, a technique was developed for locating seismic events in a laterally heterogeneous Earth (Tralli and Johnson, 1986c). This technique makes use of the regionalized tau curves for P-waves in the distance range of 10 to 100 degrees. Using equation (4), these tau curves are easily converted to travel-time curves for a laterally heterogeneous Earth (Buland and Chapman, 1983). Thus, it is possible to locate seismic sources, taking into account the information on lateral variations contained in the empirical tau curves without explicitly defining a laterally varying Earth model, and an efficient procedure was developed for doing this. This procedure was tested by locating about 100 events, including nuclear explosions in Nevada, Russia, and the south Pacific and earthquakes in California. The locations were obtained using routine arrival times of P-waves in the distance range of 15 to 95 degrees as reported by the ISC. The tests were most meaningful for the Nevada explosions because actual locations are known. Mean epicentral mislocations for twenty-eight Nevada explosions were about 3 km for this method incorporating lateral variations, whereas they were about 7 km for laterally homogeneous methods employing the Jeffreys-Bullen or PREM travel-time curves.

CONCLUSIONS

The Earth is a large and complex body, and the seismological study of its internal structure requires a large amount of data. The travel-time data collected by a global network of seismographic stations are sufficient for such a study, as long as the problem of nonuniform sampling of the Earth is explicitly considered and careful attention given to the statistical treatment of errors in the observational data. The tau method is an excellent way of analyzing data of this type.

While these initial results indicate that the travel-time data available in standard seismological bulletins have the potential to affect quantitative estimates of the three-dimensional structure of the Earth's interior, several obvious extensions and refinements of the method will be required to complete the analysis. The dimensions and dipping nature of the subduction zones have not been adequately represented by the 5×5-degree gridding of the tectonic regionalization scheme, and special studies of these regions will be required. The division of the upper mantle into seven types of tectonic regions is rather coarse, and more regions and a finer gridding may be needed. Finally, while the method of tectonic regionalization helps solve some of the problems of uneven sampling in the upper mantle, its validity decreases with depth in the mantle, and it is obvious that a more complete tomographic technique will be required in the lower mantle and core to study lateral variations in these parts of the Earth.

REFERENCES

Bessonova, E. N., V. M. Fishman, V. Z. Ryaboyi, and G. A. Sitnikova (1974). The tau method for inversion of travel times. I. Deep seismic sounding data. *Geophys. J. R. Astr. Soc.*, 36: 377–398.

Bessonova, E. N., V. M. Fishman, M. G. Shnirman, G. A. Sitnikova, and L. R. Johnson (1976). The tau method for inversion of travel times. II. Earthquake data. *Geophys. J. R. Astr. Soc.*, 46: 87–108.

Buland, R. (1986). Uniform reduction error analysis. *Bull. Seism. Soc. Am.*, 76: 217–230.

Buland, R., and C. H. Chapman (1983). The computation of seismic travel times. *Bull. Seism. Soc. Am.*, 73: 1271–1302.

Courant, R., and D. Hilbert (1962). *Methods of Mathematical Physics*. Interscience, New York.

Dziewonski, A. M., and D. L. Anderson (1981). Preliminary reference Earth model. *Physics of the Earth and Planetary Interiors*, 25: 297–356.

Gerver, M., and V. Markushevitch (1966). Determination of seismic wave velocity from the travel time curve. *Geophys. J. R. Astr. Soc.*, 11: 165–173.

——— (1967). On the characteristic properties of travel time curves. *Geophys. J. R. Astr. Soc.*, 13: 241–246.

Jeffreys, H. (1961). *Theory of Probability*, 3d edition. Oxford University Press, Oxford.

Johnson, L. E., and F. Gilbert (1972). A new datum for use in the body wave travel time inverse problem. *Geophys. J. R. Astr. Soc.*, 30: 373–380.

Johnson, L. R., and R. C. Lee (1985). External bounds on the P velocity in the Earth's core. *Bull. Seism. Soc. Am.*, 75: 115–130.

Jordan, T. H. (1981). Global tectonic regionalization for seismological data analysis. *Bull. Seism. Soc. Am.*, 71: 1131–1141.

Lee, R. C., and L. R. Johnson (1984a). Tau estimates for mantle P and S waves from global travel-time observations. *Geophys. J. R. Astr. Soc.*, 77: 655–666.

——— (1984b). Extremal bounds on the seismic velocities in the Earth's mantle. *Geophys. J. R. Astr. Soc.*, 77: 667–681.

McMechan, G. A., and R. A. Wiggins (1972). Depth limits in body wave inversion. *Geophys. J. R. Astr. Soc.*, 28: 459–473.

Rudzki, M. P. (1898). Uber die scheinbare geschwindigkeit der verbreitung der erdbeben. *Beitrage zur Geoph.*, 3: 495–519.

Tralli, D. M., and L. R. Johnson (1986a). Lateral variations in mantle P velocity from tectonically regionalized tau estimates. *Geophys. J. R. Astr. Soc.*, 86: 475–489.

——— (1986b). Estimation of slowness-dependent source and receiver corrections for P wave travel times. *Bull. Seism. Soc. Am.*, 76: 1718–1783.

——— (1986c). Estimation of travel times for source location in a laterally heterogeneous Earth. *Physics of the Earth and Planetary Interiors*, 44: 242–256.

TWENTY ONE

Love and Rayleigh Waves in Irregular Structures

Lawrence A. Drake

INTRODUCTION

Now that ocean-bottom seismometers are being operated at continental boundaries and in subduction zone regions, and Love and Rayleigh wave phase and amplitude measurements are becoming widely available (Bolt, 1977; see Nagumo et al., 1986), there is a need for computation of phase-velocity dispersion and energy scattering in realistic models of these regions. Also, on a much smaller model scale in the underground coal mining industry, longwall mining is being extensively used, and knowledge of the presence of interruptions in or damage to a coal seam ahead of the mining face is of the very greatest importance in mine planning (Ziolkowski, 1979; Buchanan, 1983).

A method for finding phase velocities and energy scattering of Love and Rayleigh waves across irregular two-dimensional structures was given by Lysmer and Drake (1972). A more complete analysis of the viscoelastic quarter-spaces at the ends of the finite-element model was given by Waas (1972, pp. 30–51). This method has been applied to the analysis of the propagation of Love and Rayleigh waves across continental boundaries (Drake, 1972a, 1972b; Drake and Bolt, 1980; Seron, 1985) and to the analysis of the propagation of Love waves across subduction zones (Bolt and Drake, 1986). It has also been extensively applied to the study of SH and P-SV waves in coal seams (Drake and Asten, 1982; Asten et al., 1984; Edwards et al., 1985). The analysis of Rayleigh waves at a continental boundary by Drake (1972b) was approximate and incomplete because computational difficulty in the oceanic quarter-space at one end of the finite-element model prevented using a negligible rigidity for the ocean layers. In 1985 Waas advised that numerical overflow in the analysis of the propagation of Rayleigh waves in a quarter-space could be avoided by normalizing the eigenvalues in the eigenvalue problem (to avoid division by a very small eigenvalue) and that he had analyzed quarter-spaces of up to 100 layers (see Waas et al., 1985).

Normalization of eigenvectors in the Rayleigh wave quarter-space problem has been simply achieved by expressing dimensions of and velocities within the quarter-space section of the finite-element model that includes water in units like megameters and megameters/s (to scale up the wave number eigenvalues). Now stable, convenient, and comparatively fast computer programs have been written for a VAX 11/780 computer to calculate the phase velocity dispersion and the energy scattering of Love and Rayleigh waves in two-dimensional irregular viscoelastic structures (Drake, 1986). For a finite-element model of forty layers and eighty columns between two horizontally layered quarter-spaces, each of forty layers, the running time for the Love wave program (per frequency) is 13 minutes, with 3.0 megabytes of memory, and the running time for the Rayleigh wave program (per frequency) is 47 minutes, with 4.6 megabytes of memory.

Because water has a viscosity of 1.14 millipascal-second $(1.14 \times 10^{-2}$ poise), and viscosity is tangential stress per unit velocity gradient, for finite tangential stress there can be no discontinuity in horizontal displacement at the base of an ocean layer. On account of the size of finite elements and the convenience of fixing the base of the finite-element model, finite-element modeling of the propagation of Love or Rayleigh waves across irregular structures introduces errors of a few parts per thousand into computed phase velocities and amplitudes of transmitted Love or Rayleigh waves. Hence, for Rayleigh-wave propagation, the most convenient way to allow for the viscosity of water-finite elements and, at the same time, to secure approximate balance between the energy of the incident Rayleigh waves and the combined energy of the reflected and transmitted Rayleigh waves, is to give the liquid elements of the finite element model a very small rigidity (for example, 1 or 0.01 bar). It does not appear to be necessary at the possibly sliding boundary to make use of a slideline option (with penalty formulation); this option is required rather for very high energy shock discontinuities (Hallquist, 1983, p. 25; 1984, p. 6).

CONTINENTAL BOUNDARY AT BERKELEY

An ocean-bottom seismometer, 235 km WNW of Berkeley and beneath 3.9 km of water, was operated from 1966 to 1972 by the Lamont-Doherty Geological Observatory (McGarr, 1969; Bolt, 1977). Because the present finite-element study is two dimensional, Love and Rayleigh waves normally incident on the continental boundary are considered, and the profile AA' in figure 1 is studied. This profile is 240 km long, extending 160 km WSW of the continental shelf near Berkeley to a region in which the ocean depth is 4.5

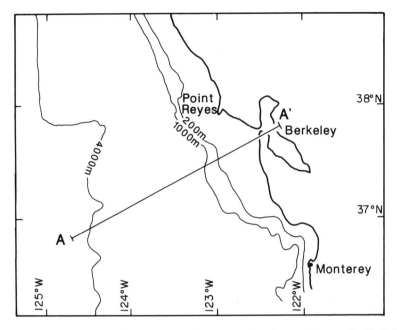

Figure 1. Section AA' of length 240 km normal to the coastline at the Berkeley seismographic station.

km. The uppermost central portion of the finite-element model for Rayleigh waves with periods between 20 and 34 s is shown in figure 2. The depth to the fixed base of this model was 450 km. A similar model with two water layers (instead of five) and a depth of 1,470 km was used for Rayleigh waves with periods between 35 and 60 s. A third model with ten water layers and a depth of 160 km was used for Rayleigh waves with periods between 10 and 19 s. Lysmer and Drake (1972) and Waas et al. (1985) recommended about eight finite elements per shortest wavelength of shear waves in any region. Hence, as periods and wavelengths decrease, smaller finite elements are used.

The thicknesses of the layers, compressional (P-wave) velocities, shear (S-wave) velocities, and densities of the region at the WSW end of profile AA' (position of a possible ocean-bottom seismometer) down to a depth of 220 km are listed in table 1. They are in general based on the oceanic model of Dziewonski et al. (1975; also see Drake and Bolt, 1980). A value of 0.01 km/s, corresponding to a rigidity of approximately 1 bar, was taken as the shear velocity in the water layer for Rayleigh wave propagation; a value of 0.001 km/s, corresponding to a rigidity of approximately 0.01 bar, gave similar results. The properties of the region below a depth of 220 km, based on the global model of Dziewonski and Anderson (1981), are given in table 2.

The thicknesses of the layers, compressional velocities, shear velocities,

TABLE 1. Horizontally Layered Structures

Ocean-bottom seismometer				Berkeley			
Layer thickness km	Compressional velocity km/s	Shear velocity km/s	Density g/cm³	Layer thickness km	Compressional velocity km/s	Shear velocity km/s	Density g/cm³
4.5	1.51	0.01	1.03	5.0	5.47	3.09	2.72
0.5	2.15	0.50	1.80	5.0	5.84	3.30	2.72
1.0	4.70	2.50	2.50	5.0	6.22	3.52	2.72
5.0	6.80	3.80	2.90	5.0	6.59	3.73	2.72
49.0	8.20	4.70	3.30	5.0	6.97	3.95	2.92
160.0	7.90	4.30	3.40	20.0	7.80	4.40	3.30
40.0	8.10	4.40	3.40	55.0	7.60	4.30	3.40
				60.0	7.90	4.30	3.40
				60.0	8.10	4.40	3.40

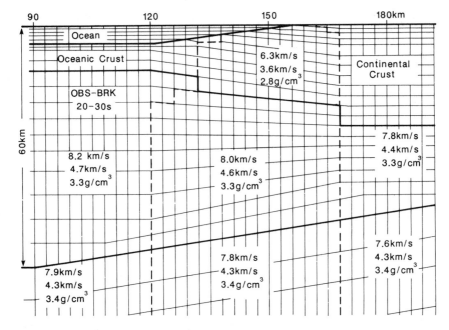

Figure 2. Central portion of the section analyzed by the finite-element method for periods from 20 s to 34 s.

TABLE 2.   Models from 220 to 1,470 km Depth

Thickness km	Compressional velocity km/s	Shear velocity km/s	Density g/cm³
50.0	8.60	4.66	3.45
50.0	8.70	4.69	3.48
80.0	8.82	4.74	3.52
100.0	9.39	5.08	3.79
170.0	10.10	5.46	3.96
200.0	11.06	6.24	4.44
200.0	11.41	6.37	4.56
400.0	11.88	6.56	4.73

TABLE 3. Phase Velocity of Rayleigh Waves

Period s	Phase velocity OBS (Dunkin) km/s	Phase velocity OBS km/s	Phase velocity BRK (Dunkin) km/s	Phase velocity BRK km/s	Mean phase velocity km/s	Model phase velocity km/s	Excess model phase velocity % of mean
60	4.0310	4.0316	3.9039	3.9058	3.9675	3.9849	0.44
55	4.0290	4.0296	3.8929	3.8949	3.9610	3.9802	0.48
50	4.0296	4.0303	3.8826	3.8846	3.9561	3.9776	0.54
45	4.0330	4.0337	3.8725	3.8745	3.9528	3.9771	0.61
40	4.0392	4.0401	3.8616	3.8638	3.9504	3.9792	0.73
35	4.0479	4.0493	3.8482	3.8506	3.9481	3.9831	0.89
30	4.0579	4.0598	3.8281	3.8301	3.9430	3.9691	0.66
25	4.0649	4.0678	3.7912	3.7939	3.9281	3.9623	0.87
20	4.0534	4.0589	3.7100	3.7141	3.8817	3.9324	1.31
15	3.9350	3.9464	3.5200	3.5241	3.7275	3.8042	2.06
10	2.2349	2.2079	3.2217	3.2253	2.7283	2.6772	−1.87

and densities in the region of the Berkeley seismographic station down to a depth of 220 km are shown on the right-hand side of table 1 (Drake and Bolt, 1980). Intermediate physical properties have been chosen for the region between the oceanic and continental structures (figure 2).

PHASE VELOCITIES AND ENERGY SCATTERING

Numerical analysis of the finite-element models (see fig. 2) gives the complex displacement of all the nodal points and the amplitudes and phases of all the reflected and transmitted Love or Rayleigh modes for a given incident Love or Rayleigh mode at a particular frequency. The mode shapes of the reflected and transmitted Love or Rayleigh waves are normalized so that the energy carried by each of them is proportional to the product of the mode frequency and wave number (Lysmer and Drake, 1972; Waas, 1972).

Phase velocities of the fundamental Rayleigh mode at periods from 60 s down to 10 s across the finite-element models of the section AA' in figure 1 are tabulated in table 3 and shown in figure 3. They are compared with the phase velocities in the regions at the ends of the models. The phase velocities in these regions were calculated by both the method of Haskell (1953) and Dunkin (1965; shear velocity in the ocean water = 0) and the finite-element method. For both the Berkeley and oceanic regions, at periods down to 20 s,

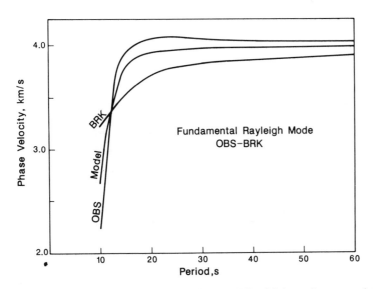

Figure 3. Phase velocity of the fundamental Rayleigh mode across the continental boundary compared with the phase velocities of the fundamental Rayleigh mode at the ocean site A in figure 1 and at Berkeley.

TABLE 4.   Phase Velocity of Love Waves

Period s	Phase velocity OBS (Haskell) km/s	Phase velocity OBS km/s	Phase velocity BRK (Haskell) km/s	Phase velocity BRK km/s	Mean phase velocity km/s	Model phase velocity km/s	Excess model phase velocity % of mean
60	4.4725	4.4730	4.2998	4.3001	4.3862	4.3937	0.17
55	4.4630	4.4635	4.2805	4.2808	4.3718	4.3808	0.21
50	4.4536	4.4540	4.2590	4.2594	4.3563	4.3679	0.27
45	4.4440	4.4445	4.2343	4.2347	4.3392	4.3537	0.33
40	4.4342	4.4347	4.2042	4.2047	4.3192	4.3383	0.44
35	4.4237	4.4242	4.1647	4.1654	4.2942	4.3196	0.59
30	4.4120	4.4124	4.1084	4.1092	4.2602	4.2794	0.45
25	4.3983	4.3987	4.0219	4.0232	4.2101	4.2146	0.11
20	4.3813	4.3819	3.8885	3.8902	4.1349	4.1390	0.10
15	4.3602	4.3608	3.7027	3.7041	4.0315	3.9853	−1.15
10	4.3357	4.3362	3.4901	3.4915	3.9129	3.8606	−1.34

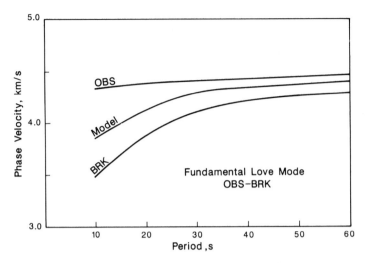

Figure 4. Phase velocity of the fundamental Love mode across the continental boundary compared with the phase velocities of the fundamental Love mode at the ocean
site A in figure 1 and at Berkeley.

the difference is less than or equal to approximately one part in a thousand.
For the ocean region, at a period of 15 s, the difference is approximately one
part in 350; at a period of 10 s, the difference is approximately one part in
eighty (later reduced by reducing the rigidity of the water in the finite-
element calculation). The mean phase velocities tabulated toward the right
of table 3 are the means of the phase velocities of the fundamental Rayleigh
mode in the oceanic and Berkeley regions, found by the method of Haskell
and Dunkin. The finite-element model phase velocities, tabulated further to
the right of table 3, are slightly greater than the mean phase velocities, except
at a period of 10 s. Mean slowness corresponds to a lower velocity than mean
velocity. The high finite-element model velocities almost certainly arise because most of the finite-element model is of oceanic structure and, except at a
period of 10 s, the oceanic phase velocity of the fundamental Rayleigh mode
is higher than the phase velocity in the region of Berkeley.

Similar values for the propagation of the fundamental Love mode from the
oceanic region to Berkeley are recalled from Drake and Bolt (1980; for that
paper the width of the finite element model was 200 km). These values are
tabulated in table 4 and shown in figure 4. Again, at the shorter periods the
finite-element model phase velocity is lower than the mean of the phase velocities found for the regions at the ends of the model by the method of Haskell.
This time, however, the phase velocity of the fundamental Love mode in the
oceanic region exceeds the corresponding phase velocity at Berkeley. At a
period of 10 s, for a path two-thirds oceanic, the travel time for the finite-

TABLE 5.   Energy Partition in Love and Rayleigh Modes

Period s	Love modes			Rayleigh modes		
	Reflected energy %	Transmitted energy, % Fundamental mode	Higher modes	Reflected energy %	Transmitted energy, % Fundamental mode	Higher modes
60	0.00	91.88	8.12	0.08	99.75	0.17
55	0.00	89.40	10.60	0.09	99.73	0.18
50	0.00	85.85	14.15	0.10	99.68	0.22
45	0.00	80.75	19.25	0.20	99.51	0.29
40	0.00	73.12	26.88	0.14	99.49	0.37
35	0.01	61.79	38.20	0.20	99.21	0.59
30	0.00	45.55	54.45	0.33	98.59	1.08
25	0.00	26.24	73.76	0.71	97.43	1.86
20	0.01	10.18	89.81	1.37	95.46	3.17
15	0.02	2.22	97.76	2.52	89.35	8.13
10	0.01	0.29	99.70	59.17	29.01	11.82

element model for the fundamental Love mode exceeds the expected travel time by one part in twenty-five. Hence, at periods of approximately 10 s, structure appears to cause a slight phase delay for the fundamental Love mode (little energy is transmitted; see table 5).

The normalized amplitudes of the horizontal and vertical displacements of the fundamental Rayleigh mode at a period of 15 s for the oceanic region at the WSW end of section AA′ of figure 1 are shown in figure 5. A rigidity of 1 bar was assumed for the ocean layer. The potential for the horizontal and vertical displacements of a single propagating Rayleigh mode in a perfectly elastic fluid at the surface of a half-space can be written as

$$\varphi = A\sin(Kz)\,\sin(\omega t - kx)$$

where A is a source term, K is $(k_1^2 - k^2)^{1/2}$, ω is angular frequency, k is a wave number in the x direction of Rayleigh mode propagation, z is depth, t is time, and k_1 is the wave number of compressional waves of the angular frequency of the Rayleigh mode in the fluid (see, for example, Ewing et al., 1957; Drake, 1972b). The value of A corresponding to the normalized amplitudes of the displacements shown in figure 5 was found from the normalized vertical displacement at the ocean surface (0.0758); k_1 at a period of 15 s for ocean water is 0.2774. Thus, the horizontal displacement at the base of a perfectly elastic ocean layer at a depth of 4.5 km for the region represented in figure 5 was found to be 0.029 normalized displacement units. The normalized amplitude of the horizontal component of a propagating Rayleigh mode found by the method of Haskell (1953) and Dunkin (1965) for a model including a surface layer of a perfectly elastic fluid includes a discontinuity of the type shown by

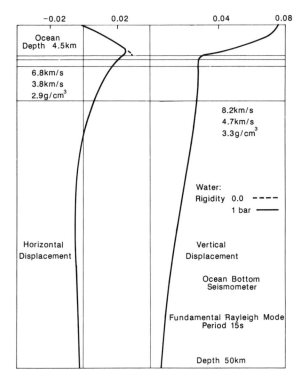

Figure 5. Normalized amplitudes of horizontal and vertical displacement of the fundamental Rayleigh mode at the ocean site in figure 1 for a period of 15 s, with and without a horizontal displacement discontinuity at the ocean bottom.

the short dashed line in figure 5. The normalized amplitude of the horizontal component near the surface and below the base of the fluid layer, and the normalized amplitude of the vertical component are shown by the continuous lines for the very slightly rigid model in figure 5.

The percentages of energy reflected and transmitted for incident motion from the ocean side of the fundamental Love and Rayleigh modes at the continental boundary near Berkeley at periods from 60 s down to 10 s are tabulated in table 5. The transmitted energy percentages are subdivided into that for the fundamental mode and the total for the remaining higher modes. The values for Love waves are recalled from Drake and Bolt (1980). The percentages of energy in the transmitted fundamental Love and Rayleigh modes are shown in figure 6. The comparatively unhindered passage of the fundamental Rayleigh mode at periods of approximately 20 s across the continental boundary, compared with the almost total absorption of the fundamental Love mode at the same periods, suggests why it is preferable to use Rayleigh rather than Love waves for the measurement of the magnitudes of

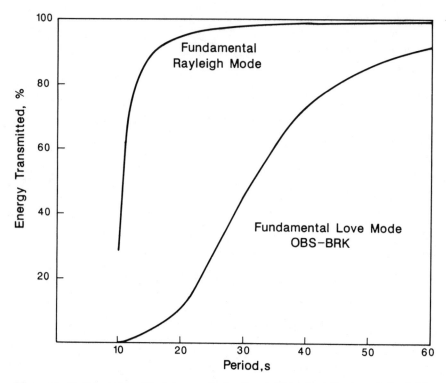

Figure 6. Energy transmitted (percent) for the fundamental Love and Rayleigh modes from the ocean site A in figure 1 to Berkeley (A').

shallow teleseisms. Also, at periods of approximately 10 s, most of the Love wave energy is scattered forward, while most of the Rayleigh wave energy is scattered back.

CONCLUSIONS

Stable, convenient, and comparatively fast computer programs have been written for a VAX 11/780 to calculate the phase velocity dispersion and the energy scattering of Love and Rayleigh waves in arbitrary two-dimensional irregular viscoelastic structures. These programs are based on the finite-element method and analyze forty rows and eighty columns of trapezoidal finite elements, as well as two layered quarter-spaces at the ends of the model. They have been applied to problems as diverse in scale as the study of continental boundaries and subduction zones down to the study of interrupted and damaged coal seams. In the study of the propagation of Rayleigh waves across regions including volumes of water, the water, because it is very slightly viscous, is assumed to have a very small rigidity (1 or 0.01 bar). If the water is taken to be, at the same time, perfectly elastic, the energy balance between incident Rayleigh waves and reflected and transmitted Rayleigh waves serves as a very useful check on the model study.

In this paper, results of a study of the propagation of Love and Rayleigh waves from the ocean side across the continental boundary near Berkeley show that, at periods from 60 s down to 20 s, the phase velocities of both Love and Rayleigh waves across the finite-element model of the continental boundary are slightly greater than the means of the phase velocities of these waves in the quarter-spaces at the ends of the model. These effects almost certainly arise because, in this period range, the oceanic phase velocities are higher than the continental phase velocities, and the finite-element model is of predominantly oceanic structure. At periods of approximately 10 s, the fundamental Love mode appears to experience a slight phase delay.

At periods from 60 s down to 10 s, the energy of the fundamental Love mode is scattered increasingly forward. At periods from 60 s down to 20 s, 95 percent of the energy of the fundamental Rayleigh mode is transmitted. Hence, Rayleigh waves with periods of approximately 20 s are useful for measuring magnitudes of shallow teleseisms. At periods of approximately 10 s, most of the energy of the fundamental Rayleigh mode is scattered back.

ACKNOWLEDGMENTS

Prof. Bruce Bolt originally suggested this problem of the propagation of Love and Rayleigh waves in irregular viscoelastic two-dimensional structures. Prof. John Lysmer (Division of Transportation Engineering, University of California, Berkeley) and Dr. Günter Waas (Hochtief AG, Frankfurt/Main, West Germany) in large measure solved it. Prof. Robert Herrmann at St. Louis University provided a computer program incorporating Dunkin's formulation for Rayleigh waves in horizontally layered structures. Finally, the staff at the Computer Centre at Macquarie University generously made computing facilities available.

REFERENCES

Asten, M. W., L. A. Drake, and S. A. Edwards (1984). In-seam seismic Love wave scattering modeled by the finite element method. *Geophys. Prospecting*, 32: 649–661.

Bolt, B. A. (1977). Ocean bottom seismometry. A new dimension to seismology. *Boll. di Geofisica*, 19: 107–116.

Bolt, B. A., and L. A. Drake (1986). Love mode dispersion across subduction zones by finite element modeling. *Geophys. J. R. Astr. Soc.*, 84: 515–528.

Buchanan, D. J. (1983). In-seam seismology: A method for detecting faults in coal seams. In A. A. Fitch, ed., *Developments in Geophysical Exploration Methods—5* Applied Science Publishers, London, 1–34.

Drake, L. A. (1972a). Love and Rayleigh waves in nonhorizontally layered media. *Bull. Seism. Soc. Am.*, 62: 1241–1258.

———— (1972b). Rayleigh waves at a continental boundary by the finite element method. *Bull. Seism. Soc. Am.* 62: 1259–1268.

———— (1986). Computer aided detection of faults in coal seams. In *Australian Coal Science 2 Proceedings*, Australian Institute of Energy, Newcastle, N.S.W., 192–197.

Drake, L. A., and M. W. Asten (1982). Wave propagation in irregular coal seams. In P. J. Hoadley and L. K. Stevens, eds., *Finite Element Methods in Engineering*. University of Melbourne, Victoria, 119–123.

Drake, L. A., and B. A. Bolt (1980). Love waves normally incident at a continental boundary. *Bull. Seism. Soc. Am.*, 70: 1103–1123.

Dunkin, J. W. (1965). Computation of model solution in layered, elastic media at high frequencies. *Bull. Seism. Soc. Am.*, 55: 335–358.

Dziewonski, A. M., and D. L. Anderson (1981). Preliminary reference Earth model. *Phys. Earth Planet. Inter.*, 25: 297–356.

Dziewonski, A. M., A. L. Hales, and E. R. Lapwood (1975). Parametrically simple earth models consistent with geophysical data. *Phys. Earth Planet. Inter.*, 10: 12–48.

Edwards, S. A., M. W. Asten, and L. A. Drake (1985). P-SV wave scattering by coal-seam inhomogeneities. *Geophysics*, 50: 214–223.

Ewing, W. M., W. S. Jardetzky, and F. Press (1957). *Elastic Waves in Layered Media*. McGraw-Hill, New York, 1–380.

Hallquist, J. O. (1983). *Theoretical Manual for DYNA3D*. Lawrence Livermore National Laboratory, California, 1–82.

———— (1984). *User's Manual for DYNA2D—Explicit Two-Dimensional Hydrodynamic Finite Element Code with Interactive Rezoning, Revision 2*. Lawrence Livermore National Laboratory, California, UCID-18756, 1–115.

Haskell, N. A. (1953). The dispersion of surface waves on multilayered media. *Bull. Seism. Soc. Am.*, 43: 17–34.

Lysmer, J., and L. A. Drake (1972). A finite element method for seismology. In B. A. Bolt, ed., *Methods of Computational Physics* 11. Academic Press, New York, 181–216.

McGarr, A. (1969). Amplitude variations of Rayleigh waves—Propagation across a continental margin. *Bull. Seism. Soc. Am.*, 59: 1281–1306.

Nagumo, S., T. Ouchi, J. Kasahara, and S. Koresawa (1986). P-wave velocity in the lower lithosphere in the western Northwest Pacific Basin observed by an ocean-bottom seismometer long range array. *Bull. Earthq. Res. Instit.*, 61: 403–414.

Seron, F. J. (1985). Love waves across the Atlantic continental margin of the Iberian Peninsula (Spanish with English abstract). *Rev. Geofisica*, 41: 219–236.

Waas, G. (1972). *Earth Vibration Effects and Abatement for Military Facilities*. U.S. Army Engineer Waterways Experiment Station, Vicksburg, Mississippi, 1–182.

Waas, G., H. R. Riggs, and H. Werkle (1985). Displacement solutions for dynamic loads in transversely-isotropic stratified media. Earthquake Eng. Struct. Dyn. 12: 173–193.

Ziolkowski, A. M. (1979). Seismic profiling for coal on land. In A. A. Fitch, ed., *Developments in Geophysical Exploration Methods—1*. Applied Science Publishers, London, 271–306.

TWENTY TWO

The Transient Regime of the Free Oscillation Spectrum: The View from the South Pole

L. Knopoff, P. A. Rydelek, and W. Zurn

INTRODUCTION

In these days of large networks and arrays, of global and especially tomographic studies, it might seem presumptuous to try to discuss single-station seismological observations. However, in the case of the seismic station at the South Pole, the geometrical symmetries are so remarkable that several useful conclusions of a pedagogic nature can be drawn that will allow us to develop a strategy for performing meaningful if not accurate observations of the free-oscillation spectrum anywhere on Earth.

All points on a conservative oscillator vibrate with the same set of eigenfrequencies. This being the case, how can we justify the use of spatial fluctuations in local measurements of the periods of the free oscillations to determine the location of lateral inhomogeneities in the Earth's interior? Why should there be fluctuations in the spatial distribution of the observed periods of free oscillations? The answers to these questions depend on the answers to other questions that test two assumptions that appear in these opening remarks: (1) Is the earth conservative; that is, is it nonattenuating? Since the answer to this question is obviously no, we ask whether the violation of the assumption of conservation is sufficient to allow us to proceed with the identification of the locations and magnitudes of the inhomogeneities in the Earth's interior? (2) How is the Fourier spectrum of a real seismogram related to the free oscillations of a conservative, or nonattenuating, Earth? The answers to these two questions are the subject of this paper.

Lateral variations in the frequencies of spectral peaks have been reported widely by many authors, for example, Silver and Jordan (1981). Our own illustrations show spectral amplitudes in the neighborhood of mode $_0S_{22}$, namely at periods near 300 s, of an earthquake in the New Ireland region,

347

observed with sibling ultralong-period instruments (Nakanishi et al., 1976) located at UCLA and the South Pole (fig. 1a), and similar observations made at one station, the South Pole, of two earthquakes on widely differing azimuths (fig. 1b). Similar period differences are found in the first instance even if the two stations and the earthquake source are located on a common great circle and in the second if the two earthquakes and the station are on a common great circle. The differences in the peak frequencies lead us to the conclusion that the peak spectral response depends on the location of both the earthquake and the seismograph. It is customary to identify the frequency of the spectral line with the peak of the response spectrum (Dahlen, 1981), and we adopt this procedure here as well. There is a reciprocity between the free-mode and the traveling-wave descriptions that is given by Jeans's formula, $ka = l + 1/2$, where l is the mode number, $k = \omega/c$, $\omega = 2\pi/T$, T is the period of free oscillations, a is the radius of the Earth, and c is the phase velocity of the corresponding traveling waves. Since the free oscillations are the standing wave system formed out of the appropriate traveling surface waves of the same period, we can use either point of view, as convenience dictates.

In this paper, we discuss exclusively observations of the spectra for modes $_0S_{20}$ to $_0S_{25}$, which have periods of roughly 300 s. These modes are usually well recorded with large amplitudes on ultralong-period instruments, and several of them are relatively free of coupling to nearby toroidal modes. Because of nonsphericity, lateral inhomogeneities, and rotation, each spectral line is composed of $2l + 1$ singlets associated with the azimuthal order number m. Each of the singlet lines in the fine structure is broadened because of attenuation. Since the attenuation-induced broadening of each line in the fine structure is considerably greater than the spacing between neighbors, and since the amplitudes of each singlet vary from place to place over the Earth, the phased sum of all the $2l + 1$ attenuation-broadened singlets will yield what appears to be a single broadened line, but one whose peak frequency varies from place to place because of the variations in amplitudes of the individual components in the sum. According to Dahlen (1981), the period and width of this peak describe the average elastic and anelastic properties of the Earth along a great circle connecting the earthquake and the seismograph, in a zeroth order approximation. Thus, although a complex peak like those shown in figure 1 contains $2l + 1$ pieces of amplitude information plus some frequency information, compaction of the more than $2l + 1$ pieces of information into one piece of frequency information and not much amplitude information causes a drastic loss of information. We must ask whether the acquisition of many pieces of this type of compacted information is sufficient to compensate for the loss of direct information about the singlets and, if so, how these data are to be interpreted to yield information about the structure of laterally inhomogeneous earth models.

LATERAL INHOMOGENEITIES IN STRUCTURE

Suppose that it is not possible to determine the laterally inhomogeneous structure of a nonattenuating Earth model from the distribution of the peaks in the summed fine-structure spectrum. Can we determine the structure in some other way? Students of introductory geophysics will reply that we can always do travel-time seismology on a nonattenuating Earth to study its laterally inhomogeneous structure. In other words, if we study the earliest parts of a seismogram, we can determine the lateral structure of a nonattenuating Earth, but if we study the complete seismogram, according to our supposition, we cannot. How do the properties of the early part of the record approach the steady-state or free-oscillation signal as we move to later times along the seismogram? As we shall see below, whether or not the nonattenuating Earth model seismogram equilibrates, that is, approaches some steady-state properties after a long elapsed time, depends on the way in which it is analyzed. Under some methods of data analysis, it may be that the seismogram seemingly never settles into a stationary state even after a very long time. If the long-term seismic signal is not stationary, harmonic analysis of any two finite samples of the seismogram will yield two different eigenfrequency estimates. Hence, in some quite realistic cases, we will find that we cannot determine the eigenspectrum of a nonattenuating earth from long but finite samples of seismograms, at least by conventional methods.

Is the fact that the Earth is not conservative the way out of the above dilemma? We may suppose that because of line broadening of the fine structure of any given mode, mode coupling will take place, thereby leading to an equilibration even of the apparently nonstationary properties taken in the nonattenuating limit. Hence we presume that a stationary spectrum should always appear in the later parts of the seismogram. If this presumption should turn out to be correct, and if one can obtain only the global average properties of the Earth from the stationary spectrum, then the location and size of the lateral inhomogeneities within it cannot be identified from these data alone. As it will turn out, if attenuation in the Earth is distributed inhomogeneously, then the very-long-term spectrum will be stationary; however, the relationship between these spectral determinations and the identification of the part of the Earth that is being sampled is not immediately obvious. In this case, the diagonal sum rule will not apply. Fortunately, for our purposes, we will see that this is a part of most seismograms that is not analyzed in most cases, even for large earthquakes, because of insufficient record length, and hence the solution to the complete problem of the interpretation of the stationary, spatially attenuating Earth is mainly of academic interest at the present time.

From the point of view of traveling surface waves, some of the same difficulties can be identified. In the early stages of a seismogram on a nonattenuating Earth, waves of a given period travel on a geodesic, which is nearly a great circle for small lateral inhomogeneities. Since the local seismic properties of different geodesics on an inhomogeneous Earth are different, the globe-circling travel times t_{gc} (and hence the equivalent periods of free oscillations) will be different from path to path. The relation between the two is $t_{gc} = (l + 1/2)T$. As the signal is scattered from the inhomogeneities, the surface wave number vector no longer points along the geodesic that includes the source and, in the later parts of the seismogram, may point in varying directions. For a nonattenuating Earth, the estimates of the eigenfrequencies in a one-dimensional case will be shown to be stationary, even though the signal continues to reverberate forever among the inhomogeneities in a nonrepetitive way, except for certain special geometries not likely to arise for a real Earth. In the language of statistical mechanics, we state that the seismic waves are fully mixed, even though the signal is not repetitive. But in the presence of lateral variations in attenuation, the wave trains that pass through or near those parts of the Earth with higher attenuation are attenuated more rapidly than those passing through less absorptive parts. We can then expect some frequency shifts to take place relative to the nonattenuating case, at least in the extremely long-term limit.

SPHEROIDAL MODES $_0S_{20}$ TO $_0S_{25}$

In principle, the fundamental spheroidal modes near a period of 300 s are in a truly complex part of the seismic spectrum. There are five perturbing influences on the estimates of the spectrum of free oscillations of the Earth, other than radial structure and source mechanism, that we must take into account in constructing a theory of the seismogram. Since four of these are small, we can assume that some sort of perturbation expansion in dimensionless parameters describing these four quantities is possible. These four properties, and their dimensionless estimates for periods near 300 s are

Rotation of the earth	$\Omega/\omega \sim 1/300$
Flattening	$e \sim 1/300$
Attenuation	$1/Q \sim 1/300$
Lateral inhomogeneities	$\eta \sim 1/300$

All of these quantities are multiplied by additional dimensionless functions of the radial properties of a spherical Earth, but let us assume that these latter are of the order of unity. This argument suggests that, unless we are very lucky, we cannot neglect any of these four influences in a perturbation expansion to determine small frequency shifts from the global averages. In the above, the Earth's rotation rate is Ω. We estimate η directly from observations described below.

The fifth parameter is the length of record, which is some function of the magnitude of the earthquake in units of the noise level of the detection, and it is our hope that the noise-to-signal ratio is also small. Usually, efforts have been made to make these records as long as possible. These enthusiasms may be misplaced if, as we believe, the most effective and available observations needed to determine the distribution of lateral inhomogeneities in the Earth are those made in the early part rather than the later, hopefully spectrally steady regime of a seismogram. As we shall show, the duration of the early phase may be of the order of 200 hours; we call this the mixing time. Since most of the efforts at identifying the Earth's spectra, by ourselves as well as others, have been made on the early part of the seismograms, we suspect that the long-time-scale spectra, which yield global average estimates, are those that have not been well determined. Since we cannot expect to obtain global average spectra from long-period records that are of short duration in comparison with the mixing time—and attenuation does not permit us to resolve the spectra of the fine structure directly (see fig. 1)—an auxiliary question we must ask is: What information concerning global average spectra is in fact to be derived from knowledge of the spatial distributions of the peak frequencies such as those in figure 1?

Despite these pessimistic comments regarding the potential equivalence of most of the perturbing influences in the period band of fundamental mode Rayleigh waves near 300 s, we can minimize the influences of two of these effects in at least one case. Because of obvious symmetries, vertical component observations made at the geographic South Pole are free of the influences of flattening and of rotation—though not of Coriolis-induced coupling to the torsional modes (Park, 1986)—at least in the early parts of the seismogram. At some late time on a seismogram at the South Pole, the signal may have become fully mixed by scattering from lateral inhomogeneities, taking into account the influence of coupling through the attenuation. At this later stage, the effects of rotation and flattening are also observed at the South Pole, by virtue of the scattering of seismic signals from nonpolar paths from these distant inhomogeneities. But since our seismograms at the South Pole are short in duration compared with the mixing time, these latter considerations do not concern us here, except in an academic sense.

OBSERVATIONS OF PERIODS OF FREE OSCILLATIONS AT THE SOUTH POLE

The unusually simple and attractive structural model derived by Masters et al. (1982) provides a convenient and useful check on observations made at the South Pole. Although their interpretation of observations of anomalous free-oscillation periods has been heavily smoothed, it nevertheless represents an excellent target for validating our own observations. Modes $_0S_{20}$ to $_0S_{25}$ are in one of the four period bands used in the analysis of Masters et al. As we have remarked, we expect that any fluctuations in period of the modes at the

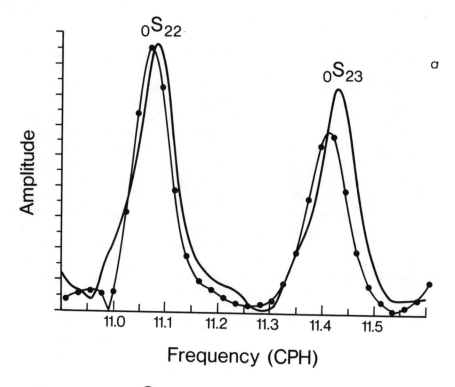

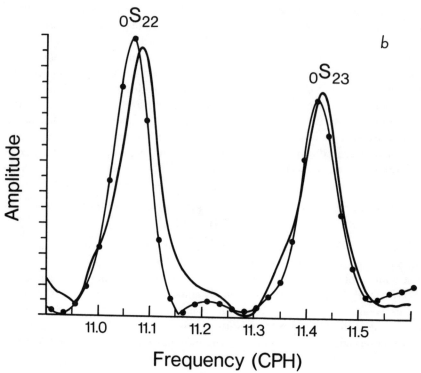

South Pole in the transient or early part of the seismogram would seem to be due almost exclusively to the influence of inhomogeneities along the great circle paths. It is later in the seismogram that the signal becomes coupled to all the perturbing influences. Harmonic analysis of the records of nine large earthquakes on essentially seven different azimuths yields the plot of the frequency shift as a function of azimuth of the source for mode $_0S_{23}$, shown in figure 2a. The length of record of each seismogram is 40 hours, which matches that of the shortest usable recording; the records were identically tapered with a Hanning window. The phase of the roughly sinusoidal graph is in good agreement with the prediction given by the model of Masters et al., and we are encouraged by the smoothness of the relative values. However, the latter property is not a prerequisite for a match in our case, since the target results were smoothed to yield an approximately sinusoidal curve of anomaly. We also note that the two pairs of events on almost the same azimuths are in excellent agreement, although this is not too unexpected, since the sources of the pairs were almost at the same location in each case; the agreement is testimony to the fidelity of recording and the large signal-to-noise ratio in both cases.

Our expectation is that the anomaly-versus-azimuth graph for mode $_0S_{22}$ should be strongly similar to the curve for neighboring mode $_0S_{23}$, since the eigenfunctions for the two cases are very close to one another. The graph (fig. 2b) shows large inconsistencies, with both our results for mode $_0S_{23}$ as well as the expectation that the general outline should be smooth and sinuous. The values of the nine points in the two cases differ by far more than the mutual standard deviations at the 2σ level. Nevertheless, the consistency of the results for the pairs of events on common azimuths in both cases points to a nonstatistical origin for the discrepancy between the two sets of data.

Inspection of similar results for modes $_0S_{20}$ and $_0S_{25}$ show that the distribution of the nine estimates of period in the former case are relatively smooth and in agreement with expectations from the distribution for mode $_0S_{23}$, while the result in the latter case is once again significantly irregular and discordant with expectations. If we average the anomalies across all four modes (Masters et al. averaged across modes 21, 22, and 23), we get a pattern that is arguably sinusoidal and whose peak-to-peak amplitude as a function of azimuth is about 1/300, while the result for mode $_0S_{23}$, our least disturbed case, is about 1/200, a 50-percent difference. We add a further question to our list: What is the cause of the rather obvious, large, and significant period shifts away from the sinuous pattern for some modes?

Figure 1a. Spectral response at UCLA (dots) and the South Pole for modes $_0S_{22}$ and $_0S_{23}$ for the New Ireland earthquake (18 March 1983, $M_s = 7.6$). Seismograms are 40 hours in length; Hanning window. 1b Spectral response at the South Pole for modes $_0S_{22}$ and $_0S_{23}$ for the New Ireland and Colombia (12 December 1979, $M_s = 7.7$) earthquakes.

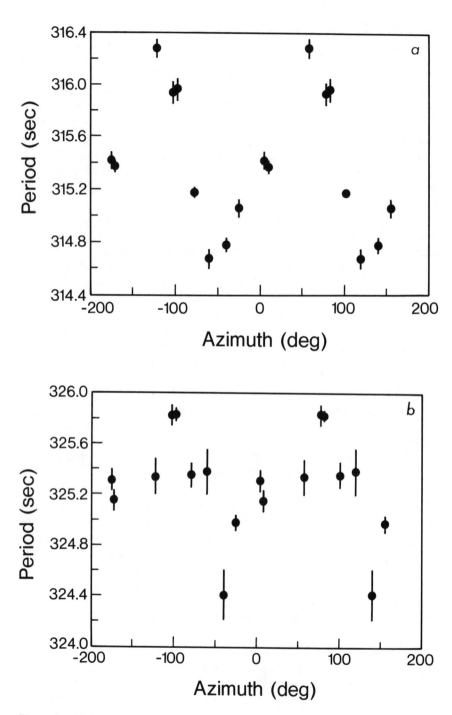

Figure 2a. Period of mode $_0S_{23}$ at the South Pole as function of azimuth for nine earthquakes. 2b Same as in figure 2a except for mode $_0S_{22}$.

A ONE-DIMENSIONAL PEDAGOGIC MODEL

In the theory of the full problem of the evaluation of the normal modes of an almost spherical Earth with all four perturbing influences, the usual solution is derived from the application of perturbation theory to a spherical, radially inhomogeneous, nonrotating, isotropic Earth model. As we have seen, none of the four perturbing influences can be neglected in the construction of the theoretical model in this period range. The theory that takes all four influences into account is extraordinarily messy algebraically. To try to gain physical insights into the nature of the behavior of seismic wave propagation in the full problem, we have had recourse to a pedagogic model, in which we have benefited from the example of Geller and Stein (1978).

Consider a twofold degenerate skeletal Earth model consisting of only two dependent homogeneous vibrating strings along which waves can propagate from the source. This is in contrast to the more appropriate condition of $(2l + 1)$-fold degeneracy in which we can imagine that $2l + 1$ strings radiate from a given source in mode l, all $2l + 1$ singlets being, in general, excited. We remove the degeneracy, that is, induce binary line splitting, by letting the velocity on one string be slightly different from that on its twin. We can imagine that this models the effect of ellipticity perturbations on a spherical Earth, since the round-trip travel time on a polar path will be less than on any other. To model scattering by lateral inhomogeneities, we let part of the signal on one string be transferred to the other string through an isotropic coupling device; for computational reasons, we transfer the simulated scattering instantly, with zero time delay between the two strings.

Given the constraints of the above model, we imagine that we have an inhomogeneous string composed of two separately homogeneous half-segments, each 20,000 km in length. The wave velocities on each half-string were taken to be roughly 5.5 km/s in the numerical simulations, with velocity differences on the two strings that ranged from about one part in 50 to one part in 180. The outer edges of the string segments are fixed; the strings are decoupled if the impedance contrast at the midpoint junction is infinite. In the decoupled case, the period of the 22d mode is about 330 s on each half-string. To introduce a weak coupling at the midpoint, we let the impedance contrast between the two strings be very large. The acoustic impedance of a string is the product of the density and the wave velocity. Since the wave velocities on the two strings are almost the same, we are obliged to introduce a large density contrast between the two strings to generate the large impedance contrast; this requirement is, of course, a nongeophysical assumption but one that will not alter any of the relevant conclusions we draw from this model. In our numerical experiments, we used values of the impedance ratio Z that varied from 10 to 50, which are essentially the density ratios. The weak coupling is intended to simulate weak scattering from seismic waves from one great circle path to the other.

The signal source on the model is chosen to be a delta function of time, for ease in numerical computation of a "theoretical seismogram." Attenuation, when present, is also chosen to have a nongeophysical property for computational purposes: we let $1/Q$ be proportional to frequency, and hence the attenuation factor independent of frequency. Under these conditions, a (delta function) signal on the string propagates without change of waveshape. A detector located along the string will record a series of delta functions that arrive at times corresponding to the multiple reflection times $(n/c_1 + m/c_2)L$, with n and m integers; the amplitudes of the pulses will vary with the values of $1/Q$ on each string and the transmission and reflection coefficients at the midpoint.

Although a simulation of earthquake motions would demand that we excite both strings with separate sources, we place the source on only one string to expose the physical relationships. Suppose that we place the detector on the same string segment as the source. In this case, we find that the detector records seismic signals in the early part of the time history that resemble a simple reverberation of a delta function on "its own" string, albeit with decreasing amplitudes. Analysis of a finite segment of this part of the time history gives a spectrum dominated by the properties of the source string as though it were homogeneous but with damping due to the energy loss by scattering; little or no evidence of binary line splitting is present, at least if the time segment is sufficiently short. Much later in the time history, we observe the effects of transfer of energy between the two strings; we expect to see a spectrum of a finite part of this portion of the time history that has a significantly different character from that of the first part of the time history. If stationarity is achieved in the later part of the time series, we expect to see binary spectral line splitting, in contrast to the spectrum of the earlier part of the record. The student should not expect that the spectrum of the stationary case will be the same as that of an interleaved pair of combs of delta functions of equal amplitudes; in the latter case the spectral peaks should occur at frequencies $nc_1/2L$ and $mc_2/2L$. The eigenvalue problem for the inhomogeneous string is the solution to

$$\tan k_1 L + Z \tan k_2 L = 0$$

which is a transcendental equation that yields the characteristic complexity expected, including the binary line splitting. For large Z, the solution to the above eigenvalue equation yields a frequency interval of splitting between the pairs of

$$\frac{\Delta\omega}{\omega} = \left[\left(\frac{\Delta c}{c} \right)^2 + \frac{1}{Z(\pi l)^2} \right]^{1/2}$$

For $1/Z$ of the order of $\Delta c/c$ (as we have suggested, these numbers are all about $1/300$) the line splitting for modes near 22 or so is dominated by the

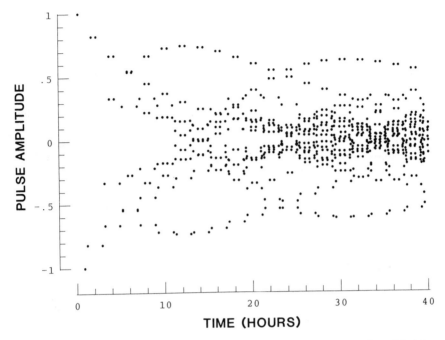

Figure 3. Forty-hour synthetic "seismogram" for an inhomogeneous string with delta function source. Impedance ratio $Z = 10$, $Q = \infty$.

velocity differences between the two segments of the string. If we extend this observation to the Earth, the fine structure in this frequency range in the stationary regime is dominated by ellipticity, rotation, and path-propagation effects; those of multiple scattering by inhomogeneities are much smaller still. At the South Pole, however, the perturbation of the frequencies of the lines in the spheroidal spectrum due to ellipticity and rotation is of course zero. The differences between the frequencies of the spectra for the comb of uniform-amplitude delta functions and the comb of pulses on the inhomogeneous string are due to amplitude modulation of the comb by the multiple scattering from the inhomogeneity.

An example of a synthetic seismogram on the inhomogeneous string is shown in figure 3 in the case in which the attenuation factor for wave propagation on the string is zero. The mixing time of these seismograms is approximately $ZlT/4$, approximately five hours. As noted, a more appropriate value of Z for the earth is about 300; we have lowered it dramatically in this example for purposes of display, as well as to be able to describe the postmixing-time behavior of the spectrum. In this case, we find that the signal is indeed mixed. That is, harmonic analysis of finite segments of the record of fixed length yields the same frequency estimates for arbitrary starting times of the segments; the frequency estimates of a record segment sufficiently long to resolve the doublet are the solutions to the eigenvalue problem but not the set for the uniform double comb in a simple way. The presence of a starting "transient" dominated by the properties of the "source string" is clearly visible on seismograms with much larger Z for which the mixing time is longer.

If we use a record segment of length too short to resolve the doublet, the shape of the spectrum appears to be that of a broadened singlet. If we fit this apparent spectral singlet with a line whose shape is that appropriate to a Q-broadened singlet, we find that the frequency of the peak is not constant with starting time for the time segment, but is nonstationary and in fact oscillates between the appropriate overtone frequencies of the two strings separately. In other words, frequency analysis of this early, premixing-time part of the record yields spectra that correspond, almost precisely, to our expectations for the homogeneous source string.

INFLUENCE OF ATTENUATION

If we add the effects of attenuation to the synthetic procedure, we identify three discernible effects:

1. There is a second time scale that defines an early, transient regime on the seismogram that may be either longer or shorter than the mixing time associated with multiple scattering. We can estimate the attenuation time scale as follows: Consider for the purposes of pedagogy (again) a coupled oscillator system with two degrees of freedom. Imagine that we have masses and springs as indicated in figure 4. Without the central coupling spring, the two oscillators are decoupled. We set the frequencies of each to be close to one another, with a notation that is purposely intended to remind the reader of the four perturbing influences on the spectrum of free oscillations of the Earth. If we couple the pair with a weak spring intended to simulate scattering by lateral inhomogeneities, we get a frequency doublet for the spectrum

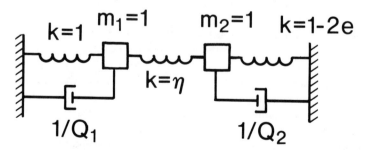

Figure 4. Slightly nondegenerate coupled oscillators with attenuation.

with individual singlet frequencies that are perturbed from the decoupled case. If there is no attenuation in the system, and we give the coupled system an initial impulse, we find that the system continues to oscillate stably for all time. If we now introduce attenuation into the model, we find that the two modes decay, as expected, and the decay rates will differ if the damping of the two masses is different. After a sufficiently long time, one mode has much larger amplitude than the other, and spectral analysis of this part of the time series for the motion of either mass will show a singlet spectral line that is attenuation broadened. The $1/e$ time for disappearance of the mode with the lower Q is of the order of rQT/π, where r is a number about 3.2 in the case of equal values of e and η and almost equal values of Q. Thus, we may expect the attenuation transition time to be roughly QT, which is about 25 hours for $Q = T$ (s) = 300. This is rather shorter than the mixing time due to scattering, which we have estimated to be $lT/4\eta$, or roughly 150 hours for $Z \sim 300$.

   Thus, for real seismograms with lengths of the order of 25 hours, the spectral structure should resemble that of a singlet with Q and peak frequency appropriate to the great circle path that includes both the stations and the seismograph, excepting effects of rotation and possibly the location of the source, neither of which has been taken into account in the modeling thus far. If longer seismograms were available, Fourier analysis of short segments would show a shift in frequency if the great circle through the station is not a path of greatest Q.

   To test the above, we performed Fourier analysis of overlapping 20-hour segments, with starting times ranging from 0 to 40 hours in 4-hour steps, of the seismogram for the Sumbawa earthquake of August 1977, which was our record of greatest useful length. Under these conditions, estimates one and six, for example, are independent. In the case of mode $_0S_{23}$, we see that the estimate of the period from these short records changes significantly over the 40-hour interval and reaches a maximum at about 30 hours after the start of the record (fig. 5), a time that is in good agreement with the estimate QT. We are not able to explore this record to observe the spectral behavior for times longer than QT.

   Mode $_0S_{23}$ was one of the modes that fit the smooth expectation model well. From the display of figure 5, we may take it that significant fluctuations in the estimates of even the "good" modes may occur if we use the early parts of the seismogram. Since the $1/e$ decay time of signal amplitude is QT/π, most of the energy in the original estimate of the periods is taken from an effective record length much shorter than the first 40 hours. We can assume that measurements reported in the literature of free-oscillation periods obtained from very long seismograms may show frequency fluctuations with record length similarly.

   2. The spectral properties of longer, real seismograms are probably only of academic interest since records of length greater than QT are not normally

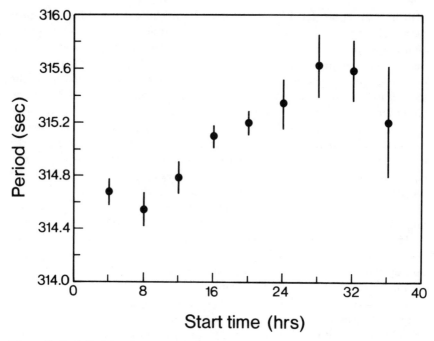

Figure 5. Period of the spectral peak for mode $_0S_{23}$ from the seismogram of the Sumbawa earthquake (19 August 1977, $M_s = 7.9$) at the South Pole. Spectra are obtained from a sequence of 20-hour long segments, each Hanning tapered. The window start time is shifted by four hours at each data point.

available. A moving-window analysis for a string seismogram similar to that for figure 5, but in this case with attenuation and in the regime $t > QT$, shows that the period of the estimate is relatively stable with time on the seismogram (fig. 6), with only a small "wow" or ripple. We infer as before that the ripple is due to the interpretation of the spectral doublet as a singlet and the fitting of this with a singlet line-shape fitting operator in a regime where the seismogram sample is of relatively short duration.

3. If we repeat the analysis of the string seismogram in the regime $t > QT$ as above, but shift the location of the source by 200 km, a small fraction of a wavelength in this mode, we find that the average value of the period estimate, except for one anomalously low value, is more than one second lower than in the first case (fig. 6). We observe that in one of the two cases, the receiver is close to a display point of resonance on "its own" string. In this case, the receiver detects only the signal scattered from the coupling (designed to simulate scattering from lateral inhomogeneities) that has the characteristic properties of resonance on the adjoining string. Thus, in this case, the signal is dominated by the properties of resonance of waves on a string segment on which it is not located.

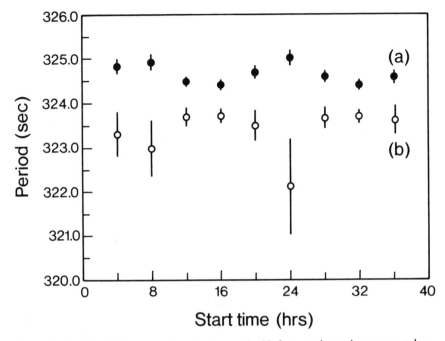

Figure 6. Period of the spectral peak for mode 23 for a string seismogram taken through a sequence of 20-hour Hanning windows shifted as in figure 5. The upper curve is for a source at coordinate 6,000 km, while the lower is for a source at coordinate 5,800 km. In each case, $Z = 50$, $Q = 200$.

We can suppose therefore that the modal periods measured in the early parts of the seismogram at the South Pole, for example, will be dominated by the properties of the great circle through the South Pole and the epicenter, unless the South Pole is at a nodal point for the radiation pattern of the mode. If the South Pole is near or at a nodal point for the standing wave pattern for the mode under consideration, then the signal at the South Pole, although weak, will yield a period for the mode that is strongly influenced by scattering from lateral inhomogeneities, and may be dominated by signals with periods characteristic of other great circle paths through the epicenter, as well as the effects of rotation and of torsional-spheroidal mode coupling.

Although the long-term properties of the seismogram in which multiple scattering dominates the properties of the signal do not concern us here, we can guess that this part of the record will be nonstationary for sample lengths that are too short to permit the multiplets to be resolved. Were this part of the record observable, the frequency of this mode would not be given by the diagonal sum rule, but would probably correspond to the singlet with the highest Q.

CONCLUSIONS

1. Most present-day measurements of periods of free oscillations are made in a transient rather than steady-state regime of the seismogram. Under these circumstances, the periods of the peak of the resonance response curves for unresolved multiplets generally characterize the properties of the geodesic (which is usually a great circle) through the station and the epicenter. It is this property that allows tomographic analysis to be performed on the data. This procedure fails when the station is at a nodal point for the mode; the nodal pattern is simply calculated as though the epicenter is at the pole of a spherical coordinate system, the focal mechanism being taken into account. If we make observations at locations remote from a nodal point, the perturbing effects of rotation, flattening, and scattering can be neglected in the zeroth order.

2. If the station is at a nodal point of the radiation pattern, significant period shifts may be observed, since the signal received at the station is derived mainly by scattering from lateral inhomogeneities, rather than by sampling the great circle path through the source.

Is there any way out of the difficulty in the use of seismograms that yield erratic period measurements, that would permit us to make use of these data without summarily discarding them? Indeed, is there some way to treat all data in the same way without having to identify which points are "good" and which "bad"?

One solution to this problem would seem to be to get rid of the standing wave pattern that produced the nodal points. Since the standing wave pattern is the result of the juxtaposition of oppositely traveling wave trains, we may delete either wave trains R_{2n} or R_{2n+1} from the time series and perform harmonic analysis on the windowed semi-seismograms. Since all the wave trains now travel in the same direction, no complexities due to standing wave patterns arise. Since the primary signal is now strong and no longer nearly zero, all perturbing effects due to scattering or mode coupling are of higher order, unless we happen to be located at a nodal point in the radiation pattern of the source. In the latter event, we can offer no solution to the problem. Barring this last eventuality, we expect that the large fluctuations observed in figure 2 should be removable. (We *are* aware that under some circumstances, wave train R_4, for example, may have a larger amplitude than R_3, a fact that cannot be explained without invoking the focusing effects of lateral inhomogeneities.) We pay a penalty, in the form of larger error bars, for dividing the record into two parts because of the poorer signal-to-noise ratio; the actual size of the error bars depends on the method used in the data analysis and the windowing of the seismograms.

The results of the phase-velocity or, equivalently, the free-mode-period analysis for thirteen seismograms recorded at the South Pole, including the original nine studied by windowing out alternating wave trains, are shown in figure 7 for modes $_0S_{22}$ and $_0S_{23}$. The inconsistencies for mode $_0S_{23}$ are now removed and, within the error bars, the results for both modes are consistent with each other. The results for modes $_0S_{20}$ and $_0S_{25}$ are similarly consistent with the first two. We do not discuss the method of data analysis of the traveling waves here; that is reserved for a subsequent publication (Gruenewald et al., in preparation).

The unsmoothed results of figure 7 show sets of long periods or low phase velocities on a narrow band of azimuths that would seem to correspond to the location of the East Pacific Rise and its antimeridian. A short modal-period anomaly is found over a broad range of azimuths with an azimuthal extremum that is asymmetric to the long-period maximum and corresponds roughly to the azimuths of the subduction zones in the Western Pacific and their antimeridian. We refrain from drawing any more detailed structural associations, since we do not know *from this analysis* where the anomalies are located on the great circles through the South Pole. Smoothing of the curves of figure 7 by a harmonic of the second degree gives good agreement with the target results of Masters et al. (1982).

Although we indicated that measurements made at the South Pole may have advantages due to symmetry over similar measurements made at non-Polar latitudes, this has not turned out to be literally true. However, the South Pole measurements have allowed us to lay bare a strategy for data analysis at almost any station on the surface of the Earth. By windowing any seismogram to delete alternating wave packets R_{2n+1} or R_n, we minimize the incidence of erratic period measurements at the expense of a poorer signal-to-noise ratio. Since the measurements are in the transient part of the signal, the phase velocity or period results can be corrected for ellipticity simply by taking into account the circumference of the great circle path through the station and corrected for rotation by taking into account the length of path in an inertial frame; we recall that the meridional component of the wave number vector for R_{2n} or R_{2n+1} is either parallel or antiparallel to the rotation of the Earth.

To respond to an earlier question, it is the fact that relatively short seismograms are used in the analysis that allows measurements to be made that permit localization of the lateral inhomogeneities through measurements of global phase travel times. How these data are correlated with the periods of the free oscillations is a matter of some complexity. Attenuation is a complicating feature for the understanding of the multiplet structure of the Earth but only on a part of the seismographic record that is not observable with contemporary instruments.

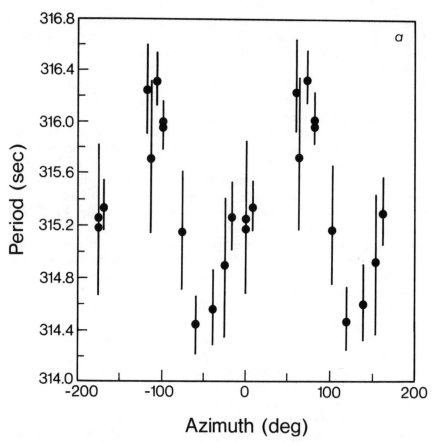

Figure 7a. Period of mode $_0S_{23}$ at the South Pole as a function of azimuth for thirteen earthquakes. Period is determined by comparing R_n with R_{n+2}. Compare with figure 2a. 7b Same as figure 7a for mode $_0S_{22}$. Compare with figure 2b.

ACKNOWLEDGMENTS

The data gathering aspects of this research were supported by grant DPP-83-14945 of the Division of Polar Programs of the National Science Foundation. The paper is publication number 3200 of the Institute of Geophysics and Planetary Physics, University of California, Los Angeles. L. Knopoff is in the Physics Department and Institute of Geophysics and Planetary Physics, University of California, Los Angeles. P. A. Rydelek is now at the Department of Terrestrial Magnetism, Carnegie Institution of Washington, Washington, D.C. W. Zurn is at the Geosciences Observatory of the Universities of Karlsruhe and Stuttgart, Schiltach, F.R. Germany.

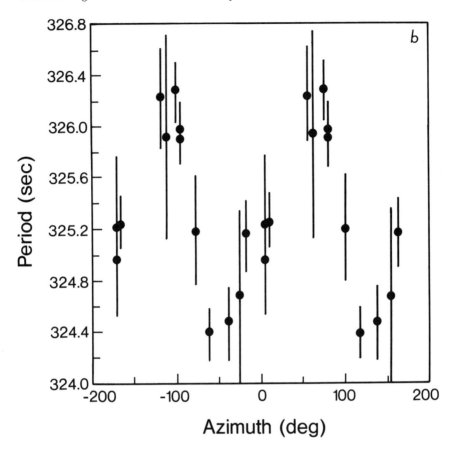

REFERENCES

Dahlen, F. A. (1981). The free oscillations of an anelastic, aspherical earth. *Geophys. J. R. Astr. Soc.*, 66: 1–22.

Geller, R. J., and S. Stein (1978). Normal modes of a laterally heterogeneous body: A one-dimensional example. *Bull. Seism. Soc. Am.*, 68: 103–116.

Masters, G., T. H. Jordan, P. G. Silver, and F. Gilbert (1982). Aspherical Earth structure from fundamental spheroidal mode data. *Nature*, 298: 609–613.

Nakanishi, K. K., L. Knopoff, and L. B. Slichter (1976). Observations of Rayleigh wave dispersion at very long periods. *J. Geophys. Res.*, 81: 4417–4421.

Park, J. (1986). Synthetic seismograms from coupled free oscillations: Effects of lateral structure and rotation. *J. Geophys. Res.*, 91: 6441–6464.

Silver, P. G., and T. H. Jordan (1981). Fundamental spheroidal mode observations of aspherical heterogeneity. *Geophys. J. R. Astr. Soc.*, 64: 605–634.

Appendix
Scientific Program

Thursday, May 28   Bechtel Engineering Center

8:00 a.m.   Registration

9:00   Opening Remarks
                 Chair: Dr. M. Niazi

9:10   Welcome to the University
                 The Vice Chancellor, Dr. R. B. Park

9:20   Remarks, Seismological Society of America
                 The President, Professor D. G. Harkrider

9:30   Remarks, U.S.G.S
                 Dr. J. R. Filson

9:40   Address: "Contributions of the Stations"
                 The Director, Professor B. A. Bolt

10:15   Coffee Break

10:30   Symposium Session I   MAPPING EARTHQUAKES
                 Chair: Dr. J. W. Dewey

10:40   "Inter-plate and Intra-plate Seismicity of the Australian Plate and its Pacific Plate Margin"
                     Dr. D. Denham

11:00   "The Need for Local Arrays in the Mapping of the Lithosphere"
                     Dr. A. Eisenberg

11:20   "Seismicity Map of North America"
                     Dr. E. R. Engdahl

11:40   "Development of Fault Plane Studies"
                     Professor A. Udías

12:00 noon   Lunch (Pauley Ballroom)
                 Luncheon Address "An Anecdotal History of the Stations"
                 Professor W. Stauder

366

1:30	Symposium Session II OBSERVATORY INSTRU-MENTATION AND PRACTICE
	Chair: Professor T. V. McEvilly
1:40	"Seismic Data Management for Hazard Assessment"
	Dr. M. J. Berry
2:00	"Statistics and Seismicity Analysis"
	Professor D. R. Brillinger
2:20	"New Global Progress and Network Design"
	Professor A. Dziewonski
2:40	"Large Scale Processing and Analysis of Digital Wave Data from the U.S.G.S Central California Microearthquake Network"
	Dr. W. H. K. Lee and Dr. S. Stewart
3:00	Coffee Break
3:30	Remarks, Seismographic Station Observing Program
	Dr. R. A. Uhrhammer
6:00	Reception (Alumni House)

Friday, May 29 Bechtel Engineering Center

8:45 a.m.	Invited Addresses
	"The World's Earthquake Observatories"
	Dr. R. D. Adams and Professor F. Gilbert
9:45	Symposium Session III ANALYSIS OF SEISMOGRAMS
	Chair: Dr. W. H. Bakun
9:55	"Deterministic and Stochastic Approaches in Seismogram Analysis"
	Professor K. Aki
10:15	"Analyses of Seismograms to Recover Physical Parameters of Seismic Sources"
	Professor J. N. Brune
10:35	"Surface Waves in Irregular Structures"
	Professor L. A. Drake
10:55	"Constraints from Seismograms on the Physical Characteristics of Explosions"
	Professor B. W. Stump
11:15	Coffee Break
11:30	Symposium Session IV REGIONAL OBSERVATORY NETWORKS: DESIGN AND ROLE
	Chair: Dr. W. D. Smith
11:40	"The Use of Dense Microearthquake Networks to Study Geologic Processes in the Earth's Crust"
	Dr. J. P. Eaton
12:00 noon	"Regional Network Seismicity Discrimination"
	Dr. J. F. Evernden

12:20	Lunch (Informal)
1:50	Symposium Session IV continued
	"Research Using the Southern California Network"
	Professor H. Kanamori
2:10	"Distributed Intelligence in Regional Networks"
	Dr. D. W. Simpson
2:30	Symposium Session V CONTRIBUTIONS TO KNOWL-EDGE OF EARTH PROPERTIES
	Chair: Professor T. Tanimoto
2:40	"Array Usages in Seismology, Past Contributions, and Future Challenges"
	Professor E. S. Husebye
3:00	"Studies Using Global Seismological Networks"
	Professor L. R. Johnson
3:20	"Symmetry Weighting Factors in Global Surface-Wave Tomography"
	Professor L. Knopoff
3:40	"Seismotectonic Features of Central Honshu Region, Japan"
	Professor T. Mikumo
4:00	Coffee Break
4:15	Report on Future Needs of Earthquake Observatories, Discussion
	Session chairs
5:00	Close
7:00	Anniversary Dinner (Faculty Club)
	Dinner Address
	Dr. R. D. Adams

Contributors

Dr. Robin D. Adams
International Seismological Centre
Pipers Lane, Thatcham
Newbury, Berkshire
United Kingdom RG13 4NS

Prof. Keiiti Aki
Dept. of Geological Sciences
University of Southern California
University Park
Los Angeles, CA 90089-0741

Dr. Michael J. Berry
Geological Survey of Canada
Geophysics Division
1 Observatory Crescent
Ottawa, Ontario
Canada K1A 0Y3

Prof. Bruce A. Bolt
Earth Sciences Building, Room 475
University of California
Berkeley, CA 94720

Prof. David R. Brillinger
Dept. of Statistics
Statistics Laboratory
University of California
Berkeley, CA 94720

Dr. David Denham
Bureau of Mineral Resources,
  Geology, and Geophysics
Division of Geophysics
GPO 378
Canberra, 2601, *Australia*

Dr. James W. Dewey
U.S. Geological Survey
Box 25046, MS 967
Denver Federal Center
Denver, CO 80225

Fr. Lawrence A. Drake, S.J.
c/o Seismographic Station
University of California
Berkeley, CA 94720

Dr. Adam Dziewonski
Harvard University
Hoffman Laboratory, 20 Oxford Street
Cambridge, MA 02138

Dr. Jerry P. Eaton
U.S. Geological Survey
MS 977, 345 Middlefield Road
Menlo Park, CA 94025

Dr. Alfredo Eisenberg
Geoexploraciones Ltda.
Galvarino Gallardo 1841
Santiago, *Chile*

Dr. E. R. Engdahl
U.S. Geological Survey
Box 25046, MS 967
Denver Federal Center
Denver, CO 80225

Dr. E. S. Husebye
Institutt for Geologi
Dept. of Geology
P.O. Box 1047 Blindern
N 0316, Oslo 3, *Norway*

Prof. Lane R. Johnson
Dept. of Geology and Geophysics

University of California
Berkeley, CA 94720

Prof. Hiroo Kanamori
California Institute of Technology
Seismological Laboratory 252-21
Pasadena, CA 91125

Prof. Leon Knopoff
Institute of Geophysics and Planetary Sciences
University of California
Los Angeles, CA 90024

Dr. W. H. K. Lee
U.S. Geological Survey
MS 977, 345 Middlefield Road
Menlo Park, CA 94025

Dr. David W. Simpson
Lamont-Doherty Geological Observatory
   of Columbia University
Palisades, NY 10964

Dr. Kenneth D. Smith
Seismological Laboratory
Mackay School of Mines
University of Nevada, Reno
Reno, NV 89557-0047

Prof. Brian W. Stump
Dept. of Geological Sciences
Southern Methodist University
Dallas, TX 75275-0395

Fr. Agustin Udias, S.J.
Catedra de Geofisica
Faculty of Physical Science
Universidad Complutense
Madrid 28040-775, *Spain*

Dr. Robert A. Uhrhammer
Seismographic Station
University of California
Berkeley, CA 94720

Index

Designer: U.C. Press
Compositor: Asco Trade Typesetting Ltd.
Text: 10/12 Baskerville
Display: Baskerville
Printer: Bookcrafters, Inc.
Binder: Bookcrafters, Inc.

48.00